P9-CDV-582

Financing the United Nations System

JX
977.8
.F5
S78

Financing the United Nations System

John G. Stoessinger

With the collaboration of *Gabriella Rosner Lande*
and *Inis L. Claude, Jr., Rowland Egger, John H. E. Fried,*
Stanley Hoffmann, Norman J. Padelford, Adamantia Pollis,
Marcia Rosenfeld, Walter R. Sharp, Howard J. Taubenfeld

THE BROOKINGS INSTITUTION · *WASHINGTON D.C.*

113351

© 1964 by

THE BROOKINGS INSTITUTION

Published May 1964

Library of Congress Catalogue Card Number 64-19923

THE BROOKINGS INSTITUTION is an independent organization devoted to nonpartisan research, education, and publication in economics, government, foreign policy, and the social sciences generally. Its principal purposes are to aid in the development of sound public policies and to promote public understanding of issues of national importance.

The Institution was founded December 8, 1927, to merge the activities of the Institute for Government Research, founded in 1916, the Institute of Economics, founded in 1922, and the Robert Brookings Graduate School of Economics and Government, founded in 1924.

The general administration of the Institution is the responsibility of a self-perpetuating Board of Trustees. The Trustees are likewise charged with maintaining the independence of the staff and fostering the most favorable conditions for creative research and education. The immediate direction of the policies, program, and staff of the Institution is vested in the President, assisted by the division directors and an advisory council, chosen from the professional staff of the Institution.

In publishing a study, the Institution presents it as a competent treatment of a subject worthy of public consideration. The interpretations and conclusions in such publications are those of the author or authors and do not purport to represent the views of the other staff members, officers, or trustees of the Brookings Institution.

BOARD OF TRUSTEES

Eugene R. Black, *Chairman*
Robert Brookings Smith, *Vice Chairman*
William R. Biggs, *Chairman, Executive Committee*

Arthur Stanton Adams
Dillon Anderson
Elliott V. Bell
Louis W. Cabot
Robert D. Calkins
Leonard Carmichael
Thomas H. Carroll
Edward W. Carter
Colgate W. Darden, Jr.
Marion B. Folsom
Gordon Gray
Huntington Harris

David M. Kennedy
John E. Lockwood
H. Chapman Rose
Sydney Stein, Jr.
Donald B. Woodward

Honorary Trustees

Daniel W. Bell
Mrs. Robert S. Brookings
Huntington Gilchrist
John Lee Pratt

Foreword

The serious financial plight of the United Nations is due to differ-ences of opinion concerning the proper role and scope of the Organiza-tion, particularly with respect to the maintenance of international peace and security. This book analyzes these divergent views and studies the financial problem in the light of the different political perspectives.

The study carries the analysis roughly through 1963. It provides data on costs of membership, budgetary procedures, and financing peace and security operations such as the United Nations Emergency Force in the Middle East and the United Nations Congo Force. It also surveys the financial history of the affiliated specialized agencies and other international organizations and considers such voluntary programs as the Children's Fund and the Special Fund. The study discusses private financial support of United Nations undertakings and explores the possibilities and limits of new sources of revenue.

For more than a dozen years the Brookings Institution has been engaged in analysis of the United Nations system. Among the more significant previous publications are: *The United Nations and the Maintenance of International Peace and Security* by Leland M. Good-rich and Anne P. Simons (1955), *Proposals for Changes in the United Nations* by Francis O. Wilcox and Carl M. Marcy (1955), *The United Nations and Promotion of the General Welfare* by Robert E. Asher, Walter M. Kotschnig, William Adams Brown, Jr., and Associates (1957), and *A History of the United Nations Charter* by Ruth B. Russell as-sisted by Jeannette E. Muther (1958). Together with the Johns Hop-kins School of International Studies, the Brookings Institution spon-sored a conference which resulted in the book, *The United States and the United Nations,* edited by Francis O. Wilcox and H. Field Havi-land, Jr. (The Johns Hopkins Press, 1961). Other studies are in prog-ress, both under the regular program of the Division of Foreign Policy Studies and under its special program of United Nations Policy Studies.

The principal author of the present study, John G. Stoessinger, is a Professor of Political Science at Hunter College of the City University of New York and Visiting Professor of International Relations at Columbia University. He is the author of a pamphlet entitled *Finan-cing the United Nations,* published by the Carnegie Endowment in

1961, and of four books: *The Refugee and the World Community* (1956), *The International Atomic Energy Agency* (1959), *The Might of Nations: World Politics in Our Time* (1962, winner of the Bancroft Prize for the best book on international relations published that year), and *Power and Order: Six Cases in World Politics* (1964).

In preparing the present study, Professor Stoessinger enjoyed the collaboration of the ten eminent colleagues to whom he pays tribute in the ensuing Author's Acknowledgments. The author and the Institution are grateful also for the thoughtful suggestions and constructive comments of an Advisory Committee consisting of Lincoln P. Bloomfield of the Massachusetts Institute of Technology, Andrew W. Cordier and Leland Goodrich of Columbia University, Lawrence S. Finkelstein and Anne Winslow of the Carnegie Endowment for International Peace, Richard N. Gardner of the Department of State, Bruce Turner, United Nations Controller and Francis O. Wilcox of the School of Advanced International Studies, The Johns Hopkins University.

The study was made possible through the generosity of the Carnegie Endowment for International Peace which provided invaluable advice as well as financing. Responsibility for the views expressed in the study, however, rests with Professor Stoessinger. The interpretations and conclusions do not necessarily represent the views of persons consulted during the preparation of the study. Neither should they be construed as reflecting the views of the trustees, the officers, or other staff members of the Brookings Institution.

Robert D. Calkins
President

February, 1964
The Brookings Institution
1775 Massachusetts Avenue, N.W.
Washington 36, D.C.

Author's Acknowledgments

In the course of my work on this book, I derived great strength from the fact that I had the good fortune of having the support of a strong research team. The acknowledgments that follow are no mere ritual obeisance.

My first debt goes to Gabriella Rosner Lande who was associated with the project as a full time research associate for a year. Dr. Lande wrote valuable papers on the historical background of financing international organizations, the World Court Advisory Opinion on United Nations Financing, and the fiscal patterns of the specialized agencies and regional organizations. She also compiled the Selected References.

Each of the other collaborators prepared research papers in his area of specialization. These papers provided the author with vital data and insights. Inis L. Claude, Jr. of the University of Michigan wrote a paper on the political framework of the United Nations financial problem. His contribution stands, with only minor changes, as Chapter 1. Rowland Egger of the University of Virginia prepared a paper on the United Nations regular budget. Norman J. Padelford of the Massachusetts Institute of Technology made contributions in five different areas: the rising cost of United Nations membership, the financing of future peace and security operations, the special voluntary programs, the specialized agencies, and private support of the United Nations. I owe him a special debt of gratitude for drawing on the resources of the Massachusetts Institute of Technology for the benefit of the project. Stanley Hoffmann of Harvard University wrote a paper on the World Court Advisory Opinion and Walter R. Sharp of Yale University made his contribution in the area of the special voluntary programs. Adamantia Pollis of Hunter College of the City University of New York wrote on the International Monetary Fund and the International Bank for Reconstruction and Development, and John H. E. Fried of New York University contributed a paper on United Nations Levies on International Activities and another on the implications of United Nations Headquarters location in New York City. Marcia Rosenfeld of Columbia University prepared two papers on new sources of revenue for the United Nations. In addition, she filled in research gaps and prepared statistical materials. Howard J. Taubenfeld of the Southern

Methodist University Law School contributed a paper on long-range possibilities of independent revenue for the United Nations.

My ten collaborators have my lasting gratitude. I have used their contributions as material for what I hope is a coherent, internally consistent book. They are blameless for its shortcomings. I assume full responsibility for the final product.

I have also profited greatly from the counsel of the distinguished group of scholars and public officials mentioned in the Foreword who consented to serve as an Advisory Committee for the project. Moreover, I have enjoyed the generous help of Arthur N. Holcombe, Chairman of the Commission to Study the Organization of Peace, Eric Stein of the University of Michigan Law School, J. David Singer of the University of Michigan, Gerard J. Mangone of Syracuse University, and Harlan Cleveland, Frank Hefner, Elmer Jackson, and Virginia C. Housholder of the United States Department of State. I am also grateful to Eric Stevenson of the Institute for Defense Analyses, Robert H. Cory, Jr. of the Quakers United Nations Program, and Albert Bender of the United States Mission to the United Nations. Alice V. R. Smith, Madeleine G. Mitchell, and Karen Petersen of the United Nations Secretariat deserve my special gratitude.

I feel deeply grateful to both the Carnegie Endowment for International Peace, which provided the financing, and to the Brookings Institution, under whose aegis the study was written. Special appreciation is due H. Field Haviland, Jr. and Robert E. Asher of Brookings for sustaining me with their counsel throughout the work, to Evelyn Breck for her capable editing, to Helen Eisenhart who prepared the index, and to Harriet Daum for her efficient secretarial assistance.

The above names by no means exhaust the list of people who have given me of their time and knowledge. I should like, in conclusion, to record my thanks to all the United Nations delegates, members of the Secretariat, officials of United Nations missions, and private individuals who have sustained me with their kindness and patience.

The study that follows is divided into three parts: past, present, and future. The emphasis, of course, is on the present—the financing of the United Nations system. But I have attempted to explore the past as prologue to the present; and the future in an act of presumptuous ambition.

John G. Stoessinger

February 1964

Contents

PART I

The Problem in Perspective

CHAPTER 1

The Political Framework of the United Nations Financial Problem

NEVER HAVE SO MANY ARGUED so much about so little money as in the United Nations. The reason is that the financial problem of the United Nations is, in reality, a political problem. The financial crisis is first a political crisis over the proper role the United Nations is to play in the national policies of its member states. Only secondarily is it a crisis over the financial burdens of membership in the Organization.

This view stems directly from the recognition that the United Nations is an agency of the multistate system, owned and operated by member states. These states undertake, cooperatively and competitively, to use the Organization to affect the working of the system and to influence their fortunes within it. The United Nations does not stand above or outside the international political system, but is clearly in and of that system. Serving as both a workshop for collaboration and an arena for conflict, the Organization is inexorably involved in the political relationships of states and is affected by political developments within them. A United Nations insulated from world politics is neither possible nor desirable. Political involvement is the price of relevance; any world organization in a position to contribute significantly to the solution of the critical problems of international relations will be subject to the buffeting of political forces.

This study is concerned with the present financial predicament and the future financial requirements and prospects of the United Nations. Before coming to grips with other aspects of these problems, however, the fact should be noted that the short history of international organizations has been marked by the tendency of states to invest only the most meager financial resources, and those grudgingly, in such institutions. If poverty is a perennial misfortune of international agencies, it is one imposed by tight-fisted states. There is thus ample precedent for the world organization's condition of financial stringency. Viewed in historical perspective, the budgets of the United Nations and the specialized agencies have been more, not less, generously supported than might have been expected. This is not to minimize the financial difficulties encountered by the international organizations of the present generation, but to note that these agencies are not unique in having troubles of this sort.

The tendency of states to exercise great economy vis-à-vis international institutions reflects the limited character of their commitment to the process of international organization. Despite the fact that multilateral institutions have become an essential part of the apparatus for conducting interstate relations in an era of impressive and increasing interdependence, the attitudes of national leaders toward such agencies are still marked by tentativeness. Thus, the notion that the United Nations is "on trial" is frequently expressed, and the question whether one is "for" or "against" the United Nations is still asked as if it were a meaningful issue. In all probability, general international organizations have passed from the status of optional experiments to that of firmly established requirements of the multistate system, and it is unlikely that many responsible statesmen are prepared to contemplate the effort to operate the international system without such mechanisms. Nevertheless, the verbalization of the view that the maintenance of the United Nations is still something of an open question indicates a basic indecisiveness in the commitment of states to international organizations.

In any case, general international organizations continue to occupy a peripheral rather than a central position in the conduct of foreign relations for many if not most states, and this political fact is expressed in the reluctance of members to provide adequate financial backing for such organizations. In some instances, statesmen doubtless hope to get something for nothing; they expect, or at least demand, substantial benefits from multilateral organizations, but are disinclined to contribute significantly to their resources. In other cases, the level of financial support may be an accurate measure of the importance that statesmen expect, or are willing to permit, international organizations to develop. Money can express more truly than words the significance attributed to international institutions and the commitment to promote or permit the growth of their capabilities. For whatever reason, the policies of states toward international institutions have typically kept those agencies in straitened financial circumstances. In the light of this background, the present predicament of the United Nations is revealed as the product of a failure to achieve a decisive break-through, not as evidence of a disastrous break-down, in the support of international institutions.

The Role of the United Nations

The cost of the United Nations is a function of the uses to which it is put. This is not to say that the most important activities of the Organization are necessarily the most expensive ones; the correlation of price and value is quite as imperfect in this realm as in many others. The world may have a cheap institutional system or an expensive one. The determination of financial requirements is dependent on political decisions regarding the activities to be undertaken by the Organization. The initial linkage between political and financial considerations is thus expressed in the question: What, in functional terms, is the United Nations to be?

A minimal consensus has emerged since World War II, to the effect that the United Nations should exist as a continuously operating center for the diplomatic interplay of representatives of most, if not all, of the world's governments. The Organization should serve as a kind of global diplomatic headquarters, providing occasions and facilities for debate and consultation, speech-making and vote-taking, declaration and resolution. This concept of the United Nations as a "static conference machinery," as the late Secretary-General Hammarskjold put it,[1] has enjoyed widespread and steady support among governments, as evidenced by the facts that virtually every state in the world has assumed the privileges of membership at the earliest opportunity and that none has yet, however frustrating and embittering its experience as a participant may have been, withdrawn from membership. Whatever reservations one may have about the value of such an international forum, it is clear that the leaders of most gov-

[1] U.N. General Assembly, Sixteenth Session, *Official Records*, "Introduction to the Annual Report of the Secretary-General on the Work of the Organization, 16 June 1960-15 June 1961," Supplement No. 1A (1961), p. 1.

ernments believe that it is eminently worthwhile—or, that their states cannot afford to be excluded from it so long as it exists.

This political consensus has been manifested in the relative lack of difficulty and controversy—at least until 1963—concerning the regular administrative budget of the United Nations. This is not to say that members have displayed unquestioning generosity with respect to this aspect of the Organization's financial requirements. The Secretary-General has had to carry on the housekeeping functions within a rapidly expanding establishment under the pressure of severe budgetary limitations, representatives of member states have frequently voiced alarm at growing budgetary requests, and the notion of a rigid budgetary ceiling has been advanced by the Soviet Union and at times by the United Kingdom.

The inclusion of particular items in the regular budget has sometimes given rise to political controversy. For example, the Soviet Union has persistently objected to appropriations for subsidiary organs that it has regarded as "illegally" established or constituted, such as the United Nations Truce Supervision Organization in Palestine and the United Nations Commission for the Unification and Rehabilitation of Korea. But only in 1963 did it refuse to pay for these operations and, like France, to pay principal and interest on United Nations bonds.

On the whole, the financial support of the routine administration of the United Nations has not been a contentious issue, for objection to particular items has usually been grounded on the claim that controversial expenditures were being smuggled into an uncontroversial budget. In principle, no state has objected to the view that members should provide the funds necessary for keeping the United Nations in business as a conference center and a supplier of essential services for international meetings. So far as the regular budget of the Organization is concerned, there is no major financial crisis, and none is in prospect. States evidently recognize the need for and the utility of a broad international forum, and they are, by and large, willing and able to pay for it. It is a reasonably safe prediction that the routine administrative cost of the United Nations will gradually increase, and that member states will, while grumbling about this trend and attempting to check it, continue to make the necessary payments.

Significant political issues arise only when the question is posed as to what, if anything, the United Nations is to do beyond the agreed minimum of providing a setting for multilateral or parliamentary diplomacy. The alternative to an organization which is merely "a static conference machinery" is one that additionally serves as "a dynamic instrument of governments," carrying out "executive action."[2] This view of the United Nations suggests an operational role for the Organization in programs within two fields, which may be roughly defined as the political and security area and the economic and social area. The Organization has in fact ventured into both realms, and the central questions for the future are whether, and how far, it shall continue thus to move. It is in connection with these operational functions that major financial and political problems may arise and become entangled. In the first place, the execution of programs in either of these fields tends to be, by the normal standards of international organizations, extraordinarily expensive. In the second place, such programs tend to be politically contentious, partly, but not entirely, because of their unusual financial implications.

To be sure, there is a middle ground between the two extremes of a world organization providing inexpensive and politically uncontroversial conference services, and an organization operating substantive programs at great cost under conditions of intense political disagreement. Expensiveness is a relative concept, as is political sensitivity. Indeed, the record shows that the United Nations has never been restricted to the minimal conference-supporting role, that it has frequently undertaken executive tasks, some of which involved minor budgetary implications, and that some of its operational ventures have not stirred political opposition within the Organization. It is doubtful that any state is committed, on either financial or political grounds, to the rigidly circumscribed conception of the Organization's function implied in the notion of "a static conference machinery." The United Nations has persistently exceeded that role, without consistently encountering financial or political difficulties.

Nevertheless, it is clear that the present financial crisis of the United Nations is the direct result of the Organization's involvement in large-scale, relatively expensive, and politically contentious executive activities. This is principally because alarming deficits have appeared in the special accounts established for the sustenance of major

[2] *Ibid.*

operations, undertakings that are incompatible with the concept that the Organization should be limited to the provision of conference facilities. While there is no effective political demand for the United Nations to remain strictly within the confines of the minimal conference, the farther the Organization is pushed beyond that limit, the greater is the risk of stirring up political conflict over its proper role.

Political and Security Operations

The ventures that have precipitated the present crisis in the United Nations are the peace-keeping operations in the Middle East and the Congo, involving the maintenance of two groups of military units assembled under United Nations direction, the United Nations Emergency Force (UNEF) and the United Nations Operation in the Congo (ONUC), and, in the case of the Congo, the effort to provide a substantial civilian assistance program as well. The lack of adequate voluntary support, and, in particular, the failure or refusal of many member states to pay their allotted shares of the costs of these activities, have created grave difficulties for the Organization in meeting its financial obligations, called into question the capability of the Organization for completing the tasks it has assumed, and raised the issue whether the United Nations can, or should, undertake similar ventures in the future. Past, present, and future are involved; default on obligations already incurred, discontinuance of present activities, and rejection of a peace-keeping executive role in emergencies to come are the possibilities that have been thrust on the United Nations.

Fundamentally, the deficits relating to UNEF and ONUC, which are the most significant elements in the Organization's present fiscal imbalance, represent political rather than economic considerations. Although a number of states presumably are in default because of financial difficulties, the greater part of the deficit is attributable to states that are unwilling, not unable, to pay. In short, the United Nations, while it supported both UNEF and ONUC, found itself overcommitted in political terms, which explains the fact that it has been and still is undersupported in budgetary terms.

This would suggest that there is inadequate political consensus within the United Nations on the use of the Organization as an instrument of what Dag Hammarskjold called "preventive diplomacy," at any rate when this involves the mustering and maintenance of significant peace-keeping forces. Since financial support presumably implies approval and refusal of support may be interpreted either as acquiescence or as some degree of disapproval, it seems clear that only a dangerously narrow political basis exists for such operations as those undertaken in the Middle East and the Congo. What are the implications of this conclusion?

One alternative is to insist on a functional retrenchment for the United Nations. The decision of the General Assembly to terminate ONUC in mid-1964 was a step in that direction. To argue that the current quasi-military ventures should be terminated as promptly and as gracefully as possible, and that the idea of launching new ones in the future should be abandoned would mean a policy of retreat from executive action in the political-security sphere. It reflects an attitude of caution, a conviction that prudent concern for the effectiveness of the United Nations requires or suggests that the Organization not court financial disaster by undertaking activities that are not firmly supported by the bulk of its membership, including, most importantly, the major powers. Indeed, financial embarrassment is not the only peril; the record of the Soviet Union in the Congo case shows that dissenters may express their opposition to executive actions in a variety of ways that damage the foundations of the Organization and imperil its usefulness. It is unreasonable, so the argument might run, to jeopardize the modest attainments and potentialities of the Organization by setting the United Nations to ambitious tasks that it cannot hope to complete successfully. In these terms, financial crisis is a warning signal that prudent men cannot afford to ignore; if it is not heeded, the United Nations may be destroyed.

A variation on the theme just stated would be to propose, not that the United Nations should never again be given assignments similar to those in the Middle East and the Congo, but that new projects of this type should be weighed with the utmost care and undertaken only if there is firm evidence of broad support, including that of the major powers. Perhaps this should be described as a "hardly ever" rather than a "never again" position. The mood is essentially the same: disinclination to endanger the United Nations by political conflict. The assumption is that political and security operations may sometimes command the necessary "critical mass" of support and therefore enjoy adequate financial backing; on this basis, it is argued, the United

Nations should be put to such uses when, but only when, these conditions prevail.

It should be noted that this position conforms quite closely to the original conception of the Organization's possibilities, as stated and implied in the United Nations Charter. The veto provision embodied in Article 27 (3) reflects the view that the United Nations cannot successfully perform significant political or security functions in the absence of unanimity among the major powers, that its existence will be imperiled if it is pushed into such futile ventures, and that constitutional safeguards are needed to prevent its being maneuvered into dangerous and unpromising situations of this sort. In essence, the position expresses belief in the political wisdom of the concept of the veto and advises adherence to the policy of restraint in the use of the United Nations in circumstances of major political dissension.

The late Secretary-General Hammarskjold appeared to espouse this position in his classic statement of the theory of preventive diplomacy, made in 1960.[3] Considering the issue of "the possibilities of substantive action by the United Nations in a split world," he virtually discarded the idea that the Organization could usefully or safely intervene in "problems which are clearly and definitely within the orbit of present day conflicts between power blocs." In such instances, he feared, it would be "practically impossible for the Secretary-General to operate effectively with the means put at his disposal, short of risking seriously to impair the usefulness of his office." Hammarskjold drew the conclusion that "the main field of useful activity of the United Nations in its efforts to prevent conflicts or to solve conflicts" should be defined as that of taking action to fill vacuums in areas of conflict outside of, or marginal to, the zones already involved in the cold war struggle, so as to minimize the tendency or diminish the incentive of great powers to move competitively into those situations. Thus, he hoped, the Organization might prevent the widening and aggravation of the bloc conflicts. He seemed to acknowledge that this kind of operation was dependent on the approval of the major cold war contestants, asserting:

> There is thus a field within which international conflicts may
> be faced and solved with such harmony between the power blocs as

[3] U.N. General Assembly, Fifteenth Session, *Official Records*, Introduction to the Annual Report of the Secretary-General on the Work of the Organization, 16 June 1959-15 June 1960," Supplement No. 1A (1960), pp. 4-5.

was anticipated as a condition for Security Council action in San Francisco. Agreement may be achieved because of a mutual interest among the Big Powers to avoid having a regional or local conflict drawn into the sphere of bloc politics.

Writing specifically of the Congo operation, he held that this was "rendered possible by the fact that both blocs have an interest in avoiding such an extension of the area of conflict because of the threatening consequences, were the localization of the conflict to fail." He stressed the role of the United Nations in "providing for solutions whenever the interests of all parties in a localization of conflict can be mobilized in favour of its efforts."

What emerges from this analysis of Hammarskjold's essay is that the father of the theory and practice of preventive diplomacy was wary of executive action by the United Nations in opposition to the will of a major power. But he was hopeful that the Organization could carry out successful and useful operations in the political and security field whenever the primary contestants in the cold war were agreed that they had a common interest in having the United Nations interposed as a neutral force to prevent their direct confrontation. While he was not explicit on this point, he clearly implied that the United Nations could not perform this function in the absence of such agreement, and, presumably, should not attempt it in such circumstances. Ironically, the final chapter of Hammarskjold's life seemed to confirm the views he had stated in 1960; the Congo operation became one that aroused bitter Soviet opposition, and Hammarskjold's efforts to maintain it in the face of that attack brought a fundamental challenge to the usefulness of his office. The Soviet rejection of the concept of the Secretary-General as executive leader of the United Nations occurred as Hammarskjold sought to carry on the Congo action in the context of a disintegrating political consensus.

Although some may read the Congo record as a warning against attempting to use the United Nations as an executive agency for political and security operations in any future case, or in any case where such use is or appears likely to become a subject of political disagreement among the major powers, others react by insisting that the Organization's development of executive functions must not be interrupted. Political opposition to the operational role of the United

Nations in this field, whether expressed in withholding financial support or otherwise, must be overridden if necessary; somehow, the Organization must be enabled to perform this function, even in the face of the determined objections of powerful states or blocs.

Political opposition represents a refusal to accept the philosophy of the veto as originally incorporated in the Charter. Concretely, it is an expression of the insistence, most notably by the United States, that the Soviet Union must not be permitted to block the development of the United Nations along lines acceptable to a sufficient number of other states. The argument that it is essential to have the Organization maintain and expand its operational role in cases like the Congo crisis is sometimes pressed so vigorously that its proponents appear to challenge the minimal consensus on the role of the United Nations; if the Organization cannot go well beyond the mere provision of conference machinery, so they seem to say, it is hardly worth having at all. It may be that this devaluation of the minimal function of the United Nations is simply a tactic adopted in the campaign to achieve the maximization of its function. If this is not the case, the political issue of the role in which the United Nations is to be cast may become doubly complex. Conceivably, there may be no possibility of attaining general agreement either to the proposition that the United Nations should function as more than a static conference machinery, or to the view that it should function as less than a dynamic instrumentality of executive action. In specific but oversimplified terms, this might mean that the Soviet Union would refuse to tolerate a maximal United Nations, while the United States would refuse to support a minimal United Nations. The difficulty of achieving consensus on executive activity by the Organization may be matched by the difficulty of achieving consensus on executive inactivity. Either difficulty could be disastrous; Soviet opposition might wreck an organization that was pushed to ambitious functions, and withdrawal of support by the United States might wreck an organization restricted to an excessively modest role.

The problems posed by states that resist the expansion of United Nations activity beyond the conference-serving function are weighty indeed, and they appear to be taken too lightly by those that insistently advocate that expansion. The Soviet Union confined its opposition to some of the minor peace-keeping ventures to verbal protests until 1963, and only then refused to pay for five regular budget items, which amounted to less than 10 percent of the total budget.[4] Nevertheless, by refusing to contribute funds, states opposing the international programs in the Middle East and the Congo have precipitated the grave financial troubles that afflict the United Nations. The bitter Soviet attack on Secretary-General Hammarskjold and its threat to demolish the institution of the Secretary-Generalship in its evolved form serve as vivid reminders of the possibility that powerful opponents of United Nations executive action could and might inflict on the Organization damage other, and more serious, than financial damage. A realistic view of the behavior of states suggests that no state is likely to give active financial or other support to a collective enterprise to which its policy is opposed, and that no major power can be expected passively to tolerate the use of an international institution for purposes that it regards as inimical to its vital interests. In such instances, neither a judicial ruling that a state is obliged to contribute funds nor a moral insistence that a state should respect majority decisions is likely to prove effective.

In the final analysis, the crucial question is how to react to the evidence that major powers are not agreed on the role that should be assigned to the United Nations in political and security affairs. From one point of view, consensus is essential; either the activities of the Organization must be restricted to fit the consensus, or the consensus must be broadened to support the developing range of activities. Financial difficulty is only a symptom of the deeper political crisis that is almost automatically precipitated by miscalculation of the limits of the prevailing consensus, or by deliberate efforts to push the United Nations beyond those limits. Caution suggests that it is imprudent so to push the United Nations, and unrealistic to expect that the Organization can succeed in such ambitious enterprises, or survive to perform more modest but still important functions if it is used in this manner. The immediate necessity is to trim functional concepts to fit consensus; the longer-term ideal is to expand consensus to support more ambitious activities. In these terms, the primary political question is how to produce general agreement

[4] For a discussion of these deductions, see Chaps. 4 and 5.

and, most importantly, Soviet agreement, on the assignment to the United Nations of an executive role in cases threatening the maintenance of international peace.

From another point of view, the lack of consensus may be deplored, but it must be essentially ignored. The problem of enabling the United Nations to operate in cases of the Congo type is defined, not as the task of expanding consensus, but as the task of carrying on successfully despite the limitation of consensus. Financial crisis does not mean that the United Nations has gone too far; it means that resources must be found for equipping the Organization to continue and even to deepen its probes in the area beyond the limits of the minimal consensus. This mood calls for the discovery of effective means for defiance of opposition, not for concessions to the obstructive capability of opponents of the expanding executive role of the United Nations. It is not concerned with avoiding financial crises, but with surmounting them.

Clearly, the issue whether the United Nations is to have a continuing series of such crises depends largely on which of these two viewpoints prevails. If the latter is dominant, financial difficulties may be expected to become a recurrent feature of the history of the United Nations. It may prove possible to deal with them, but it ought not to be assumed that states which object to the maximal concept of the political and security role of the Organization can be brought to assist in the solution of these problems.

There is, of course, a middle ground of acquiescence, between support for and opposition to an expanding executive role for the United Nations in political and security matters. Many states are willing to permit this development of the Organization's functions. Such states may support the initiation of operations with their votes, but they probably will not support the operations with their funds. Thus, while they may not contribute to the political controversies, they are likely to contribute to the budgetary deficiencies. On balance, then, states exhibiting a permissive attitude probably tend to exacerbate rather than to aid in the solution of the financial crises that may result from politically contentious peace-keeping activities.

Another middle ground must be pointed out—one which lies between the cautious insistence on executive inactivity unless general agreement on a line of action is clearly in evidence, and the audacious urge for action even in the face of formidable opposition. The limits of consensus are not always either clearly visible or absolutely rigid. In a given case, it may be desirable to initiate United Nations action despite uncertainty about those limits; the risk of damaging the Organization by pushing it beyond the limits that some important members will tolerate must be balanced against the risk of failing to exploit its potentialities by exercising undue restraint. There is a strong case for probing the limits of consensus, in the hope of discovering that restrictive views of the Organization's role are not firmly held, or that opposition in principle to United Nations executive action is qualified in the particular instance by appreciation of its potential contribution to political stability. If this probing goes too far, the precipitation of financial crisis may result, as one aspect of the political overextension of the United Nations. If it does not go far enough, the United Nations will be doomed to an underdevelopment of its capabilities for service to member states.

The decision in regard to how far to go should not necessarily be determined by considerations related to the financial health of the United Nations. Excellent reasons can be cited for pushing the United Nations as far as possible in the direction of executive activity in the political realm, but in so doing, the fact must be faced that the farther the Organization exceeds the discernible bounds of consensus, the greater becomes the probability of running into serious financial difficulties. This is a risk that cannot be denied and should not be ignored; if one opts to subject the United Nations to the risk, one should do so advisedly.

Financial nonsupport is the least serious manifestation of opposition to United Nations executive action. If a given action, supported by the United States, arouses only passive resistance by the Soviet Union (as in the case of UNEF), it is open to the United States and others to prevent financial crisis by accepting responsibility for most of the expenses. This may be sound policy; if the United States regards a United Nations undertaking as desirable, it should perhaps be less disturbed by the fact that the Soviet Union refuses to share in the cost than gratified that the latter power permits the United States and other members to use the Organization, at their own expense, for that undertaking.

The case is different when a United Nations program stirs the active opposition of a major power or a significant group of members.

As noted earlier, the Congo operation (after its initial phase) became one that the Soviet bloc was not only unwilling to support but also determined to obstruct. Soviet opposition went beyond financial deprivation to an attack on the executive mechanism of the United Nations, which indicated an urge to prevent the Organization's being used, at anybody's expense, for the conduct of such operations. When opposition takes this active form, it is clear that the United Nations has gone well beyond the limits of consensus. In such a case, the Organization incurs not only the risk of bankruptcy, which can be alleviated by subsidies provided by states favoring the operation, but also the risk of political disruption, which cannot be disposed of so handily. It may be good policy to incur this risk— but the risk must be candidly recognized and taken into account.

It is possible, of course, that a policy of active obstruction may give way to a more passive form of opposition. Soviet agreement to the election of U Thant as Secretary-General, first on an acting basis and then for a full term, may be a case in point. This suggests that the three forms which resistance to a peace-keeping operation may take —reluctant acquiescence, passive opposition, and active obstruction —are not rigidly defined and may blend into one another. The limits of consensus, too, are not rigid, and a constant testing of those limits may gradually expand the consensual basis of United Nations peace-keeping operations.

Economic and Social Operations

The issue of the operational role to be assigned to international institutions arises in the economic and social realm, as well as in the peace-keeping and security sphere. In the case of the United Nations and affiliated agencies, this is fundamentally a question of the degree to which emphasis will be placed on programs designed to promote economic growth in the developing countries. From the beginning, the organizations of the United Nations system have been involved in this kind of activity, and their commitment to such programs has steadily increased. There appears to be no significant opposition, in principle, to them. The involvement of international agencies in technical assistance and economic development activities is firmly established, and the prospects are for mounting political pressures in support of the launching of more ambitious, and more expensive, programs. In this realm, the political issue is not whether the United Nations should effect a retreat, but whether it should undertake major advances. The line of political division is not essentially the East-West boundary, as in the issue of political and security operations, but the North-South boundary; the debate is not conducted among rival great powers so much as between the states seeking international economic assistance and the industrially advanced states, which are the primary suppliers of economic aid, actual and potential. The United Nations is, and seems certain to continue to be, the major setting for the confrontation of the political demand of the developing states and the political reluctance of the highly developed ones.

In the literal sense, there is no financial crisis in the United Nations with respect to economic and social operations. That is to say, the Organization has not become involved in spending money that it does not have; it has not incurred financial obligations that it appears incapable of meeting; it has not been embarrassed by a rash of delinquencies on the part of members. In a different but more basic sense, however, there is a financial crisis in this realm. The Organization may be able to meet its commitments, but it cannot meet the needs and opportunities with which it is confronted; the crisis, in short, is that of the inadequate budget rather than the unbalanced budget. The problem lies not in excessive delinquencies, but in too meager commitments.

In the future development of the economic and social work of the United Nations and the specialized agencies, financial problems of this variety seem likely to persist. What is relevant to the political debate is not that there is great objective need for economic development programs, but that there is increasingly effective political demand for such programs, expressed particularly in speeches and votes within international institutions. There is every reason to assume that operational activities in this field will continue and, to some degree, expand; the real question is how much the states most capable of supplying resources for this work will be willing to contribute through international channels. The central political issue has to do with the nature of the response these states will make to the insistent demand of the less affluent countries.

There is a significant reversal of the identity of suppliers and con-

sumers of international services as between the operations of the
United Nations in the political-security and the economic-social
areas. While the greater part of the financial burden falls on the major powers in both instances, it is nevertheless true that these powers
are the primary recipients of direct benefit in the former instance,
and that this position is assumed by the weaker and less developed
states in the latter. This is not to deny that such an operation as
ONUC has immense political value to the Congo and its neighbors,
in helping to prevent their region from becoming the focus of
great-power competition. Nevertheless, its central aim is to enlist the
service of lesser states in helping the major powers to avoid a mutually, and, perhaps, globally, disastrous confrontation. In activities
falling under the rubric of preventive diplomacy, weaker states are
called on to do something for the great powers that the latter cannot
do for themselves. In economic and social programs, the more advanced states are called on to do something for the developing countries that these could not do for themselves.

Presumably, the world will benefit if the great powers are assisted
in avoiding a showdown and if the less advanced states are helped toward economic development, but direct benefits are differently allocated
in these two types of enterprise. Consumer demand is not the same in
both instances. The great powers are not agreed in wanting, or even
in being prepared to accept, the services that other states may be
able to render through participation in operations of the Congo
type, while the developing states display an almost unanimous urge
to secure the greatest possible expansion of United Nations activities
on their behalf. In the one case, the basic political problem is to develop a consensus among the consumers; in the other, it is to promote
agreement between consumers and suppliers. In both cases, the financial problem derives from and draws its distinctive nature from the
underlying political considerations.

The Distribution of Cost of United Nations Operations

It would be misleading to suggest that political controversy concerning the role of the United Nations turns exclusively on differing
conceptions of the nature and scope of the international activities

that should be encouraged, supported, or permitted. In principle, some states are more favorably disposed than others to the growth and strengthening of international institutions. However, the most significant differences derive less from such abstract considerations than from concrete political interests. One of the points at issue is the distribution of cost. The question is not simply what kind of activity the United Nations should undertake, on what scale of expense, but who should pay for it and on what basis of apportionment.

This issue has been avoided in financing most of the nonsecurity operational programs involving relatively high costs, by the device of building them on voluntary contributions. Member states have been left free to decide whether, and to what extent, to participate in the financial support of international enterprises. States opposed to or critical of particular programs have not been expected to support them, but at most to tolerate their being conducted under United Nations auspices with the support of other states; the operating agencies have tailored their programs to fit the budgetary resources that states have been willing to provide. If these resources have sometimes been disappointingly meager, overcommitment and political controversy over the effort to extract funds from unwilling governments have been avoided. The history of major economic and social programs in the United Nations system conforms largely to this pattern.

The story is quite different when the attempt is made to require all members to share in the support of programs, regardless of their attitudes toward the activities in question, and to establish a scale of assessment. The first really substantial programs in which the effort was made to cover a major portion of costs by this method were the quasi-military ventures, UNEF and ONUC—the programs, be it noted, that precipitated the gravest financial crisis. When the principle of compulsory financial support is adopted, two categories of questions arise: those relating to the criteria for equitable distribution of cost, and those relating to the mechanism for authoritative determination of assessments.

With regard to the question of "fair shares," several alternative criteria should be noted. States may be expected to contribute in proportion to their ability to pay. While precise computation of this factor may be impossible to achieve, this is the basis used for distributing the costs of the normal administrative budgets of the United Nations and various other agencies, and experience indicates that a rough approximation of equity can be achieved on this basis. This scheme has the merit of dramatizing the international quality of programs and the collective responsibility of states—large and small, rich and poor—for maintaining the work of the organized community.

Other devices for cost-sharing tend to move away from the principle of universal participation by member states. It may be argued that all or virtually all of the expense of a given operation should be borne by the major powers, with lesser states bearing at most a nominal part of the burden; such, for instance, was the import of some proposals regarding the support of UNEF and ONUC. Behind this argument lies the view that the special status of the great powers in the United Nations should carry with it special obligations, and perhaps the view that the great powers, having been exempted from the policing duties contemplated for them when the Charter was formulated and thus having become the beneficiaries of policing functions carried out by other states, should offer financial compensation for this shift of the peace-keeping burden. Another suggested criterion is that of guilt; the state or states that created the necessity for a given enterprise in preventive diplomacy should be required to pay most if not all of the cost. This slogan, "make the aggressors pay," has been advanced notably, but not exclusively, by the Soviet Union, in the Middle Eastern and Congo cases. The criterion of benefit has also figured in discussions of the issue. It has been applied in the sense that states receiving technical assistance and other economic aid under international programs have customarily been required to combine substantial local resources with those externally supplied. There are obvious limits, however, to the feasible application of the principle that the recipient state should pay for international assistance, since, at the extreme, it would lose altogether the character of assistance.

The problem of defining fair shares seems certain to be a major political issue in the United Nations for the indefinite future. States that oppose programs will insist that their proper share is zero. States that merely tolerate programs will argue that the actively interested states should bear all, or virtually all, of the cost. States that favor programs will differ regarding who should pay how much. Small states will argue that the great powers, having the status symbol of the veto, should carry most of the burden. Great powers, noting the regime of formal equality in the General Assembly, will think that the smaller states may be saved from the temptation to vote irresponsibly if they are sufficiently burdened with financial responsibility for the programs they may press on the Organization.

From the standpoint of functional effectiveness, the United Nations needs to lay a foundation of obligatory financial support by all or appropriately designated groups of its members under the programs it may undertake. From the political standpoint, however, disharmony is likely to result from the attempt to apply any of the criteria that have been suggested for the compulsory allocation of expenses. While individual states may take a different position on particular occasions and with respect to specific projects, it can be asserted as a general proposition that the most acceptable principle of cost-distribution for members of international organizations is that embodied in the scheme of voluntary contributions: that is, financial support should be correlated with political support; a state should give financial backing to an international activity only if and to the extent that it regards that activity as compatible with and conducive to the interests and purposes expressed in its national policy.

It should be noted parenthetically that it seems paradoxical that the economic and social programs on which there is universal agreement in principle, should be financed primarily through voluntary contributions, while the peace and security operations that have divided the Organization against itself are funded primarily through compulsory assessments. But the paradox is only apparent, since the distinction between the assessment and voluntary principles of financial support is by no means clear-cut. Though states may endorse the assessment principle, this often means merely that others should pay, even for programs they disapprove; no state wishes itself to provide backing for a program that it regards as unfavorable to its interest. The task of developing the United Nations as an effective agency involves the problem of resolving the tension between the urge of some states to achieve that end, and the urge of all states to maintain the criterion of national interest as the measure of their individual contributions to international projects. This tension may possibly be resolved, but in all likelihood not without serious political difficulty.

As suggested, the principle of compulsory financial support for United Nations operations involves not only questions relating to the criteria for the equitable distribution of cost, but also issues concerning the manner in which the determination of national assessments is to be made. Clearly, this principle can be given effect only by vesting in some international organ the competence to decide on allocations of financial responsibility. Ultimately, the question what criteria should serve as bases for allocations is overshadowed by the question what organ, acting in accordance with what procedure, should have authority to make these decisions.

Given the political and structural evolution of the United Nations, as well as the assignment of functions provided in the Charter, only one organ, the General Assembly, appears to be in line for this role. For all practical purposes, to say that major United Nations operations must be supported by obligatory rather than voluntary subscription is to say that the authority to legislate in regard to assessments must be exercised by the Assembly. This body, of course, already possesses this competence with respect to the regular budget, and the International Court of Justice has supported its assertion of the capacity to assign financial responsibilities for support of extraordinary political and security operations as well. Technically, additional authority for the Assembly may not be needed; politically, general recognition and acceptance of the Assembly's authority to determine assessments in support of all United Nations programs are essential, if the principle of compulsory financing of those programs is to be given effect. This does not mean that the Assembly must necessarily be authorized to carry out this legislative function under its existing procedural rules, which assign equal voting power to all members and require a two-thirds majority for important decisions. Conceivably, a modified decision-making process might be established by amendment of the Charter, although it would be unrealistic to assume that the political barriers to this accomplishment could easily be surmounted.

With its one-state-one-vote procedure, the political possibility of achieving general agreement to the Assembly's exercising the function of defining obligatory assessments for the support of all United Nations action programs is remote. The current financial crisis is a striking manifestation of the unwillingness of many member states to accept the exercise of this kind of legislative competence by the Assembly. The Soviet Union, viewing the Assembly from the perspective of a minority position, is clearly not inclined to support the broadening of that organ's capacity to impose financial obligations. The major

Western powers, nervously observing the adverse trend of voting patterns in a body that they formerly controlled, share that disinclination.

The position of the United States in this matter is ambiguous. Focusing on the financial troubles of UNEF and ONUC, it condemns the refusal of the Soviet Union and other states to acknowledge their obligation to pay the shares determined by the Assembly, and insists that the Assembly's authority should be upheld and respected. However, the generalization of this position would hardly be attractive to the United States. Despite its ostensible support for the proposition that the Assembly is entitled to launch whatever operations it pleases for the realization of the purposes stated in the Charter, and to bind member states to pay whatever sums it decrees for their support, there is every reason to believe that it would balk at the application of that rule in cases involving programs to which its policy was opposed. The strong pressure that the United States delegation brought to bear on the other members of the Governing Council of the United Nations Special Fund to cancel an agricultural assistance project in Cuba may be indicative of this. To assert that the Soviet Union should pay its designated part of the Congo expense is one thing, but it would be quite a different thing to admit that the Assembly is competent to establish, say, a massive capital fund, over American objections, and to obligate the United States to bear a specified portion of its cost. There is a keen awareness in the United States of the shift in the balance of voting power that is taking place in the Assembly. Correctly, or not, the United States fears increasing "irresponsibility" on the part of the Assembly. Hence, the trend of United States policy may run against, not toward, acceptance of an expanded legislative role for that organ as it is presently constituted.

For some states, the acceptability of the Assembly as the authoritative agency for defining financial obligations of members with respect to all operations would be enhanced by the adoption of an appropriate weighted voting procedure. The political demand for abandoning the procedural expressions of the fiction of the equality of members of the Assembly is mounting, although it is not clear that political resistance to any move toward weighted voting in the Assembly is likely to undergo a corresponding decline, or that political agreement on any specific scheme for reallocating voting power is in prospect. Even if the smaller states were prepared to sacrifice their disproportionate influence in the operation of the Assembly, it seems improbable that any arrangement could be devised that would enable the Assembly to inspire the confidence equally of all the great powers, or of both the Soviet Union and the United States. Two competing powers cannot both be given the assurance of control over the decisions of the Assembly; without that assurance, neither the Soviet Union nor the United States is likely to make a genuine commitment to accept and respect that body's competence to implement the principle of compulsory financial support.

Even if the competence of the Assembly in this respect were formally and firmly established, there would still remain the formidable political problem of giving practical effect to that theoretical competence. How could or would binding decisions of the Assembly be enforced? What sanctions might be brought to bear in cases of delinquency? Not a Communist leader but the Prime Minister of the United Kingdom said with respect to the financing of the Congo operation: "There is the compulsory subscription and the voluntary subscription. The only difference between them is this. The compulsory is the one that you do not pay if you do not want to, and the voluntary is the one that you need not pay unless you wish to."[5]

The Charter provides, in Article 19, that members falling into arrears equaling or exceeding assessments due for two years shall be deprived of their vote in the Assembly unless that body waives the penalty. This might prove to be a sanction of more than negligible importance, but it hardly provides an adequate guarantee that United Nations operations will in fact receive the financial backing they may require, or that budgetary decisions of the Assembly will command respect. Institutional sanctions of this general variety would seem to be the only feasible measures for backing the Assembly in its exercise of financial authority. Such measures might be self-defeating. While the threat of loss of vote in the Assembly might stimulate some states to pay their assessments, the carrying out of that threat would not enrich the treasury of the United Nations and might damage the usefulness of the Organization as an international meeting point and forum. Again, the question arises whether it is politically desirable to press for the functional maximization of the United Nations at the risk of undermining its capacity to play its minimal role in world politics. Conceivably, the attempt to lay a financial founda-

---

[5] Speech by The Rt. Hon. Harold Macmillan in the House of Commons, Dec. 14, 1961. Official text supplied by the British Information Services, New York, Dec. 19, 1961 (mimeo.).

tion for executive actions by the United Nations might destroy the
political foundation for the Organization's doing anything at all. The
consideration of sanctions for failure to pay assessments should not
proceed without due attention to the proposition that no state, and,
normally, no great power will accept compulsion to support activities
that it regards as detrimental to its national interest.

The Control of United Nations Operations

A further point at issue in the debate concerning the development
of the United Nations is the matter of direction and control of international executive actions. The question is not simply what kind of
programs the Organization should undertake, or who should bear
the resultant financial burdens, but how they should be managed
and what ends they should be made to serve.

Concretely, the Soviet Union was not so much opposed in principle to the ONUC operation or disturbed by the portion of the operational budget assigned to itself, as it was dissatisfied with the policy
direction of the United Nations intervention in the Congo and the
place allotted to the Soviet Union in the control mechanism. This
is clear from the record. The Soviet Union approved the beginning
of the Congo operation, turned against that operation only when it
concluded that ONUC was being used for purposes unfavorable to
Soviet interests, and expressed its concern by demanding an arrangement, the troika, that would give itself a powerful influence in the executive mechanism of the Organization. This effort to extend the veto
power into the "office of the chief executive" represented the insistence
of the Soviet Union that it should have, if not the power to control
policy in the positive sense, at least the power to block policy developments that it disapproved.

The Soviet Union later relinquished its demand for the troika,
presumably because of the realization that this constitutional altera-
tion was unattainable, but it had made its point: the Soviet Union
was capable of preventing the installation of a Secretary-General with
full claim to legitimacy and with unimpaired ability to exercise the
functions of the office. In withdrawing its threat to exercise this
capacity, the Soviet Union presumably expressed the mitigation of its

dissatisfaction with the conduct of the Congo operation. Nevertheless, the episode reveals the degree of unwillingness of the Soviet Union to tolerate United Nations operational policies that it regards as incompatible with its interests.

The American attitude is not fundamentally different from this. If the United States has appeared to value the veto less highly than the Soviet Union, this is essentially because the United States has had less occasion to believe that the United Nations was, or to fear that it might be, dominated by forces inimical to its national interest. If the United States has been less suspicious than the Soviet Union of the Congo operation, this is basically because the United States has had the expectation that the operation would be conducted in a manner acceptable to the West—if not favorable to the West, at least not unneutral in a pro-Soviet sense. American reaction to a United Nations operation like ONUC that the United States believed to be dominated by a pro-Soviet policy would not be substantively different, though it might be stylistically different, from Soviet reaction to the Congo operation. The record of debate concerning the establishment of a Special United Nations Fund for Economic Development (SUNFED) suggests quite strongly that the question of policy control arrangements has figured significantly in the negative position of the United States; the positive attitude of the United States toward the World Bank and the cluster of financial institutions that have grown up around that agency is obviously related to the favorable position of the United States and its Western allies in the mechanism for policy determination.

In short, members of the United Nations are not really divisible into those that oppose and those that favor an executive role for international agencies. Those that might be listed in the former group oppose United Nations operations *unless* control arrangements acceptable to themselves are made; those that might be listed in the latter group favor United Nations operations *only if* control arrangements acceptable to themselves are made.

Regardless of the formal provisions that may be made for political direction of a given United Nations operation, of either the peacekeeping or the economic variety, the dependence of such an operation on the financial backing of member states confers on states, especially the great powers, a considerable capacity to influence policy. The act of withholding payment of funds can be used by any state as an informal vote against prevailing policy, or a vote for change of policy. The power of a major state or a bloc of states to deprive a program of a large portion of the necessary financial resources is virtually the power to veto the policy being followed or considered; such power can be used as a threat to destroy a program unless policy demands are met. This is the phenomenon of the "financial veto," the capacity of the state whose financial support is indispensable to dominate policy in a negative sense. The financial method of influencing policy is available, in varying degrees, to all members of the United Nations, as a substitute for or supplement to a more formal status in the mechanisms for controlling the conduct of programs.

To accept the principle that a state can be legally bound to pay an authoritatively determined assessment in support of a given United Nations program is to restrict the right to use the financial weapon as an instrument of control. At this point, a major political question arises: Are states prepared in fact to abandon this instrument? Many states, of course, play such a minor role in financing the United Nations that the effect of their individual financial dissents is insignificant, although this does not necessarily mean that they do not value such capacity to influence policy as they possess. Other states and groups of states are aware of the fact that their importance as budgetary contributors gives them a highly effective if not a decisive voice in the management of United Nations operations, and they may be most reluctant to give up this basis for control. For instance, the Soviet bloc has indicated clearly that it values the power of financial deprivation as a partial compensation for the weakness of its formal voting capacity in the General Assembly. The United States deplores the use of the "financial veto" by other members of the United Nations, complains about the proportion of the financial burdens that is left for it to carry, and worries about the effect on the Organization of excessive dependence on United States support.

It should not be lightly assumed, however, that the United States would happily relinquish the prominent role in the direction and control of programs that is an accompaniment of its decisive importance as a contributor. At the present time the United States supports the effort to establish the competence of the General Assembly to require member states to provide financial backing for the UNEF and

ONUC operations; thus, it appears to be willing to give up its financial veto. However, this policy of the United States relates to particular programs that this country strongly supports. The policy is designed to overcome the reluctance or unwillingness of other states to provide backing for these programs. If the situation were different, the policy of the United States might well be different; if, for example, it were a matter of securing funds for an operation to stabilize the Castro government in Cuba, an operation the United States believed was being conducted for a purpose and in a manner unfavorable to its national interest, quite likely the United States would be inclined to exercise, not to relinquish, its power to hinder through financial nonsupport.

So long as policy-making organs are not so constituted as to satisfy the aspirations of major powers for directive capacity, the latter may be expected to value the possibility of using the financial veto. Even if, by some miracle of statesmanship, control arrangements acceptable to all the major powers and political blocs were devised, the retention of the capacity to exercise financial pressure on policy would be regarded by at least some of the powers as a desirable expedient for strengthening their position.

The problem of the unpredictable future looms large in the attitudes of states toward international institutions and their operations, making them wary of setting precedents that might later prove embarrassing. A government may accept a share of financial responsibility for a program already in operation, but states have a deep-seated reluctance to contract to support future programs without foreknowledge of their budgetary scope, their purposes, or their control mechanisms. The urge not to do this is a fundamental expression of the sense of sovereignty, which is, above all, the freedom of the state to set its own policy as situations arise.

This reluctance is a formidable political obstacle to the acceptance of the obligation to follow the budgetary dictates of the General Assembly in the indefinite future. Conceivably, members of the Assembly may pass a resolution formally acknowledging this obligation, but that such action would represent, in political terms, a genuine commitment to accept the obligation in all circumstances is doubtful. To retain discretionary power to lend or withhold financial support is to maintain some degree of control over the future activities of the United Nations. Since no member or group of members can be certain of dominating the United Nations in the years that lie ahead, it is understandable that great political value should be attached to this method of influencing the development of the Organization's functions. Many states, of course, give high priority to the project of making the United Nations a stronger and more reliably effective organization. This political objective is, in some degree, an offset to the political urge to retain the sovereign right of financial opposition to United Nations operations. However, pretensions of unconditional commitment to the abstract ideal of a strong and active United Nations probably have not much real depth. Underneath, one is likely to find that the degree of commitment depends on the issue of the political control of the Organization. The right to withhold financial support is for every state a political hedge against the possibility that the United Nations may come under the domination of the "wrong" elements of the international community. For the great powers, it is a reserve capacity to exercise a veto over operational policies objectionable to themselves.

Political Implications of a Financially Independent United Nations

Thus far, operations of the United Nations and the specialized agencies have been based on either voluntary contributions of states or purportedly binding assessments levied on states, or some combination of the two. Neither scheme for providing funds has proved wholly satisfactory or successful. Programs dependent on voluntary contributions have seldom enjoyed a genuinely adequate level of support. The two major operations based on assessments, UNEF and ONUC, failed so abjectly in gaining the financial support demanded of states that they threw the United Nations into an acute crisis.

There is, however, a third alternative that must be considered: the United Nations might be enabled to obtain its major financial support from sources other than states. The Organization might, in short, achieve financial independence. This is not a totally new proposition, for revenues from nongovernmental sources have played a supplementary role of some importance in financing several international projects under the auspices of the United Nations. Nevertheless, the suggestion that the Organization should derive the bulk of the funds needed for large-scale operations from sources other than governments, thus emancipating itself from dependence on either the voluntary or the compulsory support of governments, is essentially a new and untried idea.

If this plan were successfully applied, it ought to reduce or eliminate some of the political difficulties that have affected the development of the executive role of the United Nations. For example, there would be less controversy over "fair shares," if states were not called on to provide budgetary sustenance. Moreover, under such a system the implications of a neutral, or permissive, attitude of states toward United Nations programs would be more favorable to the success of those programs. When an operation is based on voluntary contributions, a state that merely acquiesces in the launching of the activity offers it no substantial support; the program may fail for lack of positive support from some of the more affluent states.

Typically, a United Nations program cannot be carried out unless it inspires a more positive attitude than permissiveness on the part of the United States. In contrast, a financially independent United Nations would be able to function on the basis of the consent of states, without requiring their active support. Mere acquiescence by a state would amount to a vote *for,* not *against,* a program. When United Nations operations are based on compulsory assessment, the middle ground of permissiveness is, in effect, eliminated. A state that regards a program with indifference is not allowed simply to stand aside; it is pressed to act as if it supported the program, and, if it refuses, it is put into the position of opposing the program and hindering its operation. On the other hand, a United Nations that could draw on its own treasury would have no need to press indifferent states to lend active financial support and thereby to risk shoving them into the ranks of the opponents of its action. In any given case, there are likely to be many states that are neither determined to hinder the Organization in carrying out a proposed international project nor willing to help it; if the United Nations were in a position to undertake the project without the financial help of its members, it could treat such an attitude as a positive resource.

However, the political difficulty posed by the definite opposition of states to United Nations operations would not be eliminated by making the Organization financially independent. States do not in every case oppose United Nations programs because they do not want to pay for them; on the contrary, in the most significant instances they are unwilling to pay for them because they oppose them. In such instances, the removal of the issue of financial support would not alter the opposition. The expression of opposition would necessarily take a new form, but it must be assumed that states which are determined to block or hamper United Nations activities would be able to contrive substitutes for the weapon of financial deprivation. The record of the Congo case indicates that the Soviet Union is willing and able to attack United Nations programs in more than one way; the attacks on Dag Hammarskjold and on the office he held were significant supplements to the refusal of the Soviet Union to meet its assessments.

United Nations operations that made no financial demands on states would still raise the possibility of contention regarding the purposes to which they were directed, and the mechanisms of policy control under which they were conducted. Indeed, a United Nations that had become financially independent might tend to inspire greater mistrust on the part of some states, for it would appear to be less responsive to the pressures of its members and more likely to become a significant force in world affairs. Such a development would no doubt be welcomed by any state in so far as it felt confident that the Organization would always act in accordance with the state's own interest; equally, it would be viewed with misgiving by any state in so far as such confidence was lacking. A world organization capable of functioning as an autonomous factor in world affairs would not be attractive to the Soviet Union if it seemed likely to exhibit a pro-Western bias in its operations, nor would it be acceptable to the West if it seemed likely to operate in a pro-Soviet manner. Again, the issue of control is the central political concern, and this issue would probably be more, rather than less, acute in the case of a financially independent United Nations.

Assuming that general agreement might be reached among members of the United Nations that the Organization should, in principle, be permitted and enabled to acquire financial resources without resort to governmental contributions or assessments, the problem of securing political agreement on the specific measures for implementing this principle would remain. This would pose many difficulties, ranging from the reluctance of states to permit the United Nations to take over valuable economic resources that they might otherwise appropriate for themselves, to the fear that a world organization vested with the power of taxation might become a kind of superstate challenging the sovereign status of its members.

If these difficulties were overcome, and the United Nations became an agency able to conduct major operations in the peace-keeping and economic fields without dependence on the financial support of states, what would be the probable results? From one point of view, the situation would be ideal. The Organization would be equipped to meet many of the basic needs of the world. It could undertake to deal with emergency situations such as the Congo case, unimpeded by uncertainty regarding financial support. It could move decisively into the realm of economic development, providing large-scale and long-term programs offering promise of genuinely constructive results. In short, the United Nations would have the prospect of doing much more of what needs to be done, of rendering increasingly valuable service to the world. States should welcome this result, as well as their emancipation from the necessity of carrying the financial burden of the United Nations. Thus runs the argument in favor of a financially independent United Nations.

There is another view, however, that deserves careful examination. A financially independent organization might be thrust by general agreement into a position of political irrelevance; instead of provoking arguments about how to use it for important political purposes, the United Nations might inspire a consensus to the effect that it should be treated as an innocuous international philanthropic agency. Its members might restrict it to operations so little related to the central issues of international relations that those operations would be as unlikely to arouse vigorous political opposition as to stimulate spirited political support. The United Nations might tend to become a sort of global "foundation," investing its funds in worthy projects but, precisely because of its financial autonomy, declining in significance as an instrument of states in their relations with each other. Losing its status as a creature of states, dependent on their sustenance, it might cease to be a center of political controversy, at the high cost of becoming an object of political indifference.

According to this point of view, the aim should be not to shift the United Nations to the periphery of world politics, where it can operate unaffected by political conflicts, but to move it ever closer to the center, where it can be used to affect the critical struggles taking place in our time. To change the figure, the danger of wrecking the United Nations on the rocks of political conflict is not to be met by anchoring the Organization in a quiet apolitical harbor, but by attempting to develop a channel of political consensus that it may successfully, and usefully, navigate. This position suggests that the dependence of the United Nations on the financial support of states may be essential to its being taken seriously by states; this dependence may weaken its executive effectiveness, but enhance its political meaningfulness.

The United Nations is an international, which is to say an intergovernmental, organization. What it can become and what it can do are ultimately determined by the governments of member states. A particular government may adopt an attitude of positive support, permissiveness, or opposition to a given program of the Organization. Regardless of how it is financed, a program requires a certain level of support from the membership of the Organization, if it is to be carried out successfully. Within limits, indifference and opposition can be tolerated; these limits cannot be stated precisely, or defined in terms applicable to every situation, but they are nevertheless very real. Much depends on the identity of the state or states declining to give active support, or registering determined opposition. The most critical difficulties arise when one of the two major powers, the Soviet Union or the United States, offers strenuous objection to a given program; in actual experience, the Soviet Union has functioned as the crucial dissenter from United Nations activities, although it is conceivable that the United States might assume that position in future contingencies.

The present financial crisis of the United Nations is a manifestation of the difficulty of sustaining an international operation against the opposition of one of the major powers. When a United Nations operation arouses the hostility of one of these powers, either before or after it has begun, there are two immediate alternatives: the operation may be abandoned in deference to that opposition, or the effort may be made to carry it on despite the opposition. As noted above, the continuation of the Congo operation in the face of active Soviet opposition appears to have been vindicated by the subsequent tempering of the Soviet attack on the operation and on the office of the Secretary-General. However, this experience provides no assurance that a similar tactic would produce equally satisfactory results in every case. The choice between defying and deferring to the opposition of a major power is a difficult one, and a general rule cannot be given regarding what should be done in such circumstances.

Shifting from the concrete situation to the problem of the long-run development of the United Nations, neither of these alternatives should be adopted, but a third course is in order: to expand, so far as possible, the consensual basis for United Nations operations. The constructive political approach, combining the best elements of realism and idealism, is to explore and exploit the possibilities of convincing the dissident power that its own best interest requires an effectively operational United Nations and that the Organization can be relied on to render impartial service, furthering the common interest in the stabilization of international relationships and the advancement of the general welfare. If the great powers can reach agreement on their mutual need for this kind of service, and can develop confidence in the capacity of the United Nations to render it in a spirit of political impartiality, the world organization will have an increasingly useful role to play in the future.

Presumably, this development will not come as a sudden and dramatic transformation. One ought not to expect a joint communiqué in which the great powers proclaim their definitive acceptance of the principle that the United Nations should move uninhibitedly toward the fullest expansion of its operational competence. Rather, one might hopefully anticipate a gradual enlargement of the area within which executive action by the Organization will be tolerated, valued, and supported. Obstructive opposition might be progressively changed, through the stages of passive opposition and reluctant acquiescence, to positive and responsible support for executive action. Toward this end, a constant probing and expanding of the limits of political consensus might best reflect a policy of realism and vision.

CHAPTER 2

Historical and Contemporary Perspectives

BEFORE THE UNITED NATIONS system itself is analyzed, historical precedents and comparative experiences will be briefly discussed. First, what were the financing patterns of the public international unions and of the League of Nations? The League learned much from the financial experience of the unions and the framers of the Charter, in turn, relied heavily on the League for clues to the effective operation of the United Nations. It is instructive to see what lessons were and were not learned from the past. Second, how have the most prominent regional organizations been financed? How relevant are their problems to those faced by the United Nations? What difficulties are duplicated elsewhere? How have these been faced? Have the regional organizations devised any new techniques that might be meaningful for the world organization? An analysis of the fiscal patterns of the major regional organizations may provide us with a better understanding not only of the financial crisis of the United Nations but also the manner in which it may be surmounted.

The Public International Unions

The public international unions were the first manifestations of international organization in the nineteenth century. They were in essence cooperative endeavors among states to facilitate economic, social, technical, and cultural intercourse. Their bailiwick was the world, and their activities included "such diverse fields as health, agriculture, tariffs, railroads, standards of weight and measurement, patents and copyright, narcotic drugs, and prison conditions."[1] Many of them exist to this day and two of the oldest—the International Telegraphic Union (1865) and the Universal Postal Union (1874) —survive as specialized agencies in the United Nations system. The

[1] Inis L. Claude, Jr., *Swords into Plowshares* (Random House, 1959), p. 35.

unions were established by treaty and were open to all countries interested in the specific activity involved.[2]

The unions procured most of their income from direct contributions by member states. The costs were relatively small and were
raised through various forms of assessment. The members of the Universal Postal Union, for example, were divided into seven classes
depending on population, extent of territory, and importance of postal
traffic. Each member was assessed a certain number of units appropriate to its class, but was given the opportunity to join a higher
category. States frequently availed themselves of this opportunity for
reasons of prestige and dignity.[3] When the annual budget of the
Postal Union had been calculated, it was divided by the total number of units, and each member state was then appropriately charged.
This seven-class system was initially adopted by the League, but was
abandoned by it in 1924. It still survives in the Universal Postal
Union today. Another type of assessment was used by the Railway
Union, which allotted budgetary units in proportion to the mileage
of railroads operated for international purposes in the member
countries. Since the costs were small, arrears were seldom a problem.
Sanctions were extremely rare. The rules of the Metric Union, for
example, stipulated expulsion if a state failed in its financial obligations for three consecutive years. In most cases, however, the national self-respect of states proved to be a sufficient guarantee of payment.

The budgetary process of the unions remained fairly primitive.
The member state in which the union placed its headquarters became
its "directing government" and usually acted as treasurer of the organization. The rules of the Postal Union, for example, provided that
the Swiss government would supervise the expenses of the union,
prepare the annual budget, and make necessary advances. The Telegraphic Union and the Sugar Union followed similar rules of procedure. While this technique resulted in some administrative savings,
it made the organization in effect dependent on the host country.
This pattern was finally broken by the Pan American Union in
Washington, which became the first international organization to be

[2] For a definitive work on these early international bodies, see Paul S. Reinsch,
Public International Unions (World Peace Foundation, 1916).
[3] C. Howard-Ellis, *The Origins, Structure and Working of the League of Nations*
(London: George Allen and Unwin, 1938), p. 433.

endowed with an independent treasury and separate fiscal account-
ability.

Perhaps the most interesting fact about these early international
organizations is that not all their revenue was derived from governments. Some of the unions supplemented their income by contributions from nongovernmental sources. The Convention of the International Institute of Refrigeration, for example, provided for subscriptions to the institute by private persons and institutions participating in the science and industry of refrigeration. Similar subscriptions
were authorized in the statutes of the International Association for
the Protection of Children, and the International Radio, Telegraph,
and Telephone Consultative Committees. Other unions augmented
their incomes through fees for services rendered. The International
Exhibition Bureau, for example, was empowered to levy fees "in
payment for services rendered to groups or to individuals."[4]

These early unions were pioneers in the process of international
organization. Their financing patterns and methods of cost sharing
influenced the framers of the League of Nations Covenant and of
the United Nations Charter. And in their more ambitious schemes
of obtaining nongovernmental revenue through private subscriptions and service charges, they adumbrate some of the more recent
proposals for strengthening the financial basis of the United Nations
system.

The League of Nations

The similarities of the financial history of the League to that of
its successor organization are so numerous as to be disturbing.[5] There
was not enough money to do all the things that were considered essential; the pressure for economy was stifling; states were inclined to
distrust the budgetary process, protest against their assessments, and

[4] The Convention Concerning International Exhibitions, Nov. 22, 1928, in Manley
O. Hudson (ed.), *International Legislation* (Carnegie Endowment for International
Peace, 1931), p. 2561.

[5] See Francis P. Walters, *A History of the League of Nations* (London: Oxford
University Press, 1952); Egon Ranshofen-Wertheimer, *The International Secretariat:
A Great Experiment in International Administration* (Oxford: Clarendon, 1956);
Herbert Ames, *Financial Administration and Apportionment of Expenses* (League
of Nations Information Section, 1928); and Seymour Jacklin, "The Finances of the
League," *International Affairs* (September 1934), pp. 609-704.

declare that they were unjustly burdened; a legend of extravagance developed and was made to flourish not only by the isolationist press and hostile governments, but to an even greater extent by statesmen who supported the organization only so long as it "kept its proper place";[6] arrears and defaults were a perennial problem; sanctions against delinquent states were considered and discarded.

The Resources and Budgetary Process of the League

The resources of the League amounted to only a small fraction of those of its successor. The average annual cost of the League, the International Labour Organisation (ILO), and the Permanent Court from 1920 to 1939 was approximately 27 million gold francs or about $5.4 million. This small sum had to pay for the wide range of political, economic, social, and legal work undertaken by the League. Since, in most instances, programs were determined by the amount of revenue available, there developed a tendency to pay more attention to the policy implications of financial decisions than to the financial implications of policy decisions. Indeed, the preoccupation with economy often tended to become obsessive. The ILO periodically lacked sufficient funds to publish its reports, the President of the Committee on Codification of International Law paid personally for the printing of the committee's minutes, and at one point officials of the League Secretariat were even induced to make a voluntary gesture entailing cuts in their own salaries.[7] A resolution fixing a budget ceiling was passed in 1926.

The cumbersomeness of the budgetary process aggravated these difficulties. The Covenant had failed to pinpoint the locus of fiscal power with the result that a struggle for authority between the Assembly and the Council disrupted fiscal procedures until 1924, when the Covenant was amended to give the Assembly sole authority to apportion expenses of the League. The problem of sharing the cost, too, was a thorny one. Until 1924, the seven-class system of the Postal Union had been used as a basis for assessments. By then, however, the members of the League rejected as undignified the idea of grouping states into classes and insisted on being listed alphabetically. After

---

[6] J. David Singer, *Financing International Organizations* (The Hague: Martinus Nijhoff, 1961), p. 40.

[7] Jacklin, *op. cit.*, p. 698.

extensive debate a new formula for calculating a state's ability to pay was agreed upon; one authority defines it as "the result of subtracting the product of population and minimum per capita subsistence from the member's gross national income."[8]

Even after the Assembly was given fiscal authority and a new scale of contributions was determined, the League budget remained the "most economical in the world."[9] Draft estimates had to pass the Secretary-General, the Treasurer, the League's Supervisory Committee, the Fourth Committee of the Assembly, and, finally, the Assembly itself. The unanimity rule in the Assembly included budgetary questions and frequently led to paralysis.

Arrears constantly plagued the League. A Working Capital Fund was established to help liquidate obligations as they arose. But the fund was often exhausted. In 1922, the Committee on Amendments proposed that the Assembly pass a resolution requiring the payment of interest on arrears at the rate then current in Geneva, but the Assembly's Fourth Committee rejected the proposal. The same committee considered the question of sanctions and concluded that "it can be maintained that the failure to pay contributions falls within the application of the paragraph permitting expulsion of states having violated any Covenant of the League," but then went on to say rather lamely that "it would seem, however, preferable at least at the present time not to apply to such cases the provisions of this paragraph." A study by the League Secretariat in 1927 endorsed this conclusion.[10] Hence, despite extensive discussions, the League never invoked penalties against financially delinquent states.

Peace-Keeping Activities

The League engaged in several minor peace-keeping activities, and also planned two major operations only one of which materialized. The fiscal principle governing these operations was that of direct benefit—the states profiting from the peace-keeping operations were expected to pay for them. The League itself would pay nothing.

[8] Howard-Ellis, *op. cit.*, p. 443.

[9] J. David Singer, "The Finances of the League of Nations," *International Organization*, Vol. XIII (Winter 1959), p. 264.

[10] For details of both reports, see "Legal Positions of States Which Do Not Pay Their Contributions to the League," Report by the Secretary-General submitted to the Council on March 8, 1927, League of Nations, Eighth Year, *Official Journal*, (April 1927), Annex 943, pp. 505-08.

The first such operation never got beyond the planning stage. When, after the Polish-led occupation of Vilna in 1920, the League sought to establish an international police force to assure the freedom and authenticity of the vote in the impending Vilna plebiscite, plans were formulated for a multinational expedition of 1,800 men drawn from Norway, Sweden, Denmark, and the Netherlands. The contributing states were to supply their contingents with necessary equipment and advance sums for transport and maintenance, but the total expense of the Vilna force was at the end of the plebiscite to be charged "to the country or countries benefiting from the expression of opinion."[11] The winner was to pay the bill. Although detailed blueprints for the force had already been drawn up, the project had to be abandoned in 1921, when it became evident that Soviet protests and continued political disagreements between the two major parties had made the entire venture impractical.

The second League experiment in peace-keeping was a success. In 1934, the League Council created an international force that operated, with the consent of Germany and France, to ensure order during and after the plebiscite in the Saar Territory. Once again, the fiscal principle adopted unanimously by the Council was that the benefiting states would bear the costs of the operation. In no case were the finances of the League to be drawn on "either for payments which [were] not reimbursable or for advances from the Working Capital Fund."[12] The arrangement stipulated that the principal parties involved in the issue, Germany and France, were to advance five million French francs each, and the Governing Commission of the Saar was to advance one million, to cover the expenses of the plebiscite. Ultimately, the winner would bear the entire cost. The money was placed in a special account to emphasize that it was not part of the League budget. The League administered the plebiscite.

Economic and Social Activities

The major economic and social operations of the League comprised the International Labour Organisation, the High Commissioner

[11] From a memorandum by the Secretary-General, League of Nations, *Official Journal,* Special Supplement No. 4 (December 1920), p. 29.

[12] Minutes of the Council's Seventh Meeting, Dec. 11, 1934, League of Nations, Fifteenth Year, *Official Journal,* No. 12, Pt. II (December 1934), pp. 1762-63.

for Refugees, the Health Organization, and the Committee on Intellectual Cooperation. The expenses of these auxiliary bodies were included in the League's regular budget. Only the most minimal allowances were made. The ILO subsisted on very meager resources. The frequent appearances of Dr. Fridtjof Nansen on the Council rostrum pleading for additional funds for refugees were one of the tragic sagas of League history. The Health Organization and the Committee on Intellectual Cooperation were similarly starved.

As a result of their perennial fiscal plight, the above agencies appealed for voluntary contributions to both governmental and nongovernmental sources. Indeed, without such contributions, they could have done almost nothing. The Nansen Office was granted an annual budget of 4,000 pounds by the League. Much larger sums were contributed by governments individually, notably Great Britain, and by private philanthropic organizations such as the Rockefeller Foundation. In addition, Dr. Nansen devised an ingenious scheme whereby all those refugees who could afford it were asked to pay five gold francs for their Nansen passports. The money was a kind of tax exacted from the richer refugees for the benefit of the poorer. It established a useful principle of organized self-help and bolstered the meager resources of the Nansen Office.

The annual budget of the Committee on Intellectual Cooperation was less than 5,000 pounds, and this amount was appropriated only after acrimonious discussions. The Assembly refused to set up headquarters for the committee in Geneva because it considered the expense too high. Only a French offer to set up the committee in Paris and voluntary contributions from several governments and private organizations made it possible for the agency to come into existence at all.

The Past as Prologue

The tragic financial history of the League was, of course, a symptom of its tragic political history. The penury exhibited by the member states stemmed from the fact that nations were loath to make the League an important vehicle of their national policies. Thus, they were unwilling to invest heavily in it, and this lack of financial support, of course, tended to relegate the organization to even greater neglect. The League was unable to break out of this circular predicament.

The framers of the United Nations Charter learned some important lessons from the League's unhappy history. First, the budgetary process became much more sensible. Fiscal authority was placed unmistakably in one organ, the General Assembly, and a struggle for power within the Organization was thus avoided; financial questions no longer required a unanimous vote but could be passed by a two-thirds majority; a provision for sanctions against delinquents was written into the Charter. In this connection, the League debates on arrears and sanctions may indicate, however, that too stringent penalties might be destructive. Costa Rica, for example, felt so offended at the League's prodding that it withdrew from the organization. Proponents of sanctions against debtors in the United Nations must ponder this precedent. The price of upholding the Charter might be depletion of United Nations membership.

In matters of peace-keeping, the League principle of "immediate benefit" has been followed in only two United Nations operations: the United Nations Temporary Executive Authority (UNTEA) in New Guinea in 1962 and the United Nations Observer Group in Yemen in 1963. In the first instance, Holland and Indonesia divided the cost between them without any expense to the United Nations, and in the second, Saudi Arabia and the United Arab Republic shared the cost. All other United Nations peace-keeping operations have been based on the principle of collective responsibility.

The builders of the United Nations system also departed from precedent in matters of economic, social, and cultural cooperation. They either created autonomous specialized agencies or set up special voluntary programs for the purpose.

On the whole, the founders at San Francisco and their successors learned their lessons well from their predecessors at Versailles and Geneva. The financial basis of the United Nations was built more securely in almost every way. The resources of the United Nations system are much greater than those of the League. These facts point to what is perhaps the most important lesson from the past: the serious financial crisis that has shaken the very foundations of the United Nations must not make us lose our historical perspective. It is true that this crisis must be surmounted if the United Nations is to grow as an instrument of peace and security and the general welfare. It is equally true, however, that the United Nations has been far better off financially than was its predecessor.

Financing Regional Organizations

In this section, the fiscal patterns of three types of regional organizations will be examined: those, like the Organization of American States (OAS) and the Council of Europe, whose purposes are primarily *political;* second, the experiments in *economic* integration in Western Europe, with emphasis on the "supranational" European Communities of The Six;[13] and, finally, the foremost Western *military* alliance: the North Atlantic Treaty Organization (NATO). These three classifications connote emphases and general types of regionalism, not rigidly defined or mutually exclusive categories.

The Organization of American States

Of all the regional arrangements in existence, the fiscal pattern of the Organization of American States most closely resembles that of the United Nations. This fact is not surprising since the OAS undertakes in the Western Hemisphere many of the tasks and responsibilities performed by the United Nations on a global scale.[14] Indeed, the political organs of the OAS, in most instances, are miniature replicas of their opposite numbers in the world organization.

The OAS regular budget is approved by a two-thirds vote in the OAS Council. Like the United Nations regular budget, it has tended to rise gradually over the years. The 1962-63 biennial budget was $13.2 million.[15] It covered the expenses of the Pan American Union's

[13] Throughout the book, the term "supranational" is applied to those organizations vested with certain powers previously exercised by national governments and in which decisions of the governing body are legally binding on the member governments and may be taken by some form of majority vote.

[14] See Arthur P. Whitaker, "Development of American Regionalism; the Organization of American States," *International Conciliation,* No. 469 (March 1951), and *The Western Hemisphere Idea* (Cornell University Press, 1954); Margaret Kiser, *The Organization of American States* (Pan American Union, 1955); Henry P. deVries, *Inter-American Legal Studies* (Columbia University, 1961); and Tenth Inter-American Conference of the Organization of American States, *Report on the Activities of the Organization of American States, 1948-1953* (Pan American Union, 1953).

[15] The figures for 1960-61 and 1961-62 were $8.3 million and $9.8 million, respectively. Until 1953, the budget never exceeded the $3 million mark.

technical and administrative offices, those of the Secretariats, and programs of the Inter-American Defense Board, the Inter-American Commission of Women, the Inter-American Statistical Institute, the Inter-American Juridical Committee, and the Committee on Cultural Action. There is also provision for a modest Working Capital Fund.

The OAS Council also determines the system of apportionment. After much discussion, it decided that "capacity to pay" would best be indicated by the relative position of each state on the current United Nations scale of contributions, with a maximum set at 66 percent of the total. Under this system, the United States paid 66 percent of the 1962-63 budget.

The budgetary process again resembles that of the United Nations regular budget. An OAS Finance Committee, analogous to the United Nations Advisory Committee on Administrative and Budgetary Questions insists on the greatest possible economy. In addition, it presses governments to pay their arrears. These have been more serious than in the United Nations regular budget. Bolivia and Paraguay have owed money since 1955. Of the twenty members, only the United States, Colombia, and Venezuela paid their 1961-62 assessments on time. Although arrears at times reach 25 percent of the entire budget, the OAS Charter makes no provisions for sanctions. These shortfalls have had serious effects on planning and have made necessary the most extreme economy in the organization's program planning.

The OAS has engaged in minor peace-keeping operations of the "United Nations Presence" or "Observer" type. These activities, all of which have been supported by the regular budgets, have included the use of commissions, military observers, the sealing of borders, and the creation of neutral zones. For example, fact-finding commissions to investigate the disputes between Haiti and the Dominican Republic in 1950 and between Costa Rica and Nicaragua in 1955 were paid for out of the regular budget. In addition, in the latter case, the United States, Brazil, Ecuador, Mexico, and Paraguay placed military personnel at the disposal of the OAS for observation purposes. Peace-keeping expenses of the OAS have always remained minuscule, however. In the 1956-57 budget, for example, only $15,826 was set aside as reimbursement to meet the expenses involved in the dispute between Costa Rica and Nicaragua.[16]

The OAS, like the United Nations, engages in economic and social

[16] Council of the Organization of American States, *Decisions Taken at the Meetings of the Council of the OAS,* Vol. IX, January-December 1956 (Pan American Union, 1957), p. 8.

activities. Most technical assistance work is supported by voluntary contributions. Annual donations to the American Program of Technical Cooperation, for example, have remained in a modest range between $1.5 million and $2 million. Furthermore, there are several technical bodies analogous to the United Nations specialized agencies that are not subsumed under the regular budget and procure their income from a combination of assessments and voluntary contributions. The Pan American Health Organization, for example, assigns annual financial quotas to its members in the same proportion as those appearing on the OAS scale. Its regular budget averages about $6 million. In addition, it receives modest donations for its malaria eradication program. The Inter-American Indian Institute is supported by an annual contribution from each member, whose quota is based on its total population and Indian population.[17] In the Inter-American Statistical Institute, quotas are assigned to member governments, professional groups, and sponsoring business firms. Partial support for the Pan American Railway Congress Association also comes from assessing private sources—railway companies and individual private members. The Pan American Institute of Geography and History, on the other hand, relies on voluntary government donations, in addition to assessments. Like the public international unions of former times, these agencies have small budgets and highly specialized tasks.[18]

The OAS has also experimented in exploring new sources of revenue. After the 1949 earthquake in Ecuador, the OAS Council adopted a resolution "to ask the governments of the countries members of OAS to consider the advisability of having each of them issue an Ecuadorian relief stamp, the total revenue from which would be devoted to the economic and financial reconstruction of that country and be placed at the disposal of that Government."[19] Stamps had frequently been issued in the past for such purposes as disaster relief, the construction of post offices, Red Cross activities, campaigns against cancer or tuberculosis, and the financing of national expositions. Here, however, postal relief stamps were to be made available for the first time through an international organization. While the sums thus realized remained modest, OAS was the first such organization that attempted to supplement its income from hitherto untapped sources.

[17] Annals of the Organization of American States, Vol. II, No. 2 (1950), p. 173.
[18] Kiser, op. cit., p. 57.
[19] Annals, Vol. I, No. 4 (1949), p. 359.

Financing the Organization of American States, then, is in most ways—though on a much smaller scale—like financing the United Nations. The regular budget is assessed; the criteria that are used to apportion expenses among members are similar to those used by the United Nations; the budget receives careful scrutiny; there is a compelling desire among delegations for economy and, usually, a shortage, not of desirable programs, but of resources with which to finance them; a problem of arrears exists; and the financing of economic and social activities relies greatly on voluntary contributions, which are seldom forthcoming in sufficient amounts.

But the gravest fiscal problem of the United Nations—financing large-scale peace-keeping operations—has not yet occurred in the OAS.

The Council of Europe

In January 1949 the foreign ministers of the major European powers drafted the Statute of the Council of Europe.[20] The Council's primary goal, as set forth in Article I, was to be the achievement of "a greater unity between its Members for the purpose of safeguarding and realizing the ideals and principles which are their common heritage." Progress toward unity was to proceed on several fronts. The statute listed an extensive range of subjects that were to be within the competence of the Council. Among them were legal matters, human rights, and cultural and social questions. While no specific reference was made to political questions in the statute, it was clearly implied that the Council was to function as essentially a political body. It was to consist of a Committee of Ministers whose members were to be the Foreign Ministers of the member states and of a Consultative Assembly whose membership was to be drawn from the legislatures of the participating countries. The original membership of the Council comprised ten states: Belgium, Denmark, France, Ireland,

[20] Important studies of the Council of Europe include: A. H. Robertson, *The Council of Europe* (London: Stevens 1961); A. J. Zurcher, *The Struggle to Unite Europe—1940-1958* (New York University Press, 1958); Robert Schuman, "L'Europe est une Communauté Spirituelle et Culturelle," *European Yearbook*, Vol. I (The Hague: Martinus Nijhoff, 1955), pp. 17-42; K. Lindsay, *Ten Years of European Cooperation* (Strasbourg, 1958); Council of Europe, *Ten Years of European Cooperation* (1958), *European Cooperation in 1958* (1959), *European Cooperation in 1959* (1960), and *A Policy for Europe Today;* M. M. Ball, *NATO and the European Union Movement* (London, 1959); and Political and Economic Planning, *European Organisations* (London: George Allen and Unwin, 1959), esp. pp. 149-56.

Italy, Luxembourg, Holland, Norway, Sweden, and Great Britain. Since then, six more have been added: Austria, West Germany, Greece, Iceland, Turkey, and Cyprus. The Council's membership policy was conceived as open-ended, and it was hoped that it might serve as a first step toward a United States of Europe.

The Council of Europe derives most of its revenue by apportioning its expenses among the member states. Each country bears the expenses of its representatives in the Committee of Ministers and in the Consultative Assembly, but the costs of the Secretariat and all other common expenses are shared in proportions determined by the Ministers on the basis of the populations of member states. In 1962, the Council of Europe's revenue, approximately fifteen million new French francs, was collected in the following manner:

COUNTRY	PERCENTAGE OF ASSESSMENT
France, Federal German Republic, Italy, and the United Kingdom	17.7 each
Turkey	9.0
The Netherlands	4.0
Belgium, Greece, Sweden	3.0 each
Austria	2.6
Denmark	1.7
Norway	1.3
Irish Republic	1.1
Iceland, Luxembourg, Cyprus	0.2 each

The modest amounts involved are paid without difficulty, and no provision for sanctions appears in the statute of the Council.

The power of the purse is shared by the Committee of Ministers and the Assembly. The former holds essential control by approving the budget estimates, but the latter has the right to express its views on the budget in advance of the Ministers' approval. This it accomplishes through a specially constituted Budget Committee. The lack of clear distinction between the Committee of Ministers and the Consultative Assembly on matters of fiscal authority is somewhat reminiscent of the early days of the League of Nations.

Since the mandate of the Council of Europe has been very vague, member states have been reluctant to support it with generous funds. The lack of specific substantive goals permeates the Council with a sense of alienation from the pragmatic every-day political realities. Nations are not very willing to finance abstract ideals that do not promise relatively quick and concrete returns.

OEEC and OECD

Western Europe has become one gigantic experimental station in economic integration. The hope that economic cooperation might contribute to the building of political communities has led to the establishment of several trail-blazing organizations. These arrangements include chiefly the Organization for European Economic Cooperation (OEEC), superseded in 1960 by the Organization for Economic Cooperation and Development (OECD); the European Coal and Steel Community (ECSC); the European Atomic Energy Community (EURATOM); and the European Economic Community, or Common Market (EEC). Behind the façade of these prosaic-sounding names pioneer work has been accomplished. The organizations they stand for have made significant contributions to building international order. Each has been unique, attuned to its own particular objectives and accumulating its own special experiences.

The nations that signed the OEEC Convention in April 1948 were all Western European: Austria, Belgium, Denmark, France, Greece, Iceland, Ireland, Italy, Luxembourg, the Netherlands, Norway, Portugal, Sweden, Switzerland, Turkey, and the United Kingdom. Canada and the United States were "associated countries." The German Federal Republic joined in 1955. Spain participated in some of OEEC's work and Yugoslavia took part as an observer. The machinery of OEEC included a Council of Ministers composed of all the member governments, an Executive Committee, several Technical Committees, and a Secretariat. Thus equipped, the organization embarked on its two main responsibilities: advice on the apportioning of American aid, and the liberalization of trade and payments in the Western European economy.

The organization's budget averaged about $5.5 million a year, two-thirds of which was used for administrative costs and the remainder apportioned for the outlays of OEEC's specialized agencies.[21] It was approved each year by the Council, acting unanimously—a rare fiscal practice in contemporary international organizations. Likewise, it was the Council's task to decide on each member's assessments and to request the Secretary-General to present it with a supplementary budget if circumstances should so require. At no time, however, was a resolution involving additional expenditures deemed effective un-

[21] The European Nuclear Agency, the Office for Scientific and Technical Personnel, and the European Productivity Agency.

til the Council of Ministers had approved an estimate prepared by the Secretary-General.

When in 1960 the OEEC was remodeled as the Organization of Economic Cooperation and Development, with Canada and the United States as full members, the objectives and administrative arrangements of the new institution remained substantially similar to those of its predecessor. In scope the new OECD was to be more "outward looking," and was to help less developed nations achieve sound economic expansion. The articles of the old convention pertaining to fiscal matters underwent a minor change: the general expenses of the organization were still to be approved unanimously by the Council of Ministers and apportioned according to a scale fixed by it, but "other expenditure shall be financed on such basis as the Council may decide." Criteria for distinguishing between "general expenses" and "other expenditures" were not established.

It is fairly safe to assume that OEEC's fiscal habits will be carried on in the OECD. Perhaps the most significant contribution of the two organizations in policy-making as well as in financing has been the evolution of the "confrontation technique"—the continuous process of intergovernmental consultation going on at all levels of the organization, which encouraged a "European way of thinking." This development has demonstrated that an organization need not be "supranational" in order to be effective. The decisive factor in the OEEC's success was not structural. It was the fact that the organization served two real and tangible purposes on which there existed a fundamental political consensus: facilitating the distribution of Marshall Plan aid and liberalizing intra-European trade. It was these well-defined purposes that saved it from the fate of the Council of Europe, in which case cooperation was defined much less concretely and sharply. Indeed, the success of the OEEC experience prompted six of its members eventually to launch a far more ambitious project in economic collaboration with completely unprecedented patterns of financing.

The "Supranational" Communities: ECSC, EURATOM, and EEC

In May 1950, French Foreign Minister Robert Schuman proposed to pool the resources of the French and German coal and steel industries under a common "supranational" authority that was to be open to other European countries. The motives underlying this far-reaching proposal were both economic and political. A more rational

organization of coal and steel production and distribution throughout Western Europe would be highly desirable. But far more important was Schuman's desire to end Franco-German enmity. By the pooling of two raw materials vital for war, the possibility of military conflict
between Germany and France would be greatly reduced. The negotiations among "The Six" took a little over two years, and in September 1952 the European Coal and Steel Community, creating a single
market for coal and steel for the 160 million people of the six participating states (France, Germany, Italy, Belgium, the Netherlands and
Luxembourg) became a reality.

The structure of ECSC is quite unique. At least one of its institutions—the High Authority—possesses "supranational" powers over the
coal and steel industries of The Six. This power applies only to those
two sectors of the member countries' economies, however, and an effective system of checks and balances was written into the treaty.
If the High Authority is the motor of ECSC, its Council of Ministers,
Consultative Committee, Assembly, and Court of Justice may be
seen as the brakes. The total structure of ECSC is a unique phenomenon, falling somewhere between a purely intergovernmental organization and a federal government. Its High Authority certainly has far more
power than the central agency of a conventional international organization, though far less than is generally yielded to a federal government.[22]

ECSC also represents a radical innovation in the financing of international institutions: the High Authority has the power to tax enterprises within the six member states, and it also has the power to borrow.
The levies it may impose on the enterprises subject to its jurisdiction
are assessed annually and are calculated according to the value of the
coal and steel production in the member countries. Paid to the ECSC
each month, the levy may not exceed a rate of 1 percent of the average
value of the enterprise's production, unless the Council of Ministers decides to authorize an increase in the quota.

The value of taxable products approached $10 billion in 1962.
Hence, income from taxation could have amounted to a maximum
of $100 million. Actually, the High Authority has never imposed the
ceiling rate of 1 percent, but has progressively reduced the tax from

[22] Important general studies of the ECSC include Ernst B. Haas, *The Uniting of
Europe* (Stanford University Press, 1958); Henry Mason, *The Coal and Steel Community* (1955); A. H. Robertson, *European Institutions* (Praeger, 1959); Political
and Economic Planning, *op. cit.;* Paul Reuter, "Juridical and Institutional Aspects
of the European Regional Communities," *Law and Contemporary Problems,* Vol.
XXVI (Summer 1961), pp. 381-99.

0.90 percent in 1956 to 0.20 in 1962. Income from taxation during the decade of 1952 to 1962 has been as follows (in thousands):[23]

1952–53	$10,620	1957–58	$29,120
1953–54	48,100	1958–59	26,060
1954–55	56,760	1959–60	31,160
1955–56	42,290	1960–61	32,280
1956–57	32,130	1961–62	28,200

Arrears in tax payments are rare. The High Authority charges 5 percent interest on each three months delay. Income from tax arrears and fines never exceeds $20,000 a year. Most of the tax income comes from enterprises in West Germany, followed by those in France, Italy, and Benelux in that order.

Under the Treaty, tax income is used to cover the administrative costs of the ECSC, assistance to workers, research, and the establishment of a guarantee fund to meet possible delays or defaults in loan repayments.

The second major source of revenue of the ECSC—borrowed funds —is also of primary importance. In order to launch the High Authority's operations, the United States Government, through the Export-Import Bank, loaned the ECSC $100 million in 1954. By 1962, the High Authority had negotiated loans totaling approximately $275 million: three public issues amounting to $120 million were raised in the United States; one of $11.6 million was offered in Switzerland; and the balance was derived from the earlier advance of the United States and from other loans contracted for the specific purpose of constructing workers' houses.

Revenues obtained from borrowing may be used by the High Authority only to grant loans to enterprises or to guarantee other loans negotiated by these industries. With the unanimous consent of the Council of Ministers, they may also be used to help finance workers' houses and installations.

In order that lenders to the ECSC would be assured that it would hold securities for their common benefit, the High Authority instituted an agreement with the Bank of International Settlements, known as the "Act of Pledge." This agreement stipulated that the High Authority's credits and securities should be placed in a portfolio representing a pledge in the hands of the bank for the benefit of all the

[23] Communauté Européene du Charbon et de l'Acier. Haute Autorité, *Budget de la communauté pour le onzieme exercise 1er Juillet 1962–Juin 30, 1963* (Luxembourg, 1962), p. 25.

community's lenders. These measures were essential since the ECSC was not itself conceived primarily as a bank.

To sum up, the financing of the ECSC is unique among international organizations. Its power to tax coal and steel enterprises in the community frees it from financial dependence on governmental contributions. And it has managed to reduce the rate of the levy over the years. Its use of the borrowing power has also been of pioneering significance. Most important, ECSC has, on the whole, been a success. Since its inception, the production of coal, coke, and iron ore has substantially increased in the member countries, trade has risen, and labor conditions have greatly improved. While these improvements, to be sure, have their roots in the general economic upsurge of Western Europe, the ECSC has been at least partially responsible.

The European Atomic Energy Community (EURATOM) was born at a meeting of the Foreign Ministers of "little Europe" in June 1955. What Robert Schuman of France did for ECSC, Paul-Henri Spaak of Belgium accomplished for Euratom. After protracted negotiations, the treaty was signed in Rome in March 1957, and after ratification by the six member states went into effect on January 1, 1958. Therewith another sector of the economies of The Six, the peaceful uses of atomic energy, was absorbed into a "supranational" community.

In contrast to the European Coal and Steel Community, EURATOM is not financially autonomous. The major portion of income is derived from assessments. Article 173 of the statute does leave the door open for the possible establishment of a levy of the ECSC type, but no steps have been taken by the members in that direction.

At present, Euratom divides its fairly modest annual expenditures into four categories: administrative; community research; national research; and those of the Supply Agency. The first two categories are financed by assessments in accordance with the following scale:

COUNTRY	ADMINISTRATIVE BUDGET (Percent)	COMMUNITY RESEARCH BUDGET (Percent)
Belgium	7.9	9.9
Germany	28.0	30.0
France	28.0	30.0
Italy	28.0	23.0
Luxembourg	0.2	0.2
The Netherlands	7.9	6.9
Total	100.0	100.0

Expenses for the support of national research programs are met by borrowing, but Euratom's financial powers in this realm differ from those of ECSC. While the latter endowed the "supranational" High Authority with competence to borrow and to lend, EURATOM gave this decisive power not to its commission but to the Council of Ministers.

The Supply Agency, alone in the EURATOM structure, enjoys a degree of fiscal autonomy. It may levy charges on transactions in order to defray its operational costs, and it may resort to borrowing to meet its needs. So far, most of its expenses have been met without difficulty from the administrative budget.

The third of the European "supranational" experiments is the European Economic Community (EEC) or Common Market. This promises to be one of the most ambitious economic schemes of our time. The idea for EEC was contained in the Spaak Report of 1956, which forcefully outlined the advantages of further steps toward economic union among The Six. The draft treaty proposed a twelve- to fifteen-year transitional period during which tariffs and quantitative restrictions for all commodities, including agricultural products, were to be eliminated among the six participating states. A single tariff schedule to be applied to outside countries was to be developed; freedom of movement for workers was also envisaged; exchange policies were to be coordinated; a common transportation policy was to be hammered out; and common provisions for social benefits were contemplated. In brief, EEC was to become an arrangement that went much further than the abolition of tariffs and quotas among The Six, yet still stopped short of complete economic union.

Once again, Paul-Henri Spaak guided the project through the delicate formative stages. As in the ECSC, each of the prospective member states saw definite advantages. The EEC Treaty was also signed in Rome in March 1957 and, together with the EURATOM Treaty, went into effect on January 1, 1958.

The institutional structure of the European Economic Community is patterned after the ECSC. A commission of nine members chosen on the basis of "general competence" plays the role of the High Authority. It is to perform its duties "in the general interest of the community with complete independence." Its "supranational" authority largely flows from the power to fix and amend the timetables for freeing the various "sectors" from trade restrictions. The Assembly of the ECSC also serves the Common Market and has the power to remove members of the EEC Commission through a vote of censure.

The ECSC Court of Justice was also made into a court of appeal in the framework of EEC. The three "communities" of The Six have a common Assembly and a common Court of Justice. In addition, EEC has a Council of Ministers, which is the link between the community and the national governments. An Economic and Social Committee similar in function to the Consultative Committee of the ECSC completes the institutional picture.

EEC's financial powers are much more limited, however, than those of either ECSC or EURATOM. It possesses neither taxing nor borrowing authority, and is completely dependent for its financial support on contributions assessed on the members by the Council of Ministers.

The European Economic Community has two budgets and two fixed assessment scales: one pertains to the regular budget and the other to the cost of the Social Fund. The purpose of the fund is the promotion within the community of employment opportunities and of workers' mobility, both geographic and occupational. The percentages assessed for each budget are distributed among The Six as follows:

COUNTRY	REGULAR BUDGET EXPENSES (Percent)	EUROPEAN SOCIAL FUND (Percent)
Belgium	7.9	8.8
Germany	28.0	32.0
France	28.0	32.0
Italy	28.0	20.0
Luxembourg	0.2	0.2
The Netherlands	7.9	7.0
Total	100.0	100.0

These scales may be amended only through unanimous decision of the council. Assessments for the regular budget are determined by the following voting formula: Germany, Italy, and France have four votes each, Belgium and the Netherlands have two, and Luxembourg has one. Votes for the Social Fund budget are weighted as follows: Germany and France: 32 each; Italy: 20; Belgium: 8; the Netherlands: 7; Luxembourg: 1.

A third budget, the EEC's Development Fund—designed to increase the social and economic development of the members' overseas territories—is financed in yet another way. This fund is supported by contributions that member nations have made for a five-year period. Initially, Belgium and the Netherlands each contributed $70 million;

Germany and France $200 million each; and Luxembourg gave $1.25 million. These sums are used to finance projects in overseas countries, territories, and former possessions of member countries.

The EEC treaty also contains a provision similar to that found in EURATOM's charter whereby the commission is charged with studying the conditions under which members' contributions might be replaced by other revenues—notably receipts from common customs tariffs, when such tariffs are brought into being.

As the above data indicates, the financial structure of each of the three "supranational" communities is completely *sui generis* and is a logical outgrowth of the function it performs. The taxing and borrowing powers of the Coal and Steel Community, the charges and dual assessment scales of EURATOM, and the potential pooling of sovereignties now underway in EEC all herald innovations in the financing of international institutions.

Financing a Military Alliance: The Case of NATO

NATO differs fundamentally from the other international institutions considered thus far. It is in essence a military alliance based on the principle of collective self-defense. The North Atlantic Pact, concluded in 1949, bound together twelve states of the Atlantic Community: the United States, Great Britain, France, Canada, Italy, Portugal, Norway, Denmark, Iceland, Belgium, the Netherlands, and Luxembourg. Greece and Turkey joined the alliance in September 1951 and West Germany's accession in 1955 brought the total membership to fifteen. Each member nation committed itself, in the event of armed attack, to take "such action as it deem(ed) necessary, including the use of armed force, to restore and maintain the security of the North Atlantic area."

"Financing" of NATO is accomplished in three basic ways: first, by furnishing manpower; this remains essentially a national responsibility. Although NATO has now established multi-national forces under a unified command, raising and maintaining these forces remain under national authority. Moreover, each member state retains complete autonomy over its defense budget. Second, the civilian administrative costs of the alliance are shared on an international basis; so are the expenses of NATO's common infrastructure program. The overall annual cost, exclusive of defense, is more than $800 million.

The raising of manpower need concern us only briefly. Each year, the resources of each member state are evaluated in terms of what it can contribute and what is reasonable for NATO to ask from it. There is no given formula for this procedure, which is called the Annual Review. General Lauris Norstad described it as follows:

> As a practical matter, we work out on quite a detailed basis the contribution of each country; each should or could provide so many divisions, so many squadrons, so many missile units, so many naval formations, specifically. We discuss this with the country concerned and there is a meeting, or a series of meetings between the military people; there is a submission then of what the country feels it can do in response to this, and there is a NATO Council meeting at ministerial level which in the last analysis considers the contribution of each country, and the commitment of the country is made on a political basis at the ministerial meetings. They are the only ones authorized to change it.[24]

These decisions are taken in the light of "what NATO expects the military forces to accomplish."[25] Political and military factors clearly take precedence over budgetary considerations.

For a time in the early 1950's, NATO weighed the possibility of sharing the costs of defense among its members according to an agreed formula. Experts attempted to work out comparable statistics on defense expenditure and national income. They hoped that the total NATO load might be apportioned among member countries according to per capita national income. However, the member states found it impossible to agree on a scale of contributions. The informal procedure of the Annual Review has thus remained in effect by default.

Unlike national defense contributions, the civilian administrative costs are apportioned under an agreed scale of contributions. The total averages around $13 million annually, and the system of apportionment has aroused little controversy. The United States, France, and Great Britain contribute approximately 24 percent each and the remaining 28 percent is prorated among the other twelve member states.

The sharing of "infrastructure" expenses, however, created considerable difficulties during the early years. "Infrastructure" describes all those fixed installations that are necessary for the effective deployment

[24] Testimony of General Norstad, *Mutual Security Appropriations for 1961*, Hearings before a Subcommittee of the House Committee on Appropriations, 86 Cong. 2 sess., p. 521.
[25] *Ibid.*, p. 522.

and operations of modern armed forces: air fields, signals, communications, military headquarters, radar warning, navigational aid stations, and port installations.

The $88.2 million cost of the initial operation in 1950, known as the "first slice," was absorbed without a definite formula by the governments of Great Britain, France, and the Benelux countries. When the "second slice" came up for discussion in 1951, attempts were made to agree on a scale of assessments. Various criteria of "capacity to pay" were considered. Most prominent among these was the criterion of the "user nation": NATO would call on each member nation to pay for infrastructure installations according to the extent to which that nation's armed forces would benefit from these facilities. However, it proved impossible to agree on a formula, and both the second and the third slice were paid for by informal agreements. Discussions over the costs of the fourth slice in 1953 revealed the procedure by which agreement was reached. Lord Ismay, NATO's first Secretary-General, described the process frankly:

> They dumped the whole problem in my lap, so I called in three assistant secretaries general, and each of us drew up our own list of what we thought the percentage of sharing should be, and then we averaged them out. I couldn't for the life of me possibly say on what basis I acted except I tried to take into account all sorts of things like the ability to pay and whether the building (of installations) would be going on in a country so that it would benefit from the construction and the money spent.
>
> Then we got into the Council meeting in April of 1953, and everybody around the table thought it was a jolly good distribution except for his own, which they thought was too high. Anyway, we went round the table and finally got agreement of each to take what was given within 1.8 percent of the total, and then we simply divided up that 1.8 percent among the fourteen, and that's all there was to it. That's why all the shares are in those funny percentage amounts.[26]

The "funny percentage amounts" were the following: Belgium, 5.09; Canada, 7.13; Denmark, 3.05; France, 13.75; Greece, 1.01; Italy, 6.50; Luxembourg, 0.20; the Netherlands, 4.07; Norway, 2.54; Portugal, 0.32; Turkey, 2.03; United Kingdom, 11.45; United States, 42.86.[27]

[26] Anne M. Warburton and John B. Wood, *Paying for NATO* (London: Friends of Atlantic Union, n.d.), p. 31.

[27] *Ibid.*, Appendix III. At the time when the shares were agreed on, Germany was not a member of NATO and Iceland made no contribution.

Once the members had agreed on these figures, there were no further difficulties and at last "the cost-sharing ghost, whose lugubrious presence had haunted previous Ministerial sessions,"[28] was banished.

In succeeding years, the percentage apportionment of infrastructure costs was as follows:[29]

COUNTRY	SLICES II–VII COST-SHARING APPROVED IN JUNE 1954 (Percent)	SLICES VIII–XI COST-SHARING APPROVED IN FEBRUARY 1957 (Percent)	SLICES XII–XV COST-SHARING APPROVED IN FEBRUARY 1961 (Percent)
Belgium	5.462	4.39	4.24
Canada	6.021	6.15	5.15
Denmark	2.767	2.63	2.87
France	15.041	11.87	12.00
Germany	—	13.72	20.00
Greece	0.750	0.87	0.67
Italy	5.681	5.61	5.97
Luxembourg	0.155	0.17	0.17
The Netherlands	3.889	3.51	3.83
Norway	2.280	2.19	2.37
Portugal	0.146	0.28	0.28
Turkey	1.371	1.75	1.10
United Kingdom	12.758	9.88	10.50
United States	43.679	36.98	30.85
Total	100.000	100.00	100.00

To sum up, the NATO infrastructure program is one of the most expensive international cost-sharing operations in existence. Perhaps the most significant observation to be made about it is the fact that, despite the political consensus existent among the membership on the overriding necessity for collective self-defense, it was not possible to arrive at a definitive formula for apportioning the expenses. In the last analysis, this had to be accomplished through informal, quite "unmathematical" devices. That it was accomplished at all was no doubt due to the fact that the membership considered the establishment of the infrastructure installations a political and military necessity. Thus, the financial problem had to be solved somehow. This experience may indeed suggest that the quest for technical formulae in the absence of political consensus may remain an exercise in futility.

[28] Lord Ismay, *NATO: The First Five Years, 1949-1954*, p. 118.
[29] NATO, *Facts about the North Atlantic Treaty Organization* (Paris, NATO, January 1962), p. 123.

Lessons for the United Nations

The overriding lesson which contemporary regional organizations seem to offer for the financing of the United Nations system is the following: an organization blessed with a high degree of political consensus and well-defined goals offering concrete advantages to the membership will have few grave problems in the financial realm; conversely, the absence of such consensus and of clearly set forth goals will tend to surround an organization with an atmosphere of obsessive frugality and thrift.

The OAS has not been blessed with a system of common values. The United States and the Latin American nations have tended to view the organization in a very different light and with very different expectations. "Hemispheric solidarity" is still an aspiration rather than a reality. Indeed, the financial history of the OAS has been a miniature of the League of Nations. The tiny budget, the problem of arrears, and the passion for parsimony are reminiscent of the League's melancholy history. Fortunately, the OAS has not been plagued by the financing of controversial peace and security operations. Its major problem is an insufficient budget, not the financing of controversial activities. Hence, the overall similarity to the League seems greater than that to the United Nations despite the structural similarities to the latter.

While political consensus in the Council of Europe may be somewhat higher than that in the OAS, this consensus has been couched in such abstract and generalized terms that it has lost a great deal of substantive meaning. Moreover, though there may be agreement on the overall goal of political unification, there are profound schisms on how this goal may best be achieved. In addition, the Council is beset by a structural difficulty that complicated the financial life of the League: the lack of clear fiscal authority in any one of the governing organs.

On the whole, the United Nations can learn little from the OAS and the Council of Europe.

On the other hand, a sense of purpose and a considerable degree of consensus have permeated the economic organizations in Western Europe. None has had serious financial difficulties, and all have been bold innovators in the quest for revenue. Formal structure seems to have made little difference. OEEC and OECD, equipped with no "supranational" features, nevertheless developed a valuable "confrontation technique," which they managed to extend into the financial realm. Herein might lie a valuable lesson for the United Nations. The even bolder innovations of the "supranational" communities are of doubtful relevance to the United Nations at its present stage of development. But they may be of inestimable value once the limits of consensus in the world organization tend to expand. In theory at least, the fiscal powers of the General Assembly under Article 17, as interpreted by the World Court, are great indeed.[30] Once political consensus broadens and deepens, the taxing and borrowing powers of the ECSC, the borrowing power of EURATOM, and the dual assessment scales and weighted voting systems of the EEC may provide an invaluable laboratory for experimentation.

The fundamental importance of homogeneity as a condition of financial adequacy is underlined once more by the financial history of NATO. Its "infrastructure" program was financed even though no scale of apportionment could be agreed on. It was financed because everyone agreed that the job had to be done.

All told, the regional organizations provide the United Nations with valuable insights from the past and for the present and future as well. Some point to follies of the past that the United Nations has largely surmounted; others suggest improvements that may be attempted in the immediate present; but most of the lessons may show their greatest value at a time when the attainment of greater political consensus among the membership will give the Organization the power to strike out in new directions in its constant search for revenue.

History teaches through analogy, not identity. The lessons from the past suggest many warnings and a few hopes. The more recent lessons of regional organizations hold out much hope for the United Nations—but only in a relatively distant future. Armed with these perspectives, an analysis of the present, the financing of the United Nations system, will be undertaken.

[30] For a full discussion of this point, see Chap. 6.

PART II

Apportioning the Costs

CHAPTER 3

The Costs of United Nations Membership

A SURVEY OF THE FINANCES of the League of Nations shows a picture of tight-fisted states starving a meagerly endowed international organization virtually out of existence. Fears are voiced in many quarters today about the finances of the United Nations, even though the Organization has been far more generously endowed. While most states are willing to contribute more funds, needs and expectations have grown and horizons have enlarged at an even more rapid rate. Hence, in relative terms, the poverty of the United Nations is as real, perhaps more real, than was that of the League. *"Plus ça change, plus c'est la même chose"* applies especially well to the financial problems of international institutions.

In the light of the above, this analysis of financing the United Nations system can begin with two general questions: first, what is the overall cost of the United Nations to its members, and second, what does it cost a nation to belong to the United Nations? These questions are of mounting concern to governments and taxpayers. The answers will shed some light on the Organization's financial crisis. They will also provide us with valuable data for the more detailed analyses to follow.

Trends in Overall Costs

The rising cost of the United Nations system to the member states can be simply stated: starting from an initial budget level of $50 million in 1946, the overall annual cost of the United Nations system has risen to almost $500 million in 1963. These costs comprise four categories: the regular budget, the peace-keeping operations, the special voluntary programs, and the specialized agencies. To these expenses must be added the many "hidden costs" of membership such as the maintenance of missions in New York, Geneva, and other major centers, and the backstopping staff at home, plus communication, information, and transportation costs.

The normal operating expenses of the Organization covered by the regular budget have risen gradually from $19 million in 1946 to $93 million in 1963. There has been no precipitous rise nor any abrupt cutback at any time. The period may be divided into three parts: an initial growth period from 1946 to 1949; a fairly sustained stabilization from 1949 to 1956 in which the overall rise was less than $10 million; and a persistent upward trend since 1957 as many new states have entered the Organization and new demands have been continually pressed on it. In this last period, the budget has risen by 65 percent over the 1956 level.

The increase in the administrative and running costs of the Organization since 1946 is understandable when it is considered that the membership has more than doubled, costs have risen, the institution has been confronted with an almost continuous succession of international crises, and there has been an unremitting demand that it concern itself with an ever-growing circle of problems and activities.

The upward curve of the United Nations regular budget would have been much steeper if the costs of some of the more expensive special programs cared for by voluntary contributions or of the large emergency peace and security operations had been absorbed. The separate financing of these activities has saved the regular budget from a much larger multiplication.

The most significant feature in the growth of costs of the United Nations is, of course, the upsurge in expenditures for peace and security operations since 1956. There is no more impressive change in the overall pattern than the sharp upward turn of expenditures occasioned by the establishment and maintenance of the United Nations Emergency Force in the Middle East (UNEF) and the United Nations Military Operation in the Congo (ONUC).

For the period from November 1956 to the end of 1963, the United Nations costs for UNEF amounted to approximately $150 million. These expenditures ran initially over $20 million a year, but since 1958 have been reduced to the $18-$19 million level.

The United Nations commitments for the military operation in the Congo amounted to approximately $400 million by the end of 1963, with $60 million expended between July and December 1960, $120 million from January to December 1961, roughly $120 million in 1962, and $100 million in 1963.

Another prominent feature of the rising cost of these operations has been the large and steadily mounting expenditure for the special programs financed by voluntary contributions. From a figure of $67 million in 1952, these had risen to $203 million by 1963. Taken as a whole, the special voluntary programs accounted for 40 percent of total United Nations expenditures in 1963.

While the portion of costs of the Organization covered by government voluntary contributions is less than one-half of total expenses of the United Nations system, it is clear that this means of support has been providing an average of more than twice the income provided by the regular budget since 1956. The amounts raised in this manner have fluctuated widely, but, on the whole, the trend has clearly been upward. The rise has been especially steep since 1959 due to the expansion of economic development activities financed by the Expanded Programme for Technical Assistance (EPTA) and the Special Fund. By 1963, government voluntary contributions provided the largest single item in the four categories outlined above.

Finally, the budgets of the specialized agencies have risen in a gentle upward curve. The rise has been strikingly similar to that of the regular budget. From $28 million in 1949, the budgets of the agencies, not including the brief life span of the International Refugee Organization, had risen to $98 million by the end of 1963.

Costs of Membership

The second question, how much it costs nations to be members of the United Nations, may be answered in two ways: first, in terms of actual amounts contributed either in dollars and cents and percentages of the total cost of the United Nations system; and second, in terms of the member's national income.

In 1962 and 1963, costs of the United Nations including assessments for the regular budget, peace-keeping operations, and specialized agencies plus voluntary contributions amounted to about $500 million. Table 3.1 shows the states in order of their payments expressed in percentages of the $500 million total. The figures do not indicate

TABLE 3.1. *Percent of Total United Nations Contributions 1961, and Regular Budget Assessment Scale 1962-63*[a]

Members in Order of Their Payments to the U.N. System	Percent of Contributions	Assessment Scale
1. United States	46.910	32.02
2. United Kingdom	8.778	7.58
3. Union of Soviet Socialist Republics	8.249	14.97
4. France	4.943	5.94
5. Canada	3.844	3.12
6. Sweden	2.012	1.30
7. China	1.939	4.57
8. The Netherlands	1.916	1.01
9. India	1.908	2.03
10. Italy	1.862	2.24
11. Australia	1.587	1.66
12. Japan	1.474	2.27
13. Ukrainian Soviet Socialist Republic	1.087	1.98
14. Denmark	.970	.58
15. Belgium	.969	1.20
16. Brazil	.752	1.03
17. Norway	.750	.45
18. Poland	.710	1.28
19. Czechoslovakia	.534	1.17
20. Argentina	.518	1.01
21. New Zealand	.477	.41
22. Mexico	.457	.74
23. Turkey	.425	.40
24. Spain	.416	.86
25. United Arab Republic	.368	.30
26. Austria	.365	.45
27. Venezuela	.349	.52
28. South Africa	.347	.53
29. Byelorussian Soviet Socialist Republic	.308	.52
30. Pakistan	.275	.42
31. Yugoslavia	.268	.38
32. Finland	.262	.37
33. Indonesia	.227	.45
34. Philippines	.225	.40
35. Rumania	.207	.32
36. Iran	.202	.20
37. Chile	.201	.26
38. Colombia	.194	.26
39. Hungary	.180	.56
40. Cuba	.144	.22
41. Thailand	.142	.16
42. Greece	.118	.23
43. Nigeria	.105	.21
44. Israel	.098	.15
45. Liberia	.095	.04
46. Peru	.090	.10
47. Portugal	.088	.16
48. Ireland	.087	.14
49. Morocco	.082	.14
50. Uruguay	.076	.11
51. Bulgaria	.070	.20
52. Iraq	.066	.09

Members in Order of Their Payments to the U.N.	Percent of Contributions	Assessment Scale
53. Burma	.064	.07
54. Sudan	.062	.07
55. Ghana	.057	.09
56. Ceylon	.053	.09
57. Jordan	.052	.04
58. Ecuador	.044	.06
59. Ethiopia	.043	.05
60. Lebanon	.042	.05
61. Malaya	.039	.13
62. Tunisia	.036	.05
63. Saudi Arabia	.035	.07
64. Afghanistan	.034	.05
65. El Salvador	.033	.04
66. Guatemala	.033	.05
67. Luxembourg	.032	.05
68. Libya	.032	.04
69. Costa Rica	.031	.04
70. Honduras	.029	.04
71. Dominican Republic	.028	.05
72. Haiti	.028	.04
73. Bolivia	.027	.04
74. Senegal	.026	.05
75. Panama	.025	.04
76. Laos	.025	.04
77. Guinea	.024	.04
78. Iceland	.024	.04
79. Nicaragua	.023	.04
80. Paraguay	.022	.04
81. Cambodia	.021	.04
82. Albania	.019	.04
83. Cameroon	.018	.04
84. Madagascar	.017	.04
85. Ivory Coast	.017	.04
86. Togo	.015	.04
87. Nepal	.015	.04
88. Congo (Leopoldville)	.014	.07
89. Yemen	.014	.04
90. Central African Republic	.014	.04
91. Mali	.013	.04
92. Cyprus	.013	.04
93. Congo (Brazzaville)	.013	.04
94. Upper Volta	.013	.04
95. Somalia	.013	.04
96. Chad	.012	.04
97. Gabon	.012	.04
98. Niger	.011	.04
99. Dahomey	.011	.04
100. Syria	.011	.05
101. Mauritania	.010	.04
102. Mongolia	.010	.04
103. Sierra Leone	.010	.04
104. Tanganyika	.010	.04

Source: Norman J. Padelford, "Financial Crisis and the Future of the United Nations," *World Politics*, (July 1963), pp. 538-39.
ᵃ The assessment percentages of Algeria, Burundi, Jamaica, Kuwait, Rwanda, Trinidad, and Tobago, and Uganda were not determined in mid-1963.

what every state paid since a number were in arrears or in default on their peace-keeping assessments in 1962. They do represent what membership would have cost if each state had paid what was assigned to it after rebates, plus the voluntary contributions that it made. This way of expressing contributions as a percentage of the total received and due to the United Nations reveals a range of 46.91 percent for the highest contributor, the United States, to .01 percent for the smallest contributors. It further reveals that 13 states bore a higher percentage of the overall support than their ratios under the regular budget scale while 97 had a lower percentage. The "over-and-above" states included only two permanent members of the Security Council—the United States and the United Kingdom. The others were Canada, Sweden, the Netherlands, Turkey, Iran, Denmark, Norway, New Zealand, Liberia, the United Arab Republic, and Jordan. These 13 states were relatively large contributors to the voluntary programs. The Soviet bloc countries stood far below their assessment levels. Their failure to pay UNEF and ONUC assessments brought their payments down by a considerable margin even below these levels. France, China, and many of the newly admitted nations were also on the low side of the normal scale. In most instances, these meager contributions can be explained not so much by reasons of economic incapacity as by the political unwillingness of states to support the highly controversial peace-keeping operations in the Middle East and in the Congo.

Perhaps a more meaningful way of expressing the cost of United Nations membership to individual states is to do so in terms of national income. After all, the above figures do not reveal what the cost of participation amounts to in the context of the resources and productivity of each country. If the payments made and due to the Organization are taken as a percentage of each state's gross national product, a fairly objective measure of the relative cost of membership can be obtained.

Gross National Product (GNP) statistics,[1] of course, do not tell the entire story about each country's means or its ability to pay. Figures are approximate at best and often difficult to verify. But GNP is a reasonably straightforward index of national capacity. It does not

[1] GNP statistics used in this study are largely based on the United Nations *Yearbook of National Account Statistics* and the *UN Monthly Bulletin of Statistics*.

TABLE 3.2. *Payments to the United Nations as a Percentage of GNP, 1961*[a]

Rank Order	Country	Percentage	Rank Order	Country	Percentage
1.	China[b]	.489	52.	Union of Soviet Socialist Republics[c]	.021
2.	Liberia	.248	53.	Albania	.021
3.	Congo (Brazzaville)	.171	54.	Peru	.021
4.	Libya	.153	55.	Burma	.021
5.	Gabon	.115	56.	Spain	.021
6.	Togo	.103	57.	Afghanistan	.020
7.	Jordan	.084	58.	Ecuador	.020
8.	Laos	.078	59.	Guatemala	.020
9.	Somalia	.071	60.	Guinea	.020
10.	The Netherlands	.070	61.	Iraq	.020
11.	Norway	.069	62.	Ireland	.020
12.	Sweden	.068	63.	Tunisia	.020
13.	Denmark	.067	64.	Venezuela	.020
14.	New Zealand	.054	65.	Chile	.019
15.	Iceland	.053	66.	South Africa	.019
16.	United Kingdom	.051	67.	Chad	.018
17.	Central African Republic	.046	68.	Niger	.018
18.	Paraguay	.046	69.	Pakistan	.018
19.	Canada	.044	70.	Brazil	.018
20.	Senegal	.044	71.	Cambodia	.017
21.	Australia	.039	72.	Mexico	.017
22.	United States	.038	73.	Ceylon	.017
23.	Iran	.036	74.	Morocco	.017
24.	United Arab Republic	.035	75.	Poland	.017
25.	France	.035	76.	Colombia	.016
26.	Bolivia	.034	77.	Ghana	.016
27.	Belgium	.033	78.	Dominican Republic	.016
28.	Lebanon	.032	79.	Israel	.016
29.	Nicaragua	.031	80.	Philippines	.016
30.	Honduras	.031	81.	Portugal	.016
31.	Haiti	.029	82.	Yemen	.016
32.	Turkey	.029	83.	Greece	.015
33.	Costa Rica	.027	84.	Japan	.015
34.	Luxembourg	.027	85.	Mali	.015
35.	Austria	.026	86.	Sierra Leone	.015
36.	El Salvador	.026	87.	Nigeria	.015
37.	Czechoslovakia	.026	88.	Ethiopia	.014
38.	India	.026	89.	Tanganyika	.014
39.	Uruguay	.026	90.	Upper Volta	.014
40.	Cyprus	.025	91.	Madagascar	.013
41.	Thailand	.025	92.	Nepal	.013
42.	Dahomey	.025	93.	Saudi Arabia	.013
43.	Panama	.025	94.	Hungary	.012
44.	Finland	.024	95.	Syria	.012
45.	Cuba	.024	96.	Rumania	.011
46.	Italy	.024	97.	Indonesia	.011
47.	Sudan	.024	98.	Mongolia	.008
48.	Argentina	.023	99.	Bulgaria	.007
49.	Cameroon	.023	100.	Malaya	.006
50.	Ivory Coast	.022	101.	Mauritania	.006
51.	Yugoslavia	.022	102.	Congo (Leopoldville)	.005

Source: Norman J. Padelford, "Financial Crisis and the Future of the United Nations," *World Politics*, (July 1963), pp. 538-39.
[a] The contributions of Algeria, Burundi, Jamaica, Kuwait, Rwanda, Trinidad and Tobago, and Uganda were not yet determined by 1963.
[b] Assessment based on resources of Chinese mainland and Formosa, but GNP is Formosa's.
[c] Separate figures are not available for Byelorussia and the Ukraine. These are included in the GNP for the USSR.

bring into question directly controversial issues such as a nation's economic effectiveness, the form of its government, or the extent of governmental control over its economy. It does afford, on the other hand, a fairly objective basis on which to compare relative resources at any given time.

Table 3.2 ranks the contributions of member states in terms of percentages of their gross national product. The principal fact emerging from this comparison is the small percentage of GNP that payments to the United Nations represent. No state contributes as much as one-half of one percent of its GNP. Few even approach this figure. The contributions of 79 states fall between .005 and .035 percent. The ranking order also reveals that those states that are the largest contributors in dollar amounts are not necessarily the largest contributors in terms of their GNP's. For example, 21 nations are obligated to pay a larger portion than the United States. The United Kingdom, the United States, France, and the Soviet Union are in sixteenth, twenty-second, twenty-fifth, and forty-eighth places, respectively. China, which is in first place, is in a special situation since its assessment is based on the resources of the Chinese mainland and Formosa, but its GNP is Formosa's. The entire range is quite wide. The contribution of the first state on the list is about one hundred times that of the last and that of the second about fifty times that of the last. In all cases more than 99.5 percent of GNP is devoted to pursuits other than the support of the United Nations and the related specialized agencies.

Hidden Costs and Hidden Savings

To complete the overall picture of the costs of membership in the United Nations, two additional factors must be taken into account: first, the cost to member governments of maintaining missions in New York City and at the headquarters of some or all of the specialized agencies; and second, the financial implications for the United States of being host country to the United Nations as an illustration of benefits that accrue to host states.

Expenditures of member governments for their missions range from the costly establishments of the United States and the Soviet Union to the modest quarters of several small nations, some of which are unable to afford United Nations missions separate from their consular offices. In all cases, expenses include office rentals, residences for top personnel, equipment, communications, transportation, and entertainment. The average cost per member state for these items is approximately $100,000 a year, bringing the total amount to something over $10 million. In addition, there are staff salaries to be paid to roughly 700 permanent delegation members of diplomatic status, and to roughly 1,000 professional personnel. These salaries come to approximately another $10 million a year. To these items must be added the costs of several hundred governmental delegates and staff who come to New York City each year for the sessions of the General Assembly. Most member states also maintain small missions or liaison offices in Geneva and the host cities of the specialized agencies. All told, the overall "hidden costs" of membership in the United Nations may amount to roughly $25 million.

The largest expenses are, of course, incurred by the United States, the United Kingdom, and the Soviet Union. The costs of their missions and staff range between $1.5 million and $2 million a year. This, however, is only a small fraction of what these nations contribute to the regular budget of the Organization. As absolute amounts go down, relative costs in terms of regular budget assessments tend to increase, however. India's annual cost of $360,000 amounts to more than 25 percent; Mexico's expense of $270,000 is the equivalent of half of its regular assessment; in the case of Indonesia, the annual cost of its representation is the same as Mexico's, but that figure is equal to its entire regular budget contribution. A number of states pay more for their missions and staff than their contributions to the regular budget. Iraq, for example, pays five times the amount. Many of the new nations from Africa run expenses that are multiples of their assessments. Extreme cases are Liberia and the Congo (Brazzaville) whose "hidden expenses" run to ten times those under the regular budget.[2] Prestige factors and costs of public relations are chiefly responsible for this. It must also be remembered that, for certain of the newer nations, a United Nations mission may obviate the need for representation in some capitals where those nations might otherwise have to be represented.

[2] The figures presented here are estimates conveytd by the missions to the author.

Turning to the special case of the United States in order to evaluate the financial impact of United Nations Headquarters on that country, three different but related questions must be answered: What is the impact of United Nations Headquarters on the economy of New York City? What is its impact on the New York City budget? What is its impact on the American economy as a whole?

Impact of Presence of United Nations Headquarters on New York City

It has often been said that the presence of the United Nations has made New York City the "capital of the world." This prestige has not remained altogether intangible. Indeed, a substantial amount of money flows into the economy of New York City every year as a direct result of the presence there of the United Nations. An estimate of specific items follows for the year 1962.

First, during 1962, the United Nations paid $40 million in salaries and wages to its staff. Of the 4,500 recipients, 3,000 were stationed at Headquarters. Their share was 64 percent, or $26 million.[3] Assuming that approximately 5 percent or $1.3 million was spent abroad, the amount that flowed into the city was about $25 million. Second, UNICEF paid $1.4 million in salaries and wages. Allowing for a similar deduction, the city gained $1.3 million. Third, staff allowances of $2.3 million were paid. Allowing the same ratios as for salaries and the same deduction, the amount is $2.2 million. Fourth, the United Nations spent $2.5 million for travel of staff including appointments, transfers, and separations. Of this sum, 40 percent, or $1 million, may have been spent in New York. Fifth, the overhead expenses of the United Nations, including equipment, maintenance, operation, rentals, utilities, supplies, and services came to $9 million. The cost for Headquarters was about $7 million. Sixth, the maintenance of missions and staff discussed above comes to $25 million. Eighty percent of this amount, or roughly $20 million, flows into the city. Seventh, New York profits from the presence of journalists and repre-

---

[3] The sources for this and the other figures in this section are: U.N. General Assembly, Sixteenth Session, *Official Records,* "Budget Estimates for the Financial Year 1962," Supplement No. 5 (1961) and "Supplementary Estimates for the Financial Year 1962," Doc. A/5223 (Sept. 24, 1962).

sentatives of nongovernmental organizations who are accredited to the United Nations. An estimate of $5,000 for each of the 250 permanently accredited journalists and of $1,000 for each transient journalist amounts to $2 million. In addition, 150 nongovernmental organization representatives are permanently residing in New York City. Their salaries plus those of several hundred transients add another $2 million.

Hence, if the above approximations are reasonable, an amount of more than $60 million flows into the economy of New York City as a result of the presence there of the United Nations.

The impact of the Organization on the New York City budget involves items on the plus and on the minus side. The city's obligation to provide added police protection is an example of the latter. During the Fifteenth Session of the General Assembly, an extraordinarily large number of heads-of-states, prime ministers, and other dignitaries congregated in New York City. This posed great problems for the police. The costs involved led to requests for a federal subsidy, which, in turn, led to a congressional hearing and a subsequent report from the city's Budget Director.

During the congressional hearings in 1961, several bills were introduced to reimburse the city for the extraordinary expenses involved.[4] A second item that came up during the hearings was the question of tax loss as a result of the Headquarters agreement exempting the United Nations from taxation by the city. The Budget Director estimated this amount at $3.4 million. On the other hand, a spokesman for the United States Department of State pointed out that the property values in the United Nations area had increased enormously as a result of the presence of the Organization, thus providing the city with substantial additional sources of revenue.

[4] Bills introduced by representatives from the state of New York were: H.R. 4441, by Hon. Edna F. Kelly, for an *ex gratia* payment of, originally, $3.1 million; H.R. 2447, by Hon. William F. Ryan, for payment of $4.4 million; H.R. 3241, by Hon. Emanuel Celler, for an *ex gratia* payment of $1.5 million; H.R. 3443, by Hon. Seymour Halpern, for an *ex gratia* payment of $4.4 million; H.R. 5209, by Hon. John V. Lindsay, authorizing "an annual payment to New York City of extra expenses incurred in providing protection to representatives or heads of foreign nations attending sessions of the UN"; H.R. 7046, by Hon. William F. Ryan for "reimbursement for New York City for the portion of the costs of its police department attributable to providing protection to the United Nations and delegates thereto."

In view of this conflicting testimony, the city was requested to submit a report on the entire question of the impact of the United Nations on its budget. In this report, entitled "Data Concerning the United Nations," which was subsequently submitted, the Budget Director stated first, that the annual costs of special police protection amounted to $1 million. More important, he declared that the advent of the United Nations had not increased property values in that area over and above what might have normally been expected since private plans for the site in 1946 had been substantial. Hence, the $3.4 million tax loss was a real one. On the revenue side, the report estimated that city tax revenues from out-of-town sightseers yielded approximately $500,000 a year and that taxes contributed by United Nations delegates and employees brought in another $400,000. On the whole, the city absorbed an annual net loss of $3.5 million.

An analysis of this report suggests that the estimates for annual tax income was too low. The report did not consider journalists and representatives of nongovernmental organizations accredited to the United Nations and their dependents. Hence, at least another $500,000 should be added to the revenue side. More important is the question of the alleged tax loss to the city. The report did not claim that the city suffered an absolute loss in the real estate taxes as a result of the United Nations exemption. It did admit that property values in the area had increased but insisted that they would have increased no less if taxable structures had been erected on the United Nations site. Whether the city would obtain more tax revenue if a commercial project occupied the site is an "iffy" question. The United Nations would then not be located in New York City, and many tangible and intangible aspects affecting the city, its budget and economy, would be different. By the same token, the city could claim "losses" for many sites that it had dedicated for nonprofit and public welfare purposes. Would not a skyscraper project on the site of the Metropolitan Museum of Art yield handsome city taxes? At any rate, the New York City report had made the $3.4 million "loss" calculation in connection with a special plea for federal help for extraordinary police costs connected with the United Nations. It was an auxiliary argument. In the same debate, the administration referred to the considerable commercial advantages accruing to the city because of the United Nations Headquarters location.

While it is very difficult to make a completely accurate calculation, the tentative conclusion may be reached from the above data that the city budget is not significantly affected by the presence of the United Nations. All factors considered, the city probably breaks about even in terms of receipts and expenditures.

Impact of Presence of U.N. Headquarters on the United States

What is the impact of the United Nations Headquarters on the United States economy as a whole? First, approximately $60 million flows into the economy of New York City every year. Second, the United Nations purchases large amounts of goods and services for its peace-keeping operations. These purchases were mentioned above but not included in New York City income. In 1962, they amounted to almost $20 million, approximately 60 percent of which, or $12 million, was spent in the United States. This figure does not include an additional amount which goes to United States shipping companies since many of these goods are purchased "U.S. pier." Third, annual UNICEF purchases come to roughly $25 million. Of this amount, at least 40 percent or $10 million is spent in the United States. Finally, over 95 percent of United Nations assets are invested in American securities, which brings another modest sum into the United States economy.

The total picture shows then, that an annual amount of roughly $82 million accrues to the American economy primarily as a direct result of United Nations Headquarters location in New York. This "hidden saving" is slightly more than the combined United States assessments for the regular budget, UNEF, and ONUC in 1962. The presence of the International Bank for Reconstruction and Development and the International Monetary Fund in Washington, D.C., increases the above "saving."

It may be safely asserted that modest increments flow into the national economies of Switzerland, Italy, France, Canada, Great Britain, and Austria as a result of the location there of specialized and affiliated agency headquarters.

The Financial Crisis

The total picture that emerges from the preceding analysis is that the cost of the United Nations has risen across the board. This rise has been sharp in some areas and gradual in others, and the overall trend may continue. The "bullish" factors operating on United Nations finances on the whole are more powerful than the "bearish" ones. The greatest upsurge has taken place in the area of peace and security. Coupled with this, the most arresting single fact about the financial situation of the United Nations has been the failure of numerous states to pay for the peace-keeping operations in the Middle East and in the Congo. It is this that produced the financial crisis of 1961-62 and brought the United Nations to the brink of bankruptcy. A look at the figures will tell the story.

At the end of 1957, 30 states had unpaid balances due on their assessments for UNEF amounting to $4 million out of the $15 million assessed. By the end of 1961 the number with balances due for that year had risen to 65. These states owed $5 million of the $19 million to be covered by assessment.

In the case of the Congo, the unpaid balances were even more grave. At the end of 1960, 67 member states had unpaid balances amounting to $19 million out of the $48.5 million assessed that year. At the end of 1961, 80 states owed $35.4 million of the $100 million assessed by the Assembly for the Congo operation. The accumulated arrears for UNEF and ONUC exceeded $80 million by the end of 1961 and $99.6 million by June 1, 1963.

The Sixteenth General Assembly took two courses of action to deal with the growing crisis: it authorized a United Nations Bond Issue of $200 million; and it requested the International Court of Justice for an advisory opinion on whether the costs of UNEF and ONUC were to be considered legally binding expenses of the Organization under Article 17 of the Charter.[5]

Deficits continued at about the same rate during 1962. At the end of that year, 69 states were in arrears on UNEF and 78 on ONUC.

[5] For an analysis of the U.N. Bond Issue and the Advisory Opinion, see Chaps. 5 and 6, respectively.

Total arrears exceeded the $100 million mark. The situation had improved somewhat, however. Approximately $140 million worth of bonds had been pledged or purchased by 58 states; and the International Court, on July 20, 1962, had answered the question put to it in the affirmative. Yet, the United Nations financial situation continued to be precarious since the bond issue was widely regarded as a "one-shot" operation, and the advisory opinion did not persuade most of those states that withheld their payments for political reasons to change their position. In March 1963 a Working Group of 21 states was unable to agree on a special scale for the financing of peace-keeping operations, but in June 1963, the General Assembly, in special session, appropriated $42.5 million for the peace forces to the end of 1963. In October 1963, the General Assembly passed a "final" appropriation of $18.2 million for ONUC until mid-1964. The mood of the Assembly by this time was clearly not in favor of any further large appropriations for peace-keeping operations.

A closer look at the states responsible for the deficits discloses two major categories: the first comprises a hard core of politically motivated delinquents year after year, and the second a growing number of states that claim financial incapacity to pay.

The Soviet bloc and most of the Arab states have made up the hard core of the politically motivated delinquents on UNEF and ONUC, and France has been a "hard core" delinquent on ONUC. China has led the list of states pleading poverty. Of the smaller countries pleading incapacity, most are in Latin America or among the emergent nations of Asia and Africa. Indeed, not one Latin American country met its ONUC assessments in full during the period 1960-62. There have been notable exceptions, however, among the new nations: Burma, Cameroon, Ceylon, Dahomey, India, and the Ivory Coast have regularly paid their obligations in full.

In sum, by the end of 1962, only one-third of the membership had met their UNEF obligations in full, and only one-fourth had paid up their assessed shares for ONUC. Two of the permanent members of the Security Council, the Soviet Union and France, had declared their unwillingness to pay, and a third, China, claimed it was not able to meet its obligations. The rest of the members in arrears or in default claimed either unwillingness or incapacity to pay as reasons for their failure.

It is clear, of course, that the major cause of the deficits is political. But the rising cost of membership has surely been a contributing factor. The fact that growing arrearages corresponded with the admission of many low-income states to United Nations membership and that they rose to 15 percent of the regular budget assessment supports this conclusion.

By the end of 1962, the total United Nations debt for UNEF and ONUC stood at $117 million. Roughly $50 million of this amount was owed for extra costs incurred in pay and allowances to ONUC and UNEF troops as well as contingent-owned equipment. The second-largest single item of $25 million was owed for airlifting operations. Troop rotation and the purchase of aircraft, operational supplies, services, and miscellaneous equipment accounted for the balance.

It is a striking fact that, if one applies the standards of national defense budgets of large powers, the amounts considered above are a pittance. And even these small amounts must be considered in broader perspective. It is true that costs of the United Nations have risen, but so have many national GNP's and national budgets. Nations have also chosen to do more things through the United Nations. In that sense, the rise in cost is an aspect of the vitality of the system. Finally, if there were no United Nations, other sections of national budgets would have to be higher. What would have been the cost to national treasuries and the world economy, for example, if there had been no United Nations during the Suez crisis of 1956? Such questions have to remain unanswered since there are too many imponderables involved.

CHAPTER 4

The Regular Budget

THE REGULAR BUDGET OF THE UNITED NATIONS for 1952-63 has ranged from $50.5 million to $93.9 million a year. This assessed budget comprises eight broad categories: first, sessions of the General Assembly and the councils; second, personnel; third, buildings and equipment; fourth, special expenses; fifth, technical programs; sixth, special missions and related activities; seventh, the Office of the United Nations High Commissioner for Refugees; and eighth, the International Court of Justice. Personnel costs are by far the largest single item and account for about 60 percent of the budget; buildings and equipment amount to somewhat over 15 percent; the six other items account for the remaining 25 percent. Hence, on the whole, the United Nations regular budget pays primarily for the "housekeeping" activities of the Organization.

Basis in the Charter

The Charter provisions on financing which, *inter alia,* govern the regular budget, are embodied in Articles 17, 18, and 19. Article 17 reads:

> 1. The General Assembly shall consider and approve the budget of the Organization.
> 2. The expenses of the Organization shall be borne by the Members as apportioned by the General Assembly.
> 3. The General Assembly shall consider and approve any financial and budgetary arrangements with specialized agencies referred to in Article 57 and shall examine the administrative budgets of such specialized agencies with a view to making recommendations to the agencies concerned.

Several observations are pertinent. In the first place, the Charter makes it clear that ultimate budgetary authority lies with the General

Assembly. As shown earlier, the Covenant of the League of Nations had omitted this stipulation and had thus precipitated a tug of war of several years' duration between the League Council and the Assembly before the latter finally gained fiscal control. In the United Nations system, this power of the purse placed the General Assembly in a strategic position. Second, the General Assembly was to apportion the budget among the member states. In this connection, the framers of the Charter at San Francisco decided to give the Assembly as much flexibility as possible, refusing to tie it down to any detailed method of budgetary procedure. Finally, Article 17 recognizes the autonomous character of the specialized agencies within the United Nations system.

Whereas in the League of Nations all technical programs were subsumed under the League budget, the United Nations system includes thirteen specialized agencies and the International Atomic Energy Agency, each with a budget and financial system of its own. Acting under the powers written into Article 17, the United Nations has signed agreements with the specialized agencies and the International Atomic Energy Agency that vary somewhat but in most cases provide for consultation by the agencies with the United Nations in preparing their budgets, and for examination of the administrative budgets and possible recommendations by the General Assembly; the agencies in general agree to "conform as far as may be practicable to standard forms and practices recommended by the United Nations." Two important exceptions are the agreements with the International Bank for Reconstruction and Development and the International Monetary Fund: these agencies, which finance their own operations from earnings and merely furnish annual reports to the Assembly, are exempt even from this perfunctory degree of supervision. In practice, the budgetary processes of most of the specialized agencies follow the United Nations pattern, with fiscal power vested in the deliberative body. This means that the United Nations system comprises a multiplicity of assessed budgets, with the General Assembly in clear control of the United Nations budget but with little control over the budgets of the specialized agencies.

Article 18, which deals with voting procedure in the General Assembly, is relevant to finance in the sense that it specifically provides that budgetary questions are to be decided by a two-thirds majority. The League of Nations required unanimity on budgetary matters and was often almost paralyzed as a result.

Article 19 incorporates one more lesson that the framers learned from precedent. Nothing in the League Covenant had provided for action in case of failure by a member state to pay its assessed contributions. As a result, members of the League had accumulated arrears without formal penalty. The San Francisco Conference, after weighing several possible penalties, decided on the loss of voting privileges in the General Assembly. As stated in Article 19:

> A Member of the United Nations which is in arrears in the payment of its financial contributions to the Organization shall have no vote in the General Assembly if the amount of its arrears equals or exceeds the amount of the contributions due from it for the preceding two full years. The General Assembly may, nevertheless, permit such a Member to vote if it is satisfied that the failure to pay is due to conditions beyond the control of the Member.

Although the Charter seems to make the suspension of voting privileges automatic unless there is formal action to the contrary by the Assembly, no procedures have been elaborated for implementing the vague wording of the article. The practice has been for the Committee on Contributions to report each year on the countries that may be in danger of losing their vote by the time the Assembly convenes, but there the matter has rested. In the two instances when states missed the two-year deadline for payments—Bolivia in 1960 and Haiti in 1963—their delegations were not present when the sessions opened, thus the question of depriving them of voting privileges did not arise. By the time of the first vote, they had discharged their debts. Most of the Western nations have taken the position that the penalty should go into effect automatically. The Soviet Union, in June 1963, took the stand that the decision to suspend a member from voting could be taken only by a two-thirds vote of the members present and voting. It based its case on Article 18 of the Charter, which requires a two-thirds majority for Assembly decisions on "important" issues, including "the suspension of the rights and privileges of membership." By the end of 1963 no nation had as yet fallen under the sanction of Article 19.

Raising the Money
The Assessment Principle

The assessment principle was implied but not spelled out in detail in Article 17. The Committee on Financial Arrangements recommended in late 1945 that the task of preparing a detailed scheme be entrusted by the General Assembly to an expert Committee on Contributions whose members were to serve for relatively long terms, be selected on the basis of "broad geographical representation and experience," and be nationals of different states. This committee, in preparing the assessment scale, was to take into account capacity to pay of a member as determined by four criteria: total national income, per-capita income, war-caused economic dislocation, and ability to acquire foreign currency.

The ten-member Committee on Contributions has a broad mandate and hence a delicate job. Its history has been quite stormy. When first confronted in 1946 with its important task—the preparation of a scale of assessments—its difficulties were compounded by the absence of complete and reliable statistical information with regard to the four criteria that were to serve as guidelines. To help the committee evaluate "capacity to pay," the United Nations Statistical Office was instructed to gather the relevant information as quickly as possible. Although the committee found "some lacunae" in the figures submitted by governments to the Statistical Office, it nevertheless proposed a scale for the first three years of United Nations operations.

The proposed United States assessment—almost half the total budget—was most controversial. The United States delegation objected strenuously on two grounds. Senator Arthur H. Vandenberg pointed out that the 49.89 percent figure was not an accurate reflection of the United States' capacity to pay. Moreover, even if the figures were accurate, it would be unwise to make the Organization so dependent on the financial contribution of one member. Instead, he proposed that no state should be assessed more than one-third of the total budget. Nevertheless, the United States agreed to a temporary assessment of 39.89 percent for 1946.

During the next ten years the United States gradually succeeded in having its assessment reduced to the one-third ceiling. At the same time, it waged a vigorous campaign to raise the Soviet share, which then amounted to 6.34 percent. A 1954 Senate Foreign Relations Committee study noted:

> . . . Senator Alexander Wiley reports that on one day in 1952, for example, he listened to a member of the Ukrainian delegation in one committee of the General Assembly speak with great pride of the remarkable economic progress his country had made since the war. The Senator then went to another committee where he heard a second member of the Ukrainian delegation explain with equal fervor why his Government was unable to increase its contribution to the U.N. budget.[1]

During the ten-year battle in the Committee on Contributions, statistical information gradually improved, war damages were repaired, the European economies recovered, and momentous changes occurred in the members' balances of payments. All these developments were reflected in the annual alterations made by the committee in the assessment scale. By 1956 a formula could for the first time be codified for a three-year period. The United States assessment was reduced to the one-third limit, the Soviet share increased to nearly 14 percent, and the United Kingdom assessment lowered to less than 10 percent.

The struggle in the Committee on Contributions, however, was not merely a reflection of the East-West struggle. The one-third ceiling suggested by the United States elicited in 1948 a Canadian demand for a ceiling on any member state's per capita assessment, in addition to the ceiling on its total assessment. The net effect was that countries with high national incomes and small populations were not to be assessed more per capita than the United States. Although the Canadian plan was vigorously opposed by the delegates from the small developing nations on the ground that it would lead to a greater financial burden for the poorer countries, it was finally adopted.[2]

Since 1956 the Committee on Contributions has had little more than routine responsibilities. The basic pattern of assessment has been

[1] Senate Committee on Foreign Relations, "Budgetary and Financial Problems of the United Nations," Staff Study No. 6, December 1954, in *Review of the United Nations Charter: Compilation of Studies Prepared . . . Pursuant to S. Res. 126,* S. Doc. 164, 83 Cong. 2 sess. (1955), p. 160. (Hereinafter cited as Senate Staff Study No. 6.)

[2] General Assembly Res. 238 A (III), Nov. 18, 1948.

set, and the changes in each subsequent evaluation have been minor. The admission of new states has made little difference in total revenues. Most of the new African nations have been assessed the minimum of 0.04 percent. Not only has the increase in membership not resulted in an appreciable reduction in the share of member states already in the Organization, but the cost of alterations at United Nations Headquarters to accommodate the increased membership has required an increase in the older members' contributions.

On the whole, three of the four original criteria determining a nation's capacity to pay are still employed by the Committee on Contributions. Total national income and per capita income are the most important of these. Countries with low per capita incomes receive up to 50 percent reductions in their assessment percentages. The criterion of "war-caused economic dislocation," while still invoked by the Eastern European countries, has been disclaimed by the committee, which has held that, since these dislocations are largely reflected in national income figures, they no longer justify special reductions. The ability to acquire foreign currencies is taken into account in that some governments are permitted to pay all or part of their contributions in local currencies. However, acceptance of local currencies is entirely dependent on the use the United Nations may have for such currencies. All told, the scale of assessment for the regular budget is determined by using total national income and per capita income figures as a base, with modifications for ceilings and floors.

The method used by the Committee on Contributions to calculate assessment scales was set forth in its 1961 report. A brief summary will suffice. Two figures are used as bases for each country: a national income figure and a population figure. The national income base for the 1962-64 scale was an average of the 1957, 1958, and 1959 figures, and the population figure was based on mid-1958. United Nations sources are used throughout, but upward adjustments are made for the national income statistics of the Soviet bloc countries. The second step is to adjust the national income of each country with a per capita income of less than $1,000 a year downward by a formula described by the committee as follows:

> A deduction is made from the national income of each country with a *per caput* income equivalent to less than $1,000. The difference between $1,000 and a country's *per caput* income is expressed as a percentage, and 50 percent of that percentage is deducted from

the country's national income for the purpose of arriving at the assessment. Thus, since the allowance is progressive, the lower the *per caput* income the more nearly the percentage deduction approaches 50 per cent of the national income, while a country with a *per caput* income of $1,000 or over receives no reduction at all.[3]

By resolution of the General Assembly, the maximum percentage is 33⅓ percent with a "principle" that no country should pay more than 30 percent. Conversely, no country is assessed below the "floor" of 0.04 percent, and each country whose percentage is less than this amount is raised to 0.04 percent. Next, if a country's per capita contribution exceeds that of the largest contributor, its percentage is lowered to the point where its per capita contribution equals that of the largest contributor. Only Canada was affected by this rule in the 1962-64 scale. When nations are admitted to the United Nations after a scale is approved, they are usually assessed a percentage that is added to the total of 100 percent, yielding a total percentage slightly above 100 percent.[4]

Surveying the present pattern of assessment, as set forth in Table 4.1, one conclusion is striking: a large portion of the United Nations regular budget is dependent on a very small minority of the membership. Sixty countries constituting over half of the membership are assessed only a little over 3 percent of the budget. Twenty countries constituting less than 20 percent of the membership contribute almost 90 percent of the total. The Big Five are responsible for almost two-thirds, the United States for almost one-third.

The collection of contributions has not posed a serious problem. Every year a number of states lag behind, but the total of arrears has never exceeded 15 percent of the entire budget. Some members fall almost two years behind but always manage to complete their contributions before the question of invoking Article 19 arises. China has been the largest single debtor and has usually been responsible for over three-quarters of the total arrears. This is not surprising, since that country continues to pay the fifth largest assessment, calculated on the basis of mainland China and Formosa, although its resources are limited to the island of Formosa. But even China manages to pay before Article 19 can be invoked.

The experience of the League of Nations had demonstrated the

[3] U.N. General Assembly, Sixteenth Session, *Official Records,* Supplement No. 10, Doc. A/4775 (1961), p. 3.
[4] *Ibid.*

TABLE 4.1. *Scale of Assessments for the Regular United Nations Budget*[a]

Member States	1959–61 (Percent)	1962–64 (Percent)	1962 Net Assessment (In U.S. $)
1. Afghanistan	0.06	0.05	37,062
2. Albania	0.04	0.04	29,650
3. Argentina	1.10	1.01	748,653
4. Australia	1.77	1.66	1,230,460
5. Austria	0.42	0.45	333,558
6. Belgium	1.29	1.20	889,489
7. Bolivia	0.04	0.04	29,650
8. Brazil	1.01	1.03	763,478
9. Bulgaria	0.16	0.20	148,248
10. Burma	0.08	0.07	51,887
11. Byelorussian SSR	0.46	0.52	385,445
12. Cambodia	0.04	0.04	29,650
13. Cameroon	0.04	0.04	29,650
14. Canada	3.08	3.12	2,312,672
15. Central African Republic	0.04	0.04	29,650
16. Ceylon	0.10	0.09	66,712
17. Chad	0.04	0.04	29,650
18. Chile	0.27	0.26	192,723
19. China	4.96	4.57	3,387,472
20. Colombia	0.31	0.26	192,723
21. Congo (Brazzaville)	0.04	0.04	29,650
22. Congo (Leopoldville)	0.04	0.07	51,887
23. Costa Rica	0.04	0.04	29,650
24. Cuba	0.25	0.22	163,073
25. Cyprus	0.04	0.04	29,650
26. Czechoslovakia	0.86	1.17	867,252
27. Dahomey	0.04	0.04	29,650
28. Denmark	0.59	0.58	429,920
29. Dominican Republic	0.05	0.05	37,062
30. Ecuador	0.06	0.06	44,474
31. El Salvador	0.05	0.04	29,650
32. Ethiopia	0.06	0.05	37,062
33. Federation of Malaya	0.17	0.13	96,361
34. Finland	0.36	0.37	274,259
35. France	6.34	5.94	4,402,972
36. Gabon	0.04	0.04	29,650
37. Ghana	0.07	0.09	66,712
38. Greece	0.23	0.23	170,485
39. Guatemala	0.05	0.05	37,062
40. Guinea	0.04	0.04	29,650
41. Haiti	0.04	0.04	29,650
42. Honduras	0.04	0.04	29,650
43. Hungary	0.41	0.56	415,095
44. Iceland	0.04	0.04	29,650
45. India	2.44	2.03	1,504,720
46. Indonesia	0.46	0.45	333,558
47. Iran	0.21	0.20	148,248
48. Iraq	0.09	0.09	66,712
49. Ireland	0.16	0.14	103,774
50. Israel	0.14	0.15	111,186
51. Italy	2.23	2.24	1,660,380
52. Ivory Coast	0.06	0.04	29,650
53. Japan	2.17	2.27	1,682,617
54. Jordan	0.04	0.04	29,650

TABLE 4.1 *Continued*

Member States	1959–61 (Percent)	1962–64 (Percent)	1962 Net Assessment (In U.S. $)
55. Laos	0.04	0.04	29,650
56. Lebanon	0.05	0.05	37,062
57. Liberia	0.04	0.04	29,650
58. Libya	0.04	0.04	29,650
59. Luxembourg	0.06	0.05	37,062
60. Madagascar	0.06	0.04	29,650
61. Mali	0.04	0.04	29,650
62. Mauritania	0.04	0.04	29,650
63. Mexico	0.70	0.74	548,518
64. Mongolia	0.04	0.04	29,650
65. Morocco	0.14	0.14	103,774
66. Nepal	0.04	0.04	29,650
67. The Netherlands	1.00	1.01	748,653
68. New Zealand	0.41	0.41	303,909
69. Nicaragua	0.04	0.04	29,650
70. Niger	0.04	0.04	29,650
71. Nigeria	0.21	0.21	155,661
72. Norway	0.48	0.45	333,558
73. Pakistan	0.39	0.42	311,321
74. Panama	0.04	0.04	29,650
75. Paraguay	0.04	0.04	29,650
76. Peru	0.11	0.10	74,124
77. Philippines	0.42	0.40	296,496
78. Poland	1.36	1.28	948,789
79. Portugal	0.20	0.16	118,598
80. Rumania	0.34	0.32	237,197
81. Saudi Arabia	0.06	0.07	51,887
82. Senegal	0.06	0.05	37,062
83. Sierra Leone	0.04	0.04	29,650
84. Somalia	0.04	0.04	29,650
85. South Africa	0.55	0.53	392,858
86. Spain	0.92	0.86	637,467
87. Sudan	0.06	0.07	51,887
88. Sweden	1.38	1.30	963,613
89. Syria	0.05	0.05	37,062
90. Tanganyika	0.04	0.04	29,650
91. Thailand	0.16	0.16	118,598
92. Togo	0.04	0.04	29,650
93. Tunisia	0.05	0.05	37,062
94. Turkey	0.58	0.40	296,496
95. Ukranian Soviet Socialist Republic	1.78	1.98	1,467,657
96. Union of Soviet Socialist Republics	13.50	14.97	11,096,380
97. United Arab Republic	0.32	0.25	185,310
98. United Kingdom	7.71	7.58	5,618,608
99. United States	32.51	32.02	23,734,542
100. Upper Volta	0.04	0.04	29,650
101. Uruguay	0.12	0.11	81,536
102. Venezuela	0.49	0.52	385,445
103. Yemen	0.04	0.04	29,650
104. Yugoslavia	0.35	0.38	281,672
Total			74,242,717

Source: U.N. General Assembly, Sixteenth Session (1961), *Official Records*, Supplement No. 10; U.N. Doc. St/ADM/Ser.B/150, Oct. 4, 1961.

ᵃ The assessment percentage of Algeria, Burundi, Jamaica, Kuwait, Rwanda, Trinidad and Tobago, and Uganda were not determined by mid-1963.

importance of a bank balance in the conduct of international administration. The Preparatory Commission of the United Nations proposed, therefore, that such a fund should form an essential part of the regular and permanent financial arrangements of the United Nations. This fund was to render the United Nations precisely the kind of service that working capital renders to any other enterprise. First, there usually is a lag between the billing of current accounts, or certification of assessments, and their collection, and the Organization must live during the interim. Second, no matter how clairvoyant the budgetary process, it is impossible to anticipate all possible contingencies, and when unanticipated contingencies arise, funds must be available to meet them. Hence, the General Assembly in 1946 authorized a Working Capital Fund from which the Secretary-General was authorized to advance "such funds as may be necessary to finance budgetary appropriations pending receipt of contributions."

Until 1962, the fund fluctuated between $20 million and $25 million. Not only was it essential for cushioning arrears, but it also financed minor peace-keeping operations such as the Truce Supervision Organization in Palestine and the Military Observer Group in India and Pakistan until these were integrated into the regular budget under the heading of "special missions."[5] Until the Congo crisis of 1960 threatened the entire financial structure of the United Nations, the Working Capital Fund was a fairly successful device for meeting emergencies. Thereafter, it was drawn on to cover some of the deficits of the peace forces and as a result was almost constantly depleted. In December 1962, over strenuous Soviet opposition, the size of the fund was enlarged to $40 million for 1963, although actual amounts advanced to the fund were considerably lower. Should the Working Capital Fund still prove inadequate, the Secretary-General is authorized to utilize cash from "special funds and accounts in his custody." Such borrowing has taken place on a number of occasions. Each year, the General Assembly also passes a resolution pertaining to "unforeseen and extraordinary expenditures." Sums of up to $2 million may be committed for this purpose without prior approval by the Advisory Committee for Administrative and Budgetary Questions, provided the Secretary-General certifies that the funds "relate to the maintenance of peace and security." At times, the Ad-

[5] For a more detailed analysis of these minor peace-keeping operations, see Chap. 5.

visory Committee permits the Secretary-General to exceed this limit. In 1958, for example, the dispatch of a United Nations Observer Group to Lebanon necessitated a supplementary appropriation of $3.7 million for that year.

In its attempt to close the gap between assessment and payment, the General Assembly has also empowered the Secretary-General to accept funds in currencies other than United States dollars. Although originally contributions were to be assessed and paid in the currency of the host country, in practice the Secretary-General has found it possible each year to accept a certain sum in other currencies. The total thus payable has fluctuated over the years between 5 percent and 35 percent of the total budget. On several occasions, it has resulted in prompt payment by states that otherwise might have accumulated arrears.

The practice of accepting nondollar payments has not created serious problems for the United Nations for two reasons. The first has been the stabilization of currencies and the progressive removal of currency exchange restrictions that have come about under the leadership of the International Monetary Fund, and in consequence of massive programs of international economic aid and investment by the United States and other major powers as well as by multilateral agencies such as the World Bank. The second has been the geographical dispersion of United Nations activities, which has increased United Nations requirements for many currencies and made the acceptance of assessed contributions in other than dollars both feasible and desirable. Approximately one-third of regular budget assessments are now collected in nondollar currencies.

Finally, mention should be made of income sources other than assessments. In 1963, it is estimated that $6,023,800 will be realized as miscellaneous income. This amount is divided into five general categories. First, funds provided from extra-budgetary accounts amount to $1.8 million. This sum includes $981,000 as reimbursement of United Nations costs in connection with the administration of the Special Account for the Expanded Programme of Technical Assistance. This is a wash transaction, and does not cover the full additional costs to the United Nations in the administration of the program. It also covers $600,000 as a comparable reimbursement of administrative expense incurred in connection with the operations of the High Commissioner for Refugees, and $203,100 is received from the United Nations Joint Staff Pension Fund, also for administrative expenses involved in the management of the fund. None of these are earnings, but rather are payments for special services rendered.

The second source of general income, in the amount of $1.7 million, originates in a variety of ways, including rental income, reimbursement for staff and services furnished to specialized agencies and others, income from interest and investments, sale of used office, transportation, and other equipment, refunds of prior years' expenditures, contributions from nonmember states, and revenue from television services and film distribution. This may be regarded as the normal income to be derived from efficient housekeeping in an operation as large as that of the United Nations. The third source is the sale of United Nations postage stamps, which from gross sales of $1.8 million in 1963 is expected to return an income of $1.3 million after paying for the Postal Administration. The fourth source is sale of publications; gross sales of $1,020,000 in 1963 are expected to produce a credit of $541,000 after paying costs of $479,000. The fifth is made up of services to visitors to Headquarters and the Palais des Nations in Geneva. Guided tours will take in $785,000 and spend $401,500, with a credit to income of $383,500; the Headquarters Gift Center will realize $184,000 for credit to income on gross sales of $642,000 after paying $458,000 in expenses. The Souvenir Shop will have gross sales of $560,000, expenses of $356,000, and will transfer a credit of $204,000 to income. The Catering Service will sell $2,133,000 worth of food, drink, tobacco, etc., but will spend $2,173,000.

Under the Financial Regulations of the United Nations, the miscellaneous income helps to finance the regular budget and serves to reduce the assessment of each member state by a modest amount.

Budget Procedure

In the search for revenue, the size and nature of the appropriations must always be kept in mind. As the Organization's revenue problems have grown, so, too, have demands for economy in expenditures. Authorizing and approving expenditures under the United Nations regular budget is a lengthy and cumbersome process. In the words of the Senate Foreign Relations Committee study: "The U.N. budget probably is given as careful a scrutiny as any budget of a similar size anywhere in the world. Representatives from member states in the General Assembly often spend days debating relatively modest sums which would be considered by some national legislative bodies in a matter of hours or even minutes."[6]

The United Nations regular budget is an executive budget and the budget cycle is virtually continuous. The estimating process is originated formally by the Secretary-General in a memorandum addressed to the several departments, offices, and services of the Organization. By late winter or early spring, departmental estimates are in condition permitting the initiation of the process of review with the examiners from the Controller's Office. Depending on the experience and determination of the departmental executive officer, this review is sometimes and sometimes not of substantive importance. In certain cases, the examiner is reviewing estimates on which he himself had made significant policy choices. In others, there appears to be a genuine confrontation of departmental and budget office positions. When the departments and the examiners are in agreement, or have defined their areas of disagreement, the budgets are collated and reviewed by the Budget Chief, who may, of course, entertain appeals from the departments and even make adjustments in their estimates. This process completed, the budget goes to the Controller, who again reviews the estimates primarily from the point of view of their conformity with the policies of the Secretary-General, although even at this level, appeal and adjustment are possible. Finally, the budget goes to the Secretary-General who, in collaboration with his executive assistant and with the Controller, and in consultation, if necessary, with his under-secretaries, makes his disposition of the document. In conformity with the instructions of the Secretary-General, the Controller then prepares the definitive version of the budget.

If the Secretary-General's budget is vulnerable in the formative stages to the actions of the several councils and their subordinate bodies, it is even more vulnerable in the intermediate stages between proposal and authorization to the General Assembly's Advisory Committee on Administrative and Budgetary Questions. This committee may be regarded as the institutional reincarnation of the old Supervisory Commission of the League of Nations.

The Advisory Committee, originally envisaged as a small group of experts sitting in their personal capacities, is in fact a twelve-man

[6] Senate Staff Study No. 6, p. 161.

body representative of the major groupings in the United Nations. It is appointed by the General Assembly, which means in practice elected by the Fifth Committee. Several of its members, in fact, sit for their countries on the Fifth Committee when the General Assembly is in session. The functions of the Advisory Committee are to examine and report on the Secretary-General's budget estimates; to advise the Fifth Committee and the Assembly on any budgetary or administrative matters referred to it; to examine, for the Assembly, the administrative budgets of the specialized agencies; and to examine and report to the General Assembly on the auditors' reports on the accounts of the United Nations as well as on those of the specialized agencies.

When the General Assembly meets in September, the Secretary-General's estimates and the report of the Advisory Committee are submitted to it and, in accordance with the financial regulations, referred to the Fifth Committee. In the course of first reading, the Fifth Committee usually attempts to arrive at a consensus on the items concerning which there is little disagreement between the Secretary-General and the Advisory Committee.

On second reading, the committee gets down to the business of reconsidering the appropriation bill. It is at this time that the spending agencies, sometimes successfully but more often not, attempt to secure the restoration of cuts made by the Advisory Committee or to overcome adverse reactions evidenced in the first reading debate. It is at this stage also that the Soviet delegate normally introduces amendments cutting radically appropriations for some departments, and eliminating appropriations for others altogether. Soviet proposals are so drastic that they generally do not receive serious consideration. At second reading, the committee also considers the problem of supplemental appropriations for the current year. These are referred to the Advisory Committee, which studies the estimate and renders a report on it. As in the case of the original estimates, the Secretary-General may comment on the report of the Advisory Committee, and essentially the same processes as those used in reviewing the original estimates are invoked for the consideration of supplementals, except for the first reading debate. When agreement has been reached on the various appropriation items, including the supplementals, a composite resolution is prepared for the appropriations. Separate resolutions relating to unforeseen and extraordinary expenses, and to the Working Capital Fund are drafted at the same time. Votes in the Fifth Committee are taken by simple majority.

Consideration of the budget by the Plenary is not purely formal, although the budget is rarely opened up completely in Assembly debate. The fact that the budget resolution in the Fifth Committee may be adopted by a simple majority while the Plenary must act by a two-thirds vote creates a situation in which losing delegations in the Fifth Committee may carry their fight to the floor with some hope of success. In practice, however, the majorities for the appropriations in committee have grown larger rather than smaller with the rise in membership of the Organization. Nevertheless, delegations have on some occasions resumed debate on specific items on which they have lost in the Fifth Committee, and while the Plenary has yet to change a budget figure proposed in committee, it has on occasion modified appropriation language in such ways as to necessitate an item-by-item vote on the estimates. Assembly approval completes the budgetary cycle.

A brief examination of the 1963 budget will illustrate the budget cycle in concrete form. In June 1962, the Secretary-General presented his budget estimates for 1963 in a 160 page document. These estimates, which did not include United Nations bond interest and principal repayment, salary increases, and capital improvements at headquarters, all to be placed in the budget later, came to $86,649,500. For six weeks in June and July, the Advisory Committee reviewed these estimates. It then recommended an overall decrease of $1,966,050. The figures adopted on first reading in the Fifth Committee were in every case those recommended by the Advisory Committee. On second reading, six of the twenty-one budget sections were adopted unanimously by the Fifth Committee, eleven without negative votes and only a few abstentions. Only the remaining four created some dissension. The closest vote of 57 in favor, 12 against, with 5 abstentions was on the item including the United Nations bond amortization. The gross budget adopted by the Plenary came to $93.9 million. Deducting income estimates and several other items, the net amount assessed to the member states came to somewhat less than $86 million. Almost immediately after final action by the Plenary, the Secretariat embarked on the task of preparing the estimates for 1964.

Problem Areas

There is ample room for improvement in the regular budget of the United Nations. A variety of proposals for strengthening its structure remain to be explored.

There has been a mounting concern in United Nations circles in recent years over the growing budget. This has been motivated sometimes by considerations of economy and sometimes by political considerations. Thus, the Soviet member of the Committee of Experts to Review the Activities and Organization of the Secretariat set up in 1960 proposed that three budgets be established: the regular budget with a net ceiling of $50 million, which should include only administrative expenses; a separate account for "extraordinary expenses and all other expenses directly connected with the maintenance of international peace and security"; and an operational budget for technical assistance and the "implementation of various types of economic, social, scientific and other programmes, projects, and measures." For each of these categories, separate agreements would be drawn up with interested member states consenting to participate.[7] The Soviet argument, which was directed particularly to peace and security operations, was that any decision by the Assembly in that area was a clear violation of the Charter's provisions and an abrogation of the authority of the Security Council.

This idea was examined and rejected by the Committee of Experts. The eight-man committee submitted a detailed report in June 1961 in which it expressed the opinion that the validity of removing operational costs from the regular budget was dubious. The committee admitted that such a separation of operational costs would reduce the 1961 budget by over $13.5 million by taking out the costs of the regular technical assistance program, special missions, the Office of the High Commissioner for Refugees, and even a part of the staff costs. While such a course would be "technically possible," the committee noted that the trend in recent years had been toward integration of all administrative costs regardless of whether they pertained to administrative functions or to operational programs. The

[7] U.N. Doc. A/4776 (June 14, 1961).

exclusion of such costs from the regular budget would reverse a policy that had received the approval of the Assembly. The Secretary-General agreed with the committee's view that: "The decision to continue to include a small amount for technical assistance in the regular budget of the United Nations was a conscious policy decision of the General Assembly, as a recognition of a minimum amount of responsibility to finance technical assistance on the part of all Member States."[8]

On balance, it seems that the elimination of minimal operational costs from the regular budget would be a case of "unscrambling scrambled eggs." The same people in the Secretariat often service both administrative and operational functions. In the words of the committee, such a separation would have to be "approximate at best." In the light of all the difficulties and relatively small returns, its prospects are most unlikely.

The proposal to fix a budget ceiling had been considered at San Francisco. Senator Arthur Vandenberg had suggested that "the United Nations must never become a rich man's club; the dues must be kept low enough so that the smallest and poorest states can afford to belong."[9] In 1950, the General Assembly's Fifth Committee warned that "if costs continued to increase, there would be a grave danger that essential activities might be severely limited by lagging contributions."[10]

The Committee of Experts again paid close attention to the budget ceiling proposal in 1961. The Soviet expert took the strongest stand and recommended that the level of the regular budget not exceed $50 million net; any increase should require the special permission of the General Assembly. The majority of the committee did not favor the fixing of a rigid ceiling. It did suggest, however, that the Fifth Committee, after approving the budget estimates for the approaching year, make known to the Secretary-General the limits within which the budgetary estimates for the year after that should be prepared. The majority further recommended that the Fifth Committee should each year examine in detail one or two of the main areas of expenditure following a prior review by the Advisory Committee on Administrative and Budgetary Questions. Such a procedure, the majority

[8] U.N. Doc. A/4794 (June 30, 1961).
[9] Quoted in Senate Staff Study No. 6, p. 165.
[10] U.N. General Assembly, Fifth Session, *Official Records*, Annexes, Agenda Item 39, Doc. A/1734 (1950), p. 62.

felt, would bring to light any lack of prudence in the normal day-to-day administration of appropriations. Finally, the majority of the committee emphasized the importance of self-imposed control in United Nations policy organs and in the Office of the Controller in the Secretariat. In his response to the committee's recommendations, the Secretary-General also rejected the imposition of a rigid ceiling, but found himself in essential agreement with the committee's more moderate proposals.

A ceiling for the United Nations regular budget is most improbable, but in view of the growing emphasis on economy in United Nations circles, it is likely that some or all of the committee's recommendations will be put into effect. The Secretariat will probably try its utmost to stabilize the budget at the present level. Yet, Secretary-General U Thant has predicted a process of "controlled expansion." Most likely, the regular budget will continue to rise in a gentle upward curve. What is certain is that the United Nations regular budget, probably the most carefully pruned in the world, will get even closer attention.

In 1963, major political differences on United Nations financing for the first time affected the regular budget. In January of that year, France notified the Secretary-General that it would refuse to pay its share amounting to $266,157 of the principal and interest on United Nations bonds. In May and June, the Soviet bloc countries followed suit and, in addition, announced their refusal to pay for four items in the regular budget: the United Nations Commission for the Unification and Rehabilitation of Korea; the maintenance of the United Nations cemetery in South Korea for members of the United Nations forces who had been killed during the Korean "police action"; the United Nations Truce Supervision Organization in Palestine; and the United Nations field service. These items and the servicing of United Nations bonds, which the Communist countries regarded as "unlawfully" voted by the General Assembly amounted to $7.8 million in the 1963 budget of which the share of the Communist countries came to $1.7 million. In addition, the Soviet bloc countries declared that they would pay their share of the $6.4 million contained in the regular budget for technical assistance in rubles and other local currencies. The French and Soviet announcements raised the question whether nations could specify portions of the regular budget to which they would contribute and, if so, how. The language of Article 17 suggests that the answer to this question is clearly "no." But the actions of France and the Soviet bloc brought the controversy over peace-keeping operations into the regular budget of the United Nations.

While the political crisis now permeates the regular budget as well, several proposals for improvement look toward the strengthening of administrative and budgetary procedure. Some of these improvements, if adopted, might put the United Nations in a better cash position. One proposal looks toward coordinating the various fiscal years of member states with the United Nations fiscal period, which follows the calendar year. Under United Nations fiscal regulations, assessments should be paid within one month after notification by the Secretary-General. These notifications are usually sent each January. But under the present arrangement, the United States Congress does not appropriate the funds for the United Nations budget until June or July and payment is made only in the second half of the year. Several other member states including the Soviet Union pay even later. Indeed, most member states pay at irregular intervals during the two-year grace period. This practice has necessitated a constant heavy drawing on the Working Capital Fund. One observer has suggested that the United States Congress appropriate money once in the spring, covering both the current year and the succeeding year. The second part of this double appropriation would then be available in the following January.[11] It is widely believed that if the United States were to take the initiative in such a plan, other governments would follow suit.

A second suggestion, made in the Assembly by Austria, would, if adopted, inject a greater degree of regularity into the revenue picture and might stimulate more prompt payment. This proposal would give each member state the option of paying regular monthly installments.[12] Still another device was suggested by the Swedish delegate to the Fourteenth Assembly: he recommended that the United Nations charge interest on outstanding contributions.[13] The International Telecommunication Union already follows this practice.

There have also been a number of suggestions for enhancing the

[11] Elmore Jackson, among others, suggested this in a speech before the Eleventh Annual Conference of National Organizations, Washington, D.C., in March 1961.

[12] U.N. General Assembly, Fifteenth Session, Fifth Committee, *Official Records,* 769th Meeting (Oct. 18, 1960).

[13] *Ibid.,* Fourteenth Session, Fifth Committee, *Official Records,* 758th Meeting (Dec. 3, 1959).

size or flexibility of the Working Capital Fund. The fund has grown over the years. Payments, however, have usually fallen short of the desirable goal, which was set at $40 million for 1963. At its four-teenth session, the Assembly had authorized the Secretary-General to seek short-term loans from governments as a way of shoring up the fund. Although the Assembly rejected, as beneath the "dignity" of the United Nations, the use of commercial loans, the question may arise again. As the United Nations Controller put it, it was to be "wondered whether the dignity of the Organization would be hurt more by recourse to borrowing or by failure to meet its legal and commercial obligations."[14] However, while having a large fund may be very desirable in a crisis situation, it does not get at the real diffi-culties of United Nations financing; in fact, it may even postpone more thorough-going remedies.

Another possibility would be to invest the miscellaneous income and build up a modest nest-egg over the years. At present, this income is used to decrease assessments of member states. If the financial regu-lations were changed, more than $6 million could be accumulated every year and used as a contingency fund at the discretion of the General Assembly. While the use of such a fund for peace-keeping pur-poses no doubt involves elements of controversy, this idea benefits from the fact that the miscellaneous income exists, and thus would not require explicit national appropriations for this purpose, even though the membership's total bill would have to be increased by the same amount.

There has been some discussion also about the possibility of in-creasing the item on "unforeseen and extraordinary expenditures." In view of the controversial nature of peace-keeping operations for which this item is largely intended, an increase seems unlikely, how-ever.

Before leaving the regular budget, a word should be said about budget coordination. Numerous writers on United Nations finance as well as public officials have advocated various types of program budgeting and a greater degree of coordination. The absence of cen-tral planning for the specialized agencies led the United States Sen-ate Committee on Expenditures in the Executive Branch to suggest as early as 1951 that control over the budgets and programs of the

---

[14] *Ibid.*, Fifteenth Session, Fifth Committee, *Official Records*, 823rd Meeting (Dec. 19, 1960).

specialized agencies be given to the General Assembly. This would entail integrating the various budgets into the regular United Nations budget, with overall control vested in the Assembly. In 1954, the Senate took the position that "member states would . . . thus be in a much better position to give overall guidance and direction to United Nations activities. Effective control over programs and projects could be established, duplication and overlapping avoided, and substantial savings brought about."[15]

That such a budget consolidation will take place is unlikely. It would require amendments to the constitutions of the specialized agencies in order to transfer control powers to the Assembly. A serious problem of membership coordination would arise, since some United Nations members do not belong to all the specialized agencies, and conversely, some agencies have members that are not represented in the United Nations. Most important has been the opposition of the specialized agencies themselves and of their "client" ministries within member governments. The tradition of autonomy has become strongly ingrained, and it is doubtful whether agencies would accept any measure of control beyond "being brought into relationship with the United Nations" under the present system. Budget coordination will probably have to continue along informal lines. Besides, the importance of coordinating machinery may be overestimated. As the Senate Foreign Relations Committee also pointed out: "Much of the difficulty arises from internal schizophrenia of governments; and if the governments of sovereign states insist on following conflicting policies in the U.N. and in the specialized agencies, reorganization of the U.N. will not cure them."[16] In the United Nations, as in other political bodies, gadgetry cannot substitute for policy.

Considered as a whole, the problems of the regular budget are not critical at this time, and the proposals for improvement are appropriately modest. There may be no major crisis over the regular budget. The heart of the crisis lies in the special operations of the United Nations to keep the peace.

[15] Senate Staff Study No. 6, pp. 174-75.
[16] *Ibid.*, p. 176.

CHAPTER 5

Peace and Security Operations Experience to Date

WHILE THE UNITED NATIONS was engaged in controversial and expensive peace-keeping operations, there was no shortage of Cassandras predicting that the Organization would end with a bang. There did exist, indeed, a real possibility that it might have ended with a whimper. A fiscal crisis was reached in 1960 which became a threat to the very life of the Organization. The heart of this crisis was in the field of peace and security. It stemmed not so much from the financial inability of some states to contribute as from the unwillingness of some to support politically controversial operations. The central issue was—and still remains—that of political consensus.

Consensus has not been an outstanding feature of United Nations peace and security operations. In Korea, there was military conflict; in the Congo, active political obstruction by a major power; in the Middle East, passive opposition; in a number of minor actions, grudging acquiescence; and in West New Guinea, positive support.

Each of the above activities required men, money, and materials—the "three M's" of any peace and security operation—but the financing patterns differed widely. The Korean "police action" was heavily dependent from beginning to end on the United States and was never budgeted through the United Nations. The establishment of the United Nations Emergency Force (UNEF) in 1956 marked the first time that the General Assembly assessed the costs of a major peace-keeping operation on the entire membership. This was a milestone for the Organization that deserves close analysis. So does the financing of the United Nations Operations in the Congo (ONUC), which turned the United Nations into a house divided and brought it to the brink of bankruptcy. On the other hand, the numerous United Na-

100

tions "Presences" and "Observers" as well as the United Nations Temporary Executive Authority in West New Guinea and the mission to Yemen were financed in a relatively simple manner. The main thrust of this analysis must turn on UNEF and ONUC.

The Korean "Police Action"

The Korean "police action" was unique and must be distinguished from other United Nations "peace-keeping" operations by the fact that military means were used to repel a military attack. The purpose of the "police action" was in fact that of an enforcement action under the Charter, although it was differently initiated and organized. This has not been true of the other United Nations operations in the area of peace and security.

This military action under the United Nations flag was fought from 1950 to 1953. The entire venture was made possible through the convergence of two circumstances: the determined leadership of the United States during the crucial weeks of June and July 1950 and the absence of the Soviet Union from the Security Council during that period.

On June 25, the day of the North Korean attack, the United States took the initiative in the Security Council and submitted a draft resolution declaring that a breach of the peace had been committed and calling on the North Koreans to cease hostilities and withdraw their armed forces. This resolution was adopted by a vote of 9 to 0 with Yugoslavia abstaining and the Soviet Union absent. At this stage the Council's hope seemed still to be a restoration of the status quo ante and peaceful settlement. On the evening of the same day, however, President Truman decided to commit the United States Government to three important steps: the neutralization of the Formosa Strait through the Seventh Fleet; the use of naval and air forces to evacuate American civilians from South Korea, and the furnishing of arms to the South Korean forces. Spurred by United States action and disheartened by a full-fledged North Korean invasion in the face of the June 25 resolution, the Security Council met again on June 27 and, twenty-four hours after President Truman's decision, recommended "that the Members of the United Nations furnish such assistance to the Republic of Korea as may be necessary to repel the armed

attack and to restore international peace and security in the area."
This time the vote was 7 to 1 with Yugoslavia voting against, Egypt
and India abstaining, and the Soviet Union once again absent.

The pattern of financing the "police action" was set by the resolution of June 27. This resolution was not taken under Article 42 of the
Charter, which would have given the Security Council authority to
order collective military measures. There were no standing United
Nations contingents to be called into action. Instead, the action "to
repel armed attack" was merely *recommended*. The result was that
the response of the member states with men, money, and materials remained voluntary.

The main manpower burden was borne by the United States and
the Republic of Korea. The United States' contribution was 50.32 percent of the ground forces, 85.89 percent of the naval forces, and 93.38
percent of the air forces; the Republic of Korea's contributions were
40.10 percent, 7.45 percent, and 5.65 percent, respectively.[1] Since almost 90 percent of the non-Korean forces fighting under the United
Nations flag (or close to two-thirds of the total force in Korea) were
United States troops, and since it had been the United States that had
taken the initiative in the United Nations, it was only logical that
the Unified Command should be primarily an American operation.
Accordingly, General Douglas MacArthur was placed in charge of the
United Nations Command, and, for all practical purposes, the United
Nations police force became identical with the Far East Command
of the United States. South Korean troops were integrated into American companies, and joint actions with other United States allies were
conducted through liaison officers. Since the United States was bearing
the largest share of the load, this preponderant American role was
accepted by all concerned as fair and proper.

Fifteen members other than the United States and the Republic of
Korea offered to contribute a total of 36,000 troops: Australia,
Belgium, Canada, Colombia, Ethiopia, France, Greece, Luxembourg,
the Netherlands, New Zealand, the Philippines, Thailand, Turkey,
the Union of South Africa, and the United Kingdom.[2] All of these
offers were accepted by the Unified Command. An offer of three in-

[1] Leland M. Goodrich, *Korea: A Study of U.S. Policy in the United Nations*
(Council on Foreign Relations, 1956), p. 117.
[2] For the percentages of contributions by these fifteen members, see U.S. Department of State, *United States Participation in the United Nations*, Publication 4583
(1952), p. 288.

fantry divisions from the Republic of China was declined for political reasons, and smaller offers from Costa Rica, El Salvador, and Panama were turned down because they failed to meet the minimum requirements set by the Unified Command. The above nations paid or offered to pay in blood to repel aggression, and thousands of men gave their lives not to a national state but for the first time in history to an international organization.

In response to a cable from Secretary-General Trygve Lie asking all member states for information on the type of assistance they were willing to give on the basis of the June 27 resolution, 53 replies were favorable to the police action. These replies may be divided into three broad categories: first, the sixteen states besides the Republic of Korea that offered troops; second, a group of thirty-seven members including the first sixteen that offered to contribute a wide range of supplies and services, including food, clothing, medical supplies, and transportation; and a group of sixteen states that found themselves in agreement with the principle of the police action, but did not offer any specific assistance.

The thirty-seven states that offered money or materials or both were the following: Argentina, Australia, Belgium, Brazil, Burma, Cambodia, China, Costa Rica, Cuba, Denmark, Ecuador, Ethiopia, France, the Federal Republic of Germany, Greece, Iceland, Italy, India, Israel, Lebanon, Liberia, Mexico, New Zealand, Norway, Pakistan, Paraguay, Panama, Peru, the Philippines, Sweden, Thailand, Turkey, the United Kingdom, United States, Uruguay, Venezuela, and Vietnam. This assistance came in the wake of a Security Council resolution passed on July 31 requesting member states to provide supplies for civilian emergency relief programs to be undertaken by the Unified Command. The range of assistance rendered was very wide and extended from almost $400 million worth of goods supplied by the United States to some $400 worth of salted fish provided for the troops by Cambodia.[3] The list of contributors included several nonmember governments. In addition, four specialized agencies, the International Refugee Organization (IRO), the International Labour Organisation (ILO), the United Nations Educational, Scientific and Cultural Organization (UNESCO), and the World Health Organization

[3] For a detailed account of military and relief assistance to Korea up to the end of 1952, see The United States and the Korean Problem: Documents 1943-1953, S. Doc. 74, 83 Cong. 1 sess. (1953), pp. 149-88.

(WHO), as well as a considerable number of nongovernmental organizations offered assistance.

Considered in perspective, four concluding observations suggest themselves on the Korean experience. First, the "voluntary" nature of the action was probably the only feasible one in the circumstances since many nations would have been unwilling or unable to contribute. Any attempt to assess the costs or to create other binding legal obligations would probably have meant no United Nations operation as such, but rather an effort to use Article 51 for some United Nations tie-in. Second, the "financing" of the "police action" was of secondary importance since the main price was paid in human lives. In this respect, the main burden was clearly borne by Korea and the United States, and without the initiative of the United States the entire venture would never have come under the United Nations aegis. But this heavy toll should not blind one to the fact that the material contributions of member states were impressive indeed. They too were very unequal, but the fact remains that thirty-seven states constituting over half the membership of the United Nations voluntarily responded with goods and services to a Security Council recommendation. Third, the generous response of the members with men, money, and materials—and even more their political support—made it possible for the operation that halted aggression and restored in effect the status quo ante bellum to be considered a United Nations one. While it would be an exaggeration to characterize the Korean "police action" as a complete success, it took a big step along the road to collective security.[4]

Minor Peace-Keeping Activities

The United Nations has engaged in several minor peace-keeping activities since 1947. These have been in the nature of "United Nations Observers" and "United Nations Presences" deployed in various parts of the globe as symbols of the world organization. It is interesting that all of these operations until 1962 were financed out of the regular budget. The first deviation from this rule was the United Nations Temporary Executive Authority in West New Guinea (UNTEA), which supervised the transfer of that territory

[4] For a definitive account of the Korean police action, see Goodrich, *op. cit.*

from the Netherlands to Indonesia between October 1, 1962 and May 1, 1963. UNTEA, which administered West New Guinea for a seven-month period, consisted of over 1,500 troops from Pakistan as well as some administrative personnel. The total costs of UNTEA, which amounted to somewhat more than $20 million, were divided equally between the Netherlands and Indonesia with no expense to the United Nations. The cost of actual peace-keeping came to less than one-third of that figure, however. The balance was spent on United Nations projects and development schemes in the course of UNTEA's existence. The second departure from the regular budget pattern occurred in the case of the Yemen Observer Group in 1963. In that case, the two major nations involved—Saudi Arabia and the United Arab Republic—divided the estimated costs of $400,000 for 200 men for a two-month period equally between them. The arrangement was extended twice for further two-month periods. In view of the severity of the financial crisis in 1963 and the hardening of the Soviet attitude toward United Nations peace-keeping operations, these two cases might well become harbingers of new financing patterns.

The most significant of these minor peace-keeping operations and their approximate costs are shown in Table 5.1. As the data reveal, some of the costs have been considerable. The Palestine Truce Organization and the Lebanon Observer Group numbered over 500 men each and, including field services, amounted to 12.6 percent and 6 percent of the 1949 and 1958 budgets, respectively. They were important precursors of the more ambitious experiments in peace-keeping. In most other years, these "Special Missions and Related Activities," as they are referred to in the regular budget, have been around 5 percent of the budget. Until 1963, none of these expenses elicited major controversies in the Fifth Committee, although delegates from the Soviet bloc repeatedly objected to the inclusion in the regular budget of "Presences" and "Observers," which they considered as inimical to their interests in the cold war. But they reluctantly acquiesced in and paid for these operations. In May and June 1963, however, the Soviet bloc countries asserted that they would not pay for the United Nations Truce Supervision Organization in Palestine nor for the United Nations Commission for the Unification and Rehabilitation of Korea. They also refused to pay for the two hundred-man field service, 75 percent of whom were assigned to the Palestine Truce Supervision Organization in 1963. These three items amounted to $3.2 million of the regular

TABLE 5.1. *Costs of Minor Peace-keeping Operations*[a]

Year	Type of Mission	Amount	Percentage of Regular Budget
1949	U.N. Truce Supervision Organization in Palestine U.N. Conciliation Commission for Palestine	$ 5,450,650	*12.6*
1950	U.N. Military Observer Group in India and Pakistan U.N. Representative for India U.N. Commission for the Unification and Rehabilitation of Korea	4,517,200	*10.1*
1951	All of above	4,126,000	*8.4*
1952	All of above	3,310,210	*6.5*
1953	All of above	2,661,900	*5.3*
1954	All of above	2,526,650	*5.2*
1955	All of above	2,227,000	*4.4*
1956	All of above	2,954,900	*5.8*
1957	All of above	2,822,600	*5.3*
1958	All of above, plus U.N. Observer Group in Lebanon	6,794,400	*11.1*
1959	All of above, plus U.N. Presence in Laos	4,022,700	*6.5*
1960	All of above	4,174,900	*6.3*
1961	All of above	4,072,750	*5.6*
1962	All of above	3,847,650	*4.6*
1963	All of above	3,856,000	*4.5*
1962 est.	U.N. Temporary Executive Authority in West New Guinea (Oct. 1, 1962– May 1, 1963)	20,000,000	No cost to U.N.
1963 est.	U.N. Observer Group in Yemen	400,000	No cost to U.N.

[a] Data compiled from estimates of the regular budget of the U.N. for various years.

budget in 1963. While the amount per se was not a large one, the constitutional and political implications of the Soviet action were most significant. The crisis over peace-keeping operations had spilled over for the first time into the regular budget of the United Nations.

The United Nations Emergency Force

It is generally accepted today that the United Nations Emergency Force was a political and military milestone for the United Nations. For the first time, an international force not dominated by a single power was constituted. What is less well known is that it also represented a fiscal milestone in the life of the world organization. For the first time, an international body decided that the costs of such an international force should be shared by the nations of the world community. This decision was to have far-reaching consequences and deserves close analysis.

The father of UNEF was Lester B. Pearson of Canada. When, on November 2, 1956, the General Assembly was locked in debate over the British-French-Israeli action in Suez, Mr. Pearson proposed that peace and security be restored through a United Nations force. The Canadian resolution passed by a vote of 64 in favor, 0 against, and 12 abstentions, and Secretary-General Hammarskjold set about improvising the force. After a great deal of delicate negotiation, over 6,000 men, contingents from ten countries (Brazil, Canada, Colombia, Denmark, Finland, India, Indonesia, Norway, Sweden, and Yugoslavia), were ready for action.[5] But it was clear that unless the question of financing was solved, the force would not get beyond the paper stage. And unless it was solved reasonably well, UNEF would be short-lived indeed. Hence the Secretary-General, in his proposals to the General Assembly, gave the matter of financing the force his most careful attention.

On November 21, 1956, the Secretary-General recommended that a Special Account outside the regular budget be set up for UNEF and that the costs of the force be shared by the member states on the basis of the scale of assessments to be adopted for the 1957 budget. In addition, he suggested an initial appropriation of $10 million to meet the immediate cash needs. As will be seen, the special account device was a crucial decision. The Secretary-General preferred it to inclusion of UNEF expenditures in the regular budget because he wanted funds for the force immediately. The latter course would almost certainly have resulted in serious delay. This technique was successful, and the General Assembly established the Special Account of $10 million on November 26 as an interim measure.

On December 3, the Secretary-General faced the central problem, that of allocating the balance of the expenses of the force, and indi-

---

[5] For complete analyses of the political and military implications of UNEF, see William R. Frye, *A United Nations Peace Force* (Carnegie Endowment for International Peace, 1957); and Gabriella Rosner, *The United Nations Emergency Force* (Columbia University Press, 1963).

cated to the Assembly that the only equitable way of meeting the costs henceforth was to share them in accordance with the 1957 scale of assessments. Although UNEF costs were financed under a Special Account, he considered them as "United Nations expenditures within the general scope and intent of Article 17 of the Charter."[6] This proposal touched off a controversy and divided the Fifth Committee of the Assembly.

The United States delegate agreed with the Secretary-General and pointed out that the committee's decision would be of crucial importance for the future of the Organization. He was supported by most of the Western nations. The statement of the delegate from New Zealand was typical: "Such responsibilities must be borne not by a fifth or a quarter of the Members or by one or two countries, but by all."[7] This view was challenged by the delegates from the Soviet bloc, who insisted that the entire cost of the operation should be borne by those countries that had precipitated the crisis—Britain, France, and Israel. The New Zealand delegation retorted that not even in the case of Korea had it been considered that the country named as aggressor by the Assembly should pay the costs of the Korean action. The Arab states supported the Soviet view and suggested that it was "morally and logically unfounded" to expect Egypt, a victim of aggression, to contribute to the costs of the force.

Several delegations expressed points of view that fell between the two extremes of the Western and Soviet positions. The Brazilian delegate suggested that countries contributing troops should have their assessments reduced accordingly. The Spanish representative proposed a formula whereby the major part of the cost would be borne by the Big Five, and the remaining portion by all member states including the Big Five. The Latin American countries, in a joint statement, disputed the Secretary-General's position. The suggestion that the costs of UNEF should be considered under Article 17, was, they asserted, "at the very least, open to question" and offered the added disadvantage that the penalty clause of Article 19 might thereby be invoked. Pointing out the primary responsibility of the Big Five for keeping the peace, the joint statement proposed that only 10 percent of the costs be assessed according to the regular scale and that the

[6] U.N. General Assembly, Eleventh Session, Fifth Committee, *Official Records*, 541st Meeting (Dec. 3, 1956), par. 79.

[7] *Ibid.*, 545th Meeting (Dec. 6, 1956), par. 3.

major part be raised through voluntary contributions from member states.

After an exhaustive debate, almost all of the Secretary-General's proposal was included in the Fifth Committee's draft resolution, adopted by the General Assembly by a vote of 62 in favor, 8 against, and 7 abstentions. By this resolution, the Assembly decided

> . . . that the expenses of the United Nations Emergency Force other than for such pay, equipment, supplies and services as may be furnished without charge by Governments of Member States, shall be borne by the United Nations and shall be apportioned among the Member States, to the extent of $10 million, in accordance with the scale of assessments adopted by the General Assembly for contributions to the annual budget of the Organization for the financial year 1957; . . . that this decision shall be without prejudice to the subsequent apportionment of any expenses in excess of $10 million which may be incurred in connexion with the Force.[8]

Since the principle of collective responsibility was established, the United States delegation declared itself willing to meet up to half the amount in excess of $10 million through a voluntary contribution, provided other governments contributed the remaining half.

The assessment pattern was now set. In each succeeding year the General Assembly assessed the largest share of UNEF expenditures in a similar manner: $15 million in 1957, $25 million in 1958, and $15 million in 1959. Each year the General Assembly went through lengthy debates before arriving at this decision. In 1960, because of pressure from the Latin American and newly admitted nations, the pattern was changed. The Assembly decided to reduce the financial burden of those governments having the least capacity to pay by applying voluntary contributions pledged prior to December 31, 1959 as a credit to reduce by 50 percent the contributions of as many governments as possible, commencing with those assessed at the minimum of 0.04 percent. The net result of this change was that the United States and the United Kingdom, the two largest voluntary contributors, assumed some of the burden of the smaller nations. The 1960 assessment under the new rule was $20 million, and those for the next three years were kept around the $19 million mark. The amounts varied from year to year because some governments, notably the United States and Canada, decided to forego their rights to reim-

[8] General Assembly Res. 1089(XI), Dec. 21, 1956.

bursement for special services such as airlifts and other means of transportation. In the 1962 apportionments, the upper limit of reductions was raised to 80 percent for states paying 0.25 percent or less of the regular budget and 50 to 80 percent for those paying more than 0.25 percent but benefiting from the Expanded Programme of Technical Assistance. Once again, voluntary contributions were to be applied to offset the resulting deficits. All in all, since the inception of UNEF, the General Assembly has assessed member states over $100 million for the force—well over the cost of the regular annual budget for the United Nations.

The decision to assess the member states did not solve the problem of financing UNEF. The heart of the problem was how to close the gap between assessment and collection. Each year up to 1962, arrears and defaults amounted to roughly one-third of the total assessment. Since voluntary contributions were less than 20 percent of the annual cost of operations, UNEF ran a serious annual deficit and had to draw heavily on the Working Capital Fund.

Up to the time of the World Court advisory opinion in 1962,[9] over one-third of the member states of the United Nations regularly defaulted in part or in full on their assessments. Some of the members in arrears, notably the newly admitted nations, conceded their legal responsibility to pay but claimed financial hardship. Theirs was primarily a practical problem and posed the least difficulty. Others, however, such as most of the Latin American countries, regarded each Assembly resolution solely as a recommendation, not as a legal obligation. They posed the problem of legal principle. And the Soviet bloc and the Arab countries, by stressing that "the aggressors must pay" raised the problem of legal obligation under the Charter in its starkest form.

The Secretary-General's position was clear: all member states had a legal obligation to pay under Article 17 of the Charter. This view was supported by a majority of the membership. It was a view that was buttressed by several arguments. First, UNEF's status was that of a subsidiary organ of the General Assembly under Article 22 of the Charter, and such an organ came within the meaning of Article 17. Second, the language of Articles 17, 18, and 19 was imperative and clearly implied that even those voting against a financial resolution were bound by the principle expressed in the statement that "the

[9] For an analysis of the World Court advisory opinion, see Chap. 6.

expenses of the Organization shall be borne by the Members as apportioned by the General Assembly." Indeed, several times in the history of the United Nations the creation of subsidiary bodies was protested by some states, but such protests never extended to the question of legal obligation to contribute to the expenses of these bodies.

On the other hand, before the World Court handed down its advisory opinion, the majority position was open to reasonable doubt. The finances of all United Nations organs were subsumed under the regular budget. UNEF, however, was financed through a special account separate from the regular budget. While the Secretary-General preferred this technique because at a time of acute emergency it might not have been possible to persuade the Assembly to include UNEF in the regular budget, this procedure opened the door to ambiguity and set an unfortunate precedent for the future financing of United Nations peace and security operations. By thus isolating the finances of the force, the Secretary-General implied that the costs of UNEF were of an extraordinary nature. Thus the question could be raised whether Articles 17 and 19 were indeed applicable in this case.

At any rate, although the numerous arrears and defaults had put the United Nations into serious financial straits by 1962, UNEF never threatened the financial structure of the Organization itself. Besides, an analysis of the assessed costs by no means exhausts the story of UNEF financing. In order to present a complete picture, a word must be said about voluntary contributions of men, money, and materials.

The average strength of the force between 1957 and 1962 was 5,300 men. By 1962, three of the original contributing countries—Colombia, Finland, and Indonesia—had withdrawn their contingents. In December 1962, the strength of the various contingents was as follows:

COUNTRY	OFFICERS AND MEN
Brazil	630
Canada	945
Denmark	562
India	1,249
Norway	613
Sweden	424
Yugoslavia	710
Total	5,133

The three Scandinavian countries raised their contingents through volunteers especially recruited for UNEF. The other four sent regular army personnel, but did not consider it necessary to replace them at home. None of the participating countries seriously weakened its military establishment through its contribution. Offers to contribute troops had been received in 1956 from twenty-four members in all, but the Secretary-General had found it wise to decline or "not to activate" fourteen of these for reasons of political sensitivity. The great powers had, of course, been excluded in principle. On balance, the offers that were deemed acceptable were sufficient to satisfy the peace-keeping requirements of the force.

Governments were also fairly generous with voluntary cash contributions. During the period of 1957-62 over $26 million, representing almost 20 percent of the entire costs of the force, was contributed by twenty-two governments. Governments made this amount available to the United Nations either through direct cash grants or by not availing themselves of reductions to which they were entitled under the financing resolutions of the Assembly. The three largest contributors were the United States, the United Kingdom, and France, which paid roughly $23 million, $2.5 million, and $400,000, respectively. The other nineteen donors, listed in order of size of contribution, were the following: Canada, Australia, the Netherlands, Sweden, Italy, Belgium, Japan, Denmark, Norway, New Zealand, Ireland, Mexico, Greece, Ceylon, Pakistan, Liberia, Burma, the Dominican Republic, and Austria. Their contributions ranged from $310,000 to $1,000.

Finally, several governments distinguished themselves by waiving claims to reimbursement for goods and services supplied. Most of these waivers were made in connection with airlifting or shipping the initial UNEF contingents to the Suez area. Thus, the United States waived an airlift reimbursement claim of $2.3 million. Canada and Switzerland waived similar claims of roughly $800,000 and $400,000, respectively. The Scandinavian countries, Italy, and Brazil chose not to bill the United Nations for smaller sums spent for transport services. In addition, several governments provided the troops with some nonessential goods and services which the United Nations considered to be "nonreimbursable" and have also incurred administrative overhead expenses in their military establishments at home. Some of these sums have not been negligible.

The total picture of UNEF support that emerges is interesting. First, all of the seven members that had troops in UNEF in 1962 had also paid their assessments. In addition, all but two of them made voluntary contributions of goods and services. They gave all three "M's" to the United Nations. Second, the heaviest manpower burden was borne by India and the largest load of money and materials by the United States. Third, the nations supporting UNEF made up a representative cross section of the membership of the United Nations. Even one Communist nation (Yugoslavia) was on the list. This suggests that, if the Korean force, organized and operated as an instrument of enforcement, came closer to the ideal of collective security in the kind of *action* it took, UNEF, though its function was limited to that of neutralization, more closely approached the collective security ideal in terms of its composition and support.

The United Nations Congo Force

Historians may differ with Mr. Hammarskjold's view that the United Nations' task in the Congo was the most important responsibility that the world organization had to assume in the first fifteen years of its life. Few, however, will disagree that the Congo problem required every resource that the United Nations could muster.

The United Nations was first called into the infant African republic to ensure both withdrawal of Belgian troops and maintenance of order in the existing vacuum that had reduced the Congo to a state of political unrest verging on anarchy and civil war. At a meeting on July 13-14, 1960, the Security Council authorized the Secretary-General:

> . . . to take the necessary steps, in consultation with the Government of the Republic of the Congo, to provide the Government with such military assistance as may be necessary until, through the efforts of the Congolese Government, with the technical assistance of the United Nations, the national security forces may be able, in the opinion of the Government, to meet fully their tasks.[10]

The Secretary-General's problems in putting together a United Nations Force for the Congo resembled those that had been faced in the Middle East, but the complications were vastly magnified. Again the force had to be improvised at a moment's notice. The Secretary-General had to race against time in order to forestall great-power intervention. Within thirty hours, troops from eight African states as well as

[10] U.N. Security Council, Fifteenth Year, *Official Records*, Supplement for July-September 1960 (Doc. S/4387), p. 16.

contingents from Sweden and Ireland arrived in the Congolese capital. In the next few days, it became clear that the new Congo force would greatly exceed UNEF in magnitude. ONUC, Mr. Hammarskjold predicted, would be "far bigger and far more complicated" with "many more nations being involved, a multilingual basis to be used, military units with very different traditions to cooperate, and a vast area to be covered."[11]

As more nations offered troops, the force was built up from an average of 10,000 men in July, 15,000 during August, 16,500 during September, to an average of 20,000 men from twenty-nine nations for the last three months of 1960. But if the force was not to be doomed to disintegration, the Fifteenth General Assembly had to consider the question of financing as a matter of first priority.

On October 24, 1960, the Secretary-General estimated the cost of the Congo force for 1960 at $66.6 million. This estimate was considered by the Advisory Committee on Administrative and Budgetary Questions, which recommended that the total costs of ONUC for 1960 be held to $60 million, and echoed a hope expressed by the Secretary-General that nations would forego reimbursement for troop transport. Both the United States and the Soviet governments informed the committee that they would waive their claims of $10 million and $1.5 million, respectively. Hence, the crucial question to be decided by the Fifth Committee was how to apportion the remaining $48.5 million among the member states.

The debate in the Fifth Committee began in a relatively mild tone. Ireland, Liberia, and Sweden suggested that ONUC's 1960 expenses be included in the regular budget and apportioned in accordance with the 1960 scale of assessments. This, the three powers maintained, would be the simplest solution and would avoid the ambiguity of the UNEF precedent. It would bring ONUC within the scope of Articles 17 and 19 of the Charter.

Pakistan, Senegal, and Tunisia instead proposed a resolution creating an *ad hoc* account for financing ONUC operations, but clearly stipulating that the 1960 costs were to "constitute 'expenses' of the Organization within the meaning of Article 17" and that assessments for it were to create "binding legal obligations."[12] This pro-

[11] *Ibid.*, 877th Meeting (July 20-21, 1960), par. 9.
[12] See U.N. General Assembly, Fifteenth Session, *Official Records*, Annexes, Agenda item 49/50 Doc. A/4676, pars. 7, 10. Adopted as General Assembly Res. 1583 (XV), Dec. 20, 1960.

cedure, too, would make the enterprise a collective responsibility but would keep it separate from the regular budget for accounting purposes. In addition, the three powers suggested the solicitation of voluntary contributions to be applied to reduce assessments of member states with the least capacity to pay. This view was supported by the United States and most of the newly admitted nations.

The Communist nations stated their intention not to contribute to any part of ONUC's expenses since, in their opinion, "the main burden . . . should be borne by the chief culprits, the Belgian colonizers."[13] The rest of the money should be raised through voluntary contributions. The Latin American countries again suggested that the expenses be paid largely by the permanent members of the Security Council.

The debate increased in intensity when the Polish delegate suggested that the proviso in the Pakistan-Senegal-Tunisia draft describing the ONUC assessments as binding legal obligations be deleted. This amendment, which would have removed ONUC from the scope of Article 19, was supported by India and Mexico in debate but was defeated by a vote of 40 to 27, with 17 abstentions. At this point, the Secretary-General offered his view to the committee. After strongly endorsing the principle of collective responsibility, Mr. Hammarskjold deplored the tendency of the delegates to approve courses of action for the United Nations without following through financially:

> Will this Organization face the economic consequences of its own actions and how will it be done? Further, if it is not willing to face the financial consequences of its own decisions, is it then prepared to change its substantive policies? There is no third alternative.

He then pointed up the resulting dilemma:

> The Secretariat finds itself in a difficult position. On the one hand, it has to pursue "vigorously" the policy decided upon by the General Assembly and the Security Council. On the other hand, it is continuously fighting against the financial difficulties with which these decisions under present circumstances face the Organization. Of course, the Organization cannot have it both ways.[14]

Finally, the Fifth Committee, by a vote of 45 to 15, with 25 abstentions, approved the draft resolution proposed by Pakistan, Tunisia,

[13] U.N. General Assembly, Fifteenth Session, Fifth Committee, *Official Records*, 775th Meeting (Oct. 26, 1960), pp. 1, 8.
[14] U.N. Doc. A/C.5/843 (Nov. 21, 1960), pp. 1, 8.

and Senegal. It recommended an *ad hoc* account for the expenses of ONUC, in the amount of $48.5 million to be assessed on the basis of the 1960 scale. It stressed that these assessments would be "binding legal obligations" on member states within the meaning of Article 17 of the Charter. It called on the government of Belgium to make a substantial contribution and recommended that voluntary contributions be applied to reduce by up to 50 percent the assessment of those states with the least capacity to pay. On December 20, this recommendation was adopted by the General Assembly by a 46 to 17 vote, with 24 abstentions. In addition, as an interim measure, the Assembly authorized the Secretary-General to incur commitments up to $24 million for ONUC's expenses for the first quarter of 1961,[15] without, however, specifying how this amount was to be raised. It did say that at its resumed session it would give "urgent consideration" to financing the costs of the Congo force in 1961 and requested the Secretary-General to submit cost estimates by March 1.

The Secretary-General, in a detailed report, estimated the 1961 costs of ONUC at $135 million. This amount included $107 million for operating costs to be incurred directly by the United Nations, and $28 million for reimbursements to governments for airlifts and other extraordinary expenses. The Advisory Committee on Administrative and Budgetary Questions, on reviewing these estimates, expressed the hope that reimbursement waivers by governments and a policy of economy for the entire operation might reduce the total to $120 million.[16] Subsequently, the Fifth Committee settled down to the difficult job of deciding on the method of apportionment.

The Fifth Committee was divided. Since the sum under consideration was the largest ever to be assessed by the United Nations for a single operation, and since the decision would obviously have far-reaching consequences, more fundamental and elaborate arguments were raised than over the 1960 assessment. Moreover, the very solvency of the Organization depended on the outcome of the discussion. The United States once again favored the principle of collective responsibility on the basis of the 1960 assessment, although it offered to waive its reimbursement rights amounting to over $10 million and to make a voluntary cash contribution of up to $4 million to be used

[15] General Assembly Res. 1590(XV), Dec. 20, 1960.
[16] See U.N. Docs. A/4703 (March 1, 1961), pp. 5-6, and A/4713 (March 4, 1961), p. 11.

to reduce the assessments of governments with a limited capacity to pay.

The Soviet Union insisted that since ONUC was a Security Council "action" in the sense of Article 48 of the Charter, the General Assembly had no right to reach a decision on the matter. Article 11 of the Charter provided that any question involving peace and security on which action was necessary must be referred to the Security Council by the Assembly. Hence, in the Soviet view, ONUC financing should not fall under Article 17 but should be governed by the unanimity principle in the Security Council. The Secretary-General stated in rebuttal that once the Security Council had taken a decision, the implementation costs fell within the meaning of Article 17 and therefore within the bailiwick of the Assembly. The Soviet position, he argued, would have the effect of extending the unanimity principle of the Big Five to matters of finance, which would lead to the paralysis of the entire operation in the Congo.[17]

The Communist countries were not alone in attacking the Secretary-General's position. The Latin American nations, under the leadership of Mexico, proposed that the ONUC costs not be apportioned under Article 17 but be considered special or emergency expenses. In an elaborate defense of this view, the Mexican delegate quoted Article 42 of the Charter with regard to enforcement action and stated that "expenses resulting from operations involving the use of armed forces, as in the Congo operation, were deliberately and intentionally excluded by the San Francisco Conference from the application of the penalty provided for in Article 19." Hence, he continued, the Secretary-General's position would lead to sanctions not provided for in the Charter. Instead, 70 percent of the ONUC costs should be borne by the Big Five, 25 percent by those states whose investments in the Congo exceeded $1 million and only 5 percent should be apportioned on the basis of the regular assessment scale. The Indian delegation, while not agreeing with the Mexican position in all its details, also favored financing the Congo force outside Article 17.[18]

The Secretary-General, in a special statement before the Fifth Com-

[17] See U.N. General Assembly, Fifteenth Session, *Official Records*, Annexes, Agenda items 49/50, Doc. A/C.5/860 (March 27, 1961), and Doc. A/PV.977 (April 5, 1961), p. 11.

[18] *Ibid.*, Annexes, Agenda items 49/50, Doc. A/C.5/862 (April 14, 1961), par. 42; and Doc. A/C.5/864 (April 14, 1961), par. 17.

mittee, countered the Mexican argument by pointing out that ONUC was not an enforcement action within the meaning of Article 42, but a military operation of essentially internal security functions in the territory of a member state. Hence, the Mexican argument, since it was based on Article 42, which had never been invoked in the Congo, was in essence irrelevant. Mr. Hammarskjold, while appreciating the concern of many delegations about the size of ONUC costs, went on to ask the committee:

> But how, from a legal and constitutional point of view, can these factors lead to a conclusion that they are not expenses of the Organization? The fact that these expenses have been substantial and un-usual—indeed unforeseeable at the time of the San Francisco Conference—cannot mean that the Charter provision must now be disregarded.[19]

France, which had already expressed misgivings regarding ONUC, refused to associate itself with this view. The Secretary-General's position was, however, supported by the United States and many Asian and African states.

The Fifth Committee adopted a draft resolution, originally sponsored by Ghana, Liberia, Pakistan, and Tunisia, which apportioned $100 million for the period January 1 to October 31, 1961 according to the 1960 assessment scale, "pending the establishment of a different scale of assessment" to defray ONUC's expenses.[20] Reductions were again granted to obtain the necessary two-thirds majority in the plenary Assembly. The upper limit of the reductions was increased to 80 percent for states paying 25 percent or less of the regular budget; and 50 to 80 percent for those paying more than 25 percent but benefiting from the Expanded Programme of Technical Assistance. Voluntary contributions were to be applied to offset the resulting deficits. The Big Five and Belgium were called on to make substantial voluntary contributions. The final vote, taken at dawn on the last day of the session, was 54 in favor, 15 against, with 23 abstentions. The Soviet bloc, Mexico, and Belgium cast negative votes, while France and South Africa abstained and subsequently refused to contribute.

Within four months, the mood of the General Assembly had

---

[19] *Ibid.*, Doc. A/C.5/864, par. 17.

[20] On October 30, the Assembly authorized the Secretariat to commit up to $10 million a month for the remainder of 1961. However, it left the mode of financing for "later deliberation."

changed considerably. Resolution 1619(XV) differed from that of the previous December in three important respects. First, while it did apportion the $100 million as "expenses of the Organization," it made no specific reference to Article 17 nor did it define the cost as a "binding legal obligation." Second, the costs were described several times as "extraordinary expenses." Third, the resolution emphasized the special responsibility of the permanent members of the Security Council for the financing of peace and security operations. The resolution was thus far weaker than its predecessor and in essence represented a regression to the UNEF pattern. The acute stage of the crisis, it seemed, had passed, and the Assembly once again found refuge in ambiguity.

The third round was fought in December 1961 over the 1962 ONUC budget. The Fifth Committee delegates went over much the same ground as in the previous debates and recommended an appropriation of $80 million to cover ONUC costs from November 1, 1961 to June 30, 1962. On December 20, 1961, the General Assembly, by a vote of 67 in favor, 13 against, with 15 abstentions, appropriated this amount with the same provisions for reductions as in April. Resolution 1732(XVI) of December 20, however, was even weaker than its predecessor. Not only were the costs referred to once again as "extraordinary," but, at the insistence of most of the small and newly admitted nations, they were also described as "essentially different from the expenses of the Organization under the regular budget." No reference was made to the costs as a binding legal obligation. The Seventeenth General Assembly in December 1962 authorized the Secretariat to commit up to $10 million a month through June 1963. However, it left the mode of financing for later deliberation pending the report of a newly established Working Group of Twenty-one, which was to report on methods of financing peace-keeping operations by March 31, 1963.

Once again, in order to obtain a full picture of ONUC support, a word must be added about voluntary contributions of men, money, and materials. Between 1960 and 1963, twenty-nine nations contributed troops; the average strength of the force during that period was around 16,000 men. The nations that had forces stationed in the Congo in December 1962 are shown in Table 5.2. As in the case of UNEF, none of these countries seriously weakened its military establishment through its ONUC contribution. The contingents were either

TABLE 5.2. *Forces in the Congo, December 1962*[a]

Country	Staff Personnel	Combat Troops	Air Personnel	Administrative Personnel	Total
Argentina	2		48		50
Austria	1			46	47
Brazil			2		2
Canada	16		19	273	308
Congo (L)		616			616
Denmark	7		5	87	99
Ethiopia	11	2,982	46		3,039
Ghana		704			704
India	77	4,618	112	928	5,735
Ireland	43	690		5	738
Italy	2		8	58	68
Liberia	4	236			240
Malaya	8	1,612			1,620
Netherlands	1		5		6
Nigeria	20	1,714			1,734
Norway	10		78	61	149
Pakistan	40		658		698
Sierra Leone	122				122
Sweden	117	651	200	84	952
Tunisia	2	1,044			1,046
Total	371	14,989	1,181	1,542	17,973

[a] U.N. Press Release CO/231, Dec. 18, 1962.

raised through volunteers, or, when regular army personnel were sent, these were not replaced at home. But the Congo force, unlike its predecessor in the Middle East, suffered considerable casualties in the performance of its peace-keeping functions.

The only nation that made voluntary contributions in cash to the Congo operation was the United States. The amounts between 1960 and 1962 came to over $30.6 million and were used to cover the deficits created through rebates permitted the poorer nations. In addition, four governments waived over $12.7 million in reimbursement claims on initial airlift and transportation services in 1960. These waivers were made by the United States, the Soviet Union, Canada, and the United Kingdom in amounts of approximately $10.3 million, $1.5 million, $650,000, and $520,000 respectively. Several governments again provided some nonessential and therefore "nonreimbursable" goods and services to the troops and incurred modest overhead administrative expenses in connection with the force.

The UNEF and ONUC assessment patterns are shown in Appendix

Tables A.3 and A.4. The total picture of ONUC support affords some interesting comparisons with UNEF. First, all nations with troops in UNEF in 1962 were also paid up on their assessments. Of the seventeen nations with troops or personnel in ONUC in 1962, all but Austria, Brazil, and Ethiopia were fully paid up. Second, voluntary contributions to ONUC were less generous than to UNEF: only the United States contributed; the amount was roughly 13 percent of the total cost up to 1962. The four waivers mentioned above came only to slightly more than 5 percent of the total expense. Once again, India supplied the greatest amount of manpower and the United States the greatest amount of money and materials. While arrears and defaults by member states on their assessments to UNEF were a serious irritation to the United Nations, they never constituted a mortal threat. In the case of the Congo force, on the other hand, arrears and defaults by late 1961 had shaken the financial structure of the Organization to its foundation.

Arrears, Defaults, and the Problem of Sanctions

At the time of the opening of the Sixteenth General Assembly, UNEF and ONUC arrears had brought the United Nations close to bankruptcy. In the case of UNEF, forty-one members owed all or part of their assessments for the 1960 budget, bringing arrears to almost 25 percent, and sixty-five members owed all or part of their 1961 assessments bringing the combined shortage to almost 30 percent of the total for the two years. With ONUC, sixty-six members had accumulated a combined shortage of almost 40 percent of the 1960 budget, and only twenty-four had paid their 1961 assessments.[21] Two of the five permanent powers of the Security Council, the Soviet Union and France, had declared their intention not to make payment, and a third, China, had defaulted.

The defaulting nations could be grouped into two broad categories. First, there were those, like the Soviet Union and France, which refused to recognize their obligation to pay under an Assembly resolution. Most of the Latin American nations, arguing that peace-keeping operations should be viewed as "extraordinary expenses" and

[21] These were: Australia, Canada, Central African Republic, Ceylon, Dahomey, Denmark, Finland, Gabon, Iceland, India, Ireland, Ivory Coast, Japan, Liberia, Malaya, the Netherlands, New Zealand, Nigeria, Norway, Pakistan, Tunisia, Turkey, United Kingdom, and United States.

should not be apportioned within the meaning of Article 17 of the Charter, adopted a milder variant of this position. Second, a number of nations, mostly newly admitted members, recognized their legal obligation but, owing to the large expense involved, had fallen seriously in arrears.

As a result, the two peace-keeping operations had become heavily dependent on one great power, the United States. Although the United States was assessed less than one-third of the 1961 UNEF budget, in effect, since its voluntary contribution was used to offset the reductions granted to fifty-one countries with a limited capacity to pay, it was paying 43 percent of the total. In 1962, these reductions were increased, and the United States assumed responsibility for a portion of the assessment of seventy-nine member states, which brought its share of the total cost to 48 percent. In the case of ONUC, the United States had assumed this larger share from the beginning.

In the light of this situation, the question arose: Could anything be done to close the gap between assessment and payment? The only legal sanction provided by the Charter was Article 19, the relevance of which, before the World Court advisory opinion was handed down in July 1962, was clear only in a single instance—the initial $48 million assessed for ONUC in 1960 as a "binding legal obligation." Article 19 had never been invoked, however, although there were some precedents on the use of sanctions in some of the specialized agencies that had equivalents of Article 19 in their charters.[22]

Even before the World Court opinion declared UNEF and ONUC costs "expenses of the Organization," there were strong arguments in favor of invoking Article 19. First, the Assembly had assessed part of the costs of the Congo force as "binding legal obligations." Not to invoke any sanction would be to make a mockery of the Charter. Second, defaulting states, if confronted with the threat of Article 19, might pay their assessments in order to avoid adverse publicity. Even the Soviet Union might decide that its vote in the Assembly was of greater value than its intransigent attitude on the Congo force. And, the African, Latin American, Asian, and Middle Eastern nations might also be prompted to honor their obligations.

[22] For a discussion of sanctions applied against delinquents in the specialized agencies see Chap. 9.

On the other hand, there was a case to be made against the use of Article 19. The heart of the Soviet contention was that the Assembly did not have the power to impose binding legal obligations in matters affecting peace and security. Many of the small nations had argued that a majority of the Assembly could not impose its will on the minority, even in financial matters. A number of the nations that had taken this position would be in arrears when the time came to apply Article 19. The Soviet Union and other defaulting nations might even decide to withdraw from the Organization. Indeed, the use of Article 19 might wreck the United Nations by depleting its membership. This danger made the literal application of the Charter a formidable problem.

The Assembly was aware of the legal ambiguity of all the UNEF financing resolutions and all but one of the ONUC resolutions. Accordingly, on December 20, 1961, it decided, by a vote of 52 to 11, with 32 abstentions, to clear up the legal controversy by asking the International Court of Justice for an advisory opinion on the question: Did the expenditures authorized by the General Assembly for UNEF and ONUC constitute expenses of the Organization within the meaning of Article 17 of the Charter?[23] Since a great number of nations were in arrears at the time and an affirmative court opinion might bring into play Article 19, a heated debate preceded the passage of the resolution.

The majority view was expressed by the delegate from Australia, who stated that the problem of financing the peace-keeping operations was primarily a political rather than a legal one and would probably not be solved by a court opinion. Yet, most of the debates had been of a legal nature, and it seemed pointless for delegations to continue to trade legal arguments instead of asking the International Court to pronounce on the legal position. Perhaps, by clarifying the legal issue, such an opinion would also help to clarify the political issue. The opposition was led by the Soviet Union, which declared that the problem was purely political and outside the competence of the International Court of Justice. All members from the Soviet bloc stated that they would not consider themselves bound by the opinion. Aside from

[23] General Assembly Res. 1731(XVI), Dec. 20, 1961. The resolution was sponsored by the United States, Brazil, Cameroon, Canada, Denmark, Japan, the United Kingdom, Liberia, Sweden, and Pakistan.

the Soviet bloc, only France voted against the resolution. The high number of abstentions, however, betrayed a considerable degree of ambivalence.

On balance, the imposition of sanctions emerged as a highly sensitive matter, which, in the last analysis, was a political, rather than a legal, problem. The tendency of many states to vote for a peace-keeping operation and not to pay for it could probably not be arrested entirely through legal means. All things considered, the prospects for strengthening the financial basis of United Nations peace-keeping operations did not seem auspicious during the early sessions of the Sixteenth General Assembly. On December 11, 1961, Acting Secretary-General U Thant warned the Assembly that the United Nations was faced with imminent insolvency if arrears and current assessments were not paid promptly. U Thant estimated that, by June 30, 1962, the gap between the debts of the Organization and its available net cash resources would exceed $100 million. Obviously, drastic emergency action was necessary to finance the peace-keeping operations beyond June 1962.

The Bond Issue

On December 20, 1961, the General Assembly adopted Resolution 1739 authorizing the Secretary-General to issue bonds in the amount of $200 million. The resolution provided that the bonds were to bear interest at 2 percent per annum and that the principal was to be repaid in twenty-five annual installments by including in the regular budget each year beginning in 1963 an amount sufficient to pay installments of principal and interest charges. The bonds were to be offered to member governments of the United Nations, members of the specialized agencies, and of the International Atomic Energy Agency, and, if the Secretary-General with the concurrence of the Advisory Committee on Administrative and Budgetary Questions should so determine, to nonprofit institutions or associations. The sale of bonds was to continue until December 1962.

While the idea of the bond issue was proposed to the General Assembly by Acting Secretary-General U Thant, the formal sponsors of Resolution 1739 were Canada, Denmark, Ethiopia, the Federation of Malaya, the Netherlands, Norway, Pakistan, Tunisia, and Yugoslavia. The vote on the resolution was 58 in favor, 13 against, 24 abstaining, and 9 absent.[24]

The issuance of bonds by the United Nations was clearly seen as an emergency measure. Indeed, a preambular paragraph of Resolution 1739 states "that, under existing circumstances, extraordinary financial measures are required and that such measures should not be deemed a precedent for the future financing of the expenses of the United Nations." Nevertheless, the bond proposal was not entirely without precedent. When the United Nations had set up Headquarters in New York, it had borrowed $65 million from the United States on an interest-free basis with an amortization period of thirty years. These amortization payments have been included annually in the regular budget of the United Nations and have been promptly paid. Indeed, the proviso that the bonds were to be repaid through the regular budget was not only to ensure collective responsibility but also to make certain that Article 19 could be invoked against defaulting member states.

The debate in the Fifth Committee, which preceded the passage of Resolution 1739, was animated and frequently heated. Strong support for the bond issue came from the delegates of the United States, Canada, Australia, Ireland, Ethiopia, Ghana, Ceylon, Burma, and the Netherlands. Philip M. Klutznick of the United States said that if all members paid their arrears on the peace-keeping operations, the Organization could forget about the proposal; but since the opposite seemed to be true, the committee could not leave the Acting Secretary-General with a political mandate but without the means to carry it out. Any amount less than $200 million would be insufficient to

[24] *In favor:* United States, Argentina, Australia, Austria, Bolivia, Burma, Cameroon, Canada, Ceylon, Chad, Chile, Colombia, Cyprus, Denmark, Ethiopia, Federation of Malaya, Finland, Ghana, Guatemala, Guinea, Iceland, Indonesia, Iran, Ireland, Israel, Italy, Ivory Coast, Japan, Laos, Lebanon, Liberia, Luxembourg, Madagascar, Mali, Mauritania, Morocco, Nepal, the Netherlands, New Zealand, Nicaragua, Niger, Nigeria, Norway, Pakistan, Panama, Paraguay, Peru, Senegal, Sierra Leone, Somalia, Sweden, Turkey, Thailand, Tunisia, United Kingdom, Upper Volta, Venezuela, and Yugoslavia.
Against: Albania, Belgium, Bulgaria, Byelorussian SSR, Cuba, Czechoslovakia, France, Hungary, Mongolia, Poland, Rumania, Ukrainian SSR, and USSR.
Abstaining: Afghanistan, Brazil, Cambodia, Central African Republic, China, Congo (Leopoldville), Dominican Republic, Ecuador, El Salvador, Greece, Haiti, India, Iraq, Jordan, Libya, Mexico, Philippines, South Africa, Spain, Sudan, Syria, Togo, United Arab Republic, and Yemen.
Absent: Congo (Brazzaville), Costa Rica, Dahomey, Gabon, Honduras, Portugal, Saudi Arabia, Tanganyika, and Uruguay.

put the United Nations house in order. The proposal was to be seen as a one-time emergency arrangement to keep the Organization alive.

This view was supported by the Canadian delegation, which, citing the commentaries of Goodrich and Hambro on Article 17 of the Charter,[25] observed that, since the arrangements for apportioning the expenses of the Organization by the General Assembly had not been defined in detail, the Assembly was free to choose unusual methods of raising funds, provided the principle of collective responsibility was observed.

The opposition was led by A. A. Roschin of the Soviet Union who declared that the deficit in the United Nations did not exist because certain states did not pay their contributions but because UNEF and ONUC were illegal under the Charter. A bond issue would make the United Nations a tool of the bondholders. It was a maneuver to enable the United Nations to engage in similar illegal "peace-keeping" activities. Moreover, there seemed to be a serious inconsistency between the draft resolution financing the Congo operation for 1962, which clearly stated that this expense was to be kept apart from the regular budget, and the proposed bond issue, which was to be repaid out of the regular budget although it was clearly intended for "peace-keeping" purposes. The French delegation echoed this last sentiment when M. Viaud expressed doubts about the bond proposal, which, he feared, would cause confusion between two categories of United Nations expenses, ordinary and extraordinary. Many of the small and newly admitted states expressed strong reservations about the proposal, and Chile insisted on the inclusion of the preambular paragraph defining the issue as an isolated emergency measure. The final vote in the Fifth Committee on December 19 was 45 in favor, 11 against, with 21 abstentions. Passage by the Assembly took place one day later after most delegates had restated their original positions.

Congress and the Bond Issue

The passage of the bond resolution by the General Assembly was only the first step in securing the $200 million loan for the United Nations. In many member nations, only legislative approval could

[25] Leland M. Goodrich and Edvard Hambro, *Charter of the United Nations: Commentary and Documents* (World Peace Foundation, 1949).

authorize subscription to the bond issue. Most crucial, of course, was to be the decision of the Congress of the United States. When the American delegate to the United Nations voted in favor of the bond resolution, he stated that only the Congress could authorize the purchase of such bonds and that his vote was to be considered as subject to this condition. Indeed, the most intense legislative battle over the bond issue took place in the Congress of the United States.

On January 30, 1962, President Kennedy sent a special message to the Congress which supported the bond resolution and requested the appropriation of $100 million for the purchase of the bonds. Exhaustive hearings on the bill were held in the Senate Committee on Foreign Relations during February and March. The bond issue was defended by top-level members of the administration, including Secretary of State Dean Rusk, the Assistant Secretary of State for International Organization Affairs, Harlan Cleveland, the United States Representative to the United Nations, Adlai Stevenson, and the United States Representative to the Economic and Social Council, Philip M. Klutznick. The merits of the bond plan were seriously questioned, however, by several members of the Committee on Foreign Relations, particularly Senators George D. Aiken and Bourke B. Hickenlooper. These debates in the committee were perhaps the most crucial phase in the history of the bond issue.

There were several strong arguments adduced in favor of the bond proposal. First, it was claimed that the bond issue would ensure the principle of collective responsibility since the principal and interest payments on the bonds would come out of the regular budget, thus compelling nations to pay or else to risk the loss of voting privileges in the General Assembly. Second, it was asserted that the United States would save money in the long run because, since the bonds would be paid back out of the regular budget over a twenty-five-year period, the United States would contribute to UNEF and ONUC operations on the basis of the regular contribution scale, then 32 percent, instead of 48 percent as heretofore. Third, since the Secretary-General would be permitted to sell bonds not only to member states of the United Nations, but also to members of specialized agencies and possibly to nonprofit institutions, this offered the prospect of new financial resources. For example, Germany and Switzerland, two nonmembers, would, it was hoped, purchase some of the bonds. Fourth, it was argued that the twenty-five years permitted for repayment would make each annual installment small enough so that the burden on some of the smaller countries would not be unreasonable. The administration defended the view that the bond proposal appeared to be the best temporary device to finance the two peace-keeping operations until a pay-as-you-go plan could be agreed on. Moreover, the bond issue was not to be deemed as a precedent for financing the United Nations and was not intended to relieve nations in arrears of their responsibilities toward the two peace-keeping operations. The proceeds were expected to be large enough to carry UNEF and ONUC until the end of 1963.

While no member of the committee proposed that the United States withhold emergency financial assistance from the United Nations, there was considerable concern about whether the bond technique was the wisest course of action. Senators Aiken and Hickenlooper suggested as an alternative that the United States should make a three-year loan of $100 million to help the United Nations over its financial emergency. The interest rate should be 3 percent a year.

The two senators, who received considerable support in the committee, questioned the bond device on a number of grounds. First, it was felt that, although the bond issue was not to become a precedent, it would encourage further fiscal irresponsibility by member states who were in arrears. Many might decide that if the United States bought one-half of the bonds, this amount would suffice to relieve them of their responsibilities. Thus, a short-term loan coupled with a vigorous attempt to collect arrears on past assessments would be preferable. The bond issue would simply postpone the moment of truth and encourage irresponsible nations to shift their burdens to others. Second, support for the bond issue in the General Assembly itself had not been overwhelming. While 58 nations had voted in favor of the bond resolution, 13 had voted against it, and 33 had abstained or had been absent, indicating that perhaps as many as 46 states did not support the proposal. Third, whether repayment through the regular budget could compel delinquents to pay was dubious. Since Article 19 of the Charter stipulated that a nation could only be deprived of its vote if the amount of its arrears exceeded the contributions due from it for the preceding two full years, nations disapproving of peace-keeping operations could simply withhold that part of their share of the regular budget that was designated as repayment of the bond issue. As this amount would be only a fraction of the total contribution to the regular budget, Article 19 could not be invoked for ten years or more. The Soviet Union, for example, whose assessment of the regular budget was roughly 15 percent or $9 million a year, could legally refuse to pay its annual portion of the bond repayment, amounting to approximately $1.5 million, until its total arrears would mount up to twice its annual contribution, that is, $18 million. In other words fully twelve years might elapse before the Soviet Union could be legally deprived of its voting privileges in the General Assembly unless sanctions could be imposed retroactively for all accumulated debts going back to 1956. Moreover, it was feared that a bond issue would be a disguised form of assessment under which subscribing states initially would pay up the arrears of delinquent states. And when the bonds came due, the redemption money would come not from the states in arrears but from those that had paid their assessments faithfully and subscribed to the bonds as well.

After weighing these conflicting considerations, the Committee on Foreign Relations, by an 8-to-7 vote, reported favorably on the bond bill. The alternative of a straight $100 million loan was narrowly rejected. The majority, however, decided to protect the United States by including the proviso that the President would be authorized to purchase $25 million worth of bonds without limitation, but that the purchase of additional bonds up to $100 million would have to be matched by the aggregate amount purchased by other nations. Furthermore, in order to ensure repayment of the American bought bonds, the majority of the committee required that amounts corresponding to principal and interest payments due to the United States were to be deducted from the annual contributions of the United States to the regular budget. The committee also made clear that the bond issue was not to set a pattern for the future financing of peace-keeping operations, but was to be regarded as an extraordinary one-time remedy for the financial ills of the United Nations.

The narrowness of the vote was a source of considerable anxiety to the administration. It was feared that a hostile majority might develop on the floor of the Senate. Even if the bill passed the Senate, the passage was highly uncertain in the House of Representatives. Consequently, the White House supplanted the State Department as the administration's intermediary with the Senate, in the hope of achieving an overwhelming Senate majority for the President's proposal. The result was agreement on a revised form of the bill; the money was to be designated as a loan but made available for the purchase of United Nations bonds by the President at his discretion. This compromise in which the President maintained the substance of his proposal and the senators won their semantic point of designating the fund as a loan produced a favorable vote on the Senate floor of 70 to 22 in June 1962. The bill as finally passed retained the original matching proviso as well as the condition that bond repayments be deducted annually from the United States' contribution to the regular budget. It also included a clause to the effect that the United States should use its best efforts to promote a pattern of United Nations financing that would make unnecessary any future large-scale borrowing.

The telling argument against a straight $100 million loan, which won over the opposition, was the fact that such a loan would certainly have precipitated a financial crisis after three years, since in all likelihood, the world organization would have had no resources to repay the loan. Moreover, the Senate shared the hope of the administration that the bond plan would compel all members to pay their share of the costs of peace-keeping operations. The Aiken-Hickenlooper loan project would not have furthered the principle of collective responsibility.

The fight in the United States Senate over the bond proposal was not solely, perhaps not even primarily, the result of a difference of opinion over the respective merits of a bond issue or a straight loan. The bond controversy became a catalyst and brought into the open doubt, suspicion, and ambivalence about the United Nations as a whole. The role of the United Nations in Katanga, the rising power of the African and Asian nations in the General Assembly, and the increasing intransigence of the Soviet position all stimulated a reassessment of the world organization. The difficulties that the bond proposal experienced in the United States Senate could largely be explained in terms of a genuine and serious questioning about the role of the United Nations, especially its peace-keeping function, in the foreign policy of the United States.

The battle in the House of Representatives was no less intense. In September 1962 that body, by a vote of 256 to 134, passed a bill that permitted the United States merely to match purchases of other members of the United Nations up to $100 million. The Senate version would have permitted outright purchase by the United States of $25 million. In the end, the more restrictive version was adopted by the Congress.

The legislative struggle in the United States over the bond issue was by no means the only one. The bond issue became a source of controversy in the British House of Commons, but it never became linked to a general debate about Britain's role in the United Nations. The government pledged itself to purchase up to $12 million of the bonds by the end of 1963, an amount that was 20 percent less than its proportionate assessment to the regular budget. In deciding on the amount and timing of the purchases, the government declared that it would be guided by its own currency position, the cash needs of the United Nations, and the efforts of financially delinquent members to meet their obligations. Like the United States, the British Government saw the measure as a one-time emergency provision. Criticism developed along fairly nonpartisan lines. Some Labour members felt that Great Britain ought to purchase $15 million worth of bonds, an amount proportionate to its assessment. Several Conservative members, on the other hand, asked the government to make sure that certain "voluble members" of the United Nations paid up "before any more British money was sunk into the organization." On the whole, however, the bond bill encountered less opposition in Britain than it did in the United States.

Amounts Pledged

By October 1, 1963, 65 nations had subscribed to the bond issue, many of them subject to legislative approval. The total amount purchased had reached almost $150 million. The United States had purchased bonds worth almost $75 million, representing the total actually bought by the other members. Only in the United States had the condition of legislative approval posed a serious threat. Everywhere else, parliaments approved the pledges of their delegations with relative ease. Tunisia's pledge of $485,000 was for almost five times its annual contribution to the regular budget. The following eight purchased double their annual contributions to the regular budget:

Denmark	$2,500,000	Liberia	$ 200,000
Ethiopia	200,000	Nigeria	1,000,000
Finland	1,480,000	Norway	1,800,000
Italy	8,960,000	Sweden	5,800,000

Japan's pledge of $5 million exceeded its regular assessment by

10 percent. Australia's pledge of $4 million, New Zealand's pledge of $1 million, and Iran's pledge of $500,000 exceeded their assessments by 20 percent, and Malaya's pledge of $340,000 exceeded its assessment by 30 percent. The following seven countries pledged subscriptions exactly proportionate to their assessments:

Austria	$ 900,000	Luxembourg	$ 100,000
Canada	6,240,000	Morocco	280,000
Iceland	80,000	Netherlands	2,020,000
Ireland	300,000		

Thirty-eight countries pledged amounts smaller than their proportionate assessments:[26]

Afghanistan	$ 25,000	Lebanon	$ 8,271
Brazil	100,000	Libya	25,000
Burma	100,000	Mali	20,000
Cambodia	5,000	Mauritania	4,082
Cameroon	9,569	Pakistan	500,000
Ceylon	25,000	Panama	25,000
China	500,000	Philippines	750,000
Cyprus	26,175	Saudi Arabia	20,000
Ecuador	12,000	Sierra Leone	28,000
Ghana	100,000	Sudan	50,000
Greece	10,000	Tanganyika	2,800
Honduras	10,000	Thailand	160,000
India	2,000,000	Togo	10,000
Indonesia	200,000	Turkey	100,000
Iraq	100,000	Uganda	10,000
Israel	200,000	United Arab Republic	250,000
Ivory Coast	60,000	United Kingdom	12,000,000
Jamaica	20,000	Venezuela	300,000
Jordan	75,000	Yugoslavia	200,000

Five nonmember states also pledged subscriptions: The Federal Republic of Germany pledged $10 million and Switzerland $1.9 million, amounts roughly corresponding to these two nations' assessments in the specialized agencies of which they were members. Kuwait, South Korea, and Vietnam pledged $1 million, $400,000, and $10,000, respectively.

By late 1963, it appeared that about three-fourths of the $200 million bond issue would be subscribed by governments. A survey of the subscribing member states showed that none of those who denied the legality of the peace-keeping operations offered to purchase bonds. However, several members that had regarded UNEF and ONUC financing as "extraordinary expenses" decided to subscribe. Most in-

[26] Monthly statements of the U.N. Secretariat.

teresting, eighteen countries that had been in arrears on their peace-keeping assessments, Afghanistan, Austria, Cambodia, Cameroon, China, Ecuador, Ethiopia, Iran, Italy, Ivory Coast, Jordan, Lebanon Panama, Sudan, Togo, United Arab Republic, Venezuela, and Yugoslavia, also decided to pledge. Some of these, like the United Arab Republic, for example, were able to provide financial assistance without overtly compromising their previously stated positions. As was to be expected, the staunch supporters of the principle of collective responsibility in peace-keeping operations also turned out to be the most generous bond subscribers.

The Working Groups and the Special Session of 1963

It was always clear to even the strongest supporters of the bond issue that the measure would have to be regarded as a stop-gap emergency device pending a permanent solution of the problem of financing peace-keeping operations. As early as April 1961, conscious of the necessity of devising a more adequate method of financing peace-keeping operations in the future, the Fifteenth Assembly, at its final plenary meeting, had decided to place on the agenda of the sixteenth session "as a matter of prime importance and urgency" an examination of methods for covering the cost of peace-keeping operations and the relationship between such methods and existing administrative and budgetary procedure. This resolution had grown out of a Canadian draft in the Fifth Committee envisaging the creation of a United Nations Peace and Security Fund that could be used to finance operations like UNEF and ONUC.

In accordance with the resolution, a Working Group of Fifteen was established.[27] In the summer of 1961, it received from twenty-one states their observations on principles to be applied in determining a special scale of assessments for peace and security, and on other matters relevant to its study.[28] On November 15, 1961, the Working Group reported

[27] The Working Group consisted of representatives of the following states: Brazil, Bulgaria, Canada, China, France, India, Italy, Japan, Mexico, Nigeria, Sweden, USSR, United Arab Republic, United Kingdom, and United States.

[28] Communications were received from Albania, Bulgaria, Chile, Norway, Peru, Mexico, Burma, China, Colombia, Indonesia, New Zealand, Pakistan, South Africa, USSR, United States, Greece, Iraq, Luxembourg, Philippines, the Netherlands, and Liberia.

its findings to the Fifth Committee. In essence the report was a catalogue of individual opinions, which largely retraced the ground that had been gone over in earlier debates on UNEF and ONUC financing. Only one positive recommendation emerged from the discussions —the suggestion to ask the International Court for an advisory opinion on the applicability of Article 17 of the Charter to peace-keeping operations. While most of the members of the group had recognized that the financing of peace-keeping operations was a collective responsibility, they had not succeeded in reaching agreement on a scale of assessments. Indeed, the Working Group had not been able to make a single substantive recommendation.

Perhaps the most useful aspect of the report of the Working Group of Fifteen was the attempt to identify, through extensive discussion, the major issues to be explored and resolved. Eight such categories were identified in the report;[29] sources of authority for peace-keeping operations; collective responsibility in financing peace-keeping operations; applicability of Article 17; an advisory opinion from the International Court of Justice; sources of funds; apportionment of costs of peace-keeping operations; safeguards and limitations; methods and procedures for administrative and budgetary arrangements. The issues raised in the first four categories were clarified when, on July 20, 1962, the World Court declared in a 9 to 5 advisory opinion that the costs of UNEF and ONUC were to be considered as legally binding obligations on the entire membership.

The Seventeenth General Assembly, on December 19, 1962, after a debate that covered familiar ground, decided to "accept" the advisory opinion by a vote of 76 in favor, 17 against, and 8 abstentions. It also re-established the Working Group and increased its membership to 21. The additional members were Argentina, Australia, Cameroon, Mongolia, the Netherlands, and Pakistan. The group was asked to report its findings on special methods of financing peace-keeping operations, including a possible special scale of assessments, by March 31, 1963.

In the Working Group of 21, Soviet bloc countries stuck to their contention that only the Security Council had the right to impose assessments for peace-keeping operations. The United States stiffened its position and declared its opposition to any special scale of assessments for UNEF and ONUC for the last six months of 1963 that

[29] U.N. Doc. A/4971 (Nov. 15, 1961), p. 3.

would involve an assessment for the United States in excess of 32.02 percent. The new argument of the United States was based on the assumption that the regular scale made ample adjustments for low per capita income countries and the belief that the financing of UNEF and ONUC for the last six months of 1963 should be handled on an *ad hoc* basis by methods that would not necessarily constitute a pattern for the future. Argentina, Brazil, Cameroon, India, Nigeria, Pakistan, and the United Arab Republic proposed that the industrialized countries pay most of the cost. Under their proposal, only the first $5 million of any peace-keeping operation should be raised by assessing the entire membership on the regular scale. Between 50 percent and 95 percent of the costs above $5 million should be met by assessing the five permanent members of the Security Council and other developed countries. The United Kingdom introduced a compromise proposal under which the Assembly would impose assessments of $10 million according to the regular scale for the last six months of 1963, with the assessments of the developing countries to be halved if they paid promptly. The deficit would be met by voluntary contributions from the industrialized countries. The United States refused to agree to this plan. Although the Working Group was unable to submit any proposal, its report to the General Assembly emphasized the sentiment in favor of some sort of reduction in payments for members with "a limited capacity to pay."[30]

The General Assembly met in special session during May and June of 1963. Intense negotiations produced the passage of seven resolutions that provided a breathing spell in the continuing financial crisis. The first two resolutions, which appropriated the sum of $42.5 million for UNEF and ONUC for the last six months of 1963, were a compromise between the industrialized and the developing countries. Under the terms of the resolutions, the first $3 million for ONUC and the first $2.5 million for UNEF were to be raised according to the regular scale. Assessments for the developing countries for the remaining $37 million were to be reduced by 55 percent. The resolutions further recommended that the deficits created by these reductions be made up by voluntary contributions from the following twenty-six countries: Australia, Austria, Belgium, Byelorussia, Canada, Czechoslovakia, Denmark, France, Finland, Hungary, Iceland,

[30] U.N. Doc. A/5407 (March 29, 1963).

Ireland, Italy, Japan, Luxembourg, the Netherlands, New Zealand, Norway, Poland, Rumania, South Africa, Sweden, the Ukraine, the United Kingdom, the United States, and the Soviet Union. These voluntary contributions were made contingent on the payment by the developing countries of their assessments. It was also agreed that services and supplies, acceptable to the Secretary-General, could qualify as voluntary contributions. The two resolutions were seen as *ad hoc* arrangements and were not necessarily to constitute precedents for the future. The votes on the UNEF and ONUC resolutions were 80 to 11, with 16 abstentions, and 80 to 12, with 15 abstentions respectively. Only the Soviet bloc countries voted against the UNEF appropriation, but were joined by France in the vote on ONUC.

The struggle that produced the above resolutions was a three-cornered one: the developing countries held out for a 65 percent reduction, but they settled for 55 percent. The United States softened its attitude somewhat and retreated from its position announced in the Working Group that it would pay no more than 32.02 percent. The $2 million, which it pledged as a voluntary contribution, brought its total contribution to 37 percent. The Soviet Union hardened its position considerably during the special session: first, it hinted at a possible walkout if any money were appropriated for the peace-keeping operations; second, it declared its refusal to pay for a number of minor peace-keeping operations as well as for United Nations bond amortization payments, all of which had been included heretofore in the regular budget; third, it insisted that the Observer Group to Yemen, which was organized during the special session, be approved by the Security Council and that a provision relating to financing be included in the preamble of the resolution; finally, it asserted that the deprivation of a member's vote under Article 19 was not automatic, but could be decided only by a two-thirds majority of the members present and voting. Nevertheless, the General Assembly passed both financing resolutions by large majorities.

The Assembly also passed a resolution on general principles to serve as guidelines for the sharing of the costs of future peace-keeping operations involving heavy expenditures. This resolution affirmed the principle of collective responsibility, but also stated that economically more developed countries should pay more of the burden while economically less developed countries had a limited capacity to pay; it reasserted the special responsibility of the Big Five and endorsed the soliciting of voluntary contributions without prejudice to the principle of collective responsibility; and at the insistence of the Arab states, it asserted that the General Assembly should give special consideration to the situation of member states that were "victims of, and those which [were] otherwise involved in, the events or actions leading to a peace-keeping operation." The resolution passed by a vote of 92 to 11, with 3 abstentions. Only the Soviet bloc countries voted against.

In its fourth resolution, the Assembly appealed, by a vote of 79 to 12, with 19 abstentions, to member states to clear their accounts and also urged those members that objected to the peace-keeping operations on political or juridical grounds to make a special effort to make payment without prejudice to their position. Fifth, the Assembly requested the Secretary-General to consult with member states and interested organizations on the desirability of establishing a United Nations Peace Fund to be made up of voluntary contributions from member states as well as organizations and individuals. The vote was 91 to 12 with 2 abstentions. The Assembly also recommended the continuation of the Working Group of 21 and extended the deadline for purchases of United Nations bonds to December 31, 1963. The respective votes were 95 to 12, with 2 abstentions, and 93 to 12, with 4 abstentions.

In all seven resolutions, the majorities were unusually large. In no case did the affirmative votes fall below 80. Indeed, with the exception of the Soviet bloc and France, the special session ended with a powerful reaffirmation of the principle of collective responsibility for United Nations peace-keeping operations.

The Eighteenth General Assembly, impressed by a request from Congolese Premier Cyrille Adoula, appropriated $15 million in October 1963, by a vote of 76 to 11 with 20 abstentions, for a reduced ONUC force of 5,350 men to remain in the Congo until June 30, 1964.

Under the terms of the resolution, the total amount authorized was $18.2 million. The difference between the appropriation of $15 million and the authorization to spend $18.2 million was accounted for by an offer from the Congolese Government to contribute the equivalent of $3.2 million toward the costs. Of the $15 million appropriation, $3 million was apportioned among the member states in accordance with their regular scales of assessment for 1964. For the balance of $12 million, the developing countries once again received reductions of 55 percent, to be made up by voluntary contributions from the industrialized countries. Toward that end, the United States, Canada, and several Western European countries pledged to make donations totaling $1.3 million. Once again, as in the special session, it was agreed to make these special donations contingent on payment by the developing nations of their assessments and to accept services and supplies acceptable to the Secretary-General as voluntary contributions.

In essence, the terms of this final ONUC appropriation were similar to those agreed upon at the special session six months earlier. But two significant differences were manifest in the voting pattern. France, pleased by the inclusion of a cut-off date, decided to abstain, and Belgium supported the majority and decided to pay its assessment for the last six months of the force. Only the Soviet bloc and Cuba voted against the resolution.

In December 1963 the Eighteenth General Assembly, by a vote of 77 to 11 with 20 abstentions, appropriated $17.75 million for the United Nations Emergency Force for 1964. Of this amount, $2 million was assessed according to the regular scale, and the developing countries were granted reductions of 57.5 percent for the balance. The Assembly expressed the hope that "this *ad hoc* assessment would be the last one presented to the General Assembly." Obviously the majority of the members were in no mood to continue massive peace-keeping operations indefinitely. The combined cash appropriations for UNEF and ONUC for 1964 amounted to less than one-fourth of those appropriated for 1963.

Patterns of Financing

An overall survey of the financing of peace and security operations from 1956 to 1963 affords some interesting conclusions. First, the great variety of financing patterns: Korea, UNEF, ONUC, UNTEA, Yemen and the United Nations Observer Groups and United Nations Presences. Most of these have been *sui generis,* and no easy generalizations are possible. This highly diversified pattern points up the *ad hoc* quality of these operations, but it also highlights the adaptability and gift for improvisation that the United Nations has exhibited. The bond issue, which largely financed UNEF and ONUC between July 1962 and June 1963, is a case in point. Second, the Assembly has stubbornly asserted the principle of collective responsibility. The Soviet bloc, France, and most of the Arab states have challenged this principle almost throughout, but the Western nations and most of the members from the developing areas of the world have supported it. The latter, however, have consistently presented the view that the industrialized nations, especially the Big Five, should assume a larger part of the financial burden. Indeed, all the "rebate" resolutions on the financing of UNEF and ONUC were compromises between the industrialized and the developing nations. In effect, they came close to establishing special assessment scales for peace and security purposes. The greatest dilemma throughout, however, has not been that of financial limitation, but that of political opposition.

Perhaps the most astounding phenomenon about the peace-keeping operations has not been the enormous difficulties with which they have been financed, but the fact that they have been financed at all—most of them on a basis of collective responsibility. In historical perspective, this is quite an accomplishment, as a moment's reflection about the fate of the League of Nations shows. The League, in the last analysis, repudiated the principle of collective responsibility for peace-keeping. The United Nations has not yet completely accepted it, but the fact that it has managed to establish and to finance a continuing procession of temporary operations demonstrates its growing usefulness and vitality. In that sense, what has not killed the United Nations, has made it stronger.

CHAPTER 6

The World Court Advisory Opinion

THE PROBLEM OF FINANCING peace-keeping operations did not remain confined to the political and fiscal realms of the United Nations. As shown in Chapter 5, it also came before the world's highest judicial tribunal, the International Court of Justice. The judicial phase of the Organization's financial crisis is of sufficient importance to merit separate treatment. This chapter will analyze the majority and minority opinions on the main issues with which the Court had to deal, and explore the implications of the advisory opinion for the future of the United Nations.

When the General Assembly, on December 20, 1961, requested the World Court to give an advisory opinion, it asked for guidance on the following question:

> Do the expenditures authorized in General Assembly resolutions . . . relating to the United Nations operations in the Congo . . . and to the operations of the United Nations Emergency Force . . . constitute expenses of the Organization within the meaning of Article 17, paragraph 2 of the Charter of the United Nations?

The World Court asked for written statements from the members of the United Nations, and received twenty-one such statements, as well as three letters whose authors referred to their governments' views previously expressed in discussions in the General Assembly. In May 1962, oral proceedings were held before the Court; nine states, whose views had already been communicated to the Court in the written statements, were represented in the oral proceedings. On July 20, 1962, the opinion of the Court was announced: by a vote of 9 to 5, the Court stated that the expenditures authorized in the General Assembly resolutions dealing with the financing of UNEF and ONUC "constituted 'expenses of the Organization' within the meaning of article 17, paragraph 2 of the Charter." Of the nine judges in the majority, three, Sir Percy Spender, Sir Gerald Fitzmaurice, and Gaetano

140

Morelli, wrote separate opinions, and one, Judge Spiropoulos, made a separate declaration. Each of the five dissenting judges, President Winiarski, Jules Basdevant, V. Koretsky, Lucio M. Moreno Quintana, and J. L. Bustamante, wrote his own dissenting opinion.

The Dialogue on the Court

If the advisory opinion handed down on July 20, 1962, was one of the most significant in the history of the World Court, it was also one of the most fractured. There was disunity within the ranks of the majority as well as within the minority; the judges differed not only on their answers, but also on the way in which they felt the question should have been phrased by the General Assembly. All this gives an air of great complexity to the opinion. The arguments and conclusions of the five judges who spoke for the majority opinion, Vice-President Alfaro and Judges Badawi, Wellington Koo, Tanaka, and Jessup, will be considered first; then the four concurring and five dissenting opinions will be discussed.

The five majority judges at the outset rejected the contention that the alleged political character of the problem precluded a juridical opinion; they maintained that the request made of the Court was in keeping with the role of the Court: the interpretation of a treaty provision in the United Nations Charter. Next, the majority turned its attention to a French draft amendment that had been rejected by the Assembly during the debates in December 1961 on the question whether the Court ought to be asked for an advisory opinion. The French amendment would have asked a "previous" question: Were the Assembly resolutions themselves in conformity with the Charter? In other words, France would have had the Court pronounce on the legality of the basic resolutions before deciding whether the costs incurred as a result of these resolutions were "expenses of the Organization." This draft amendment had been rejected because most delegations believed this distinction to be too blurred, or agreed with the delegate of Canada who maintained that it would be "invidious for . . . [the] Assembly to go to the Court and put into question a large number of its own decisions taken over a number of years."[1]

[1] U.N. General Assembly, Sixteenth Session, *Official Records*, Annexes, Agenda Item No. 62 (1961); and U.N. Doc. A/PV.1086 (Dec. 20, 1961).

The majority opinion, in reference to the proposed French amendment, declared that the Assembly's rejection of it should not preclude an investigation of the resolutions themselves if the Court should find such an investigation relevant: "The Court must have full liberty to consider all relevant data available to it in forming an opinion in a question posed to it for an advisory opinion."[2]

The majority then turned to an examination of Article 17, paragraph 2 of the Charter in an attempt to identify "expenses of the Organization." Did these expenses imply "regular" and "administrative" expenses only? The majority noted that Article 17 (1) of the Charter spoke of the "budget" of the United Nations, while paragraph 3 of the same article spoke of the "administrative budgets" of the specialized agencies. Hence, the Court concluded that the framers of the Charter, recognizing a distinction between "administrative" and "operational" budgets, would have inserted the word "administrative" before "budget" in Article 17 (1) had they intended the budget to be limited to administrative expenses.[3] Actually, the United Nations had from the beginning included operational items in the regular budget, such as the annual appropriations for "special missions and related activities," "unforeseen and extraordinary expenses" relating to the maintenance of peace and security, as well as a variety of expenses for technical assistance, programs of economic and social development, human rights activities, public administration, and narcotics drug control. There was therefore no basis for interpreting the term budget in its narrowest sense.

The five judges then examined Article 17 in relation to the general structure and intent of the Charter. They noted that Article 17 placed control over the finances of the United Nations in the General Assembly, and that the Assembly was not precluded from dealing with expenses relating to the maintenance of peace and security. They observed that, while the Security Council had primary responsibility for operations in this realm, its responsibility was not exclusive. When expenditures related to this end were not otherwise provided for, the Assembly had the authority to apportion them among member governments. The provision of Article 11, paragraph 2, whereby

[2] International Court of Justice, *Certain Expenses of the United Nations (Article 17, paragraph 2, of the Charter), Advisory Opinion of 20 July 1962: I.C.J. Reports, 1962,* p. 157. (Cited hereinafter as *Opinion.*)
[3] *Ibid.,* p. 159.

"any such question [relating to the maintenance of international peace and security] on which action is necessary shall be referred to the Security Council by the General Assembly either before or after discussion," did not restrict the Assembly's authority in all matters concerning peace and security. This article, declared the Court, referred to action of a coercive or enforcement character. But if the "action" was not of an enforcement nature, the last sentence of Article 11 (2) did not apply.[4]

Article 43 of the Charter was also found inapplicable to the question at hand.[5] The majority found that, while expenditures for enforcement action were within the sole authority of the Security Council, those of other actions relating to peace and security constituted "expenses of the Organization within the meaning of Article 17, paragraph 2."

The Court then passed on to an examination of the peace-keeping expenditures in terms of the overall purposes of the United Nations.[6] It noted that an expenditure that was not made for one of the purposes of the Organization could not be viewed as an "expense of the Organization," but went on to say that if an expense was in harmony with the overall purpose of the United Nations, but was made "by the wrong organ, [this] was irregular as a matter of internal structure, but would not necessarily mean that the expense incurred was not an expense of the Organization."[7] Cases in which the body corporate or politic might be bound by an *ultra vires* act of an agent were not unfamiliar to national and international law. Having said this, the Court proceeded to the two central questions: First, were UNEF and ONUC related to the purposes of the United Nations? Second, were these two peace-keeping operations the type of noncoercive, nonenforcement action that came under the jurisdiction of the General Assembly?

UNEF, the Court declared, had been created by the General Assembly without a single dissenting vote in order to promote and maintain peace and security in the Middle East. It had been established with the consent of the states most intimately concerned, including that of the host state, Egypt, and its duties had clearly been envis-

[4] *Ibid.*, pp. 162-63.
[5] *Ibid.*, pp. 165-67.
[6] *Ibid.*, p. 167.
[7] *Ibid.*, p. 168.

aged as noncoercive in character. Hence, the Emergency Force was obviously not an enforcement measure. The Court dismissed the view that the establishment of a separate account for UNEF's expenses implied that the funds were not to be derived from contributions assessed on the members by the General Assembly. The majority thus concluded that, since the inception of UNEF, its costs were to be regarded as expenses of the Organization within the meaning of Article 17 (2).

Turning to the operation in the Congo, the Court pointed out that ONUC had been initially authorized by the Security Council without a dissenting vote, and that it had been invited by the government of the Congo in order to maintain international peace and security. The Court rejected the argument that the resolution establishing ONUC violated fundamental Charter provisions, which endowed the Security Council rather than the Secretary-General with the authority to carry out decisions involving the maintenance of peace and security. After reviewing the various resolutions pertaining to the operation, the majority concluded:

> In the light of such a record of reiterated consideration, confirmation, approval and ratification by the Security Council and by the General Assembly of the actions of the Secretary-General . . . it is impossible to reach the conclusion that the operations in question usurped or impinged upon the prerogatives conferred by the Charter on the Security Council. The Charter does not forbid the Security Council to act through instruments of its own choice: under Article 29 it may establish such subsidiary organs as it deems necessary for the performance of its functions; under Article 98 it may entrust "other functions" to the Secretary-General.[8]

Moreover, since ONUC's operations did not entail the use of armed force against a state that the Security Council, under Article 39, had defined as an aggressor or peace-breaker, and since ONUC did not take military action against a state, its actions, like those of UNEF, did not involve "enforcement measures." Hence, the Security Council did not have exclusive jurisdiction in the matter.

Thus, as in the case of UNEF, the majority came to the conclusion that the costs of ONUC were to be regarded as "expenses of the Organization." The Court was not deterred by the fact that the Assembly had twice decided "that the extraordinary expenses for the United

[8] *Ibid.,* pp. 176-77.

Nations in the Congo [were] essentially different in nature from the expenses of the Organization under the regular budget and that therefore a procedure different from that applied in the case of the regular budget [was] required for meeting these extraordinary expenses."[9] The majority felt that its conclusions were supported by the two Assembly resolutions themselves, which had stated that the decision to use the regular scale of assessment had been made "pending the establishment of a different scale of assessment to defray the extraordinary expenditure: The only alternative—and that means the 'different procedure'—contemplated was another *scale* of assessment and not some method other than assessment. 'Apportionment' and 'assessment' are terms which relate only to the General Assembly's authority under Article 17."[10]

An examination of the text of Article 17 (2) of the Charter thus led the majority to the conclusions that UNEF and ONUC were in keeping with the purposes of the Organization, that they were noncoercive in character, and that, therefore, the expenditures incurred by them were to be regarded as "expenses" within the meaning of Article 17 of the Charter.

The majority opinion was supported by four concurring opinions. Judge Spiropoulos, in an explanatory "declaration," answered the Assembly's question in the affirmative on the ground that the expenditures had been incurred by a two-thirds vote of the Assembly for what were clearly legitimate purposes of the United Nations. He felt that the Assembly's rejection of the proposed French amendment indicated that it did not wish that the Court concern itself with the "prior" question of the legal validity of the resolutions themselves. Similarly, Judges Spender and Morelli declared that the validity of the resolutions themselves was not relevant since the expenditures they authorized clearly came within the meaning of Article 17. Judge Fitzmaurice, while concurring with the majority, indicated that "although given expenditures [were] expenses of the Organization, there may not necessarily or always be an obligation for every Member State to contribute to them."[11] He suggested that "expenses of the United Nations" could broadly be divided into obligatory and permissive ones, the former being of a peace-keeping nature and the lat-

[9] General Assembly Res. 1619(XV), April 21, 1961, and 1732(XVI), Dec. 20, 1961.
[10] *Opinion*, p. 179.
[11] *Ibid.*, p. 198.

ter economic and social in character. The former type of expense should be shared by all members, but dissenters should not be bound to contribute to the latter. He warned that unless Article 17 were interpreted in this more restricted sense, "the Assembly could vote enormous expenditures, and thereby place a heavy financial burden even on dissenting States, and as a matter of obligation even in the case of non-essential activities. This would be reading a lot into such a provision as Article 17, paragraph 2."[12]

Of the dissenting justices, Judge Koretsky expressed the most radical opposition to the majority and concurring opinions. To him, the entire issue appeared fundamentally as a political, rather than a legal one. The resolutions authorizing the UNEF and ONUC expenditures were invalid and themselves based on prior resolutions that had been carried out illegally. He considered UNEF and ONUC as enforcement actions falling within the meaning of Article 39 since there had been breaches of the peace and acts of aggression involved. He rejected the majority's narrower interpretation of enforcement action and saw the two operations as destructive to the balance established by the Charter between the Security Council and the Assembly, a balance that gave the primary role in peace and security operations to the former. Hence, since the operations had been conceived and carried out in direct violation of the Charter, there existed no obligation to pay for them.[13]

President Winiarski also denied the legality of the UNEF and ONUC resolutions. He pointed out that not only had many members refused to pay because they thought the operations to be illegal, but the resolutions themselves had preserved a separation "between the normal administrative expenses of the Organization and those called for by exceptional circumstances." And even if the expenditures in question were "expenses of the Organization," no legal obligation to pay necessarily followed, since resolutions of the Assembly had the status of recommendations only.[14]

Judges Moreno Quintana and Bustamante felt that the "previous" question of the validity of the Assembly resolutions themselves was at the heart of the matter and deplored the fact that the proposed French amendment, which would have clarified the issue, had

[12] *Ibid.*
[13] *Ibid.*, pp. 253-87.
[14] *Ibid.*, pp. 227-34.

been rejected by the Assembly. Judge Quintana indicated that the resolutions had been illegal for "any use of armed force intended for whatever purpose implie[d] by definition enforcement action."[15] According to Judge Basdevant, the Assembly's failure to ask this more basic "previous" question had led to inexactness in the way in which the request for an advisory opinion had been framed. This failure of the Assembly to comply with Article 65, paragraph 2, of the Statute of the Court requiring "an exact statement of the question upon which an opinion is required," made it impossible for Judge Basdevant to concur with the majority.

The Advisory Opinion and the Charter

An analysis of the advisory opinion suggests three fundamental constitutional issues on which the arguments of the fourteen judges hinged. An attempt to cull these basic principles from the legal labyrinth of the arguments may make it easier to assess the opinion's contribution. These basic issues seem to be: first, the legal role of the General Assembly in the realm of peace and security operations; second, the nature of the Assembly's fiscal powers; and third, the role of the Court itself in interpreting the Charter.

On the first issue, the Court clearly affirmed the right of the Assembly to establish subsidiary organs for the purpose of maintaining international peace and security.[16] The "primary" responsibility of the Security Council in this realm was admitted but limited to the kind of "action" that was "indicated by the title of Chapter VII of the Charter, namely 'Action with respect to threats to the peace, breaches of the peace, and acts of aggression.' "[17] Recommendations made by the Assembly or the Council establishing subsidiary organs for peace and security purposes were not enforcement actions. Both UNEF and ONUC had been established on the basis of such recommendations. The Court implied that when the nature of the action in question was somewhat obscure, the decision should be governed by the fun-

[15] *Ibid.*, p. 246.
[16] For a discussion of the legal issues involved in the creation and maintenance of U.N. forces by the Assembly and the Council, see Gabriella Rosner, *The United Nations Emergency Force* (Columbia University Press, 1963), and E. M. Miller, "Legal Aspects of the United Nations Action in the Congo," *American Journal of International Law*, Vol. LV (January 1961) , pp. 1-28.
[17] *Opinion*, p. 165.

damental and overriding purpose of the Organization, the maintenance of peace and security. It rejected the concept of a rigid separation of functions between the Security Council and the General Assembly.

As mentioned above, two judges in the minority rejected, and the three others seriously questioned, the competence of the Assembly in matters of peace and security. They felt that the separation of powers between the General Assembly and the Security Council should be maintained.

An analysis of the opposing positions on this issue reveals striking similarities to the debates preceding the "Uniting for Peace" Resolution in 1950. During these discussions, the majority of the member states had asserted the competence of the Assembly to consider any case in which "there appear[ed] to be a threat to the peace, breach, or act of aggression," with respect to which the Council, "because of the lack of unanimity of the permanent members, fail[ed] to exercise its primary responsibility." Indeed, the "Uniting for Peace" Resolution had formalized this view over the objections of the Soviet Union.

The Soviet delegate had also maintained then that assumption by the Assembly of the power to recommend collective measures was in violation of the principles of the primary responsibility of the Security Council and the unanimity of the great powers. Furthermore, the "Uniting for Peace" Resolution had directly violated the provision of Article 11(2) of the Charter according to which the Assembly must refer to the Council, either before or after discussion, any question on which "action is necessary." The supporters of the "Uniting for Peace" Resolution, on the other hand, had replied that despite the Council's primary responsibility, members of the United Nations were obliged to act collectively to keep the peace. Although the Assembly could not take "binding decisions," it could, under its broad powers, make recommendations that, if backed by large majorities, "would naturally carry considerable weight and would spur Member States to action."[18]

[18] U.N. General Assembly, Fifth Session, First Committee, *Official Records*, 354th Meeting (Oct. 9, 1950), p. 66. See also Leland M. Goodrich and Anne P. Simons, *The United Nations and the Maintenance of International Peace and Security* (Brookings Institution, 1955), pp. 431-32.

The arguments of the majority judges and the objections of Judges Koretsky and Winiarski were in fact a repetition of the arguments over the "Uniting for Peace" Resolution. The majority opinion in effect reaffirmed the principles of that resolution, and the minority with equal determination wished to prevent any such extension of the General Assembly's mandate.

It may well be that the most significant contribution of the opinion was in the second fundamental problem area: the Assembly's fiscal powers. The Court found no limitation on the Assembly's authority in the financing of peace-keeping operations that did not constitute enforcement action:

> The provisions of the Charter which distribute functions and powers to the Security Council and to the General Assembly give no support to the view that such distribution excludes from the powers of the General Assembly the power for the financing of measures designed to maintain peace and security.[19]

The financial powers of the Assembly, declared the Court, extended to all financial requirements of the organization, as long as these requirements were consonant with the purposes of the United Nations and outside the purview of Chapter VII.

In its reasoning on this matter, the Court relied heavily on the principle of ultimate effectiveness, determined in this instance by the overall purposes of the United Nations. This was not without precedent in the history of the Court. For example, the real basis of the Court's Advisory Opinion in 1949 on *Reparation for Injuries Suffered in the Service of the United Nations* was the assumption that certain powers must be implied in the Charter as being essential to the purposes of the Organization: "Under international law, the Organization must be deemed to have those powers which, though not expressly provided in the Charter, are conferred upon it by necessary implication as being essential to the performance of its duties."[20]

The Court broadened this interpretation even further in 1962 by asserting, as noted above, that even if the financial action had been taken by the wrong organ, this did not necessarily mean that the expense incurred was not an expense of the Organization. Both national and international law contemplated cases in which the body cor-

[19] *Opinion*, p. 164.
[20] I.C.J. Reports 1949, p. 182.

porate or politic may be bound, as to third parties, by the *ultra vires* act of an agent.

A survey of the literature on the doctrine of *ultra vires* reveals considerable conflict of opinion. On the one hand, a distinguished group of international lawyers—Anzilotti, Cavagliori, Bittner, Verdross, Basdevant, and Willoughby—maintain that the *ultra vires* act of an agent does not legally bind the body corporate.[21] On the other hand, an equally distinguished group of writers—Strupp, Schücking, Politis, de Visscher, Challey, Hyde, and Kosters—hold the opposite view.[22] The advisory opinion clearly aligned the Court with the latter group.

In view of the great financial powers which the majority opinion saw fit to vest in the General Assembly, it followed quite logically that the Court should regard the assessments imposed by the Assembly for UNEF and ONUC as legally binding obligations on the entire membership. In this connection, the Court noted carefully that:

> . . . The functions and powers conferred by the Charter on the General Assembly [were] not confined to discussion, consideration, the initiation of studies and the making of recommendations; they [were] not merely hortatory. Article 18 dealing with *"decisions"* [did] indeed include certain recommendations, but others [had] dispositive force and effect. Among these latter decisions, Article 18 include[d] suspension of rights and privileges of membership, expulsion of Members, and "budgetary question."[23]

The Court noted further that the "decision" to approve the budget had a close connection with paragraph 2 of Article 17,

> . . . since thereunder the General Assembly [was] also given the power to apportion the expenses among the Members and the exercise of the power of apportionment creates the obligation, specifically stated in Article 17, paragraph 2, of each Member to bear that part of the expenses which is apportioned to it by the General Assembly. When these expenses include expenditures for the maintenance of peace and security, which are not otherwise

---

[21] *Research in International Law*, Pt. 3. Law of Treaties, Draft Conventions Prepared for Codification of International Law, Supplement to *American Journal of International Law*, Vol. 29 (1935), p. 999.

[22] *Ibid.*, p. 1008. See also Herbert W. Briggs (ed.), *The Law of Nations: Cases, Documents, and Notes* (Appleton, 1952), pp. 844-47; Edvardo Vitta, *La Validité des Traités Internationaux* (1940); and Clive Parry, "The Treaty-Making Power of the United Nations," *British Yearbook of International Law, 1949*, pp. 108-49.

[23] *Opinion*, p. 163.

provided for, it is the General Assembly which has the authority to apportion the latter amounts among the Members.[24]

The majority was especially careful in presenting its case for the legally binding effect of the UNEF and ONUC assessments, and the minority was especially bent on disproving that assertion. The Court was not alone in its disagreement on this matter. This is readily demonstrated by a survey of the literature on the subject.

In Sir Hersch Lauterpacht's view, there are two kinds of legal obligation: some are "rudimentary, elastic and imperfect . . . intangible and almost nominal," such as the obligation of member states to give due consideration in good faith to resolutions of the Assembly. Others are "automatic" and require that "full effect" be given to them. He stressed that "in some matters, such as the . . . *approval of the budget and the apportionment of expenses,* the full legal effects of the Resolutions of the General Assembly are undeniable."[25] James L. Brierly writes that *"apart from its control over the budget,* all that the General Assembly can do is to discuss and recommend and initiate studies and consider reports from other bodies."[26] Francis O. Wilcox and Carl M. Marcy agree with this dictum,[27] but Hans Kelsen goes further: the term "recommendation" in the Charter may have several meanings. A recommendation of the General Assembly in the field of the maintenance of international peace and security may possibly be binding.[28] Leland M. Goodrich and Edvard Hambro declare that Article 17(2) "empowers the General Assembly to apportion the expenses of the United Nations among the Members and places the members *under the obligation* to bear these expenses."[29] Finally, Daniel S. Cheever and H. Field Haviland express a practical view on Assembly resolutions: "It is not so much their legal character

[24] *Ibid.,* p. 164.

[25] *Voting Procedure on Questions Relating to Reports and Petitions Concerning the Territory of South-West Africa,* I.C.J. *Reports,* 1955, p. 115. Italics added. F. Blaine Sloane, "The Binding Force of a 'Recommendation' of the General Assembly of the United Nations," *British Yearbook of International Law,* Vol. XXV (1948), pp. 1-33, agrees with Lauterpacht's view.

[26] *The Law of Nations: An Introduction to the International Law of Peace* (5th ed., Oxford University Press, 1955), p. 107. Italics added.

[27] *Proposals for Changes in the United Nations* (Brookings Institution, 1955), p. 348.

[28] *The Law of the United Nations: A Critical Analysis of its Fundamental Problems* (Praeger, 1951), p. 459.

[29] *Charter of the United Nations: Commentary and Documents* (World Peace Foundation, 1949), p. 184. Italics added.

as 'recommendations' which determines their effectiveness but rather the quality, quantity and intensity of community support behind them."[30]

It is fairly clear from the above cross-section of opinion, that a majority of jurists and scholars seem to feel that, while there are definite limits to the Assembly's authority, its resolutions pertaining to financing and apportionment of expenses are legally binding in character. The advisory opinion further strengthens this interpretation.

The third contribution of the opinion may be found in its relevance to the evolving body of international constitutional law on the United Nations Charter. The Court was asked by the General Assembly to interpret a treaty provision. This had occurred several times in the past.[31] In that sense, the advisory opinion of 1962 was not unorthodox and "seemed to fit comfortably within the scope of accepted judicial interpretation."[32] But the Court has never been the sole interpreter of the Charter. No agreement had been reached at San Francisco on the question: By whom is the Charter to be interpreted authoritatively? This power was not bestowed unequivocally on any one organ of the United Nations. In this connection, one authority has written:

> The easiest, the most primitive, and the most unsatisfactory solution is to say that each individual Member has the right to decide for itself how to interpret the Charter. . . . The next solution is that each organ of the United Nations should decide its own competence. This is in practice what happens in the Constitution of many individual States.[33]

The latter course of action is in effect what has happened in practice

[30] D. S. Cheever and H. F. Haviland, *Organizing for Peace: International Organization in World Affairs* (Houghton, 1954), p. 89. The Court in its opinion also seemed to be aware of the importance of community support behind a resolution by stressing the fact that UNEF and ONUC were created without dissenting votes and financed time and again by two-thirds majorities.

[31] For example, the following cases inter alia involved Charter interpretation: Admission of a State to the United Nations 1948; Competence of Assembly Regarding Admission to the United Nations (1950); Reparation for Injuries Suffered in the Service of the United Nations (1949); International Status of South-West Africa (1950).

[32] James Fergusson Hogg, "Peace-Keeping Costs and Charter Obligations—Implications of the International Court of Justice Decision on Certain Expenses of the United Nations," *Columbia Law Review*, Vol. LXII (November 1962), p. 1246.

[33] Pollex, "The Interpretation of the Charter of the United Nations," *British Yearbook of International Law, 1946*, pp. 50-57.

at the United Nations. The 1962 advisory opinion contributed further to the evolving trend of interpreting the Charter through combined action of the Assembly and the Court. One seems to be on sound legal grounds when maintaining that interpretation of the Charter has been achieved when the Court adds its support to the position taken on repeated occasions by a two-thirds vote of the General Assembly, and the Assembly in turn accepts the Court's opinion. Whether the Assembly's request for an advisory opinion in 1962 and the Court's subsequent role were politically wise in addition to being legally sound is a question that is far more difficult to answer.

The Advisory Opinion and the Financial Crisis

It is not easy to evaluate the impact of the advisory opinion on the financial structure of the United Nations. The Court has confirmed the Assembly's role in peace-keeping activities and has also underwritten its authority to impose legally binding assessments on the member states. This means that, in financing peace-keeping activities, a two-thirds majority of the General Assembly may bind the entire membership, including those states that vote against. In that sense, the opinion signifies a tentative step toward the principle of international taxation of states by the world community. More broadly, it lends support to the principle of majority rule in international relations. The Court also gave the Assembly or the Security Council free reign to establish other noncoercive forces in the future and to arrange for their financial support, provided they are in accord with the purposes of the United Nations. On the whole, therefore, the Court gave its approval to Dag Hammarskjold's conception of the United Nations as a "dynamic instrument" capable of "executive action" toward "increasingly effective forms of active international cooperation," as against the notion of the Organization as a mere "static conference machinery."

The practical effect of the opinion on the treasury of the United Nations is not likely to be too significant. Although the Seventeenth General Assembly decided to "accept" the opinion by a large majority of 76 in favor, 17 against, with 8 abstentions, while the Sixteenth had

requested it by a vote of only 52 in favor, 11 against, with 32 abstentions, the politically motivated delinquents have not been eager to
abide by the opinion. A considerable number of other nations in arrears, on the other hand, were guided by the opinion and cleared their
accounts as indicated in Table 6.1. But their payments amounted to
only a small part of the unpaid assessments.

The opinion also makes it possible for the Assembly to invoke
sanctions if it chooses to do so. The Court has not pronounced on
this matter, and there is no precedent for sanctions in the United Nations. As noted in the preceding chapter, the heart of the problem of
sanctions is not legal, but political. To ignore the possibility of invoking Article 19 altogether would be to ignore the implications of the
advisory opinion; but to insist on sanctions might lead to an exodus
of disgruntled states from the United Nations. On balance, if Article
19 has to be invoked, it should be made clear that the thrust of the
sanction is not against a given state, but for the law of the Charter.

The political import of the opinion was reflected in each of the
ten different statements. All the judges labored under the difficulty of
applying legal tools to what was also a controversial political issue.
It is true that the Assembly asked the Court a legal question; but
it is equally true that its request for an advisory opinion was also an
attempt to exert pressure on a stubborn minority. It is probably not
an accident that all the judges save one—Judge Badawi of the United
Arab Republic—took voting positions that were congruent with those
of their national governments.

In its broadest form, the issue at stake may be described as that of
majority rule versus state sovereignty. The advisory opinion advanced the cause of the former and, by so doing, affirmed the power
of the General Assembly. It in effect reversed the stand taken by the
Permanent Court of International Justice in 1927 in the Lotus case,
which had asserted the principle that limitations on the sovereignty
of states cannot be presumed, with its implication that what is not explicitly surrendered by states is retained.[34] This great power of the
Assembly may be used constructively and with a sense of fiscal responsibility; but, as Judge Fitzmaurice warned, it could also be used
by impatient majorities eager to push vast economic and social programs to impose large assessments on a reluctant minority by decid-

[34] P.C.I.J., Series A, No. 10.

TABLE 6.1. *Payments Made Since World Court Advisory Opinion as of October 1, 1963*
(In U.S. dollars)

Nation	UNEF	ONUC
Argentina		250,000.00[a]
Austria		568,875.00[a]
Bolivia	7,345.00	8,768.60
Brazil	18,934.00	2,080.00
Cambodia		27,298.00
Chad		13,035.98
Colombia	41,732.91	177,825.50
Congo (Brazzaville)	8,745.00	16,452.00
Congo (Leopoldville)	1,362.00	11,196.00
Costa Rica	8,000.00	
Dahomey	1,158.93	6,246.06
Ecuador		34,534.62
El Salvador	12,497.00	22,013.00
Ethiopia	65,084.50	34,365.50
Gabon		7,925.00
Ghana	1,676.00	14,341.00
Greece	160,116.00	137,869.50[a]
Guinea		33,664.00[a]
Indonesia		206,930.00
Iran	3,663.00	
Italy		3,318,544.00[a]
Laos	4,457.00	23,977.00[a]
Lebanon		9,904.98[a]
Libya		27,298.00[a]
Luxembourg		7,949.00
Morocco	29,451.00	
Nepal	25,410.80	17,474.34[a]
Nicaragua	1,665.50	
Paraguay	5,876.00	9,686.50
Philippines	47,329.00	85,191.00
Sierra Leone	1,196.00	7,277.00
Somalia		6,813.93
Sudan		26,416.50
Tanganyika	1,196.00	7,277.00
Thailand	2,940.00	25,465.00
United Kingdom		377,242.92
Venezuela	46,528.00	302,916.50[a]
Total	$496,363.64	$5,826,853.43

Sources: United Nations Documents ST/ADM/SER.B/162-173, 175, 177, and 179.
[a] Made first payment.

ing that such expenditures were "expenses of the Organization appropriate for the fulfillment of one of the stated purposes of the UN." Majority rule per se does not guarantee progress toward order in the relations of states. Nor will the advisory opinion clear the way for a definitive solution of the financial crisis. But it may be an important building block if the Assembly chooses to build on it with wisdom, prudence, and imagination.

CHAPTER 7

Financing Future Peace and Security Operations

IT IS ALMOST CERTAIN that the need for United Nations peace-keeping will arise again in the future. If so, the resolution on "general principles" for future peace-keeping operations passed in the special session of the General Assembly in June 1963 will provide only the most superficial guidance. The discussion that follows is an effort to explore, in a specific and systematic manner, various possibilities of strengthening the financial basis of future United Nations operations in the peace and security field. It is grouped into three parts: first, the enlargement of reserve and emergency funds; second, an analysis of the problem of cost apportionment; and third, concrete proposals.

The Enlargement of Reserve and Emergency Funds

There are some proposals that may not be thoroughgoing remedies, but are in the nature of stop-gap emergency relief until more permanent solutions may be found. A first step in this direction was taken by the Seventeenth General Assembly in December 1962 when it enlarged the Working Capital Fund from $25 million to $40 million for 1963. This may help somewhat in reducing deficits and may provide partial, stop-gap financing for the initial phase of future operations.

Building a Contingency Fund

In 1960, the Advisory Committee on Administrative and Budgetary Questions recommended the enlargement of the annual budgetary allotment provided for unforeseen and extraordinary expenses.

An increase of from $2 million to $5 million a year, it was felt, was politically feasible. So far, however, no action has been taken on this proposal. A variant of this recommendation would be to set aside the miscellaneous income for unforeseen and extraordinary expenses. Instead of helping to reduce members' assessments, this sum of roughly $6 million a year would be permitted to accumulate as a contingency fund. The advantage of this plan would be that the money is available—it would not have to be specially raised. However, to carry out this recommendation, the financial regulations would have to be changed, and the plan would no doubt encounter the political objection that it would be a disguised way of raising the assessments of member states.

A Peace and Security Fund

Moving into more ambitious proposals, a plan to establish a standing United Nations Peace and Security Fund has been the subject of continued discussion during recent years. In 1960, the Advisory Committee suggested the establishment of such a fund at a level of $20 million to $25 million, to be financed partly from the regular budget and partly by voluntary contributions.

Secretary-General Dag Hammarskjöld was a firm supporter of this plan. In a special appearance before the Advisory Committee, he declared that he saw such a fund or a similar arrangement as indispensable to the future solvency and efficiency of the United Nations. In his view, a Peace and Security Fund would have two purposes. First, it would cover expenditures within certain limits authorized by the General Assembly for specific purposes. Second, and more important, it would provide for additional expenditures within a prescribed amount, for unforeseen security costs, on certification of need by the Secretary-General.[1]

The manner of financing both UNEF and ONUC has not been inconsistent with the principle of this approach. In each case, albeit for different reasons, a separate, special account was set up within the United Nations for handling receipts of income and paying obligations incurred in the operations. Separate assessments were sought in each instance plus voluntary contributions. Thus it can be said that a precedent has been set for separate funding of peace and security operations involving a combination of assessment and voluntary contri-

[1] See U.N. Doc. A/C.5/843, XV (Nov. 21, 1960).

butions. The creation of a single, permanent, consolidated fund for this purpose remains to be agreed upon.

The advantages of such a procedure would be numerous. In addition to the two mentioned by the late Secretary-General, this plan would make possible the accumulation of a larger net amount by permitting and encouraging voluntary contributions to this end. The separate fund arrangement might also have the advantage of permitting more flexibility in fiscal proceedings.

Another separate fund would, on the other hand, further complicate United Nations accounts. States inclined to be evasive or indifferent about paying for peace and security actions where their own interests are not immediately involved might conceivably be under less compulsion if payments were to be made to a separate Peace and Security Fund than if the amounts had to be paid into the regular budget.

When the Working Group of Fifteen was considering various ways of increasing United Nations financial resources, only the Soviet Union and Bulgaria registered opposition to the suggestion of studying the establishment of a Peace and Security Fund. Their position was based on opposition to any move that would take peace and security matters out of the hands of the Security Council and tend to increase the powers of the General Assembly or the Secretary-General. Otherwise, more accord was displayed within the Working Group on action along this line than on any other proposal placed before the committee. This may, therefore, suggest that there would be somewhat more readiness to proceed along this path than some others in the near future.

Another alternative would be a United Nations Peace and Security Fund open to voluntary contributions from both governments and private sources. The advantages of such a plan, if approved by the General Assembly, would be: its flexibility in permitting those who wished to contribute to do so while affixing no stigma to those who felt constrained to offer no contribution; avoidance of the imposition of additional assessments on the low-income states; circumvention of the problem of having to determine the amounts to be paid by individual states and what to do in the event of refusals to pay; and its provision of a channel for individuals, private or religious groups, foundations, or other organizations that may wish to make financial contributions to the United Nations for peace and security.

When the suggestion of a voluntary fund not necessarily restricted to government subscription was raised before the Working Group of Fifteen, wide differences of opinion immediately arose. Seven states— France, Italy, Japan, Nigeria, Sweden, the United Arab Republic, and the United States—supported the idea. Three—Bulgaria, the Soviet Union, and the United Kingdom—were opposed to the motion. These governments took the position that since the Organization was one of states, it was the responsibility of states to support it. This responsibility should not be undermined or diluted. Two states—Brazil and Mexico—abstained from voting on the proposal, and three—Canada, China, and India—reserved their opinion. During the special session of the General Assembly in 1963, Ghana urged the establishment of a crisis "Peace Fund" to be made up of voluntary contributions from governments and private sources. The Assembly passed a resolution recommending a study of the desirability of establishing such a fund.

This plan is open to certain shortcomings and raises some fundamental questions. First, the amount the United Nations might realize from a voluntary fund would be uncertain and dependent on many variables beyond its control. Second, a wholly voluntary fund would depart from the basic principle that peace and security are every member's business. Third, such a fund would allow those who have refused to pay their share of UNEF and ONUC expenses not only to continue evading their responsibilities, but also to engage in irresponsible criticism without assuming any of the burdens. Fourth, if private contributions were to become a substantial portion of the fund, as a result of major gifts by large foundations, charitable trusts, wealthy individuals or businesses, would not private, nongovernmental representatives be tempted to claim a voice in determining how and when such monies should be expended? Thus a voluntary fund does not seem advisable.

A third way of financing a Peace and Security Fund would be for member nations initially to make funds available on an interest-free loan basis. The fund would then be maintained by assessing all member states on the basis of "capacity to pay" over a fixed period of years.[2] The author of this plan declared that the ultimate size of such a fund could be fixed only after thorough study, but speculated that during the next three to ten years, the amount required might be as

[2] Calvin J. Nichols, *Financing the United Nations: Problems and Prospects* (Center for International Studies, Massachusetts Institute of Technology, February 1961), p. 31.

high as $500 million, of which the United States might be expected to advance 50 percent or more on a loan basis. This comes closer to the mark of what the United Nations should have available in the event of a serious crisis, but the political opposition to such a plan would be almost impossible to surmount.

Another way of starting the fund would be to base it on a special scale of assessments that would take into account the special responsibilities of the permanent members of the Security Council for the maintenance of international peace and security.[3] This, in a sense, would perpetuate the rebate formula of financing UNEF and ONUC. As a variation of this proposal, one authority has suggested that the fund could be started with the proceeds of the bond issue.[4] However, it is not likely that any money will be left over from bond proceeds to start such a new venture.

There has been some discussion of establishing a fund to which "interested members" could contribute if the necessity for a peace-keeping operation were to arise. Such an arrangement gives rise to a number of questions. First, this procedure may place onerous burdens on some states while allowing others to contribute nothing at all. Moreover, the United Nations would have no way of knowing how much money could be counted on. It is also very probable that in the sensitive area of peace and security, states willing to contribute substantial amounts to the fund would wish to have some kind of control over its use. Theoretically, states choosing not to contribute to an "interested members" voluntary fund would have no legal grounds for objecting to such funds being placed at the disposal of the United Nations, provided the General Assembly had control of these funds on a par with all other funds contributed to the Organization.

Perhaps a majority in the General Assembly could be mustered for the establishment of a voluntary fund in which the members of an advisory committee, council, or governing board, made up of contributors, would have a veto power over expenditures from the fund, by some system of weighted or preferential voting. But there would be heavy opposition to approval of a voluntary fund in which the contributing members could compel an outlay for peace-keeping ac-

[3] Elmore Jackson, "The Constitutional Development of the United Nations: The Growth of its Executive Capacity," *Proceedings of the American Society of International Law,* Vol. 55 (1961), pp. 78-88.

[4] Arthur Larson, "Road Map for the UN," *Saturday Review* (April 28, 1962), pp. 11-13.

tivities irrespective of the wishes of the General Assembly. There would also be considerable reluctance to appropriate money in anticipation of unknown events.

The strongest argument for full financing by the "interested members" may be that this is the most feasible method of providing such resources. The example of West New Guinea would support this contention. But to this pragmatic need the concept of collective responsibility would then have to be sacrificed.

Before leaving the problem of establishing a Peace and Security Fund, a word must be said about political control. At whose discretion should this fund be used: the Security Council; the General Assembly acting under the Uniting for Peace Resolution; the Secretary-General; or a combination of these? These questions cannot be separated from the problem of raising the money for a Peace and Security Fund.

A Bond Issue for Peace and Security Operations

Another suggestion in the general area of emergency financing has been made to the effect that the United Nations treat the $200 million bond issue not as a "one-shot" affair, but as a precedent for covering future peace and security operations.

Proponents of this idea declare that the issuance of bonds could provide a source of revenue since some governments might be ready to loan money at reasonable rates of interest. Moreover, the bond system would afford an effective "double vote" means of keeping United Nations peace and security operations within "realistic" limits. A bond issue would have to be authorized by a two-thirds vote of the General Assembly, which would not be likely unless the United States and other principal contributors to the United Nations were in favor of such a move, and the income would amount to relatively little unless these same members subscribed, a decision that would rest in their own hands.

Opponents, on the other hand, maintain with equal vigor that the $200 million bond issue was deliberately designated as not constituting a precedent for the future. Assurances in this respect had been given to the United States Congress by Secretary of State Dean Rusk, Assistant Secretary of State Harlan Cleveland, and Ambassador Adlai Stevenson. The reasoning of "changed circumstances" might be accepted by a future Congress under different conditions. But given the measure of opposition revealed in the Eighty-seventh Congress, a change of heart is not likely to come readily. Opponents of further use of bonds for peace and security operations also argue that reliance on such a method in the future might lead to a serious weakening of the Organization and of its capacity for swift and effective action in crisis situations.

Experience with the $200 million bond issue seems to indicate that there is a measure of approval of this method of handling emergency financial needs. The number of states that have voluntarily purchased the bonds or pledged amounts equal to or in excess of their regular assessment rates may be indicative of considerable favorable sentiment. The argument that the bond issue was not supposed to be a precedent may not be very serious, for previously tried actions have usually tended to be repeated in the United Nations.

There are, of course, aspects to the bond technique that could become drawbacks in any extensive employment of this method. A good deal of negotiation would be needed before the United Nations organs could be sure, in a highly contentious situation, whether substantial amounts would be pledged and purchased. Most governments are uneasy about the circumstances in which the funds would be used and thus reluctant to pledge in advance. There might also be serious difficulties in a future situation, similar to the one the United Nations faced in 1956, when two major crises occurred simultaneously in widely separated geographic areas in both of which the Organization could be called on to make a major effort. Furthermore, resistance may be encountered to substantial amounts being added to the regular budget for the repayment of bonds and the accrued interest. The Soviet bloc and France, as indicated earlier, refused in 1963 to pay their share of the $4.7 million earmarked to cover the first interest and principal repayment of the United Nations bond issue.

There is no obvious simple solution to the problem of emergency financing. In general it appears that the present legal level of the Working Capital Fund is satisfactory. But it would be advisable to have the amounts available within the regular budget for unforeseen and extraordinary expenses increased and to make the miscellaneous income available as a contingency fund, although there seems little likelihood of this.

The establishment of a separate fund specifically designated for peace and security purposes, combining voluntary contribution and assessment features, may offer a good possibility for building up a stand-by reserve to meet at least the initial costs of a peace and security operation.

The Problem of Cost Apportionment

Reflection suggests that this aspect of the problem involves three issues. (1) What type of cost apportionment should be used: direct assessment, voluntary contributions, or some mixture of the two? (2) If a direct assessment method is to be employed, should this be in accordance with the normal scale for the expenses of the regular budget or some special scale? (3) If a special scale is to be established, on what principles should it be based?

Type of Apportionment

The financing formulas adopted at the Sixteenth General Assembly and at the special session in 1963, indicate that a strong sentiment prevails within the presently constituted Assembly that (1) some portion of the expenses should be borne by assessment on all; (2) this should be lightened by from 50 to 80 percent for the developing nations; (3) members of the Security Council have a "special responsibility" for permanent peace and security operations and should bear a substantially larger percentage of the total than they do of the regular budget; and (4) voluntary contributions should play a large part in meeting the overall costs.

It seems safe to assume that, barring radical changes in national positions, sentiment will continue to favor a mixture of assessment and voluntary contributions. There are several advantages in the mixed system. Assessment of some part of the cost to all member states emphasizes the collective responsibility of all states, but simultaneously recognizes the capacity of some to bear larger amounts of the total than others. Retention of the voluntary element permits interest and calculations of special responsibility to enter the picture. By providing for a portion of the total expenses to be paid by voluntary contributions by the larger and wealthier powers, this reduces the amounts to be assessed on all members and thus alleviates the burden on the young and developing states and those with frail economies. On the whole, the mixed system seems preferable.

Scale of Apportionment

The second basic issue is whether the amounts to be covered by assessment should be divided according to the regular scale of apportionment or by some separate, special scale.

The principal argument in favor of using the regular scale for whatever portion of the expenses is to be defrayed by assessment is that this scale has been worked out with care over the years. It has been found generally satisfactory for covering normal expenses. It is based on considerations of capacity to pay, and it is accepted by the membership. These are valuable considerations. The regular assessment scale appears suitable for continued coverage of the relatively low costs involved in minor peace-keeping activities such as United Nations "observer groups" and "presences." Meeting the costs of fairly large-scale operations such as UNEF and ONUC, however, raises problems of a different magnitude.

A small state, like Costa Rica, for example, with a GNP of only $375 million, like all others at the minimum level of assessment (.04 percent), in 1961 was assessed $27,478 for the regular budget. Its assessments for the specialized agencies amounted to $52,508. Over and above this, it pledged $40,000 to the special voluntary programs, making a total of $119,986 due to the United Nations. If the regular budget scale had been applied for UNEF and ONUC expenses, the additional cost to Costa Rica would have resulted in a 40 percent increase in the cost of United Nations membership for this small country, an increase that is not negligible in a state with a small GNP that has not reached the so-called "take-off" point in economic development.

A developing country more nearly in the middle of the scale would also face a problem if the regular scale were used. Indonesia was in the .46 percent portion of the assessment scale (1959-61) with a GNP of $9.1 billion. Its regular budget assessment for 1961 was $322,867, plus $330,275 for the specialized agencies, and it made voluntary contributions amounting to $200,000, a total of $862,142. The application of the regular scale for UNEF and ONUC would have brought the combination of its assessed obligations and contributions to $1.4 million. In its case the UNEF-ONUC assessments would have increased the cost of United Nations membership by 64 percent.

Granting that an outlay of half a million dollars for peace and security activities by a state with a GNP of nearly $10 billion is a relatively small item in itself, this amount might be used instead to purchase three hundred tractors to improve food production, or an equivalent amount of machinery, textbooks, or medicine, all of which are among the things that are urgently needed for economic and social development.

To a country in Indonesia's position—and 84 percent of the members of the United Nations now have a national income so low as to put them in the class contributing less than 1 percent on the regular assessment scale—the progression of assessments for helping to meet the UNEF and ONUC costs may well be frightening. Where is this to end? This is a natural question in the minds of statesmen in all countries struggling to hasten economic growth toward the envied levels of the Western nations.

On the other hand, the peace-keeping operations have contributed to the stability so necessary for economic development in the new nations. The larger flow of capital to them has more than offset their contributions. They are willing to put up considerable amounts to obtain approval of United Nations development projects, and their living and entertainment allowances at United Nations headquarters are fairly high. These indicators suggest that many of the new nations might be able to afford payments based on the regular scale, but tend to place too low a value on peace and security operations.

For the United Kingdom and the United States, at the other end of the scale, the assessments for UNEF and ONUC ($9.2 million for the United Kingdom and $38.3 million for the United States in 1961) have added much smaller percentages to the totals of their overall payments to the United Nations—32.1 percent and 23.4 percent, respectively. This is due to the fact that large voluntary contributions have increased their total payments far above the amounts represented by their assessments.

The sharply mounting magnitude of peace-keeping operations since 1957 has led to increasing opposition to distributing these costs by the regular scale of assessments. This factor has also been responsible, in some instances at least, for the defaults in payments, and for the appeals to the great powers to make larger voluntary contributions in order to lighten the load on those less able to pay. And it has contributed in a large measure to the pressure for a different system of sharing the burden. Had it not been for the voluntary contributions made by the United States and a few other states, the amounts that would have had to be parceled out in assessments would have been considerably larger.

What do these amounts mean in terms of a lightened load for other members of the United Nations? The $9.8 million voluntarily contributed by the United States for UNEF in 1958 is equal to the total assessed to the entire membership for UNEF in 1962. For every country at the .04 percent end of the scale this meant a saving of $3,900. For a country at the .46 percent assessment point, such as Indonesia, this was a saving of $43,875 in what it would otherwise have been assessed for UNEF in that year. Again, the $15 million voluntarily contributed by the United States for the Congo operation in 1961 is almost exactly what was assessed to the full membership for UNEF in 1959. For every .04 percent payer, this gift meant a saving of $6,082. For a country such as Indonesia at the .46 percent point in the scale (1959-61), the saving was no less than $71,461 in 1961.

These voluntary contributions were correspondingly beneficial to other nations in need of economic and technical assistance. For example, the $15 million contribution meant a saving of $107,955 to Mexico, which was at the .71 percent mark; $155,091 to Brazil, which was at the 1.02 point; and $374,043 to India. These are by no means inconsequential benefits for countries with frail economies.

The total of the United States voluntary contributions to UNEF and ONUC combined from 1957 to 1962 amounted to roughly three million dollars more than the United Nations regular budget for 1959. Thus under the 1959-61 assessment scale, United States voluntary contributions averaged over the six years saved each of the .04 percent contributors approximately $25,000; the .32 percent members (e.g., the United Arab Republic), $200,000; the .46 percent members (e.g., Indonesia), $300,000; those generally in the same position as Mexico, $440,000; and those at 1 percent (e.g. Brazil and Argentina) between $630,000 and $690,000.

These United States voluntary contributions were made to help relieve the burden of assessment that would otherwise have fallen on the new and developing states with a limited capacity to pay. One possibility of dealing with costly peace and security operations would be for the United States to continue to make voluntary contributions rather than to work out a new special scale of assessment. This would be simple and would avoid laborious negotiations over a special scale. But the United Nations could never be sure of what it could count on and might become too heavily dependent on one donor state. It can be said, of course, that the experience with the UNEF and ONUC assessments shows that the United Nations cannot count on some major members of the Organization to pay their assessments. Voluntary contributions from the United States, however, have been a more reliable source of income than assessments from some other states.

While it appears that there is a great deal to be said for going on with the type of arrangement whereby the United States voluntarily contributes amounts of money to reduce the burden of the poorer states, this method of cost apportionment lacks stability in the long run. The United States was prepared to make voluntary contributions to UNEF and ONUC, but might not be prepared to do the same for a future peace and security operation. It would be more logical to have a special scale so that all member states would know in advance what percentage they would have to pay. Agreement on such a scale would also involve a new commitment to pay on the part of all participating members.

A Special Scale of Apportionment

Considerable support for developing a special scale was manifest in the two Working Groups and in the special session in 1963. Although there were wide differences of opinion on the principles on which a scale should be based, there was more sentiment in favor of this method of funding the costs than of using the normal scale of apportionment. The numerous resolutions passed by the Assembly granting reductions to the low-income states receiving technical assistance and asking the great powers and other states able to do so to cover the deficits resulting from the reductions represented a step in the direction of establishing a special scale. So did the compromise solution adopted at the special session in 1963.

The opposition to apportionment of the large expenses of UNEF and ONUC on the basis of the regular scale of assessments has focused on three factors, which point to possible bases for a special scale. These were summarized as follows for the United States Congress:

> . . . First, it was contended that the Charter contemplated that peace and security actions should be carried out primarily by the

five permanent members of the Security Council who would furnish their troops without cost to other U.N. members. Accordingly, it was argued that the five permanent members of the Security Council should pay considerably more than their ordinary assessment percentages for peace and security operations such as UNEF and ONUC, particularly since in neither case were they furnishing manpower. Second, it was maintained that in accordance with principles of equity the "aggressors" who made U.N. peace and security actions necessary, plus "parties in interest," should pay all or most of the expenses. Finally, it was argued that regardless of other considerations, some member states had such limited financial resources that they simply could not contribute on the basis of the regular scale of assessments to the expenses of such costly operations as UNEF and ONUC.[5]

RESPONSIBILITY OF BIG FIVE FOR COSTS. One of the most insistent suggestions put forward by the newer and smaller powers is that the permanent members of the Security Council should pay a higher rate of assessment for peace and security operations than other members of the United Nations. Article 24 of the Charter and the record of the San Francisco Conference proceedings are cited as a basis for this proposition.[6]

Various specific proposals have been advanced for a scale of apportionment built on such a principle. These have ranged from the suggestion that the permanent members of the Security Council should be assessed for all costs relating to international peace and security, to the proposal that they should pay 80 percent of all direct expenditures, or 70 to 80 percent of all costs above a certain level determined by the General Assembly, perhaps as low as $5 million.

There are good arguments for some such scheme. Under the Charter, the permanent members of the Security Council were granted special privileges and have assumed a special responsibility for the maintenance and enforcement of international peace and security. The United States, the United Kingdom, and France are among the

---

[5] *Purchase of United Nations Bonds*, Hearings before the House Committee on Foreign Affairs, 87 Cong. 2 sess. (1962), p. 340. Statement prepared by the Department of State.

[6] There was an interesting division in the Committee of Fifteen on the proposition that each of the permanent members of the Security Council has a responsibility for paying proportionately more than other member states. Supporting this were Brazil, India, Japan, Mexico, Nigeria, and the United Arab Republic. Opposing were Canada, China, Italy, Sweden, the United Kingdom, and the United States. France abstained, and Bulgaria and the Soviet Union reserved their opinion.

wealthiest member states in the United Nations and the income of the Soviet Union has grown impressively. They possess the largest armaments and heavy industries and are the principal sources of investment capital. In power terms, they have a vital interest in preventing the outbreak of a general war and the explosion and spread of limited conflicts.

While not denying their responsibility for international peace and security, the larger powers have appropriately pointed to the basic principles of the Organization—the sovereign equality of states and the obligation of all members to give the United Nations "every assistance in any action" it takes. Hence, the other member states should be assessed for some portion of the expenses. Thus, there would be a recognition of the responsibility of all states for the activities of the Organization. With sovereign equality must go acceptance of responsibility.

The present state of international relations, as well as the financial crisis, suggest that there is little hope of gaining general political acceptance among the Big Five themselves, in the near future at any rate, of a scale built explicitly on the principle of the permanent members of the Security Council assuming primary responsibility for covering peace-keeping costs incurred by the Organization. Even if this were voted by the General Assembly over Soviet and French objections, or those of other permanent members, it is certain that these states would ignore the action, refuse to pay assessments based on such a scale, and place the United Nations in the embarrassing position of having to call for payments or try to extract payments from the great powers. This could lead to a break-up of the Organization.

MAKING THE AGGRESSOR PAY. Certain Arab states have insisted that those states that invaded Egypt, together with their friends and allies, should pay all or the bulk of the costs entailed in stationing UNEF in the Gaza Strip on the grounds that their actions were responsible for creating the situation that necessitated the creation and continuance of UNEF. The Soviet Union and its allies have supported this proposition, arguing that the "aggressor" must be made to pay the costs.

There may be some justice in the notion that aggressors should recompense those whom they injure and make restitution for property destroyed. Many peace settlements have been postulated on this principle. But the circumstances of modern international relations are too complex, there are too many factors involved, and too many variants in the situations in which force is used or coercion attempted, to make the principle of "making the aggressor pay for the remedy" a workable base for constructing a long-range scale of assessments. Supposing, for example, this principle had been the operative one for covering the costs of the United Nations defense of the Republic of Korea. How would the Organization have obtained from the North Korean Government and Communist China, whom it designated as "aggressors," reimbursement for the United Nations Unified Command and all the troops, naval and air forces, and supplies sent to Korea? Moreover, there may be cases not involving an aggressor. The proposal seems unrealistic in the light of the present structure of the United Nations and the state of the world. A world government with powers to adjudge guilt and force compliance would be needed to obtain collections.

SPECIAL CONSIDERATION TO LOW-INCOME STATES. A wide cross-section of the newer and developing countries has repeatedly urged not only the necessity but also the desirability of granting special consideration to those whose economic and financial conditions are such that they must have external assistance to develop. This is the principle which was in effect substantially followed in the resolutions financing the costs of UNEF and ONUC.

There is one major problem connected with this principle, which we have already encountered: How is the balance that is left after the reductions are made to be covered? The assumption of course is that it will be divided up among the states having greater capacity to pay. But on what basis? Equality, pro-rata according to the regular scale, or pro-rata according to some other scale? Or, is this to be left—as it has been so far—in the hope that some state or group of states will voluntarily contribute the necessary amounts to make up the difference? This is one of the most important items of unfinished business in connection with developing a special scale of apportionment.

OTHER BASES FOR A SPECIAL SCALE. In addition to the ideas discussed above, four other considerations might be taken into account in framing a special scale. One proposal suggests that a major factor that should be considered in the construction of a special scale is the direct benefit accruing to a member state or group of states as a result of a particular peace and security action.

Several methods for estimating such "benefits" in the case of peace and security operations have been suggested. At the Fifteenth Session of the General Assembly, the Latin American nations proposed that a relevant factor might be the total value of all national investments in an area from both public and private sources.

Wide differences of view developed in the two Working Groups on the principle of taking special benefits into account in constructing a scale of assessment. But it seemed to most members that, even if political opposition could be surmounted, the problem of compiling objective data would pose formidable obstacles.

Another consideration that might form a basis for fixing the scales of payment might be the regional concept. A situation involving some area or parties in a large continental region is often primarily of concern to neighboring states and much less so to states in other parts of the world. This is, of course, not always so, and there are many degrees of involvement on the part of the United Nations members in different localized disturbances. A situation between Argentina and Chile, for example, may be a matter of concern primarily to the countries of the American hemisphere. Likewise, in a situation between Thailand and Burma, Uruguay's stakes are limited. This suggests that in some form the regional consideration might be added to the list of factors to be taken into account in fixing a scale. The theory would be that the interests of the states in a region are most particularly served by restoring peace or preserving order; therefore, as special beneficiaries, they might reasonably be expected to pay more, relatively speaking, than states in other parts of the world. Difficulties can be anticipated, however, in finding a formula that would be generalized enough and be sufficiently flexible to cover the variety of situations that might arise and that would at the same time obtain the necessary majority support in the General Assembly.

Another proposal that has been advanced both within and outside of the United Nations is that the scale of assessment for peacekeeping purposes be related to national armaments expenditures. Such a plan, proponents declare, would ensure that those nations that spend the largest sums for their own national security should contribute the most to the preservation of international peace and security since they have the most at stake in keeping the peace and an apparent capacity to pay for it.

If it is assumed that the United States, the Soviet Union, and the entire rest of the world combined spend $150 billion a year for armaments, then if each nation were to pay to the United Nations only 1 percent of its national defense budget, this would give the Organization at least $1.5 billion a year.[7] The difficulties inherent in such a scheme, however, aside from the problem of securing the consent of member states, are perhaps so obvious as to make further discussion unnecessary. Unless a major change in the international climate should occur in the near future, it is reasonable to predict that few member states would be willing to furnish complete information on their defense expenditures or allow the requisite scrutiny of their defense establishments. Another difficulty would be the fact that of the seven countries whose defense expenditures constitute the bulk of world defense expenditures, two are not members of the United Nations: West Germany and Communist China. Others would hesitate to approve a scale that did not apply to or at least take into account the expenditures of these states.

Finally, it has been suggested that, in the construction of a special scale, reimbursements should be granted to those nations that contribute troops or supplies to a peace-keeping operation. It has been pointed out that most of the troops constituting UNEF and ONUC come from the poorer nations of the world. India, for example, has been the backbone of the two peace forces. Manpower is the most important contribution, and if the United Nations had to pay the entire cost of the troops, peace-keeping would be a far more expensive proposition.

Although there is a great deal of merit in this argument, it is at least probable that the contributing states found the Gaza Strip and the Congo valuable training grounds for their forces, and, with the possible exception of India, none was forced seriously to weaken its military establishment as a result. The task of expressing manpower contributions in monetary terms and the job of including materials and services in a special scale would also pose serious problems. Might some nations not be tempted to dump surplus foods instead of paying their assessments? Who would determine the value of contributions in foods and services? All these considerations would make the construction of a troop-and-services reimbursement formula a complex task indeed.

[7] Leslie Fishman, "An Economic Plan for Disarmament," *Bulletin of the Atomic Scientists* (March 1962), p. 37.

While arguments can be made for giving special attention to each of the foregoing considerations, the principles of sovereign equality and collective responsibility expressed in the Charter imply in practical terms that *something* should be assessed on *all* members.

This interpretation rules out any scale of assessment that would throw all of the costs of any operation on one combination of members and relieve others of paying anything. Furthermore, it requires the creation and use of an index of ability to contribute or capacity to pay as a fundamental criterion. Determination of this criterion is the most important and sensitive aspect of constructing the special scale.

In the regular budget, capacity to pay is generally accepted as being primarily indicated by GNP and GNP per capita statistics of member states. Beyond this the Assembly has also ruled that no assessment should exceed the per capita rate of the highest contributor and that "special graduated reductions of up to 50 percent are given to states having low per capita incomes."[8]

As shown in Chapter 4, the Committee on Contributions has been chary about publicizing in more than general terms the criteria used in calculating specific membership assessments and recommending them to the General Assembly. Yet a comparison of current GNP and assessment ratio figures shows a high degree of correlation, indicating that GNP and GNP per capita are in effect the guiding bases of assessment. As shown also, comparisons of GNP and GNP per capita with the normal scale of assessments demonstrate that adjustments are made by the Committee on Contributions for poor countries with large populations like India and for rich countries with small populations like New Zealand.

In developing a special scale of assessments, two main factors are involved: (1) an economic factor—what has to be raised and what the members can afford to pay; and (2) a political factor—acceptability.

ECONOMIC FACTOR IN A SPECIAL SCALE. Turning first to the economic factor, GNP and GNP per capita are only two elements of many that might be included in an index of capacity to pay. Other economic variables such as a country's balance of international payments, governmental liquid reserves, percent of GNP controlled by the central

---

[8] For a more detailed analysis of regular budget criteria, see Chap. 4.

government, contributions to other international agencies, rate of economic growth, "material product," and level of national resources, all might with justification be used as elements of a multi-variable index of ability to pay.

Professor Paul Rosenstein-Rodan of the Massachusetts Institute of Technology has suggested that the concept embodied in progressive taxation, as evidenced for example in United States income tax legislation, might be applied to per capita, or per family, income in the developed countries in order to determine their share of the burden of international aid to the developing countries.[9] The concept is equally suggestive for the United Nations itself. Although all members might be expected to share in the financing of the United Nations, a nation in which per capita income is, say $1,200, can presumably afford to make a higher contribution out of its second $600 of income per head than out of its first $600, and thus contribute more than twice as much per inhabitant as the nation in which total income is only $600 per head. Similarly, the nation enjoying an income of $2,000 per capita can probably afford to contribute at a considerably higher rate on the last $800 of per capita income than on either its first or its second $600.

Comparative positions in international balance of payments, as well as liquid reserves, may afford further useful clues to the abilities of various nations to pay for costs of the United Nations. Differing exchange rates, varying burdens of indebtedness, the problem of estimating purchasing power equivalents, and other complications impose difficulties, however, in using these criteria as exclusive or principal bases of determining capacity to pay.[10]

There are several practical reasons for using GNP as the point of departure for a special peace-keeping scale. As noted in Chapter 3, it is a relatively straightforward and stable index of national capacity. It does not stress directly such politically sensitive issues as the effectiveness of a nation in mobilizing its economic resources, its type of governmental system, or the extent of governmental control over the economy. It lends itself to predictability better than some other criteria.

[9] P. N. Rosenstein-Rodan, "International Aid for Underdeveloped Countries," *Review of Economics and Statistics* (May 1961), pp. 101-37.

[10] See doctoral dissertation by James E. Price, entitled, "Financing of International Organizations by Membership Contributions," submitted to the Department of Economics and Social Science at the Massachusetts Institute of Technology, Aug. 31, 1962.

Provided the Committee on Contributions, or whatever other body may be constructing a special scale, has the authority to take into consideration special situations relating to population, per capita income, economic growth rates, and other elements in making decisions with respect to the scale, GNP and GNP per capita appear to afford the most generally satisfactory basis on which to locate relative capacity to pay for peace and security operations.

POLITICAL FACTOR IN A SPECIAL SCALE. The political factor may present more formidable obstacles than the economic. There is bound to be political resistance by some states to almost any scale. Leaving aside for the moment the Soviet and French refusals to pay anything for ONUC, there may be additional difficulties. For example, State A at the upper end of the scale may object to a large quota lest this encourage voting majorities in the General Assembly to take actions involving large financial outlays. United States apprehensions about the SUNFED scheme were a case in point. State B, at the other end of the scale and of GNP, may likewise object to a special scale with higher assessments lest this further cut into the limited means at its command for its own economic and social progress.

Keeping in mind these political difficulties, it is nonetheless necessary to make an effort to construct a scale in accordance with "objective" criteria of capacity to pay. GNP figures, as has been noted, do not give the whole answer to each nation's ability to contribute. Other factors, especially per capita income, must be borne in mind in particular situations: A small country like Denmark or New Zealand can be rich and still have a smaller GNP than a large country that is poor, like India.

If GNP is used as a basis of rating ability to contribute, member states tend to fall into five general divisions: (1) less than $1 billion GNP; (2) GNP from $1 billion to $6 billion; (3) GNP from $6 billion to $20 billion; (4) GNP from $21 billion to $50 billion; and (5) GNP of over $50 billion. These are somewhat arbitrary divisions, of course, but the clusterings of states are reasonably distinct.

In 1962 about 50 percent of the member states, that is, fifty-two countries, had a GNP of less than $1 billion. Within this large segment of the membership were no fewer than forty states with a GNP of less than $500 million a year.

Little can be expected from most of these states over and above what they are already contributing to the United Nations in terms of their payments to the regular budget, the specialized agencies, and to the special voluntary programs. Although there may be exceptional cases, such as Kuwait, where particularly valuable natural resources are brought into production, most of them will need virtually everything they have or can be given in economic and technical assistance for their own growth if they are to move forward during the development decade. Their assessments will have to be kept very low in any special scale for peace and security purposes.

If the states having a GNP from $1 billion to $6 billion are grouped together, thirty members fell within this category in 1962. The majority within this group—twenty states—have a GNP of less than $3 billion. These states, like those in the very low income group are in the membership category that is currently assessed less than 1 percent under the normal scale of apportionment for the regular budget. Most of these countries are classifiable as being in some stage of "developing economies." With eleven exceptions, the states in this grouping, as well as all of the countries in the lowest income class, are currently receiving aid either from the Expanded Programme for Technical Assistance or the Special Fund or both.[11]

Clearly, there are substantial differences in the accumulated and natural wealth, the industrial capacity and the foreign trade of these countries. Chile and Saudi Arabia, for example, have natural sources of wealth and exports that greatly exceed those of Ceylon and Ireland. Some states are obviously moving more rapidly than others from traditional to modern societies. Some have much heavier burdens of indebtedness, or other costs, to discharge than do others. And some, like China (Taiwan) and Israel are bearing heavy national defense costs, while others are expending little in that direction. In short, there is a considerable differential in ready ability to contribute within this group. But on the whole, most of the states, save the eleven exceptions noted above, will be able to pay only limited amounts for United Nations peace-keeping activities for years to come until their economic growth proceeds beyond present levels.

In the GNP range extending from $6 billion to $20 billion will be found twenty members. And in a distinct bracket, set off from the others by a gap of from $11 billion to $20 billion, are four other states with a GNP ranging from $31 billion to $41 billion. Between them

[11] The nonrecipient countries are Austria, Bulgaria, Byelorussia, Czechoslovakia, Denmark, Finland, Hungary, New Zealand, Norway, Rumania, and South Africa.

these two groups of states had a GNP of $382.45 billion, which amounts to 29 percent of the estimated total GNP for all members of the United Nations in 1962. They are currently assessed 27 percent of the costs of the United Nations by the normal scale of apportionment.

These groups include many of the countries commonly thought of as the "middle powers." With notable exceptions, and with the addition of some of the states in the lower income groupings, these are the countries that have supplied important elements of UNEF and ONUC as well as members of commissions of inquiry, truce supervision missions, and other minor peace-keeping operations of the United Nations.

There is fairly solid economic capacity in both of these groups of states. Notwithstanding the large differences in economic advancement and per capita income, most of them are in a position to make additional payments for peace-keeping operations without much difficulty. Furthermore, their ability to contribute should increase materially in the future.

There are only four states in the United Nations with a GNP of over $50 billion. These are France, the United Kingdom, the Soviet Union, and the United States. Together they account for 64 percent of the total GNP of the United Nations membership. Their current assessment under the regular scale of assessment amounts to 60.51 percent.

Although all of these states are in different situations, and two of them have refused to pay for the Congo operation, they are nevertheless clearly the states with the greatest ability to contribute to the support of peace and security activities. It is natural that the United Nations should look to these permanent members of the Security Council to carry the largest assessments. Mathematically speaking, it would not be unreasonable if these states were asked to contribute collectively the equivalent of their percentage of the total GNP.

Proposals for Financing Future Operations

The preceding discussion highlights several principles on which a special peace and security scale should be based. First, some portion of the cost must be borne by all members. Second, a reduction element must be built into the scale to protect the poorer states. Third, the deficits created by the reduction must be absorbed by those states with a higher capacity to pay. Fourth, the scale should be a flexible one and subject to periodic review and readjustment. Four alternative scaling plans that would incorporate these principles are considered below, with a view to determining which of them would yield optimum results.

Plan One

The simplest procedure would be to take the combined assessment-rebate-voluntary contribution formula hammered out at the special session of the General Assembly in 1963 and apply it to future actions.

This would maintain apportionment of agreed total amounts in accordance with the regular scale of assessments, subject to (1) 55 percent reduction of assessments for the low-income states and others receiving assistance under the Expanded Programme for Technical Assistance, (2) appealing to those able to make voluntary contributions to do so, and (3) applying these contributions to cover the deficit resulting from the reductions in assessments.

The advantages of maintaining and generalizing this formula would be that the Assembly has sanctioned it in practice and that laborious and possibly futile negotiations over a new scale would be avoided. On the other hand, the formula has serious limitations. It places a large dependence on voluntary contributions; it makes no provision for covering the annual deficit resulting from reductions; and it does not come to grips with the politically motivated deficits, like those produced by the Soviet Union and France.

Plan Two

A second alternative would be to continue use of the regular assessment and rebate features of the 1963 ONUC and UNEF financing arrangement. But instead of leaving the deficit arising from the 55 percent reductions to be made up by voluntary contributions, this plan would apportion the deficit among those nations not eligible for rebates under the reduction formula at their regular assessment rates and add this to their assessments.

This plan would retain the advantages of the first and, at least theoretically, reduce the dependence of the Organization on voluntary contributions by apportioning the deficits arising from reductions. However, the other drawbacks of the first plan still apply here. In addition, there might be stiff resistance in the United States Congress to an upward scaling of the American assessment despite the fact that the United States total contribution to UNEF and ONUC approached 50 percent if voluntary contributions are included.

Conceivably, the Congress would be willing to consider a 37.74 percent assessment for peace and security expenses if twenty or more other nations were to increase their payments at the same time and voluntary contributions were no longer needed. One variation that might be built into this or any other plan would permit the percentages to be borne by the wealthier states to rise as the costs rise beyond certain norms and the percentages to be paid by the poorer states to be lowered. This technique was used by the Assembly at its special session when it appropriated $42.5 million for UNEF and ONUC for the last six months of 1963.

To generalize from this precedent, all states above $1 billion GNP might pay their normal scale proportion toward a deficit resulting from reductions on assessments so long as the peace-keeping costs range from $10 million to $100 million a year. Deficits resulting from reductions on assessments covering expenses from $100 million to $200 million might be apportioned among states having a GNP above $9 billion. Deficits stemming from assessments covering expenses above $200 million might be apportioned only among the states having a GNP above $25 billion. To make this progressive scale more equitable, GNP figures might be considered in conjunction with per capita income in each case.

Such an arrangement would introduce a sliding scale that would lighten the loads for the lower income states as the costs of peace-keeping operations rise by correspondingly raising the amounts to be paid by those with greater capacity.

Plan Three

A third plan would be to continue the present separate assessments for peace and security costs at the regular scale with the reductions for the developing countries as now provided, but to cover the deficit resulting from the latter out of an increased "Unforeseen and Extraordinary Expenses" item in the regular budget, possibly including the miscellaneous income as well.

Judging from the 14.02 percent rebated on the Congo assessments, such a plan would mean an increase of $14 million to $21 million in the regular budget to make up rebated amounts granted in a peace and security operation of the magnitude of say $100 million to $150 million a year. This would involve adding to the assessments of all member states, but would be done as a part of the regular annual assessment and at the normal scale of apportionment.

The primary advantage of this method of making up the rebated portion of special assessments would be the avoidance of a conflict with the United States. Neither the Congress nor the General Assembly would have to be asked to change the rates of assessment.[12] A second advantage would be that this procedure would broadly distribute the amount to be made up and would eliminate dependence on voluntary contributions.

Assuming, as this plan does, that the states granted rebates on the special assessments for peace-keeping operations would continue to pay their assessments for the regular budget at the full normal level, this would mean that these states would themselves be losing 21.62 percent of the rebated amount through their payments to the regular budget.

To counteract the effect of asking for this increased payment on the regular budget, the idea might be considered of raising the rebates on the special peace-keeping assessments from 80 to 90 percent and from 50 to 65 percent, respectively, to give an added differential for contributions toward making up the deficit. By doing this, the ac-

---

[12] The limitation was placed by the U.S. Congress on American contributions in Public Law 495, July 10, 1952, which reads as follows:

"No representative of the United States Government in any international organization after fiscal year 1953 shall make any commitment requiring the appropriation of funds for a contribution by the United States in excess of $33\frac{1}{3}$ per centum of the budget of any international organization for which the appropriation for the United States contribution is contained in this Act: *Provided*, however, that this section shall not apply to the United States representatives to the inter-American organizations.

"No representative of the United States Government to any international organization of which the United States is now a member shall, unless specifically authorized in an appropriation Act or other law, make any commitment requiring the appropriation of funds for a contribution by the United States in excess of $33\frac{1}{3}$ per centum of the budget of such international organization." (66 Stat. 549, 550-51.)

tual expenditures of the states accorded reductions would still be approximately what they are under the present reduction plan.

If such a procedure were followed on the model of the November 1961 to June 1962 ONUC assessment, the additional rebate suggested would add $2.1 million to the $11.4 million original rebate deficit, making a total of $13.5 million to be made up out of the "Unforeseen and Extraordinary Expenses" item of the regular budget and possibly out of miscellaneous income. By adding to the regular budget assessment of each of the countries on the reduction list its normal scale proportion of this total deficit, approximately $2.9 million would be paid in toward the "Unforeseen and Extraordinary Expenses" item, leaving $10.6 million to be added from among the higher income countries. The United States portion of this amount would be $4.3 million to be added to the amount otherwise paid for the regular budget.

The amounts added to the regular budget could, if not used, be applied to reducing the amount needed for unforeseen and extraordinary expenses on the following year's budget. Alternatively, the unexpended amounts could be allowed to accumulate as a "savings bank account" when the ONUC and UNEF expenses are reduced. These might be transferred to the Working Capital Fund earmarked for draft when a future emergency arises. Or they might be employed to initiate a special Peace and Security Fund along the lines discussed at an earlier point. Thus, the rebates could be covered and a reserve eventually started without resort to creating a new scale of assessment.

Plan Four

A fourth alternative would be to develop a separate scale for peace and security expenses that would provide a straightforward ratio of assessment for each state without resort to reductions, deficits, and payment of the deficit either by voluntary contributions or reapportionment.

Such a scale could be constructed around the same basic data as the regular scale: GNP and GNP per capita figures. Its cardinal feature would be starting the minimum percentage of payment at a much lower point for the very low income states and gradually raising the percentages as total GNP and GNP per capita rises.

Such a scale could have as its minimum starting point .008 percent instead of .04 percent. This would correspond almost exactly with the 80 percent reduction authorized in 1960 on the assessments of the developing countries with limited capacity under the terms of the ONUC and UNEF financing resolutions. The reductions might then decrease by slowly graduated steps closely corresponding to rising GNP and GNP per capita and the rising points on the normal scale until the plus $9 billion GNP rate and normal apportionment point of 1 percent were reached, at which reductions from the normal level would stop.

Above this point there might be slowly graduated increases in the apportionment rate, corresponding again to rising GNP and GNP per capita, and the rising points on the normal scale. The United States presents a special problem here. The congressional limit of $33\frac{1}{3}$ percent permits an addition of only 1.3 percent although GNP and GNP per capita indicators would place a United States contribution around a 40 percent mark.

Table 7.1 illustrates a special scale constructed on the above principles and adjusted to the limits imposed by the United States congressional ceiling. Variations could be made in the reductions or increases as the Committee on Contributions might see fit.

This plan would retain the advantages of the first and second proposals and, in addition, would eliminate the need for rebates, deficits, voluntary contributions, or complicated reapportionments. It would, however, require sixteen states to assume increases in their assessment percentages. The sample scale does not provide for uniform up-scaling, but, on the contrary, drops off in percentage terms when it reaches the four largest givers. This feature may have to be modified in order to obtain a two-thirds majority in the Assembly. On a uniform up-scaling, the percentages of France, the United Kingdom, the Soviet Union, and especially the United States would be considerably higher.

It appears that a special scale constructed along some such lines is to be preferred to the present cumbersome arrangement or any other built around the procedure of reductions and deficits to be taken care of either by voluntary contributions or some scheme of reassessment. The plan, of course, does not provide a solution for a deficit that may result from the unwillingness of some states to pay their assessments or a temporary incapacity of some to contribute. This problem applies to almost any scale that has a realistic chance of

TABLE 7.1. *Illustrative Special Scale of Assessments for Peace and Security Expenses*

	Normal Assessment		Percent of Total	
40 states at	.04 to be assessed	.008 =	.32%	80% reduction. GNP $30–559 million
11	.05	.008	.09	
1	.06	.01	.01	
4	.07	.02	.08	
3	.09	.03	.09	
1	.10	.04	.04	
1	.11	.04	.04	
3	.13–.14	.05	.15	
3	.15–.16	.07	.21	
3	.20	.08	.24	
3	.21–.23	.10	.30	
2	.24–.26	.12	.24	50% reduction. GNP+$4.5 billion
1	.32	.20	.20	
2	.36–.38	.22	.44	
3	.40–.41	.24	.72	
4	.42–.45	.27	1.08	
3	.52–.53	.38	1.14	
2	.56–.58	.45	.90	
1	.74	.66	.66	
1	.86	.77	.77	
2	1.01	1.01	2.02	No reduction. GNP+$9 billion
1	1.03	1.05	1.05	*Increase begins.* GNP+$13 billion
1	1.17 Czechoslovakia	1.20	1.20	
1	1.20 Belgium	1.30	1.30	
1	1.28 Poland	1.38	1.38	
1	1.30 Sweden	1.50	1.50	
1	1.66 Australia	1.86	1.86	12% increase. GNP+$17 billion
1	1.98 Ukraine	2.25	2.25	
1	2.03 India	2.35	2.35	15% increase. GNP+$30 billion
1	2.24 Italy	2.55	2.55	
1	2.27 Japan	2.52	2.52	
1	3.12 Canada	3.60	3.60	15% increase. GNP+$37 billion
1	4.57 China	4.57	4.57	(Special case) GNP $1.70 billion
1	5.94 France	6.50	6.50	9% increase. GNP+$60 billion
1	7.58 U.K.	8.18	8.18	8.18 87.8% increase. GNP+$73 billion
1	14.97 USSR	16.17	16.17	8% increase. GNP+$169 billion
1	32.02 USA	33.32	33.32	4% increase. GNP+$525 billion
104	100.00%		100.00%	

Source: Data developed by Norman J. Padelford. See "Financial Crisis and the Future of the United Nations," *World Politics*, Vol. XV, (July 1963), p. 562.

adoption. However, voluntary contributions, or reapportionment of deficit amounts, or the floating of new bond issues may be the only approaches to this problem.

Perhaps the only way in which a special scale could meet the problem of political unwillingness to pay is to introduce an opting-out clause. Under such a plan, each member would be entitled to refuse to pay for peace-keeping operations that had been authorized over its opposition. It might be possible to set up a subsidiary organ of the General Assembly or the Security Council to control such operations, composed only of those not opting out. This would mean that only the payers would share in the control. While such a proposal, if adopted, would require "bailing-out" operations, it frankly faces the fact that no power—especially no major power—can be expected to pay for an operation that it regards as inflicting a diplomatic or military defeat on itself. Indeed, this plan would be viable only if the opposition manifests itself in its passive form and remains limited to nonpayment. If it assumes proportions of active obstruction, the nations doing the "bailing-out" would have to risk in addition the disintegration of the United Nations itself.

Procedures and Safeguards for the Future

A few thoughts remain to be added on certain methods, procedures, and safeguards that may usefully be built into arrangements relating to the financing of peace and security activities.

First, any special scale of contributions that is established should have maximum and minimum percentages of contribution. This has been a fundamental feature of the normal scale. It has a similar place in any special scale so that all may know in advance what the ceiling and floor will be. This is as important to the states at the lowest extremity of the scale as it is to the Congress of the United States, which must appropriate the large amounts asked of that country.

Second, any scale of allocation should be applicable to expenditures not exceeding certain fixed limits. These can be generously fixed if this is the mood of the General Assembly. But in the field of peace and security operations in particular, where expenditures can run very high, it may be desirable to have some bounds beyond which the Assembly may not go without going back to the member states for a fundamental review of the financial arrangements.[13] Voluntary contributions may of course be solicited and received to cover any amounts exceeding the initially agreed limits.

Third, it might be desirable to make some provision for a definite period of application of the rates laid down in a special scale at the end of which the apportionments would be reviewed and revised in the light of changed conditions and then applied anew for similar succeeding periods of time. This is particularly important during the next ten to fifteen years as many of the newer and presently low income countries respond to the challenge of development.

[13] When this question came up in the Working Group of Fifteen, ten states supported the principle of installing a specific limit. The United States was one of these. No state opposed it. The remaining members of the group abstained.

Fourth, if authority to activate the special scale is to remain in the hands of the General Assembly, as in other financial matters, there should be some safeguarding provision built into the system that would forestall hasty, ill-considered activation of the assessment scale. One possibility would be to have a stipulation that, in matters relating to peace and security expenses, the necessary two-thirds majority in the Assembly must have the concurring participation of two-thirds of all the states having a GNP in excess of say $5 billion, including at least two of the highest income members. This would ensure that no assessment could be imposed on the states that currently have 92 percent of the total GNP of the United Nations membership without a good measure of agreement on their part. It seems that some formula along these lines would be desirable as a protective measure.

Fifth, it may be advisable to link a future peace and security operation to a payment plan by setting forth the financial provisions in the initial resolution creating the new force. This thought is prompted by a perusal of the records of UNEF and ONUC. The establishment of the former was authorized by the General Assembly without a dissenting vote (64-0-12), but the vote on the initial financing resolution was 57 in favor, 8 opposed, and 9 abstaining. The latter was set up by the Security Council without a negative vote. But the Assembly votes on financing the 1960, 1961, and 1962 costs were 46-17-24, 54-15-23, and 67-13-15, respectively. By June 1, 1963, 51 nations were in arrears or in default on their UNEF assessments, and 54 had paid in full.[14] The respective figures for ONUC for June 1, 1963 were: 62 in arrears or in default, and 42 paid in full. This indicates that a large number of even those nations which vote *for* the financial resolutions cannot be counted on to make payment. Tables A.1 and A.2 show the votes on approving and financing UNEF and ONUC and also the balances due June 1, 1963.

As a result of this situation, several countries have proposed that in cases in which emergency action of one of the principal United Nations organs has major financial implications, the initial resolution should contain a section clearly setting forth the terms under which the program would be financed. A vote for the resolution would thus carry with it a more direct commitment to help pay the bill.

To link a peace-keeping operation to a payment plan is well worth

[14] The term "arrears" is used when partial payment has been made; the term "default" when a state has made no payment.

exploring, but there are some problems to be kept in mind. The commitment to pay would still be relatively unenforceable. More important, it might be more difficult, and certainly slower, under such conditions to get a peace-keeping resolution through the Assembly in the first place. In the meantime, the crisis might get out of hand. The question must therefore be asked whether it is better to rush troops to a trouble spot and worry about payment later, or to make sure at the outset that the United Nations can pay its bills.

Finally, it may be advantageous for the General Assembly to create an office of United Nations Under-Secretary of Finance to deal directly with the highest fiscal officers of member governments concerning payments to the Organization. A person of high national cabinet standing and world repute appointed to such a post could be most helpful in procuring earlier payments of assessments. He could also be instrumental at times in stimulating voluntary contributions when these are needed in conjunction with peace-keeping activities. And as a man of wide experience with financial matters of large scope, he could be an invaluable aide and counselor to the Secretary-General. The appointment of Mr. Eugene R. Black as Special Financial Consultant to the Secretary-General in 1963 to help speed the payment of arrears was a step in that direction.

The Heart of the Matter

On surveying the proposals for strengthening the financing of United Nations peace and security operations, one is impressed by the number and tenacity of the obstacles. Most require for their adoption conditions within the United Nations that do not prevail at this stage of the Organization's development. No special scale, no matter how carefully constructed, can solve the problem of politically motivated deficits, like those of France and the Soviet Union. The heart of the matter is the issue of political consensus.

Nations are reluctant to supply the United Nations with greater revenues. They want to be in a position to withhold their financial support in the event that they disapprove of what the Organization is doing. To relinquish control over money would be to relinquish control over programs. Some member states do not yield an inch on this point, others are willing to take a first step, and a few have already made a beginning. These differing conceptions of what constitutes the national interest may well hold the key to the financial future of peace-keeping operations.

The politics of financing peace-keeping confronts each nation with its own peculiar dilemma, which it must attempt to resolve by reconciling the dictates of its national interest with those of the international community as a whole.

The fiscal policy of the United States has vacillated between two different views of the meaning of the peace-keeping operations to the United States national interest. At times the United States has viewed the Organization in much the same manner as it has tended to view its alliances. But at other times—and these have been no less prominent—the United States has perceived the United Nations as a neutral mediator in the East-West and colonial struggles.

In both these cases, the United Nations has been seen as an instrument of United States national policy—in the first, the policy was to fight the cold war through the United Nations, and in the second, to try to ameliorate it. This is not a dichotomy in re the United Nations, but in re United States policy. Therefore, the United States has had no problem in reconciling these two conceptions in the case of the two peace-keeping activities in the Middle East and the Congo. Both these activities coincided with United States interest in preventing either unilateral intervention by another great power or a competitive intervention by the United States and the Soviet Union. Thus, the ideal of a neutral international organization, too, was fulfilled. The United States has never been tested in a situation in which it might be called on to take a stand on a United Nations peace-keeping operation that it might define as inimical to its national interest. United States opposition to Special Fund aid to Cuba in 1963 suggests that the answer would probably be in the negative. Would the United States, for example, be willing to pay its assessed share of a peace force dispatched by the General Assembly to prevent aggression against the revolutionary government of Fidel Castro in Cuba?

The Soviet attitude has had the virtue of consistency, but little else. Its minority position in the United Nations has led it to view with growing uneasiness the shift from the Security Council, where it has a veto, to the General Assembly. Recent events, particularly the United Nations action in the Congo, have confirmed its fears that the Organization can and will act on occasion despite strong Soviet opposition. Here, the Soviet financial veto has become a formidable weapon.

The new nations face their own unique dilemma in the determination of fiscal policy for the peace-keeping operations. On the one hand, they consider UNEF and ONUC of great value since, after all, "it could happen here." Many regard the sealing off of their countries from the East-West struggle as central to their national interest. But, on the other hand, they say they can ill afford the potentially large expense of such sealing-off operations.

All this demonstrates that the national interests of member states dictate a policy of fiscal caution. This caution is manifest in varying degrees: relatively mild in the case of the United States and the Western nations; more pronounced in the policies of the new and uncommitted nations; and so intense in the case of the Soviet Union and other Eastern European countries as to result in outright refusals to pay.

In the light of the above, proposals that are to have a realistic chance of adoption must remain fairly modest. It may be that the General Assembly will not be able to agree on a permanent peace-keeping scale acceptable to two-thirds of the membership. In that case, financing such operations along the lines of a Korea-type consortium or through an immediate *ad hoc* pledging arrangement when a crisis erupts may have to be considered. It is indeed possible that in the foreseeable future no single formula or set of principles or criteria can be applied to any and all peace-keeping operations. The method of financing may have to be determined each time on an *ad hoc* basis, and the solution adjusted to the particular facts of the case. In some instances, as in the case of the United Nations Temporary Executive Authority in West New Guinea in 1962, or the United Nations mission to Yemen in 1963, it may perhaps be possible to divide the costs between the parties concerned without expense to the United Nations.

The present arrangement for financing peace and security operations should be viewed as a temporary expedient. It is cumbersome. It leaves a substantial amount to be provided by uncertain means, either voluntary contribution or reapportionment among some undefined group of members of the United Nations. It should be replaced as soon as possible by some more stable system.

It would be advantageous to seek establishment of a new special scale of assessments for peace and security expenses based on GNP and GNP per capita figures as suggested in Plan 4 outlined above. Maximum amounts should be fixed beyond which the Assembly cannot go without a new mandate from the membership. Such a plan would improve on the cumbersome arrangement now in force. It would call on every member for some payment. It would be scaled in such a way as to give the very low income states all of the benefits presently being derived from the rebate system. It would permit a broad spreading of the load and would be an equitable arrangement simple to administer.

Pending adoption of such a scale, the present arrangement could be improved by use of Plan 3 outlined above covering the deficit created by the reduction for the developing countries by transferring this amount to the regular budget, paying for it out of the "Unforeseen and Extraordinary Expense" item and miscellaneous income, and adding it to the budget to be reimbursed out of regular assessments. This would call on all members to pay something toward removal of the deficit.

It may become necessary to face up to the starkest of realities and permit members to refuse payment for a peace and security operation that they oppose. Here the distinction between passive and active opposition outlined in Chapter 1 becomes crucial. When supporters of an action encounter passive opposition only, that is, nonpayment, they may find it prudent to go ahead if they are willing to pay for the entire operation themselves and are reasonably confident that the opposition will not take an active form. But when a major power takes an attitude of active opposition, supporters would be advised to go ahead with the action only if they are prepared to run the risk of driving the opposing state out of the United Nations or if they are reasonably confident that the active opposition will be reduced to passive opposition. The launching or continuing of an operation in the face of either passive or active opposition by a major power is to ask for financial crisis, and any state which asks for such a crisis ought to be prepared to face the consequence of that action, namely, to relieve the crisis.

CHAPTER 8

The Special Voluntary Programs

WHILE PEACE AND SECURITY OPERATIONS have been in the nature of sporadic and unpredictable crash programs, economic and social activities have been stable, long-term, and steadily growing commitments of the United Nations. There has been no opposition to them in principle. The political issue in this realm has not been whether these programs should exist, but how quickly and by how much they should be expanded. Indeed, of the total expenditure of close to $4.5 billion by the United Nations system for all purposes over the period of 1946 through 1963, approximately two-thirds has been spent on economic and social activities.[1]

In the light of the above, it may seem strange that most of the Organization's economic and social operations subsist solely on the generosity of governments and private citizens' groups throughout the world, while the major portion of peace and security funds is raised through compulsory assessments. Logically, it should perhaps be the other way round. The primary reason for this development is the fact that voluntary contributions offered the only practical basis on which most of the economic and social programs could get started.

The most important of these special voluntary programs are the United Nations Children's Fund (UNICEF), the United Nations High Commissioner for Refugees (UNHCR), the United Nations Relief and Works Agency for Palestine Refugees in the Near East (UNRWA), the Expanded Programme of Technical Assistance (EPTA), the Special Fund, and most recently, the Congo Fund. Two temporary operations, the International Refugee Organization (IRO) and the United Nations Korean Reconstruction Agency (UNKRA),

---

[1] This figure does not include the expenditures of the International Monetary Fund and the International Bank for Reconstruction and Development.

191

were terminated in 1952 and 1958, respectively.[2] Government contributions have provided most of the support for these voluntary programs. Only the Children's Fund and the High Commissioner for Refugees have received substantial private donations.

To include these programs in the regular budget would have aroused the opposition of most member states, not only on grounds of excessive expense but also because some of the programs, such as UNRWA and UNKRA, had a fairly limited impact and were to benefit only a relatively small number of states.

This pattern has given each member state the freedom to contribute to each program in accordance with its ability—or its willingness—to pay. This has often been a disadvantage since it has made the programs dependent on the decision of states to grant or to withhold funds. But at times the independent financing of the special programs has resulted in a larger allocation of funds. In the case of the United States, for example, Congress was willing to contribute more than one-third of the budgets of some of the programs because they were not conceived as permanent obligations. Moreover, several states that are not members of the United Nations, notably the Federal Republic of Germany and Switzerland, have made substantial contributions. Many governments have liked the voluntary contribution feature because it has given them a greater sense of self-determination than the assessment system. Governments also have taken pride in the "over and above" element implied in a voluntary contribution.

Despite these cogent reasons for the independent financing of the special voluntary programs, there is little logic in the distinction between them and the regular budget. It would be inaccurate to refer to the latter as a purely administrative budget and to the voluntary programs as exclusively operational. As shown previously, the regular budget includes operational items. Similarly, the voluntary programs must make allowances for administrative expenses. The following chapter will show that some of the specialized agencies also make use of the voluntary contribution device to finance operational programs.

As can be expected, the base of support has been very uneven.

[2] IRO is a case *sui generis*. It was a nonpermanent specialized agency with a large operational budget that was financed by a mixture of assessment and voluntary contributions from its eighteen member governments. For a detailed account see John G. Stoessinger, *The Refugee and the World Community* (University of Minnesota Press, 1956), pp. 91-95.

Only forty governments, for example, chose to contribute to UNKRA, but UNICEF is being supported by almost the entire membership of the United Nations. Contributions are generally announced at annual pledging conferences, but many of these pledges are subject to parliamentary approval in the member states. To encourage governments to make their pledges as generous as possible, a special body was created by the General Assembly in 1952—the Negotiating Committee for Extra-Budgetary Funds. This ten-member body tried to stimulate contributions by appealing to governments and private sources. It also attempted to close the gap between pledges and actual payments and constantly searched for untapped resources.[3] In these tasks it was not very effective and ceased to function in 1961. Since then, there has been almost no fiscal coordination among the voluntary programs. In essence, each must ensure its own livelihood.

The Children's Fund

The oldest of the voluntary programs is the United Nations Children's Fund. Until 1950, UNICEF focused on emergency relief to children of war-devastated countries. After that its mandate was broadened to emphasize continuing child-care programs, particularly in underdeveloped countries. While most forms of technical assistance concentrate primarily on advisory services, UNICEF has been a supplier of such basic goods as powdered milk, anti-malaria insecticides, BCG vaccine, and factory equipment for the production of fish flour, soya milk, and antibiotics.

Financing throughout the emergency period was haphazard and depended primarily on contributions from the United States. UNICEF made its first allocations in 1947 on the basis of a $15 million grant from the United States as well as some of UNRRA's residual funds. Until 1952, United States contributions accounted for more than 70 percent of the entire budget. The United States contribution proved to be the keystone of UNICEF, not only because of its size but also because of a matching formula conceived by the United States government in order to stimulate contributions from other countries. This

[3] The 1960-61 members of the Negotiating Committee were: Brazil, Canada, France, Ghana, Ireland, Norway, Pakistan, Senegal, United Kingdom, and the United States. See discussion of the committee, pp. 212-13.

device worked quite successfully and brought government contributions between 1946 and 1953 to more than $125 million. An average of thirty countries contributed, with Australia, Canada, France, New Zealand, and Switzerland as the next largest contributors.

The year 1953 was a dividing line in the financial history of UNICEF. The fund was put on a permanent basis and as a result its support broadened considerably. Fifty-five governments made contributions in 1953 and over one hundred governments contributed by 1962. Approximately $23.5 million, which amounted to 80 percent of the entire UNICEF budget in 1962, was given by governments. The rest was raised through donations from private sources and the sale of UNICEF greeting cards.

Several observations are in order about the present financial pattern of UNICEF. In the first place, the United States has gradually reduced its matching percentage over the past eight years. In 1960 it stipulated that its contribution must not exceed 48 percent of the total. In 1961 this ratio was further reduced to 46 percent, by 1962 to 44 percent, and in 1964 it stood at 40 percent. Since the list of donors has grown each year, however, and most individual contributions have also increased, the amount of the United States donation has risen as well.[4]

Secondly, many of the developing nations have made unusually high pledges to the fund. In 1962, thirty nations contributed a higher percentage of the annual UNICEF budget than their proportionate assessment for the regular United Nations budget. In spite of their low per capita incomes, many of these governments make contributions to the fund that compare favorably with the relative support from a number of wealthier countries. The reason for this is, of course, the fact that UNICEF is primarily a supply agency to the poorer countries. In 1962, for example, countries assisted by the fund were contributing over 20 percent of the government grants to UNICEF; of the twenty largest donors, nine were receiving aid from UNICEF.[5]

The members of the Soviet bloc ignored UNICEF until 1953, but since then have been regular contributors. The annual Soviet contribution for the past three years has been $500,000. This contribution

[4] For a review of UNICEF financing, see Ellen Frey-Wouters, "The United Nations Children's Fund" (unpublished doctoral dissertation, Columbia University, 1958), Chap. 4.
[5] Brazil, India, Iran, Italy, Japan, Mexico, Philippines, Turkey, and Yugoslavia.

and those of the other East European countries add up to a little over 3 percent of the total.

In sum, government contributions to UNICEF have grown steadily since 1953, when they amounted to about $14.3 million, and now approach $24 million. Further growth, however, will largely depend on higher contributions from governments other than the United States. This is so because the United States hopes to maintain its matching percentage at 40 percent. Now that virtually all the states of the world are contributors to UNICEF, greater financial support from other governments will be needed to make fully available to the fund the amounts pledged by the United States. Such a trend seems indeed to be in the making. Some of the largest contributors pledged sizable increases for 1962: the Federal Republic of Germany increased its support by 140 percent over 1960; France by 48 percent; the Soviet Union by 41 percent; and Australia, Canada, India, Sweden, Switzerland, and the United Kingdom—the other main contributors—all raised their support considerably.

UNICEF, like EPTA and the Special Fund, has used a device whereby the value of its effective resources exceeds by far that of the contributions received from donor governments. By a system of "matching" on the part of countries assisted, UNICEF obtains further funds. The governments of assisted countries provide an average of $2.00 to $2.50 for every $1.00 from UNICEF. Thus, in addition to the almost $30 million for programs allocated by the fund in 1962, this system of "local matching" committed governments receiving aid from the fund to spend the equivalent of $75 million over and above the allocations from UNICEF. While there is probably some tendency to overstate the value of the contributions in kind made by host governments, their matching funds not only enable UNICEF's resources to go further, but help to assure that a project is rooted in the country as a basic responsibility of its government.

UNICEF also employs a variety of distinct fund-raising techniques. In the main, initiatives by its own staff are relied on. UNICEF's relatively long life, the powerful "magic" appeal of children, and the fact that the Executive Director has remained the same man ever since the fund's establishment, have combined to produce a set of special techniques tailored to the susceptibilities of individual governments. Through extensive travel, the Executive Director over the years has been able to establish close personal relations with key government officials in the welfare domain, which he has successfully used for fund-raising purposes. Responsibility for persuading governments to contribute in an increasingly generous manner is delegated in substantial degree to the field staff of UNICEF, which is in constant contact with government bureaucracies in many national capitals. There is hardly a case in which the negotiation for financial support is left entirely to headquarters. On the other hand, neither is there negotiation by the field staff with which headquarters is not familiar within a reasonable period of time.

UNICEF has from experience found it particularly important to time its approaches to governments in relation to budget preparation periods. In addition, a special effort is made to agree on reasonable goals to suggest to national ministries. Such goals are said to emerge from discussions with regional directors of UNICEF or are recommended by field staff familiar with the circumstances, or constitute figures that the Executive Director considers in the realm of possibility. There is no yardstick by which these amounts can be measured, but frequently the example of governments giving outstanding contributions is used to induce others to increase their donations.

The UNICEF staff endeavors to persuade all countries to contribute, if only in token amounts. This undertaking has been conspicuously successful in that the number of contributors has increased from only twelve in 1947 to more than one hundred in 1962.

A word is in order regarding UNICEF's attitude toward the role of the Negotiating Committee for Extra-Budgetary Funds, to which reference was made above. Except in certain "stubborn cases," when a high-level letter to a government seemed advisable, this committee was not considered very useful to UNICEF. The feeling in UNICEF circles was that the committee was best geared to serve the refugee programs, whereas UNICEF could more effectively attract government support through its own direct appeals. "The child," observed UNICEF's Executive Director, "represents the potential of the nation." Making the most of this kind of appeal, UNICEF has been able to win almost universal support through its own unique character.

Perhaps the most interesting fund-raising technique used by UNICEF is its appeal for contributions from nongovernmental organizations such as churches, schools, and citizens' groups. Indeed, UNICEF has come to depend on some regular income from private sources. The first experiment was launched in 1946. It was the United Nations Appeal for Children, a world-wide campaign for nongovernmental contributions to meet emergency needs of children, adolescents, and expectant mothers. Private groups in forty-five countries and thirty nonself-governing territories contributed $11 million to UNICEF by the end of 1948. The drive was eminently successful, but it was never duplicated. It had hinged on a unique humanitarian appeal at the end of the war when the condition of millions of children was especially desperate in many countries. From 1951 to 1955, annual private contributions to UNICEF never exceeded $1 million. Since 1956, the figure has risen slowly, largely because of organized collections by children in the United States and Canada on Halloween. The total for 1962 was $1.9 million, most of which came from the United States. A similar amount is realized annually from the sale of UNICEF greeting cards throughout the world. But all told, private contributions and income from greeting cards amount to only 20 percent of the annual UNICEF budget.[6]

On balance, the United Nations Children's Fund has been characterized by both originality and persistence in the ways it has found to raise money for its wards throughout the world. Arrears have never been a serious problem in UNICEF. The Latin American countries have been somewhat tardy in paying their pledges, but few countries are more than two years behind on their payments. All things considered, the financial picture of UNICEF has been steadily improving.

Refugee Programs

The United Nations has always been concerned with the problems of refugees. Indeed, since the end of World War II there has been a procession of temporary agencies under United Nations auspices to deal with the uprooted.

First, the International Refugee Organization (IRO) was called into being as a successor to the United Nations Relief and Rehabilitation Administration (UNRRA), which had managed to repatriate the great majority of refugees dislocated during World War II. The IRO was to explore repatriation or resettlement opportunities for

[6] For a further analysis of private contributions to the United Nations, see Chap. 10.

those refugees who still found themselves in displaced persons camps when UNRRA ceased operations in 1947. The organization was set up as a "non-permanent specialized agency," and it was originally hoped that it would be financed by assessing the member states of the United Nations. However, since many of the refugees were anti-Communists who refused to be repatriated to their former homes in Eastern Europe, the Soviet-bloc countries refused to share in the work of the IRO. Moreover, the primarily European emphasis and the expense of resettling or repatriating close to a million and a half people prompted more than half the members of the United Nations to refrain from participating. In the last analysis, the birth of the IRO depended on a large United States financial contribution. The United States Senate decision to ratify the IRO constitution was influenced by two considerations: first, the IRO was to be a nonpermanent organization, and second and equally important, the United States would save money by joining. A sum of $130 million was being spent annually for the upkeep of refugees located in the United States zones of Germany and Austria. The following exchange in the Senate Foreign Relations Committee was decisive:

> SENATOR VANDENBERG: Then is it fair—I want to get this overall relationship—is it fair to say that IRO involves a total expenditure of $73,000,000 for an operation which has cost and is costing $130,000,000 under existing auspices?
> GENERAL HILLDRING: That is correct, Senator.
> SENATOR VANDENBERG: So that we are saving, so far as dollars and cents are concerned, $57,000,000 by this switch over to IRO; is that correct?
> GENERAL HILLDRING: Based on the record alone.[7]

The initial United States contribution of $73 million breathed life into the IRO. It amounted to almost 60 percent of the total. The United Kingdom contributed 15 percent, France 4 percent, and fifteen other governments offered smaller amounts. The membership of the organization never exceeded eighteen. Nevertheless, the IRO was the most expensive single operation ever undertaken under United Nations auspices. By 1952 it had spent $428.5 million. The United States consistently contributed 60 percent. Indeed, its contribution to the IRO during the organization's existence amounted to between 40 and 70 percent of total United States expenditures on international or-

[7] International Refugee Organization, Hearing on S. J. Res. 77, Senate Committee on Foreign Relations, 80 Cong. 1 sess. (1947), p. 39.

ganizations up to that time. Significantly enough, the IRO had to cease operations after 1951 because of the unwillingness of the United States to contribute further to an organization whose target date for completing its work had originally been mid-1950.[8] Although homes had been found for over a million people, there remained a hard core of refugees, many of them old or sick, for whom opportunities for resettlement would be difficult to find.

Even long before the IRO was closing its doors, millions of new refugees resulted from the upheavals in China, India, Korea, and the Middle East. The refugee was evidently a lasting phenomenon, and the IRO, instead of achieving—as had been hoped and intended—a complete solution of a temporary problem, only succeeded in achieving a partial solution of a long-term one.

The successor to the IRO was the Office of the United Nations High Commissioner for Refugees (UNHCR), established in January 1951 to bridge the gap shortly to be left by the IRO in the field of international protection. By then, interest in the refugee problem had sunk to a low ebb, and the General Assembly refused to grant the High Commissioner operational authority. The Office was equipped with a small administrative budget of $300,000 and, much like the Nansen Office of the League of Nations, was to concern itself solely with the legal protection of refugees. Indeed, the statute setting up the Office stipulated that "the High Commissioner shall not appeal to governments for funds or make a general appeal, without the prior approval of the General Assembly."[9]

After a determined drive by the High Commissioner, however, the Assembly relented in 1952 and authorized him to become an international mendicant. He was given authority to appeal for $3 million for emergency aid "to the most needy groups." Only fourteen governments responded, with a little over $700,000. The financial needs of the office were so acute that the gold bar awarded to the League's High Commissioner Fridtjof Nansen by the Nobel Peace Prize Commission in 1922 was sold for emergency relief purposes. Fortunately, as will be seen below, private groups came to the help of the Office at this point and saved it from complete fiscal paralysis.

In 1954 the High Commissioner made another appeal to govern-

[8] For an analysis of private contributions to the refugee program, see Chap. 10.

[9] Art. 10 of the statute, reproduced in *Yearbook of the United Nations, 1950* (1951), pp. 585-87. Originally established for three years, the High Commissioner's mandate has three times been extended for five-year periods.

ments for a United Nations Refugee Fund (UNREF) to promote permanent solutions for certain groups of refugees within his mandate. Although the target was set at the modest sum of $16 million over a four-year period, the response for 1955 and 1956 was poor. A few governments contributed roughly 30 percent of the annual target. However, the exodus of some 200,000 refugees as a result of the November 1956 Hungarian revolution precipitated such unprecedented world-wide publicity for the refugee problem in general, that UNREF was able to collect $14.5 million out of the projected $16 million from member governments by the end of 1958. Thirty-one nations contributed, the United States leading with 35 percent. Australia, Belgium, Canada, Denmark, France, the Federal Republic of Germany, the Netherlands, New Zealand, Norway, Sweden, Switzerland, and the United Kingdom also made substantial contributions.

In 1958, the Thirteenth General Assembly proclaimed World Refugee Year, to begin on July 1, 1959. Its aim was to focus interest on refugee problems, encourage additional financial contributions from all possible sources, and "encourage additional opportunities for permanent refugee solutions."[10] Ninety-seven countries and territories and thirty-nine national committees participated. The United Kingdom alone raised almost $25 million—more than one-fourth of the total. Some countries extended the project beyond its June 1960 deadline, and various committees were continued on a permanent basis. To date, over $100 million has been raised; of this amount, $15 million went to the High Commissioner's program and some $4 million to the United Nations Relief and Works Agency for Palestine Refugees in the Near East. A large proportion of the total figure went directly to voluntary organizations working with the refugees. Lately, however, governmental interest in the refugees has slackened, as indicated by the decrease in governmental pledges from over $6 million in 1960 to under $4 million in 1961 and 1962.

As in the case of UNICEF, private donations have played an important role in the life of the Office of the High Commissioner. In 1952, a $2.9 million grant from the Ford Foundation enabled the High Commissioner to rehabilitate a considerable number of "hard-core" refugees living in European camps. Indeed, it was this private grant that made it possible for the Office to embark on operational work for

---

[10] General Assembly Res. 1285(XIII), Dec. 5, 1958.

the refugees. In that sense, it served as a pump-primer to the General Assembly, which later reluctantly endorsed the operational aspects of UNHCR's program. A second occasion arose in connection with World Refugee Year. In 1959, private contributions to UNHCR exceeded $1 million, constituting 20 percent of total income. In 1960, for the first time in the history of any United Nations program, contributions from private sources exceeded those from governments. A determined world-wide fund-raising campaign netted over $9 million, one-third more than the amount contributed to the office by governments.

During 1961 and 1962, $1.5 million was raised through an ingenious stamp plan under which seventy-five postal administrations issued special stamps to commemorate World Refugee Year; there was also a coordinated plan for selling these stamps and first-day covers. Three-fourths of the proceeds went to UNHCR and one-fourth to UNRWA. This plan was a major feature of the World Refugee Year campaign through which the Office of the High Commissioner wished to dramatize the urgency of the refugee problem. It may be assumed that the publicity generated by the stamps in turn stimulated further contributions to World Refugee Year.

The second program is the United Nations Relief and Works Agency for Palestine Refugees in the Near East, established to help meet the basic necessities of the hundreds of thousands of Palestinian Arabs who left their homes for neighboring countries in 1948. The political situation has been stalemated ever since, and UNRWA has had to clothe, feed, and shelter approximately one million refugees on a financial basis described by the commissioner-general as "a matter of grave concern." While UNRWA's income for normal operations has become stabilized at around $34 million, expenditures, increased by rising costs, have exceeded income. The deficit has had to be met from rapidly diminishing working capital. United States government contributions have consistently amounted to almost 70 percent of the total; that country, the United Kingdom, Canada, and France have through the years provided almost 95 percent of the income, with thirty-three countries making up the remainder in 1962. UNRWA, therefore, is virtually at the mercy of its largest contributor, and each year the Congress of the United States has threatened to cut off financial support if no terminal solution is found for the refugee problem. No such solution is in sight.

The United Nations Korean Reconstruction Agency was a large-scale, temporary operation established in 1950, to plan and supervise rehabilitation, relief, and refugee work in Korea, and terminated in 1958. It too was dependent on United States financial support, to the extent of almost 70 percent of the $149 million spent for UNKRA. The United Kingdom contributed close to 20 percent, and thirty-eight other nations shared the remainder.[11] When the United States decided in 1957 to pursue its program of military and economic aid to Korea unilaterally rather than through the United Nations, UNKRA's relief and rehabilitation operations came to a standstill and the Agency was disbanded in 1958.

Development Programs

Voluntary contributions from governments support three United Nations programs dealing with economic development. The first of these, the Expanded Programme of Technical Assistance, was launched in 1950; the second, the Special Fund, began operations in 1959; and a fund for the economic development of the Congo was set up in 1960. Financing follows a similar pattern in all three programs. EPTA and the Special Fund differ from most of the other voluntary programs, however, in that their existence rests more clearly on the presumption of permanence.

Although the United Nations and various specialized agencies had carried on a modest technical assistance program almost from the beginning, the impetus for EPTA came out of Point Four of President Truman's inaugural speech of January 1949. Subsequently, the United States proposed to the United Nations Economic and Social Council (ECOSOC) that a concrete program be elaborated for enlarging technical assistance activities. Since 1950, when EPTA began operations with $20 million provided by fifty-four nations, contributions have steadily increased. In 1955, seventy nations pledged over $27 million. And by 1962 pledges from ninety-eight governments stood at $50.5 million.

Like the other voluntary programs, EPTA was launched with a sizable contribution from the United States, which amounted to 60

[11] See Gene M. Lyons, "American Policy and the United Nations Program for Korean Reconstruction," *International Organization,* Vol. 12, No. 2 (Spring 1958).

percent of all government contributions. Since then the United States has gradually reduced its "matching" percentage, and during the past few years has insisted that its contribution not exceed 40 percent of the total. But, as in UNICEF, the number of donors and the size of contributions have gone up so that the United States has also pledged increasingly larger amounts. The United Kingdom contributes 8 percent and France and Canada over 5 percent each. The developing countries themselves contribute 10 percent. The Soviet Union and other East European countries began to contribute in 1953 and have been responsible for slightly more than 4 percent of the budget.

Again, as in UNICEF, the actual impact of EPTA is larger than its financial resources would indicate. Recipient governments are obligated to pay for the local costs of EPTA projects, which amount to more than twice the annual budget of EPTA itself.

The Special Fund was set up for the purpose of financing preparatory and "pre-investment" projects that would make it possible for technical assistance and development to yield optimum results. In keeping with its mandate, the Special Fund has concentrated on relatively large projects. Financing has been virtually a carbon copy of EPTA. The total government contribution has been slightly above that for EPTA—$38.5 million in 1960, almost $47 million in 1961, $60 million in 1962, and $72.5 million in 1963. Again, the United States limits its contribution to 40 percent of the total. Governments increasingly regard the financing of EPTA and the Special Fund as a joint operation. Several, in fact, make a single pledge to both programs. Some, like India and Japan, make their pledges contingent on the attainment of a given minimum of total government contributions to the two programs.

The fund-raising procedures for EPTA and the Special Fund have much in common with those used by UNICEF. Prior to the establishment of the Fund, most of the initiative was taken by the Technical Assistance Board (TAB) secretariat. In this connection, the Executive Chairman of the TAB sought every opportunity—on his numerous field trips, in the meetings of the Technical Assistance Committee (TAC), ECOSOC, and General Assembly committees—to bring to the attention of governments the growing demands on the program. It was stressed that EPTA was a program with which they should feel a sense of partnership: it was after all "their" program. This partnership concept has been invoked with moderately good results. The number of contributions from the developing countries has risen steadily over the years, even though many of these contributions are still in token amounts. Most of the newly independent nations of Africa can scarcely afford to give more.

The experience of the TAB secretariat was that direct informal contacts with those national units that were concerned with the policy, administration, and budgeting of technical assistance or economic planning activities, were likely to produce more effective results than approaches by way of foreign offices or even finance ministries.

The advent of the Special Fund brought to the fore the idea of setting an overall program "target" for it and EPTA together as a means of stimulating expanded government support. By Resolution 1240(XIII), the General Assembly in 1958 envisaged $100 million as such a target. Two years later, the Assembly raised the target to $150 million, and again, in 1961, it urged governments to review their contributions to the two programs so that their combined budgets for 1962 might reach this level. While government pledges for 1962 and 1963 fell short of that figure, they did amount to $105 million and $123 million, respectively.

A dynamic force behind the drive for Special Fund resources has been Paul G. Hoffman, Managing Director of the Fund, who has served as a kind of *de facto* "finance minister" for United Nations economic and social operations.

In a sense, the money-raising work "in the field" on behalf of EPTA and the Special Fund may be said to culminate in the announcement of annual pledges, which takes place at the special Pledging Conference held during the early part of the General Assembly's regular session. The precedent for this arrangement dates back to the initial year of EPTA, when a special conference was held to record the first pledges from supporting governments. Behind the arrangement, continued ever since, was the notion that it would be good psychology to invite governments "to stand up and be counted" rather than to depend merely on official written requests for contributions. The annual Pledging Conference serves as a sort of deadline for pledges. Even so, a considerable number of delegates are not in a position to make firm or unconditional pledges at the conference. Some pledges depend on subsequent approval by national parliaments; others on final executive or treasury action to be taken later. Each year a number of additional pledges are made directly to program headquarters during the first months of the financial year following the Pledging Conference in the fall. This situation leaves program administrators in a state of some uncertainty as to how much money they may expect to receive for the ensuing year. Pledges themselves, once announced, however, are usually considered firm obligations, and there have not been many cases in which national parliaments have failed to approve them.

All this does not mean that EPTA and the Special Fund do not have their share of fiscal difficulties aside from the chronic one of never having enough money to go around for allocations to worthwhile projects. In EPTA, a special problem has been the difficulty of inducing recipient governments to pay promptly their "local cost" obligations. This situation led the Technical Assistance Committee in 1960 to authorize the executive chairman of TAB to defer the implementation of new projects in the case of any country which, at the end of a particular year, was in arrears on its local cost obligations in an amount exceeding the equivalent of $3,000. This action was designed to strengthen the hand of the TAB secretariat in its endeavor to reduce the amount of unpaid local costs. Notwithstanding, arrears in local cost payments continue to present something of a problem, particularly since the matching condition imposed by the largest EPTA contributor, the United States, includes local cost payments by recipient governments in the computation of total contributions from other governments. If, for 1962, there were $3 million in paid-up local cost obligations, this would generate $1.2 million in additional United States EPTA money, which could reach but not exceed 40 percent of the all-inclusive total for the year, according to the conditions set by the Congress.

In addition to the above difficulties, there are two other problems. The first of these grows out of the uncertainties of the pledging system; the other has to do with the difficulty of using some of the currencies in which pledges are paid. Uncertainty about the timing of contributions within a given year sometimes compels TAB to cut back program allocations. More important, both EPTA and the Special Fund have attempted to circumvent the hazards of annual financing by initiating two-year programing in 1961 and "project-programing" in 1963. Governments are being encouraged to make pledges for periods longer than a year. While some of the Western European governments, notably in Scandinavia, have been receptive to the idea, the United States has been somewhat hesitant to go along with it. Nevertheless, a considerable amount of project-programing is already in effect.

The problem of currency utilization is even more complex. Despite constant exhortations to governments to make their contributions as far as possible in convertible currencies, EPTA and the Special Fund have received numerous inconvertible contributions. It became particularly vexatious in EPTA when the Soviet Union began to make contributions in 1954. In its initial pledge the U.S.S.R. specified that its contribution, in rubles, was nonconvertible. During the period 1954-57 most of the Eastern European countries made similar but much smaller nonconvertible contributions.

EPTA soon experienced difficulty in making use of these currencies, partly because only a few countries, mainly in the Middle East and in South Asia, then found Soviet or East European experts acceptable. This situation prompted TAB to negotiate with the Soviet Union for partial convertibility of its EPTA contribution. By the end of 1956, this was granted up to 25 percent of the total annual pledge of one million rubles.

Nevertheless, lack of convertibility for the larger part of these "difficult" currencies made it necessary for TAB to resort to various ingenious expedients, one of which was to devise "special" projects. Such projects had to be financed primarily by rubles allocated to recipient countries as a distinct part of their annual programs. This practice aroused protest in TAC and ECOSOC meetings in 1956, both from the Soviet Union, which objected to "being singled out" in this manner, and by the United States, which argued that "rubles were being 'pushed' " by TAB. Expressed differently, these "ruble projects," it was contended, might well develop into a permanent bilateral program, administered for the Soviet Union by the United Nations under the guise of a multilateral program. By the end of 1956, only about 32 percent of the Soviet and Eastern European contributions had been spent. At its summer session during that year, ECOSOC adopted a resolution aimed at ending "special projects." This resolution further urged contributing countries to make their contributions in convertible currencies—a provision admittedly pointed at the Soviet Union.

Since 1956, the difficulty of using Soviet and Eastern European currencies has been somewhat lessened by a slightly increased demand for Soviet experts and larger purchases of Soviet equipment. But the problem has by no means disappeared. In 1961 the Soviet Union doubled its contribution to EPTA, a move which, at least temporarily, increased the difficulty of using it entirely. A backlog of two million unused Russian rubles existed at the beginning of 1962.

Although the Soviet bloc countries have caused the greatest difficulty in the matter of currency utilization, a number of other governments restrict the convertibility of their contributions in whole or in part. As late as 1959, the contributions from forty-nine countries were entirely nonconvertible while fifteen others were partially so. In response to a strong appeal from the Executive Chairman of TAB, forty-two countries made their contributions fully convertible in 1961. Further progress was made in 1962 and 1963.

Thus far the Special Fund's problems with currencies have been less serious than those experienced by EPTA. However, since the number of projects in operation is steadily growing, it may become necessary to exert pressure on governments for full convertibility. In one respect, the Fund's situation is more favorable than that of EPTA because it spends more than the latter on project supplies and equipment and can, like UNICEF, shop all over the world for its requirements. In a cautiously optimistic vein, the Managing Director of the Special Fund told its Governing Council in May 1961 that "I myself am satisfied that with careful management, and drawing upon the experience gained earlier under other programs, we will face no insuperable difficulties in the utilization of the currencies available to us."[12]

Before leaving the financing of the development programs, a word should be said about the United Nations Fund for the Congo. This fund was established by the General Assembly at its fourth emergency special session on September 20, 1960. It was decided to aim at a figure of $100 million for financial assistance to the fledgling republic. By 1962, only twenty governments had responded with a disappointing total of $49 million. Of this total, the United States contributed $38 million, or slightly more than three-fourths, while four countries —the United Kingdom, West Germany, Sweden, and Canada—gave 20 percent. Fourteen other governments, most of them Western, contributed the remaining 5 percent .

[12] U.N. Doc. SF/L.52 (June 14, 1961).

The Pattern of Contributions

Turning from the analysis of the voluntary programs to some general comparative patterns, several interesting observations are suggested. First, contributions to the voluntary programs always exceed expenditures under the regular budget of the United Nations. Indeed, on several occasions they have amounted to two or three times the total subscribed to the regular budget. Contributions to the IRO alone far exceeded the regular budget during the period of 1947-50. Second, despite a great deal of fluctuation in contributions, on the whole, the trend has been upward. This has been especially true of UNICEF, EPTA, and the Special Fund which have won close to universal support, including that of several nonmember nations. The more modest response to the refugee appeals, UNKRA, and the Congo Fund suggests that where programs are set up chiefly for the benefit of a single country or a social group such as the refugees, the response is likely to remain limited.

If the pattern of voluntary contributions by governments is compared with that of the assessed budget, several significant factors emerge. First, the role of the United States is even more dominant in the voluntary programs than in the assessed budget. While its contribution varies from 70 percent of the total in UNRWA to 40 percent in EPTA and the Special Fund, it is quite clear that the United States contribution is financially controlling over all the voluntary programs. The IRO and UNKRA which ended when the United States financial contributions ended are cases in point. All told, the United States has paid well over half of the aggregate amount spent on all the voluntary programs since their inception.[13] Moreover, the United States contribution in every instance has been above its proportionate contribution to the regular budget. On the whole, American willingness to bear a heavy share of the burden during the initial stages made these programs possible and, in some cases, carried them until other countries, persuaded of their value, assumed an increasing share of the load.

The Soviet Union and other East European countries ignored the

[13] For United States contributions to these programs, see *United States Contributions to International Organizations,* H. Doc. 131, 88 Cong. 1 sess., App. Table 6.

voluntary programs completely until 1953. After the death of Stalin, they not only joined some of the specialized agencies, but began to make contributions to UNICEF, EPTA, and, in 1959, to the Special Fund. Not only was the new Soviet leadership willing to experiment with new ideas, but it was apparently impressed with the evidence by mid-1953 that UNICEF and EPTA were not going to fail, that their popularity would increase, and that more harm to the Soviet Union would result from remaining outside than from participating. The annual East European contributions to the three programs have amounted to less than 5 percent of the total—roughly one-third of the percentage these nations are assessed in the regular budget. No Soviet-bloc contribution has ever been made to the refugee programs or to the Congo Fund.

The United Kingdom has paid for about 8 percent of the voluntary programs, approximately the same ratio as its share of the regular budget. France has pledged 3 percent, roughly half its proportionate share of the assessed budget. And China's contribution has been an infinitesimal 0.05 percent. As a rule, the developing nations of Africa, Asia, the Middle East, and Latin America contribute in a slightly higher proportion to the voluntary programs than to the regular budget. A comparison of the proportionate contributions in 1962 to the four principal voluntary programs—UNICEF, UNRWA, EPTA, and the Special Fund—with those to the regular budget reveals that besides the United States only the United Arab Republic has given a higher percentage to all four programs than to the regular budget. Six countries gave a higher percentage to three of the four programs. These were Canada, Denmark, Iran, Norway, Sweden, and Turkey. Twenty countries were on the plus side in two of the four programs. Three states—the Netherlands, Norway, and the United Arab Republic—more than doubled their assessment percentages in two of the four programs and twenty-three states doubled their assessment ratios on one of the voluntary programs.

Taking the voluntary programs as a whole, the amounts contributed by most states over the years have shown little correlation to their proportionate contributions to the regular budget. Table A.5 shows for selected years the special programs financed by voluntary contributions.

Improving the Financing of the Voluntary Programs

Proposals for improvement may be grouped into two broad categories: budget coordination and the strengthening of the voluntary contribution principle.

To begin with the first problem, it has been suggested that the merger of the two major long-range development programs—EPTA and the Special Fund—should result in some reduction in overhead costs and more effective coordination of program planning. This question was debated at some length in an "Ad Hoc Committee of Eight" set up by ECOSOC in 1961 to study the working relations of the two programs. It was contended by certain members of this committee that the existing administrative arrangement, although already in part a joint one, was unduly complicated and confusing for many recipient countries.

The discussion proved inconclusive, and the committee contented itself with recommending that a study be made of the possible advantages and disadvantages of a partial or complete merger in due course, without running counter to the basic objectives of each program. It was not conclusively demonstrated in the committee that a merger would necessarily result in a reduction of overhead costs.

A more radical proposal has been that the voluntary principle be abandoned altogether and that the major programs now supported in this manner be incorporated into the regular budget of the United Nations alone, or of the United Nations together with the specialized agencies concerned. This proposal has the virtue of logic and fiscal simplicity to commend it. By now, nearly the entire membership of the United Nations makes contributions to EPTA, the Special Fund, and UNICEF. Furthermore, both the United Nations and several of its affiliated agencies contain operational program elements in their regular budgets, thus providing a precedent, if need be, for expanding them to include the costs of the voluntary programs of a permanent character. Would this not assure more dependable revenue and provide a more favorable outlook for steady program progress? So the argument runs. An examination of various implications of the proposal, however, makes the case for it much less attractive than at first glance.

First, there is no convincing evidence that, other things being equal, the "absorbed" activities would receive more favorable financial treatment than they now enjoy under the voluntary pattern. Contributions to EPTA and the Special Fund have risen more sharply than the assessed contributions to the regular budget and the specialized agencies. Second, absorption would probably involve the setting up of a special assessment scale for the former voluntary program. As already noted, the pattern of support for these programs has been substantially different from the regular budget scales. The Soviet bloc, probably France and a considerable number of middle and minor powers would insist on this as the price of their acquiescence in the new arrangement. The difficulty of arriving at a consensus on the special assessment quotas can easily be imagined. Indeed, the chances are that total contributions would decline, or at best, not increase appreciably, under an assessment pattern.

Strong objection to the transfer of EPTA and the Special Fund to the United Nations regular budget would almost certainly be forthcoming from the specialized agencies. From their standpoint this would be viewed as giving to the chief policy organ of the United Nations the decisive voice in determining the nature, scope, and resources of such program activity. Even though the agencies would continue to participate in the execution of the formerly independent programs, their policy role would probably diminish. Moreover, the special programs would tend to lose their identity and concurrently, a good deal of the impact of their appeal. Would, for example, the General Assembly be disposed to act favorably on budgetary proposals from the Secretary-General for field activities in the economic and social sphere if they involved substantially larger contributions from a voting majority of the member states on a compulsory basis?

The case of UNICEF illustrates the fear of loss of program identity. UNICEF's functions would probably be distributed among WHO, FAO, and the United Nations Bureau of Social Affairs. If this happened, in the view of UNICEF's leadership, the "magic appeal" of children might disappear and with it much of the support UNICEF now receives from its special clientele. In effect, this might mean a financial withering away of the program rather than a constructive "consolidation." And some of the contributions from nonmember states might be lost if the voluntary programs were absorbed.

The case for program consolidation or for absorption into the regular budget is not a good one on financial grounds. Indeed, it is likely that the livelihood of the voluntary programs is better assured if the voluntary principle is maintained and strengthened. The greatest problem confronting the programs is to increase the funds available to them. Basically, the outlook is good here.

Insofar as it is possible to venture any firm prediction on the fate of the United Nations system in these critical times, it would probably be that, short of a general debacle, the work of the Organization in the field of economic and social development will not only retain its present popularity but will expand in scope and intensity. Even political controversies like the 1963 crisis over the Special Fund project in Cuba are not likely to interrupt this long-range trend. One of the most enthusiastic actions of the 1961 General Assembly was the unanimous adoption of a resolution proclaiming the current decade as the "United Nations Development Decade." In his "Proposals for Action during the United Nations Development Decade," issued in the spring of 1962, Secretary-General U Thant suggested an expansion of the resources of EPTA and the Special Fund by at least $25 million annually. This would give the United Nations, at the end of the decade, annual resources of about $300 million for development purposes.

There have not been many techniques either used or suggested to elicit more generous contributions from governments. The only instrument devised so far by the General Assembly has been the Negotiating Committee for Extra-Budgetary Funds, which went out of existence in 1961.

The Assembly at its twelfth session introduced the procedure of convening an *Ad hoc* Committee of the Whole Assembly for the announcement of pledges of voluntary contributions to the two United Nations refugee programs. This procedure, repeated annually, was first adopted at the suggestion of the Negotiating Committee in an attempt, through the increased publicity, to focus attention on the problem of refugees and thus to bring about an improvement in the financial support of these programs. The Negotiating Committee also recommended each year that, in order to ensure maximum attendance, as much advance publicity as possible be given to the pledging conferences, and that they be scheduled at times when no other meetings were being held.

It is difficult to assess the effectiveness of the Negotiating Committee. While it is true that pledges rose in the latter years of its existence, it is not likely that the committee exerted a major influence on the decisions of member states. In the last analysis, voluntary contributions were precisely what the term connotes—voluntary.

Another technique that has been suggested is to present to governments the claims of all the programs in a single package on the order of a "community chest" or "united fund" appeal. The adoption of such a procedure would reduce the number of separate claims for money submitted each year to the member states of the United Nations. Including all the specialized agencies and all the voluntary programs, such claims now range between fifteen and twenty for states belonging to the entire cluster of United Nations organizations. Any consolidation of budgetary claims would presumably be viewed with favor by national treasuries and parliamentary committees in most member states.

Here again, however, the application of this seemingly more orderly arrangement would involve some of the same objections noted above in connection with the discussion of proposals for program consolidation. The vested interests behind each of the present programs, both at the policy and the staff levels, would no doubt resist lumping them together for fear of jeopardizing the effectiveness of their special appeal for contributions. There is the further complicating fact that some of the programs, such as UNRWA and UNHCR, do not have a world-wide appeal, or are for political or other reasons shunned by certain governments. Would the "packaging" arrangement have to allow for the imposition of conditions by donor governments in the form of "opting out" clauses for certain specified programs? If such a right were resorted to by a large number of governments, much of the value of the unified approach would be dissipated. In addition to these difficulties, it would be necessary to develop some mechanism for distributing the proceeds of the united appeal among the beneficiaries. This operation might provoke lively interprogram competition. What kind of mechanism would be most acceptable to all the rival interests concerned? The Fifth Committee of the General Assembly? A special interprogram group at the senior staff level? Or some other type of body? A generally acceptable answer would not be easily found. It should also be remembered that there can be no completely unified approach to governments for international "welfare" funds so long as the specialized agencies retain their organizational autonomy. In this connection, the idea of a consolidated budget for the United Nations system as a whole has been debated over the years without any appreciable impact. This being the case, one wonders whether the value of partial consolidation would not largely be offset by the loss of separate program appeal. The evidence suggests that specially highlighted drives have on occasion been quite successful. World Refugee Year may be a case in point. Similarly, the value of resourceful and vigorous directors is beyond a doubt.

It might be possible to devise some objective formula by which governmental contributions would, while remaining nominally voluntary, follow an ascending curve on some agreed equitable basis of distribution. As in the area of peace and security operations, a combination of GNP per capita, with ceiling allowances made for the wealthier nations and floors for the developing states, may provide the most practicable basis for constructing such a scale. It is relevant to note that the governments of Sweden and Norway, in their response to the Secretary-General's request to governments for comments on what should be done in respect to the United Nations Development Decade, indicated that they were planning successive increases in their foreign aid contributions, 1 percent of the national income being set as the target to be reached in ten years.

Another possibility would be for the Secretary-General, on occasion, to project himself into an appeal and to throw the full weight of his office behind it. Secretary-General U Thant's initiative on the Development Decade would be a case in point.

In the final analysis, the financial future of the voluntary programs is likely to depend much more on the development of a vigorous consensus for their support than on any particular procedural arrangement for raising money. The fact that such a consensus already exists to a considerable degree augurs well for the future of the voluntary programs. A constant testing and gradual expansion of the limits of this consensus might truly bring economic and social welfare within the reach of all in our generation.

CHAPTER 9

The Specialized Agencies

A STUDY OF FINANCING the United Nations system must include the system in its widest sense. Experience is by no means limited to the headquarters of the world organization. In Montreal, Rome, Paris, Geneva, Washington, and Vienna, there have emerged significant repositories of experience in international public finance—the specialized agencies. Some precede by several decades the founding of the United Nations, others were not created until after its inception. These important members of the United Nations system are not simply miniatures of the central body in their financial structures. Rather, financing of their programs takes many forms.

The specialized agencies of the United Nations may be roughly divided into three groups. The first group, for lack of a better term, may be called the "development" agencies. They are "development" in the sense that they are intended to improve world economic, social, and cultural conditions. The second group are the communication agencies, whose major purpose is to broaden and facilitate communication among nations. The third group are essentially financing institutions and are related to the United Nations only in a very loose sense. While all of these agencies are members of the United Nations system, they have developed their own unique organizational patterns. Each has its own membership policy. Some, like the International Bank for Reconstruction and Development (IBRD) and the International Monetary Fund (IMF) do not include the Soviet bloc countries. Others, like the Universal Postal Union (UPU), the International Labour Organisation (ILO), the United Nations Educational, Scientific and Cultural Organization (UNESCO), and the World Health Organization (WHO), are virtually universal in their inclusiveness. Many comprise nations or territories that are not members of the United Nations.

Some nations have withdrawn from, and then rejoined, the specialized agencies. The Soviet bloc countries, for example, boycotted the ILO, UNESCO, and WHO for almost a decade, but decided to rejoin in the mid-1950's. Each specialized agency has its constitution and its executive and deliberative bodies. Each elects a chief administrative officer as director-general or as secretary-general. Each has evolved in a tradition of independence. Several agencies have come to provide valuable testing grounds for experimentation in different patterns of international administration. All illuminate the problems and progress in the development of sound international financial structures.

The problems of the specialized agencies are similar to those of the voluntary programs. There is no immediate financial crisis, and the few politically motivated delinquencies do not threaten the lives of the agencies. But there is constant tension between donor and recipient states. The former are reluctant to increase their commitments and to make larger contributions with each passing year. The latter maintain that there is never enough money to go around and exert constant pressure for expansion.

The budgets for 1963 of the agencies in the first two groups reached $97.7 million—roughly the amount of the United Nations regular budget. Organizations are financed in all cases from assessments. In addition, they receive allocations from the Expanded Programme of Technical Assistance (EPTA), and, in some cases, voluntary contributions.

Some degree of fiscal coordination exists between the United Nations and the specialized agencies. As indicated in Chapter 4, Article 17 of the Charter provided the basis for agreements between the agencies and the parent body, which give the Assembly the right of perfunctory supervision of the budgets of the "development" and "communication" agencies, but not of the IBRD and the IMF. In practice, there has been almost complete decentralization of financing in all the agencies.

The following analysis will set forth the basic financial patterns of the agencies and will emphasize those features that are unique to each.

Development Agencies

The five agencies included in the "development" group are the International Labour Organisation (ILO), which was established to better conditions of labor; the World Health Organization (WHO), which hopes to attain the highest possible level of health for the peoples of the world; the Food and Agriculture Organization (FAO), which hopes to raise the levels of nutrition and to improve agricultural technology; the United Nations Educational, Scientific, and Cultural Organization (UNESCO), which was set up to improve understanding among nations through research and the exchange of scholars and scientists; and the International Atomic Energy Agency (IAEA), whose purpose is to use the energy of the atom in the cause of peace. The ILO is the oldest of this group.

The International Labour Organisation

The ILO is unique among international organizations in that it includes representation not only from governments but from employers and workers as well. This tripartite system makes itself felt in the financial structure of the organization.[1]

The International Labour Conference adopts the annual budget of the agency, after approval by the Governing Body, and fixes the scale of assessments. In 1962, the ILO budget was $11.6 million. As the largest contributor, the United States paid 25 percent of the assessed budget—considerably less than its proportionate contribution to the United Nations or to the other specialized agencies. The minimum percentage was 0.12.

There is no mathematical explanation for the low United States percentage. It is probably because of the fact that the ILO was established at a time when the United States did not loom so large in the world economy and that the organization managed to survive during the early years without the United States as a member. Despite objections by several ILO members, American lawmakers have tended to take the low percentage for granted. When the Senate Committee on

[1] For discussion of the system, see Bernard Béguin, "ILO and the Tripartite System," *International Conciliation*, No. 523 (May 1959).

Foreign Relations discussed the matter of raising the legislative ceiling on contributions to the ILO, there was never any question of raising the *percentage* ceiling.[2]

On the whole, the employer members of the ILO have tended to be more economy-minded than their worker colleagues. The organization has increasingly been confronted by larger needs as a result of its expanded membership, its goal of recruiting a larger staff, and its hope of making special efforts in Africa where the requirements of newly independent countries are very large. Accordingly, the budget has expanded over the years. Larger credits have not, however, been voted without considerable debate. For 1963, the Director-General asked for a budget amounting to $14.9 million.[3] The increase proposed over the 1962 budget was about $3.3 million or 28.4 percent. While some of the government delegates of the Financial and Administrative Committee of the agency voiced objections to this increase,[4] the employer members were the most critical.[5] The worker members, on the other hand, extended full support to the Director-General's proposals: "It is not sufficient to pay lip-service to the need to help the developing countries; it is essential to provide the [International Labour] Office with the funds which will enable it to give as much effective help as possible to these countries."[6] Budget estimates for 1963 finally approved by the Financial and Administrative Committee and adopted by the Governing Body amounted to $14.2 million—an increase of $2.6 million or 22.02 percent over the previous budget.

It is by no means certain that the budget will keep pace with growing needs. The American percentage contribution will probably remain the same. The United Kingdom, another large contributor, has frequently opposed the rate of expansion proposed by the Director-General. And the Soviet Union, which re-entered the organization in 1954 after an absence of fifteen years, has not been an exponent of an increased budget. Indeed, at a meeting of the Governing Body in 1961, the Soviet delegate recommended that the expenditure estimates for 1962 should be considerably reduced.

[2] *Contributions to the International Labour Organisation,* Hearings before the Senate Committee on Foreign Relations, 85 Cong., 1 sess., April 16 and June 18, 1957.
[3] International Labour Conference, 46th Session, *Financial and Budgetary Questions* (1962), p. 99.
[4] For example, the delegates of the Federal Republic of Germany, Canada, France, the United States, the U.S.S.R., and the United Kingdom. Speaking for proposed increases were the representatives of Venezuela and India. See *ibid.,* pp. 82-99.
[5] *Ibid.,* p. 84.
[6] *Ibid.*

Many of the problems besetting the ILO budget are reflections of political dissatisfaction. The U.S.S.R., for example, has objected to budgetary provisions in the program, such as the Committee on Forced Labour, that it has found contrary to its political interests. In the United States, unofficial charges were frequently made to the effect that the ILO was Communist-dominated, was not pursuing its original objectives, and was interfering in the internal affairs of nations. The directors of the United States Chamber of Commerce and of the National Association of Manufacturers in 1956 asked for a thorough congressional and executive study of the organization in order to ascertain whether the United States should continue to participate. Although these studies cleared the ILO of the charges, continued political criticism left an impact on the finances of the organization.

In addition to these difficulties, the ILO faces on a smaller scale a problem which, in the United Nations, has come to have major repercussions: the tendency of some states to support programs with their votes, but not to follow through with their funds. The Director-General's statement to the Financial and Administrative Committee of the ILO in 1962 was reminiscent of many similar statements made by the United Nations Secretary-General before the Fifth Committee:

> What is baffling is when these great statements of policy are made and these tremendous decisions are taken on resolutions so that the aspirations of people all over the world are aroused and I am asked to act on it and build a budget and bring it—and then you say "No."[7]

Like the United Nations, the ILO also has problems in collecting contributions. Arrears are sometimes considerable. Stringent sanctions prevail in this regard. Nations that have defaulted in their assessments for more than two years may lose their voting rights in all the ILO organs—in the General Conference, the Governing Body, the committees, and the election of members to the Governing Body.[8] Only the ILO and the IAEA provide penalties of so grave a character. Moreover, the ILO Director-General has standing orders to inform the General Conference of those states that have lost their voting privileges. By a two-thirds majority, however, the conference may permit defaulting states to vote if it is satisfied that the failure to pay is due to conditions

[7] *Ibid.*, p. 104.
[8] Art. 13, par. 4 of the ILO Constitution.

beyond the control of the member in question. In 1961, for example, special arrangements were made and approved by the conference in regard to contributions due from Bolivia, China, Spain, and Hungary.[9] At other times, notably in 1954 and 1955 in the case of Hungary, member nations have not been permitted to retain their voting privileges so long as they are in arrears.

The ILO also shares in EPTA's voluntary resources and, in this regard, like the other agencies, has had to face considerable uncertainty in planning. To meet this uncertainty, the organization has generally tried to remain undercommitted. A special congressional study on international organizations evaluated this procedure and recommended in 1954 that the ILO's example be followed in other international organizations.

To sum up, the financing of the ILO has been heavily suffused with political considerations. Both the United States and the Soviet Union have been wary of the organization on political grounds. Many of the ILO's difficulties have not been unlike those the United Nations has faced on a larger scale. Nations have failed to support their own policies with funds; arrears have often been considerable; and there has been strong resistance to budget increases. Perhaps most interesting, the ILO has applied sanctions against delinquents and, in most cases, received payment as a result. Whether this is a lesson for the United Nations, where the issue of defaults and sanctions is much more heavily surrounded by political considerations, is doubtful.

The World Health Organization

Assessments on member states are the World Health Organization's principal source of income. WHO's constitution stipulates that the World Health Assembly shall apportion the expenses of the budget among member governments on a scale determined by the Assembly. In addition, allocations from EPTA and the Special Fund provide WHO with further revenue.[10] In 1962, the World Health Assembly appro-

[9] International Labour Conference, 45th Session, *Financial and Budgetary Questions* (1961), p. 107.

[10] In the first years of its existence, the agency also had at its disposal a United Nations loan of $2.2 million, $4 million from UNRRA funds, and monies derived from the assets of the Office International d'Hygiene Publique. UNICEF, too, helped to finance expenses for some joint operations which could not be financed from WHO's resources alone. See *The First Ten Years of the World Health Organization* (Geneva, 1958), pp. 117-26.

priated a budget of $24.9 million. The figure for 1963 approached the $28 million mark.

The agency's assessment pattern is similar to that of the United Nations regular budget. Criteria for apportioning expenses among member states follow closely those of the United Nations, taking into account the difference in membership. No one state contributes more than one-third of the organization's expenses. In 1962, the United States paid 31.71 percent of the agency's assessed budget, a decrease from the first assessment of 38.76 percent. More than one-half of the funds were provided by the United States, the Soviet Union, and the United Kingdom together. Three-fourths of the contributions to the assessed 1962 budget were made by eleven states, each of which contributed more than $250,000: Canada, China, France, Germany, India, Italy, Japan, the Ukrainian Soviet Socialist Republic, the U.S.S.R., the United Kingdom, and the United States.

WHO has always had difficulties with arrears. A number of these were caused by uncoordinated fiscal cycles in member states and by difficulties in obtaining hard currency. In 1949, the trouble was exacerbated by the refusal of the Soviet bloc countries to consider themselves members of the organization and to pay their assessed contributions. As a result, WHO was forced to fix two annual budgets—a "budget level" on which the assessments on active and inactive members were based; and an "effective working budget," which determined the authorized level of expenditure for the year and showed amounts assessed on active members only. This complication became necessary because the World Health Assembly decided in 1952 that the constitution gave it no authority to omit members from the scale of assessments.

Article 7 of WHO's constitution was never applied against the inactive states. This article reads:

> If a Member fails to meet its financial obligations to the Organization or in other exceptional circumstances, the Health Assembly may, on such conditions as it thinks proper, suspend the voting privileges and services to which a Member is entitled. The Health Assembly shall have the authority to restore such voting privileges and services.

In 1956, when a number of inactive states returned to active membership, the World Health Assembly considered the problem of their accumulated arrears. It was decided that contributions for the years during which they had been active should be paid in full. But during the years of inactivity, a token payment of 5 percent of the contributions assessed each year would discharge the obligations of the inactive members. These sums could be paid in equal annual installments over a period of not more than ten years.

In practice, the Assembly has not applied sanctions against the former "inactive" states even though they have been tardy in making their token payments. And when Bolivia, which was six years in arrears in 1961, made special provision to pay one-tenth of its arrears for the period 1955-61, WHO's Executive Board recommended that no sanctions be invoked against that country. On the whole, arrears have been a major irritant, but never a threat to the work of WHO.

The organization's second source of revenue consists of allocations from EPTA, which have increased steadily over the years. The amount that WHO receives annually depends on total governmental contributions to EPTA during the year, as well as on priorities placed by national governments on health programs. Hence, WHO, like the other specialized agencies, encounters some difficulty in planning future projects, because the sums available for any year are accurately known only six months after the annual program has been approved by the Health Assembly. EPTA allocations to WHO for 1961—the first year of the 1961-62 biennium—amounted to $7.1 million, to which must be added appropriations from the EPTA Contingency Fund amounting to $145,386. This total of $7.3 million was almost 25 percent above that for 1960.[11]

Voluntary contributions to support special programs are a third source of revenue. In 1960, the Health Assembly established a Voluntary Fund for Health Promotion, which included four subaccounts to be credited with voluntary contributions received in any usable currency. These were a general account for undesignated contributions; a special account for smallpox eradication; a special account for medical research; and a special account for community water supply.

A word should be said about the financing of WHO's malaria eradication program. A special voluntary account for malaria eradication had been established by WHO in 1955. Contributions were solicited from governments, foundations, industries, labor organizations, institutions and individuals. While the balance remaining in the account amounted to $12.4 million at the end of September 1960, this sum was

[11] See U.N. Doc. A/5007 (Dec. 4, 1961).

found insufficient to ensure the continued financing of the campaign.[12] The Fourteenth World Health Assembly therefore decided to incorporate the costs of the program into the regular budget of WHO, beginning in 1962. Incorporation was to proceed by stages over a three-year period: $2 million was added to the effective working budget for 1962; $4 million was included in the budget estimates for 1963; and by 1964, the full costs of the malaria eradication program are to be absorbed into the regular budget. To bring this about, the World Health Assembly adopted a reduction formula similar to that created by the United Nations General Assembly for peace-keeping operations. "As a transitional measure to preclude placing too heavy a burden on countries carrying out malaria programs," the following formula was to apply:

(1) all active Members carrying out malaria programs, (a) whose assessments are 0.50 percent or less, or (b) whose per capita income is low, shall be eligible for credits of 75 percent towards the payment of their share of the $2,000,000. . . .

(2) The Members eligible for credits shall be determined by the World Health Assembly. . . .

(3) The credits referred to herein shall be covered by the cash balance available in the Malaria Eradication Special Account. . . .[13]

The absorption of the costs of the malaria eradication program is especially interesting because it represents a case in which a special account was incorporated into a regular assessed budget without excessive difficulties.

Perhaps the most interesting feature of WHO is the fact that it is the only specialized agency that has persistently discussed and studied the problem of raising additional funds through original money-raising schemes. As early as 1949, the delegate from Belgium suggested that a World Health Defense Fund should be set up through an international loan from the World Bank, and guaranteed by all the member states.[14] President Eugene Black of the World Bank, how-

---

[12] An additional $4.8 million was required to finance the malaria eradication operation in 1961. "First Report of the Standing Committee on Administration and Finance," World Health Organization, Twenty-sixth Session, *Official Records*, No. 106, Executive Board (1960), p. 26.

[13] Res. WHA 14.15. In interpreting clause (b) of the resolution, the Assembly included those members of WHO which had requested credits and which were eligible for assistance from EPTA.

[14] World Health Organization, Second World Health Assembly, *Official Records*, No. 21 (1949), pp. 126-27.

ever, stated that the proposed loan would involve a substantial departure from the normal lending activites of the IBRD and would raise serious questions of interpretation of its Articles of Agreement. Moreover, he pointed out that, if states were able to give the guarantees required for a loan, they should be able to undertake corresponding commitments to increase WHO's annual budget:

> It is hard for me to see what real advantage WHO would gain from such an operation. In order to meet the requirements of our Charter, it would be necessary for those WHO members which are also members of the Bank to guarantee, jointly and severally, the payment of principal and interest on any loan that might be granted. If the countries are willing to assume this obligation, would they not be equally ready to undertake corresponding long-term commitments to meet WHO's annual budgets, thus obviating the necessity for a loan? And would not the latter arrangement be a more direct and more satisfactory solution of the problems?[15]

The scheme was rejected by the Third World Health Assembly in 1950. Instead, it suggested a new scheme: the issuance of special world health stamps or labels for purchase by the public on "a purely voluntary basis during such period or periods as the Members may consider convenient, the monies thus raised being divided between the World Health Organization and the country concerned on an agreed basis."[16]

In considering the question, the Executive Board felt that it would not be feasible for the organization itself to promote the sale of stamps because of the costs involved and possible conflicts with existing national campaigns. Instead, the Fourth World Health Assembly decided to issue special WHO seals on a voluntary basis. Each member state was to decide whether to offer these seals to its nationals and what their price was to be. The proceeds of the sale would be divided between WHO and the government concerned, the agency receiving

---

[15] Text of letter from the President of the International Bank for Reconstruction and Development to the Assistant Director-General, Department of Administration and Finance, WHO, in *Official Records,* Third World Health Assembly (1950), Annex 15, p. 558. In the discussion of the Assembly's Committee on Administration, Finance, and Legal Matters, only the delegate of the Netherlands spoke in favor of the Belgian scheme. The United Kingdom, Australia, and Canada strongly opposed the proposal. The United States delegate declared that "the Organization was receiving a certain support from Member Governments and he did not consider that it was opportune to ask them to do more." See *ibid.,* pp. 395-96.
[16] Res. WHA 3.97 in *ibid.,* p. 58.

25 percent and the government retaining 75 percent, "to be used for health programmes in its country for purposes in conformity with the principles set forth in the Constitution of the World Health Organization."[17] To finance the issue of the seals, a special revolving fund was set up and $5,000 transferred to it from the Assembly Suspense Account.[18] Later, proceeds from sales were to be applied to this fund. Each year the World Health Assembly was to receive a report from the Director-General on the operations of the fund and decide "what part of the fund, if any, shall be used to supplement the regular budget of the Organization."[19]

In 1951, the Director-General dispatched a letter to member states soliciting their agreement to the sale of WHO seals. However, only eleven governments responded favorably. In view of this unenthusiastic response and because of protests made by nongovernmental organizations that were dependent on similar projects for their revenue, the agency's Executive Board asked the Fifth World Health Assembly to reconsider the question as a whole. During the general debate, the delegates from the United States and Canada expressed serious doubts about the wisdom of WHO's competing for funds with "voluntary organizations" that depended for their livelihood on similar campaigns. The Health Assembly decided, however, that it was in fact impossible to raise funds without recourse to a method that had been used previously. While the sale of WHO seals in certain countries might indeed affect the income of some private groups, this in itself was not sufficient ground for abandoning the project. Hence, despite strong misgivings, the World Health Assembly approved the continued supply of the seals to member states on request. But the response continued to be meager. In 1952, requests were received only from Afghanistan, Cambodia, India, Indonesia, Israel, Korea, Laos, Panama, Thailand, Vietnam, and Yugoslavia, and in 1953 only seven countries participated. At the end of 1953, after providing for the cost

[17] World Health Organization, Fourth World Health Assembly, *Official Records,* No. 35 (1951), Sixth Meeting of the Committee on Administration, Finance and Legal Matters, p. 244.

[18] The Assembly Suspense Account is made up of budget surpluses and consists of a non-cash portion representing unpaid contributions due from members (including inactive members), as well as a cash portion from any unused balance of contributions. The World Health Assembly decides on the ultimate use of these sums. From time to time they have been applied for the purpose of financing part of the regular budget.

[19] *Official Records,* No. 35, p. 244.

of printing the 1954 seals, there remained only a balance of $5,200. In 1955, the World Health Assembly discontinued the scheme.

In 1961, in order to supplement its income for the malaria eradication program, WHO initiated yet another scheme—the issue of malaria eradication stamps. Governments were invited to issue the stamps on April 7, 1962—World Health Day—and to make contributions to WHO in one of three ways: to donate a quantity of the stamps to the organization for philatelic sale; to pay WHO a portion of the proceeds from national sales of the stamps; or to apply the stamp revenue toward national malaria eradication programs.

Almost the entire membership of WHO participated in the plan. Income for 1962 from donated stamps and governmental payments from national sales amounted to approximately $1 million. In addition, at least an equal amount of money was applied by governments toward their national programs. On the whole, the malaria eradication stamp scheme was a modest success and has set a meaningful precedent.

In summary, the financial structure of WHO has several interesting features. First, WHO has the largest budget of all the specialized agencies. Second, the fact that several countries had "inactive" status for a number of years resulted in large arrears and forced the organization to fix two annual budgets. Third, WHO has constantly sought to enhance its income. It established a number of "voluntary" funds and pioneered in the incorporation of a special account into the regular budget. Finally, WHO has shown considerable originality and persistence in its attempts to tap new sources of income.

The Food and Agriculture Organization

As is true of the other "development" agencies, FAO's financial resources must be viewed in relation to needs, and needs are virtually unlimited—certainly not definable in precise amounts. The funds required for agriculture in the developing countries can only be defined in the light of answers to two questions: how far and how fast? Until 1953, FAO's annual budget was $5 million. During the years following, it steadily increased and amounted to $30 million for the biennum 1961-62. This budget can hardly meet the ever-rising demand even though, as FAO declared in a report to the Economic and Social Council, the responsibility for the development of agriculture rests on the member governments themselves; FAO's role is primarily one of providing information, expert assistance, and guidance.[20] While FAO can hardly hope to meet the agricultural needs of the developing part of the world, it has not faced grave financial problems within the present scope of its activities.

The FAO scale of contributions basically follows the United Nations pattern, although the membership differs somewhat since the Soviet Union is not a member of the FAO and Czechoslovakia, Hungary, and China (Taiwan) have withdrawn from the organization. The arrearage problems of the FAO are similar to those confronted by WHO.

FAO is the largest single beneficiary of EPTA. Its annual allocation is determined to some extent, of course, by voluntary contributions to EPTA. In this area, some larger financial difficulties have emerged. As indicated in the preceding chapter, the operating problems involved in voluntary financing are considerable. In 1954, for example, Burma's rinderpest livestock disease control project had to be planned for three years to be effective, but it was impossible to promise employment to the necessary technicians for as long as two years. The FAO, like EPTA, is confronted by problems of planning in the face of a good deal of financial uncertainty.

The FAO also engages in a number of special programs that are supported by voluntary contributions in cash or in kind. Noteworthy among these is a Desert Locust Project, which in 1962 was supported by $2.5 million from the Special Fund, $1.3 million in voluntary cash contributions from twenty-eight governments, and considerable quantities of goods and services contributed by governments.

The World Food Programme should also be mentioned in this connection. Under joint administration by the FAO and the United Nations, it hopes to accumulate $100 million worth of surplus foods in voluntary contributions for use in promoting development in low-income countries. By the end of July 1963, fifty-three countries had pledged $89.9 million in commodities, services, and cash, although cash pledges were small and commodities received were not always those most needed. On the whole, however, the outlook for the World Food Programme seems good.

The FAO, like WHO, has experimented with a stamp scheme. In

[20] U.N. Food and Agriculture Organization, *Forward Appraisal of FAO Programs, 1959-64* (Rome, 1959), p. 8.

1962, the organization invited member governments to issue "Freedom from Hunger" stamps on March 21, 1963. Again, governments were asked to donate stamps to the FAO or to make the proceeds of sales available for the "Freedom from Hunger" campaign. Moreover, it was hoped that additional revenue would be obtained from large philatelic sales. Total income is estimated to be comparable to the WHO malaria eradication stamp scheme, that is, about $1 million.

The FAO's income, then, depends on assessments and voluntary contributions. As EPTA's largest beneficiary, the FAO is more dependent than most other "development" agencies on voluntary contributions. Like WHO, but not with the same persistence, the FAO has experimented with special voluntary programs and novel methods of increasing its income in order to keep pace with rising needs and expectations.

The United Nations Educational, Scientific and Cultural Organization

UNESCO's regular budget, like that of most of the other specialized agencies, has risen steadily over the years. From a level of $8.2 million a year in 1950, appropriations have risen to $39.9 million for the biennium 1963-64, an increase of more than 100 percent in a little over a decade. Two factors are worth noting about the size of the UNESCO budget: the penury of most member states until 1954, which forced one Director-General to resign; and the unusual largesse of the General Conference in the late 1950's, which prompted it at times to appropriate sums larger than those requested by the Director-General.

The early years of UNESCO's life were marked by continuous battles over budget ceilings. Two major powers—the United States and the United Kingdom—led the opposition against the budget increases urged by Dr. Torres Bodet, the Director-General, who resigned in 1954. Besides the usual motive of economy, this negative attitude had its roots in political considerations. In the United States, UNESCO had come under attack from a number of groups, including the American Legion, which claimed that many Americans connected with UNESCO had records of affiliation with subversive or Communist-front organizations, and that UNESCO had attempted to infiltrate the American school system and promote world government. While these and other charges were found to be unsubstantiated by a subcommittee of the House Committee on Foreign Affairs,[21] they may have contributed to the caution displayed by the United States toward increases in the UNESCO budget.

In addition to pursuing a policy of extreme economy, a number of governments failed to meet their obligations during the early years. China found it impossible to meet its assessments; the Soviet Union boycotted UNESCO for nine years; and Poland, Czechoslovakia, and Hungary were in considerable arrears. Pressures on these states to pay up were unsuccessful at the time. Sanctions were discussed extensively but not applied in practice.

The realization that contributions from the "inactive" members could not be counted on, led to the establishment of a dual budget in 1951—an "assessment level" budget and a "spending level" budget, as employed by the World Health Organization.

In 1954, however, the situation suddenly improved. When the new Director-General, Luther Evans, asked for considerable budget increases, his recommendations were accepted. Two years later, the General Conference of UNESCO acted with even greater largesse: responding to an urgent appeal for help from the developing countries and overriding United States, Soviet, and British objections, the conference—led by the Asian and Latin American countries—voted $1 million more for the 1957-58 budget than had been requested by the Director-General and the Executive Board.

There are several reasons for this about-face. First, the newly admitted nations, realizing the growing need for education, pressed for program expansion and larger appropriations. Second, the return of the Soviet bloc countries to UNESCO not only brought new contributions but stimulated lively competition between the two major powers for leadership in the fields of educational, scientific, and cultural endeavor. This competition expressed itself in more generous contributions to UNESCO's budget. Moreover, the role of UNESCO had changed by the mid-1950's from the classic type of intellectual cooperation into one that emphasized direct services to member states, especially those in the earlier stages of economic development.

At present, over one hundred states share the regular budget. Expenses are apportioned according to the United Nations scale of as-

[21] *The United Nations Specialized Agencies,* Report of the Subcommittee on International Organizations and Movements of the Committee on Foreign Affairs, July 1, 1957, especially pp. 6-7.

sessment, suitably adjusted to take into consideration the difference in membership of the organizations and the following special features: (a) states that are members of UNESCO but not members of the United Nations; (b) states that are members of the United Nations but not members of UNESCO; (c) the principle that no one member state should in normal times contribute more than one-third of the budgetary appropriations of UNESCO; (d) special percentages granted to certain member states: for example, no nation is to pay a higher per capita contribution than the nation paying the highest contribution.

In 1962, the United States paid 31.4 percent of the assessed budget. The other major contributors were the Soviet Union (13.18 percent), the United Kingdom (7.53 percent), France (6.19 percent), and West Germany (5.16 percent). The floor of the scale is identical to that of the United Nations: 0.04 percent.

The problem of arrears on the regular budget is far less serious than it was in the early years. The government of China, which at one point was more than $5 million in arrears, negotiated a special arrangement with UNESCO whereby some of its arrears were canceled as "beyond its control" and the remainder was to be paid in annual installments over a period of fifty years. At the same time, the contribution of China was reduced by almost 50 percent.

In the case of the "inactive" states from the Soviet bloc, another special arrangement was made when they decided to re-enter the organization in the mid-1950's: payment of a small percentage of their arrears was to be made over periods ranging from nine to twelve years.[22] On the whole, the condition of the UNESCO regular budget has been steadily improving during the past decade.

In addition to its income from assessments, UNESCO receives allocations from EPTA and the Special Fund. For the biennium 1963-64, these are estimated at $15 million and $34.4 million respectively, both of which are substantial increases over the funds allocated previously. Also, in order to meet special needs of member states, UNESCO in 1959 had set up a special account to be supported by voluntary contributions. In this respect, contributions of $700,000 in 1959-60 and $155,000 in 1961-62 in support of a program of International Action

---

[22] U.N. Educational, Scientific and Cultural Organization, Eighth Session, *Official Records,* Proceedings of the Administrative Commission (Montevideo, 1954), Vol. I, p. 567.

to Safeguard Archaeological Monuments of Nubia in Egypt, were encouraging.

The total financial picture presented by UNESCO is one of gradually rising resources. The early years were characterized by an attitude of economy. Since 1954, however, the politics of great power competition and the needs of the developing countries have militated in favor of steadily increasing funds from both assessed and voluntary contributions. While these resources have by no means kept pace with needs and expectations, they have nevertheless increased in greater proportion than those of many of the other specialized agencies.

The International Atomic Energy Agency

The International Atomic Energy Agency, an autonomous member of the United Nations system, was set up in 1957 to "consecrate the atom to man's life rather than dedicating it to his death." Since then, the agency—which is concerned solely with the peaceful uses of atomic energy—has been serving as a transmitter of atomic energy "know-how" to educational institutions, laboratories, hospitals, and agricultural stations in the developing areas of the world, by means of fellowships, experiments, research contracts, conferences, publications, and the setting up of nuclear reactors.

Under the statute of the IAEA, administrative expenses, such as staff salaries, costs of meetings, and expenditures required for the preparation of agency projects, are assessed on member states on roughly the same basis as contributions to the United Nations regular budget. The IAEA budget for 1962 was $6.3 million. The Director-General prepares the estimates, which must pass the careful scrutiny of the Board of Governors. The board, in turn, submits them to the General Conference for approval by two-thirds majority. The conference may not change these estimates without referral once more to the Board of Governors.

The IAEA statute contains an article on sanctions, with a proviso similar to that found in the ILO constitution. A member state in arrears for two or more years will "have no vote in the agency." Only one nation, the Republic of Paraguay, has lost its voting privileges. Otherwise, arrears have not posed a serious problem.

What differentiates the agency's finances from those of other organizations within the United Nations system is that expenses incurred in connection with particular technical assistance projects and the supply of atomic energy materials are not to be met by assessment. The supplying of materials, the statute declares, is to be conducted on a business basis. Those countries that furnish materials to the IAEA are to be reimbursed by the agency, while the recipient states, in turn, make payments to the IAEA for the materials supplied. Such transactions are designed to produce revenue for the agency that is to be applied to the costs of technical assistance projects.[23]

At the statute conference, considerable discussion took place in regard to the supply of materials. Many states viewed the charges to be imposed on project agreements between the agency and recipient states as an important source of income. However, the developing nations argued that materials supplied by the agency would have to be furnished at less than cost and that an agency subsidy would be necessary so that the cost to recipient states could include surcharges for safeguards and handling and yet compete effectively with bilateral programs. Opponents of this view pointed out that a subsidy policy would induce an artificial lowering of the world price of source materials.[24]

No consensus was reached on this issue and the statute was left flexible enough to permit the furnishing of materials at any price:

> The Board of Governors shall establish periodically a scale of charges, including reasonable uniform storage and handling charges, for materials, services, equipment, and facilities furnished to members of the Agency. The scale shall be designed to produce revenue for the Agency adequate to meet the expenses and costs . . . (of any materials, facilities, plant, and equipment acquired or established or provided by the Agency), less any voluntary contributions which the Board of Governors may . . . apply for this purpose.[25]

In practice, since the agency has engaged in only a few transactions involving the supply of source materials, the above provisions have hardly been implemented. Indeed, technical assistance and other operational activities have had to depend for their sustenance on an "operational budget" consisting exclusively of voluntary contributions. The response to requests for funds for this purpose has been disappointing. The Board of Governors stated in 1962 that, unless

[23] See International Organization and Conference Series, *The International Atomic Energy Agency*, U.S. Department of State Publication 6696 (August 1958), pp. 13-14.
[24] See John G. Stoessinger, "Atoms for Peace: The International Atomic Energy Agency" in *Organizing Peace in the Nuclear Age*, Report of the Commission to Study the Organization of Peace (New York University Press, 1959), p. 151.
[25] Art. XIV of the statute.

contributions increased, the successful fulfillment of the agency's statutory responsibilities would be seriously jeopardized. In 1959 and 1960, pledges of voluntary contributions represented 78.9 percent and 66.4 percent, respectively, of the target figure of $1.5 million decided on by the General Conference for each of these years. For 1961, this figure was increased to $1.8 million, of which 70 percent was pledged. A similar amount was contributed in 1962. Of the thirty countries contributing, the United States, the United Kingdom, and Canada have consistently made the largest pledges, with the Soviet Union contributing token amounts each year.

An interesting feature of IAEA is its borrowing power. The statute, in Article XIV, explicitly gives the Board of Governors authority to exercise borrowing powers on behalf of the organization "without, however, imposing on members of the organization any liability in respect of loans entered into pursuant to this authority." This right to borrow had been the subject of lively discussion during the statute negotiations. Borrowing for day-to-day operations had been rejected by all states, but the United States had favored the use of loans to finance the construction of agency facilities, such as storage buildings for fissionable materials. Repayment of these obligations would be made from donations and charges. The Soviet Union had opposed this view and taken the position that borrowing would encourage extravagance. So far, no use has been made by the agency of this authority.

In sum, the IAEA has had few difficulties with its regular assessed budget. Its major problem lies in the area of operational development. Since voluntary donations have been meager and the system of charges has hardly become operative, and there has been no occasion to exercise the borrowing power, the IAEA has been able to supply only a fraction of the funds required for the development of atomic energy. Hence, the problem of the solvency of the IAEA looms large if expansion of operational activities is to proceed at a reasonable rate. The crucial obstacle here is political: the bypassing of the agency by the United States and other donor nations in favor of bilateral agreements has relegated the IAEA to a secondary role in the development of the peaceful uses of atomic energy. An East-West agreement in September 1963 to extend the IAEA's safeguards system to large nuclear reactors may be the beginning of a reversal of this trend. If this is so, it is likely that the agency will command more substantial financial resources.

Communication Agencies

Some of the communication agencies antedate the United Nations, but all of them are now part of the United Nations system. Included in this group of specialized agencies are the Universal Postal Union (UPU), the International Telecommunication Union (ITU), the International Civil Aviation Organization (ICAO), the World Meteorological Organization (WMO), and the Intergovernmental Maritime Consultative Organization (IMCO). Each has unique financial features.

The Universal Postal Union and the International Telecommunication Union

The financial structures of the Universal Postal Union (UPU) and the International Telecommunication Union (ITU) have three distinctive features: the grouping of states into classes for the purpose of expense apportionment; the practice of charging interest on arrears; and supervision and advance of credits by the Swiss Postal Administration.

Both of these agencies antedated the League of Nations. Indeed, the early League assessments had been based on the UPU class system. Today, UPU members are grouped into seven classes of payment units subdivided into from twenty-one to one unit. Included in the first class are the United States, the United Kingdom, France, West Germany, Italy, Japan, the Soviet Union, Australia, Brazil, Canada, China, Spain, India, New Zealand, Pakistan, the Union of South Africa, and Argentina. Among those in the lowest class are Saudi Arabia, Cambodia, Iraq, Iceland, Somalia, Jordan, Laos, Lebanon, Liberia, Libya, Monaco, the Philippines, San Marino, Sudan, Syria, the Vatican, and Yemen. When a new member is admitted to the Union, the government of the Swiss Confederation determines, in agreement with the government of the country concerned, the class 'in which it is to be placed.

The ITU arranges its members into classes ranging from thirty units to one-half unit. The United States, the United Kingdom, and the Soviet Union are in the top class while nineteen small nations are assigned to the lowest.

Both the UPU and the ITU charge 3 percent interest on arrears during the first six months after the date on which contributions are due and 6 percent thereafter. These charges usually net each of them somewhat over 100,000 Swiss francs a year. The financial relations with the host government have been very smooth in both cases.

Turning to actual expenditures, the UPU appropriated 4.3 million Swiss francs for 1962, an amount that was well within the budget ceiling authorized by the UPU Congress. Financing the UPU has presented no difficulty since the concrete services rendered by it have been well worth the modest expenses involved.

In 1962 the ITU budget was fixed at $3.2 million. This, for the first time, was a consolidated budget. Previously, the ITU's budget had been divided into "ordinary" and "extraordinary" expenses, each financed in a different way. The "ordinary" budget had covered the normal expenses of the secretariats of the permanent organs and of the General Secretariat, while the "extraordinary" budget had covered the expenditures of the meetings of the various bodies of the ITU. The former had been assessed on all members and associate members, but the latter expenses had been met only by the participants involved (including governments, international organizations, and private operating agencies). Now, all members and associate members contribute to the consolidated budget. Until 1962, the ITU had been the only organization in the United Nations system in which private companies had been assigned a portion of costs.

Unlike the UPU, the ITU is faced with an acute financial problem. Outer space communications and related matters require urgent attention, but the ITU lacks sufficient credits for their support. This is due to the fact that a budgetary ceiling was established for five years by the 1960 Plenipotentiary Conference. This ceiling can be changed only under exceptional circumstances with the agreement of member states to be secured by referendum. The next conference is not scheduled until 1965. Aside from this problem, the finances of the UPU and ITU have been stable and almost completely unaffected by controversy.

The International Civil Aviation Organization

The financial pattern of the International Civil Aviation Organization differs in a number of respects from arrangements of other specialized agencies.[26] First, while "capacity to pay" is still the major criterion for apportioning the organization's expenses, this formula carries only 75 percent of the total. The factor responsible for the remaining 25 percent is the "interest and importance of civil aviation."[27] Second, member states are asked to *consent* to the place allocated to them in the scale. Third, ICAO prepares its budget only every three years.

> This policy was considered desirable as States are more likely to meet their contributions promptly if they are satisfied that their place in the scale is such as to compare favourably with the position of other states of like status and that their position in the ICAO scale is comparable to that in the scale of other international organizations.[28]

At its twelfth session in 1959, the ICAO Assembly approved budgets in the following gross amounts in Canadian currency: $4.7 million for 1960, $4.9 million for 1961, and $4.9 million for 1962. Of this, 32.95 percent was paid by the United States whose assessed percentage contribution to ICAO in 1960 was higher than that made to any other organization within the United Nations system. By 1963, the United States contribution had been reduced to 31.8 percent. No Soviet bloc country is a member of ICAO.

Arrears have been somewhat of a problem despite the "consent" clause in the scale of contributions. Foreseeing this possibility, the convention had provided that the assembly might, in case of arrears, suspend a nation's voting power in both the assembly and in the council. Use of this power was made on several occasions: in 1948, for instance, the voting powers of Bolivia, El Salvador, Nicaragua, Paraguay, Poland, and Jordan were suspended.[29] In 1952, similar sanctions were employed against Bolivia, Czechoslovakia, El Salvador, Guatemala, Jordan, and Poland.[30] The states in question subsequently cleared their accounts. By 1962, arrears were not significant.

In addition to the distinctive features of its regular budget, ICAO

[26] The budgetary process is fairly typical. Financial arrangements are determined by the assembly and are administered by the council, whose agent in these matters is the Finance Committee. See Arts. 49(e), 54(f), and 61 of the convention.

[27] ICAO Doc. 7456, A8-P/2, 8/4/54, p. 62.

[28] Jacob Schenkman, *The International Civil Aviation Organization* (Geneva Librarie E. Droz, 1955), p. 192.

[29] ICAO Doc. 5692, Res. A2-1, p. 1.

[30] ICAO Doc. 7367, 7A-P/1, 31/3/53, Res. A6-2, p. 106.

is unique among the specialized agencies in the creation of joint support programs involving international financing. Under these programs, a number of ICAO members maintain radio and weather stations in the North Atlantic on a cost-sharing basis. The nations involved contribute services, facilities, or cash payments based principally on the criterion of direct benefit. For example, an eighteen-nation joint support agreement, coordinated by the ICAO, regulates the operation of nine floating ocean stations in the North Atlantic. They are supplied with ships by Canada, France, the Netherlands, Norway, Sweden, the United Kingdom, and the United States, while cash contributions are made by Australia, Belgium, Denmark, West Germany, Iceland, Ireland, Israel, Italy, Spain, Switzerland, the United States, and Venezuela, all of whose aircraft fly the North Atlantic. The ICAO budget and the joint support program have remained relatively stable over the years.

The World Meteorological Organization

Fiscal stability is also a feature of the World Meteorological Organization. Its budget is a modest $710,268 for 1962. The Third World Meteorological Congress in 1959 approved a maximum expenditure of $2.7 million for the third financial period of the agency, January 1, 1960 to December 31, 1963. Noteworthy in the financial picture of WMO is the fact that it operates on a four-year budgetary cycle. This system has been popular with member states since they have been able to calculate their future obligations. However, the long budgetary cycle has made it difficult to keep abreast of rapid developments in meteorology and the requirements of newly independent states.

The budget has increased very slowly. WMO relies heavily on national meteorological organizations. For the most part, the secretariat merely plays the role of coordinator and catalyst; the technical work is undertaken by commissions and working groups, each of which is comprised of experts nominated by national organizations. Thus, the services of competent experts in the world are made available to WMO at little or no expense to itself, since even travel expenses are often paid by member states. In 1961, the United Nations Advisory Committee on Administrative and Budgetary Questions commended this procedure.

This committee also lauded the fact that the publication of the meteorological data of the International Geophysical Year (IGY) and International Geographic Co-operation (IGC) is being carried out on a self-financing basis.[31] The committee, in fact, invited all United Nations organizations to consider the adoption of similar methods before embarking on any new large-scale publications program.

The Intergovernmental Maritime Consultative Organization

The youngest of the specialized agencies, the Intergovernmental Maritime Consultative Organization (IMCO), which came into being in 1959, has the smallest budget. At its second session in 1961, the IMCO Assembly authorized a maximum expenditure of $892,350 for the second financial period (1962-63), and appropriated $471,100 for 1962 and $421,250 for 1963. The 1962 budget represented a 63.3 percent increase over that for 1961.

While it is too early to evaluate the financial structure of IMCO, it is fairly safe to say that, so long as it shares the essentially nonpolitical character of the other "communication" agencies, its finances will increase gradually and will not encounter major difficulties.

Financial Agencies

The four agencies included in this group are: the International Monetary Fund, which promotes exchange stability through short-term loans for member nations in temporary balance-of-payments difficulties; the International Bank for Reconstruction and Development, which grants long-term loans to nations for the development of their resources; and the International Finance Corporation (IFC) and the International Development Association (IDA), which are affiliates of the International Bank.

The Fund and the Bank

The financial structures of the International Monetary Fund and the International Bank for Reconstruction and Development bear no resemblance to those of the other specialized agencies. These are in

---

[31] The revenue from sales of publications is credited to a publications fund for the purpose of increasing the publications program.

essence banking institutions and not dependent on annual assessments or voluntary contributions. Indeed, these agencies are self-financing and have consistently operated at a profit.

Membership is very broad. All nations outside the Soviet orbit except Switzerland are either members or are currently applying for membership. Although the Soviet Union participated in the Bretton Woods Conference, it never ratified either the IMF or the IBRD agreement. Czechoslovakia, Poland, and Yugoslavia were charter members of both organizations; but Poland withdrew in 1950, and Czechoslovakia was expelled in 1954. In recent years, no formal move has been made by any Communist country to seek membership.

The absence of the Soviet bloc countries has eliminated the kind of violent political controversy that characterizes the United Nations and some of the development agencies. The power of the major Western nations, especially the United States, is clearly controlling in both agencies. These countries are the heaviest financial contributors and have a preponderance of voting strength. Weighted voting, dependent on financial contributions, characterizes the agencies. The weighting of votes in the IMF and the IBRD is shown in Tables A.6 and A.7.

The financial structure of the IMF is geared to its major purpose: the promotion of exchange stability by providing short-term credits to alleviate temporary balance-of-payments disequilibria in member states. The IMF obtains its financial resources from subscriptions paid by its members. The subscriptions are determined by quotas assigned to each country which are calculated on the basis of a formula taking into account a country's national income, its holdings in gold and United States dollars, and its volume of imports and exports. These quotas determine voting strength and the amounts that may be drawn from the currency pool. The quotas are subject to review every five years and underwent an across-the-board rise in 1959. Quota changes must be approved by a four-fifths vote in the Board of Governors, and no country's quota may be changed without its consent. The total resources of the IMF now exceed $15 billion. This amount determines the limits of its lending power.

The fiscal structure of the IMF eliminates the problem of arrears. The Articles of Agreement, however, provide a number of sanctions for violations of obligations. These include the denial of credit facilities and suspension or expulsion from membership. Sanctions were applied only once—in the case of Czechoslovakia, which was expelled for refusing to submit information considered essential for the determination of its quota. It is unlikely that the IMF will have financial difficulties of the kind encountered by the United Nations.

The lending operations of the IMF generate revenue that more than covers administrative expenses. Members pay charges for their gold or currency purchases and, in addition, the IMF earns income by investing a part of its holdings. Total income from charges and investments in 1962 amounted to $33.1 million, which was more than four times the administrative budget. The surplus is placed in a reserve that enables the IMF to embark on various subsidiary activities such as the study of economic conditions or the launching of limited training programs in member countries.

Turning to the problem of the relevance of the International Monetary Fund to United Nations finances, it should be obvious from the above that the IMF is, for all practical purposes, a separate body. It may be, however, that it could provide some limited indirect assistance to the United Nations.

The IMF's short-term loans to some of its members that have balance-of-payments difficulties may make it possible for those members, among other things, to pay their arrears to the United Nations regular budget and the specialized agencies. Such loans may be extended as transitional measures while developing nations adopt sounder monetary policies or adjust their balance-of-payments difficulties. Any direct IMF loans to the United Nations or a specialized agency are precluded by the Articles of Agreement of the IMF.

The IBRD is as autonomous an organization as the IMF with again only indirect relevance to United Nations financing. Whereas the IMF deals with balance-of-payments difficulties by extending short-term credits, the IBRD is charged with long-term investment, primarily for developmental purposes. Initially, the IBRD concentrated on the reconstruction of war-devastated areas, but since the late 1940's its attention has shifted to the developing nations of the world.

The IBRD views itself essentially as a bank. Loan applications are considered in terms of their financial soundness and the borrower's ability to repay both principal and interest. Interest rates have varied between 4 and 6 ¼ percent.

Like the IMF, the IBRD is completely self-financing. Its initial capital stock was set at $10 billion. Shares were allotted to members based on criteria similar to those determining the quotas for the IMF. In 1959, the capital stock of the IBRD was increased substantially and several members, for example Canada, West Germany, and Japan, more than doubled their subscriptions. By 1962, the subscribed capital of the IBRD exceeded $21 billion.

The IBRD has consistently accumulated reserves. With the exception of its first year of operations, earnings have always exceeded expenses. For the fiscal year ending June 30, 1962, its total expenditures came to $118 million, whereas gross income was over $218 million.[32] In the same fiscal year, administrative expenses amounted to $12.7 million, of which $1.9 million was spent for project studies, missions, and training programs.[33] Obviously all administrative and technical expenses can be met easily by current earnings.

Earnings over and above expenses are placed in either a Special Reserve or a Supplemental Reserve. By the end of 1962, these funds had accumulated to $700 million. As in the IMF, the question of sanctions against delinquents is largely irrelevant. Once initial subscriptions are paid, the IBRD is financially independent. States may be suspended from membership by the Board of Governors in case of failure to fulfill any obligations to the IBRD. But there has never been a default in repayment of principal and only minor adjustments in interest payments. Indeed, the problem of the IBRD is not one of arrears or defaults, but one of surplus. Reserves have continuously been on the rise, and while no formal proposals have been made to reduce interest rates or to pay dividends, such suggestions are made occasionally by debtor governments.

Like the IMF, the IBRD has been engaging in a number of technical assistance projects. Originally, these projects had been limited to technical advice in the planning of investment, but were gradually expanded to include a wide range of surveys and studies, an Economic Development Institute for training purposes (partly supported for the first few years by the Ford and Rockefeller Foundations), and a Development Advisory Service. The latter is composed of experts who serve as advisors to developing countries. The IBRD also, on request, sends survey missions to analyze economic conditions in the develop-

[32] See International Bank for Reconstruction and Development, Comparative Statement of Income and Expenses, *Seventeenth Annual Report, 1961-62*, Appendix B.
[33] International Bank for Reconstruction and Development, Administrative Budget; *ibid.*

ing countries. Costs of such missions are shared by the IBRD and the requesting government. All in all, the various technical assistance activities of the Bank have been expanding. As noted above, services to member countries cost the Bank approximately $1.9 million in 1961-62, and were scheduled to rise sharply in the ensuing fiscal year.

The International Finance Corporation and the International Development Association

These agencies are affiliated with the IBRD and are governed by weighted voting. The IFC, which came into existence in 1956, and is smaller in membership than the IBRD or the IDA, promotes economic development through investment in association with private capital and management, without governmental guarantee, in the developing areas. The IDA, which joined the United Nations system in 1960, makes loans to developing countries on terms that are more lenient than those of the IBRD, so that it can assist countries unable to service additional debts on IBRD terms. The IDA underwrites projects that IBRD would reject. Thus, it has extended loans for municipal water supply projects, the developing of harbors, and technical training. To date, all IDA credits have been interest-free except for an annual service charge of $3/4$ of 1 percent, and have been repayable over a fifty-year period with a ten-year period of grace.

Of the four financial institutions considered so far, the IDA possesses the greatest flexibility. Except for a provision specifying that its resources must be used to aid the economies of the developing areas, no restrictions are imposed on the terms of its loans, or on eligibility for the use of its funds. In fact, Article V, Section 2 (c) states:

> The Association may provide financing to a member, the government of a territory included within the Association's membership, a political subdivision of any of the foregoing, a public or private entity in the territories of a member or members, or to a public international or regional organization.

The IDA's most serious limitation is its modest capital subscription of $1 billion.

Some comments should be made about the relevance of the IBRD and the IDA for the finances of the United Nations. Periodically, casual proposals are made to the effect that profits of the IBRD be used to meet the financial difficulties of the United Nations. As these difficulties have become more acute, demands that the IBRD come to the assistance of the United Nations have been voiced in the legislative bodies of a number of states. There have been no formal proposals, however, toward this end by either the United Nations or the IBRD.

Actually, within the framework of the Articles of Agreement of the IBRD, loans to the United Nations or to any specialized agency are precluded. The articles authorize loans to members or to private enterprises provided these have a governmental guarantee. Moreover, loans to the United Nations Working Capital Fund or to the regular budget or loans for peace and security operations are not in line with the purposes for which the IBRD is authorized to use its resources, namely, economic development. Hence, the prospects for IBRD loans to the United Nations are unfavorable for two reasons: the United Nations is not an appropriate borrower, and most of its activities do not fulfill the requirements for IBRD credit.

Although it is improbable that IBRD loan funds can be made available to the United Nations, the use of the Bank's surplus to supplement certain United Nations activities is not precluded. While it would be argued that the surplus is intended for lending and the backing of guarantees, it might be possible for the IBRD to earmark a percentage of its annual profits for assistance to United Nations activities that are in line with the objectives of the Bank. The recent expansion of the activities of the IBRD in the technical assistance realm might be a first step in that direction.

The obvious United Nations programs that might qualify for such assistance are the Expanded Programme of Technical Assistance and the Special Fund. These two voluntary operations are consistent with the economic objectives of the IBRD, and are not politically controversial. Moreover, as indicated in Chapter 8, the uncertainty of voluntary contributions makes effective long-range project planning extremely difficult. IBRD assistance would inject a higher degree of predictability into such planning.

The Articles of Agreement of IDA, as we have seen, are more permissive than those of the Bank and do not foreclose loans to the United Nations or the specialized agencies. IDA shares the goal of economic development with the IBRD and hence IDA credit, like IBRD loans, would probably also have to be earmarked for the economic and social activities of the United Nations. IDA has very limited resources, however, and these are committed to the needs of the developing countries.

A variation of the above proposal would be to make a part of the Bank's surplus available to IDA. IDA might use the IBRD surplus funds either to extend its own operations in economic development, or to lend the money to the United Nations development programs or the specialized agencies for the furtherance of their own operations.

The above suggestions, while permissible under the charters of the IBRD and the IDA and logical in the context of the Development Decade, would presume a major policy change in the governing organs of these two institutions. Whether such a change is politically feasible is problematical.

Conclusions

A survey of the financial picture of the "development" and "communication" agencies indicates that their fiscal experiences have been similar in broad outline, but disparate in detail. While expenditures in 1962 ranged from about $24 million for WHO to $400,000 for IMCO, all the budgets have risen during the past few years. This is illustrated in Table A.8. The rise has been accomplished in the face of considerable resistance from member states, especially in those agencies which, like the ILO and UNESCO, have been permeated with political controversy. The expansion has encountered little resistance in the "communication" agencies. This overall upward trend is likely to continue.

The assessment pattern in most agencies follows that of the United Nations regular budget rather closely, as may be seen in Table A.9. There are deviations, however. The UPU and the ITU prefer a class system and ICAO employs special criteria to compute its assessment formula. Further differences are evident in the budget cycles: WHO and the ITU prepare annual estimates, the FAO and IMCO use biennial cycles, and ICAO and WMO employ three and four-year cycles, respectively.

The United States has the highest assessments in all the agencies, although its percentage contribution has been gradually decreasing over the years. The range in 1962 extended from 32.95 percent in ICAO to 4.21 percent in the UPU.

Arrears have been a problem in most of the agencies, and all provide penalties in their charters for delinquent states. Actual arrearage patterns have been similar throughout, although each agency has dealt with its difficulties in its own way. WHO and UNESCO made special arrangements to deal with the arrears of "inactive" members. The UPU and the ITU have charged interest on delayed payments. The FAO and ICAO suspended the voting privileges of delinquent states in their deliberative bodies. The ILO deprived such states of their votes in all of the organization's organs. In most cases, these sanctions have worked relatively well. The IBRD and the IMF expelled Czechoslovakia from membership.

Most of the agencies receive allocations from EPTA and some from the Special Fund. While these allocations have increased overall revenue, they have also resulted in "budget squeezes" in most of the development agencies, notably the FAO and UNESCO, as a result of unreimbursed administrative costs incurred in carrying out EPTA and Special Fund work. Several agencies have also set up special accounts supported by voluntary contributions, and WHO and the FAO have pioneered in the creation of special stamp schemes in order to raise additional revenue.

The multiplicity of fiscal patterns in the specialized agencies has given rise to repeated demands for more effective coordination or consolidation. The arguments used on both sides recall those made in connection with the special voluntary programs. Critics point out that the present mosaic of independent organizations, each with its own budget and fiscal system, is extremely complex and confusing. It gives rise to duplication of effort. Only effective budget coordination would produce effective programing and project coordination. The present system encourages competition among the specialized agencies for larger portions of funds and results in a number of special accounts to which voluntary contributions are invited, raising the question whether numerous appeals for such donations do not result in dissipation and even a decline of the total voluntary effort. Above all, the critics claim, the present arrangement does not permit efficient central planning.

However, the arguments on the other side are even weightier. As early as 1951, a committee of the United States Senate which studied the problem warned that:

> . . . Effective coordination can be achieved only if some measure of real control over the budgets and programs of the specialized agencies is given to the General Assembly. This, in turn, can be

accomplished only by amendment of the constitutions of the specialized agencies, designed either to afford to the General Assembly effective control over programs and projects of the agencies, or to provide for the inclusion of the budgets of the agencies within a consolidated budget of the United Nations, to be approved by the General Assembly.[34]

The possibility of establishing a consolidated budget has been discussed several times by the General Assembly. The recommendations were negative every time. It was decided that consolidation would necessitate not only constitutional amendments, changes in the character of delegates to the Assembly to allow for the inclusion of specialists competent to evaluate agency programs, and the lengthening of Assembly sessions, but also the devising of a solution for the difficulty of divergent membership in the agencies. Moreover, the agencies have a tradition of autonomy; program identity might be lost in the shuffle; and the objections of "client ministries" in the agencies would be almost insuperable. On balance, the virtues of consolidation have probably been exaggerated.

The IMF and the IBRD are relevant to United Nations financing largely in their ability to provide financial assistance to their own members and to supplement certain United Nations development programs. The possibility of direct IBRD contributions from its surplus to EPTA and the Special Fund is remote. The IDA Articles of Agreement are more permissive than those of the Bank, and do not foreclose loans to the United Nations or the specialized agencies, but the capital available to the IDA is urgently needed for projects in low-income countries.

[34] *United States Relations with International Organizations,* Report of the Committee on Expenditures in the Executive Departments, S. Rep. 90, 82 Cong. 1 sess., p. 57.

PART III

The Search for Revenue

CHAPTER 10

Private Support of the United Nations

THE UNITED NATIONS CHARTER opens with the significant words: "We the peoples of the United Nations." A quarter of a century earlier, the framers of the Covenant of the League of Nations had seen themselves as "High Contracting Parties." This difference symbolized a significant evolutionary trend that had taken place during the interwar period: international organizations were still in essence the creatures of states, supported and controlled by them, but private citizens, through nongovernmental organizations, had become more important. The "High Contracting Parties" of the League had not had much patience with nongovernmental representatives at Geneva. "Open covenants openly arrived at" was meant to apply to diplomatic intercourse among statesmen rather than to the general public. This picture has changed somewhat at the United Nations. A broad cross-section of nongovernmental organizations is closely involved in the deliberative processes of the world organization. A considerable number of different ethnic and church groups, citizens groups, and other interested parties enjoy consultative status in United Nations organs and make their influence felt on the delegations at all stages of the policy-making process. While it is true that governments still dispose, it is equally true that nongovernmental organizations frequently propose. Hence, it is appropriate that, in the search for new sources of revenue, the role of private support in the overall picture be analyzed first.

The Role of Private Support

Private contributions have played a part in the financial picture of the United Nations since the first year of its existence. The question has never been whether private support should play a part, but how its possibilities and limits in an organization of nation states should be defined.

There are various ways of looking at private contributions to the United Nations. They may be seen as a supplement to government payments to increase the overall revenues of the Organization. They may be viewed as a means of providing a floor under the regular budget, thus reducing the financial burden on some of the poorer countries. They may pay for certain special programs or projects, particularly those of a humanitarian, cultural, or social nature. From the contributors' point of view, they may be regarded as a means of satisfying the desire of individuals and groups to "do something" tangible for the United Nations.

Actual contributions from private sources have fallen rather neatly into these categories. Some, like donations to World Refugee Year or the United Nations Children's Fund, have provided amounts over and above those contributed by governments. Purchases of gifts and stamps at United Nations headquarters have added to the Organization's miscellaneous income and helped to reduce regular budget assessments. Gifts by foundations and individuals have made possible the purchase of basic facilities that would have had to be financed by governments. And many contributions, large and small, have been motivated by the general desire to assist "a good cause." Whatever the motives that lie behind private contributions to the United Nations, they all beg the basic question: What is the appropriate place of such support in the world organization?

The United Nations is in essence an institution created by and for the use of states. It is the responsibility of the member governments to ensure that the amounts required to support it are in fact available. Article 17, paragraph 2, of the Charter is quite explicit about this: "The expenses of the Organization shall be borne by the Members as apportioned by the General Assembly." This does not say, however, that private, nongovernmental contributions may not be received. It does say that it is up to the member states to pay the expenses of the Organization. Beyond that, the field is open.

It seems in keeping with the purposes and principles of the Charter that the United Nations receive and even encourage private contributions to give "the people of the world" a stronger stake in the continued growth of the Organization. Such contributions should never have the effect of promoting fiscal irresponsibility by allowing member states to vote for given programs without having to follow through financially. But this danger seems remote indeed. Private support has played a modest role in the overall United Nations financial picture and is not likely to surge upward sharply in the foreseeable future. The major burden will continue to be borne by governments. Broadly speaking, most of the private support has been contributed to supplement humanitarian programs or to enable the United Nations to establish essential physical facilities. Private gifts in these areas merit detailed consideration.

The Extent and Place of Private Support

Although the main beneficiaries of private donations have been refugees and children, there have been significant contributions to the United Nations for land and buildings, and others for specific or undesignated purposes.

Refugee Programs

Since its establishment in 1951 the Office of the United Nations High Commissioner for Refugees has made a series of appeals for assistance to resolve the most pressing refugee problems. These have comprised in particular a United Nations Refugee Emergency Fund, 1952-54; a four-year United Nations Refugee Fund (UNREF), 1955-58, to promote permanent solutions for refugees in camps; and a Special Fund for Refugees from Hungary, 1956-60.

For the two-year Refugee Emergency Fund in 1952-54, $159,227 was received by the High Commissioner's Office from private sources. During the four-year period of UNREF, private receipts mounted to more than $2.1 million. For the Special Fund for Hungarian Refugees, $726,551 was contributed by private donors.

G. J. van Heuven Goedhart, the first United Nations High Commissioner for Refugees, was particularly successful in eliciting several large grants from American foundations. The Rockefeller Foundation made a grant of $100,000 in 1951 to underwrite a comprehensive survey of the refugee situation. The following year, as noted in Chapter 8, the Ford Foundation made a grant of $2.9 million for a "pilot program" to see what could be done to achieve local integration. A supplemental grant of $200,000 was made by the Ford Foundation in 1954. In the same year the Nobel Peace Prize was awarded to the High Commissioner's Office for its achievements, thereby adding another $35,000 to its resources. With the help of these funds the High Commissioner was able to aid over 37,000 refugees, of whom 11,280 were permanently settled. As a result, there was an atmosphere of hope in refugee camps throughout Europe. In the words of James M. Read, former Deputy High Commissioner, "The intervention of private organizations in the discharge of what was essentially a governmental responsibility threw a bright spotlight on the refugee problem and made it impossible for governments to belittle it."[1]

The most successful device for eliciting private support on behalf of refugees was the inauguration of World Refugee Year (WRY) in 1959. This plan, first advanced by four young Englishmen after the example of the International Geophysical Year,[2] aimed at stimulating sufficient public concern about the refugee problem to enable the United Nations agencies to clear a large number of camps.

According to the 1961 Report of the High Commissioner to the General Assembly, more individuals "participated personally in WRY than in any other initiative taken by the United Nations since its foundation." The result of this was that the $9 million contributed to the United Nations High Commissioner's Office from private sources in 1960 exceeded government contributions by one-third. Substantial amounts were raised by unions, employer groups, citizens' associations, and individuals in ten countries. The following table gives the approximate amounts of the WRY contributions from private sources in these ten countries.[3]

United Kingdom	$3,300,000	Sweden	$ 360,000
United States	2,200,000	The Netherlands	300,000
West Germany	590,000	Australia	270,000
Canada	400,000	Switzerland	240,000
Norway	360,000	Denmark	220,000

While the High Commissioner's Office received WRY contributions from thirty-six other countries, the donations from the above ten countries amounted to more than 90 percent of the total.

The United Nations Relief and Works Agency for Palestine Refu-

---

[1] James M. Read, "The United Nations and Refugees—Changing Concepts," *International Conciliation*, No. 537 (March 1962), p. 14.
[2] *Ibid.*, p. 27.
[3] Channeled through the United Nations High Commissioner for Refugees.

gees in the Near East (UNRWA) has also been active in seeking private support and received approximately $5 million between 1950 and 1962. The United Nations Korean Reconstruction Agency (UNKRA), however, received only $5,000 during its entire lifetime. The very existence of these agencies stimulated a considerable amount of giving that was channeled through nongovernmental organizations. Indirectly, the United Nations agencies benefited considerably from these donations.

The Children's Fund

No United Nations appeal to the general public has had a more enthusiastic response than that of UNICEF.[4] Tremendous numbers of small donations from children as well as adults come into UNICEF each year. These gifts both help to sustain routine social welfare projects and provide a reserve fund for emergency situations to help victims of war, political upheaval, or disasters caused by nature. From 1947 through 1962, UNICEF received almost $28.3 million in contributions from private sources. Annual figures are shown in the table below.

1947	$ 16,000	1955	$ 786,748
1948	5,904,000	1956	1,007,013
1949	5,014,000	1957	1,303,059
1950	1,513,000	1958	1,268,142
1951	236,000	1959	1,526,070
1952	144,000	1960	1,910,848
1953	828,000	1961	2,670,006
1954	461,000	1962	3,735,877

As noted in Chapter 8, the large amounts contributed in 1948 and 1949 were the result of urgent and poignant needs in the war-devastated areas of Europe and the Orient. The decline after 1950 can be attributed to the ending of the emergency programs and the simultaneous stepping up of appeals on behalf of refugees.

The rise in giving to UNICEF since 1956 can be ascribed in considerable measure to original fund-raising techniques devised by the Fund itself and to strengthened national committees working on its behalf. One of the most successful steps taken to reach out to the "grass roots" level in the United States was the inauguration of the "trick or treat" Halloween drives, getting solicitation cans into the

[4] See Chap. 8 for a discussion of UNICEF.

hands of children on a door-to-door basis across the nation. Such activities, stimulated by the United States UNICEF Committee, together with extensive advertising, have begun to encourage the notion that one should give each year to UNICEF as one gives to the United Givers' Fund, the local hospital, or to church or college.

Similar efforts have been started in Canada, the Federal Republic of Germany, Sweden, Switzerland, and the United Kingdom with good results. Table A.10 shows private contributions by countries to UNICEF during the period 1959-62.

The UNICEF Greeting Card Fund has been one of the unique devices adopted by the United Nations for eliciting private support. While receipts from the sale of gift cards cannot strictly be construed as charitable giving, they are in fact bought because individuals want to support UNICEF, and the designs for them are donated by artists from many lands. They also serve to publicize UNICEF in a most effective way and thus stimulate further interest in its operations.

The annual sales of the colorful cards, with greetings in the five official languages of the United Nations and designs by outstanding artists, have brought UNICEF the following net income from 1950 to 1962:

1950	$ 4,200	1957	$ 336,965
1951	16,274	1958	660,812
1952	76,335	1959	769,892
1953	99,703	1960	1,019,097
1954	153,638	1961	1,116,603
1955	226,913	1962	1,600,000 (est.)
1956	259,346		

UNICEF greeting card sales were first promoted in the United States, and were then expanded to include other countries where the custom of exchanging greetings during the Christmas season was already prevalent: the United Kingdom, Canada, Australia, New Zealand, and most European countries. The sale of the UNICEF cards has generally paralleled the monetary donations to UNICEF. Table 10.1 shows where the sales of cards in excess of $10,000 have taken place. Over 20 million cards are sold every year.

UNICEF national committees have experimented with still other devices. One such experiment in the United States has been the placement at Boston's Logan International Airport of a UNICEF Collection Box for foreign currency. Located in a prominent position at the international arrival room, the UNICEF box and sign encourage

TABLE 10.1 *UNICEF Greeting Card Fund*[a]

(In thousands of dollars)

Country	1959	1960	1961
United States of America	584	657	914
United Kingdom	205	209	248
Canada	68	99	86
Germany	50	68	122
France	51	67	82
Netherlands	36	49	62
Australia	36	43	55
Norway	25	37	34
Sweden	26	31	51
Denmark	20	27	45
Italy	13	25	20
Switzerland	9	20	32
India	11	19	24
New Zealand	13	17	Below 10
Belgium	13	14	15
Pakistan	11	14	15
Philippines	13	13	Below 10
Peru	7	11	12

Data from Office of the Comptroller.

travelers to deposit whatever silver and other foreign currency they may have left on arriving in the United States. Attempts to place boxes at other international terminals have also been initiated. Thus, even small coins and bills may further the work of a United Nations agency.

Contributions for Land, Buildings, and Special Projects

A number of large private contributions made to the United Nations stand in a category by themselves. These are headed by a gift of $8.5 million given by Mr. John D. Rockefeller, Jr., in 1946 for the acquisition of the land adjoining the East River in New York City that became the headquarters of the United Nations. This gift enabled the Organization to situate itself in one of the world's great urban centers, at the meeting point of the principal lines of world transportation and communication, and at the heart of international finance.

In 1949 the Rockefeller Foundation made a $68,000 grant to the United Nations for assisting research work on special projects in the field of economics. This gift was timely in enabling the staff to undertake long-range research relating to economic development at a moment when this was needed for subsequent planning and action but could not be financed through the regular budget.

In 1959, the Ford Foundation made a grant of $6.2 million for the construction of a United Nations Library at the corner of First Avenue and Forty-second Street. Like the planting of a young tree, this will bear fruit for years to come. The library already provides storage space for official records, reference works drawn from all over the world, and congenial surroundings in which delegates, United Nations officials, and scholars may gather information.

Though few in number, these large acts of private philanthropy have in each instance moved into the United Nations picture in a timely and statesmanlike manner. Without the gifts from the Rockefeller and the Ford Foundations, the Organization would have been delayed, to say the least, in obtaining the excellent quarters and present plant that it possesses in New York. Hence, private gifts have, in a real sense, been a key that has made it possible for the United Nations to have a commanding place and facilities in which to conduct the business of world affairs.

Other Moves to Aid the United Nations

In addition to the gifts described above, there has been a spontaneous outcropping of private donations intended for other specific purposes or for the United Nations in general. For example, between 1960 and 1962 $86,000 was received in unsolicited contributions from private groups and individuals for technical assistance activities in Africa.[5] And during the same period, members of the Society of Friends in the United States sent nearly $100,000 to the United Nations "to share in the economic betterment of other peoples and areas."[6] Another step was the launching of a "Shares in the Future, Inc." movement in 1961 intended to focus "efforts on peace and disarmament instead of on negative efforts to survive a nuclear war." Certificates were issued in symbolic terms of being "payable in the strengthened hope of a peaceful world." The funds obtained through this were sent to the Freedom from Hunger campaign. A further experiment had its

[5] United Nations Press Services, Office of Public Information, Note No. 2580, April 30, 1962.
[6] Robert H. Cory, Jr.. "Gifts to the UN as a Witness for Peace," *Friends Journal* (April 15, 1962).

origin in the midst of a national debate in the United States about the desirability of fall-out shelters. A North Carolina group, declaring it to be preferable to help build "shelters for the shelterless rather than tombs for ourselves," resolved to raise funds for the United Nations to launch self-help housing projects in Somalia and other countries of Africa. The group adopted the slogan "The U.N. Our Shelter" in connection with its money-raising efforts.

Some people have sent monetary gifts to the United Nations without designation with a view to contributing to the peace-keeping or other political functions of the United Nations. Checks have also been sent since the financial crisis arose, apparently with the purpose of compensating, even in small measure, for the refusal of some member governments to bear their share of the costs of the Organization.

No United Nations organ is permitted to accept private donations unless specifically authorized by the General Assembly. Undesignated gifts are customarily treated as "miscellaneous income" and are applied to the regular budget to help reduce member nations' contributions. Customarily, the Controller has returned checks designated for the furtherance of peace-keeping activities. It has been the view of the Secretary-General that these operations are the province of official decisions, and that if the Organization accepted gifts for such purposes, this might involve it in the moral dilemma of having made a commitment that could conceivably be at variance with the will of its members. One thing that might be done would be to have the General Assembly establish a special account to which private contributions of this nature might be credited. These amounts could then be used constructively as the Organization might deem best. If the Peace Fund proposed at the 1963 Special Session of the General Assembly should become a reality, it would be a logical recipient of private gifts.

The story of private contributions shows that people, in their own ways, have attempted to implement the principles embodied in the United Nations Charter. Some of these private efforts have shown originality and demonstrated considerable persistence over the years.

Increasing Private Contributions

On the basis of past performance, it is reasonable to believe that the limits of private giving may not be exhausted. The experience with special appeals such as World Refugee Year and UNICEF suggests that there is an extensive reservoir of good will toward such activities. Much has hinged on the nature of the appeal, the amount of organized effort placed behind it, the effectiveness of the national organizations set up to promote it, the measure of government support or discouragement given to such drives, and other variables such as the strength of competing interests at the time or the effects of deductibility credits for income tax purposes. These are all elements in the picture. On the whole, there is still a considerable potential for increasing private contributions to the United Nations. The following ideas all look toward this end.

A substantial broadening of private donations must rest on an enlarged program of public information concerning the needs and opportunities for private support. For this purpose, public education campaigns adapted to different cultural and economic environments would be essential. What would work well in New York City would not necessarily produce optimal results in Cairo or São Paulo. Money, as well as official encouragement at the United Nations and within the member states, would be needed to produce results. The complete shutting-off of private gifts to UNICEF and other activities that occurred in Czechoslovakia after the Communist takeover in February 1948 demonstrates how vital the role of government sanction can be. Given an open door, the Organization might be able, through thoughtful educational campaigns, to enlist additional private support.

The record also suggests that specially highlighted occasions, such as World Refugee Year, can be effective in arousing public support. There is, of course, a limit to the number of such appeals that can be mounted within a given period of time without running into the law of diminishing returns. It would not be wise to have more than one at a time under United Nations auspices. Yet, how would the Organization choose among many worthy causes? If conflicts developed among the various voluntary agencies because of this dilemma, the idea would be self-defeating. Thus, although World Refugee Year was a success, there are limits to the usefulness of this method of fund-raising.

Another idea which merits careful consideration is the possibility of private subscription to United Nations bonds. The General Assembly resolution of December 20, 1961 directed that the bonds should be offered in the first instance to member states and to official institutions. But it also specified that "if the Secretary-General, with the concurrence of the Advisory Committee on Administrative and Budgetary Questions, shall so determine," they could subsequently be offered to "nonprofit institutions or associations."

This last clause would permit the sale of bonds to charitable trusts and foundations, or to educational institutions, trade unions, and other associations that might wish to subscribe. The implication of the resolution seemed to be that this would not be done until the possibilities of official purchases had been exhausted.

There was nothing in the 1961 resolution authorizing the sale of bonds to private individuals. A General Assembly resolution amending the action of the Sixteenth Session would be needed to authorize direct individual participation. The way could perhaps be opened if the Secretary-General and the Advisory Committee permitted some of the larger foundations and institutions wishing to show their support of the Organization's peace-keeping activities to purchase some of the bonds.

The United States has been the only country where serious debate regarding private subscriptions to the bonds has taken place. No less than seven bills and amendments relating to this matter were introduced into the Congress. Several sessions of the Senate and House hearings on the bond issue touched on this topic with over a dozen witnesses testifying specifically in this regard. The aim of the proposed legislation was generally the same: to authorize the Treasury to issue United Nations bonds for sale to the general public, including individuals, corporations, and associations. These bonds would be in small denominations, the highest being $100, and would bear 2 percent interest annually. There was some discussion on how the money so collected should be used. A number of legislators believed that the money should be earmarked as a replacement fund for loans made to the Organization under the government bond purchase bill; others felt that the funds should be available to the President "in support of the activities of the United Nations." The Eighty-seventh Congress adjourned without taking action on any of these proposals.

Two answers are possible to the question whether United Nations bonds ought to be opened to private subscription. First, it is true that this method permits tangible expression of popular support for the United Nations on the most crucial level, that of peace-keeping. The "peoples of the United Nations" would thus be given a stake in this primary responsibility. On the other hand, it may be said that such a method would blur the distinction between private, individual action and governmental responsibility. Some observers maintain that it would be better to establish in each country a nonprofit organization through which individuals could purchase the bonds. Such a procedure would be within the sense of the 1961 resolution authorizing the bond issue and would allow national identification of donations.

Even if it is agreed that it is desirable to have member governments issue bonds, several other fundamental questions must be answered. How are the monies so collected to be used? Are they to be employed to replace government funds expended or are they to be considered as supplementary contributions? Should they be earmarked only to underwrite specific projects or should they be for general support of the United Nations? Should tax incentives in the form of tax exemptions or tax credits be given to encourage individual purchases? Or should these bonds not be subject to existing tax laws? Decisions on these issues must be made before any plan for individual purchases of United Nations bonds can be viewed as an effective method for increasing private financial support for the United Nations.

To date, no country has granted tax deductibility credit for contributions to the United Nations. Only in the United States has there been serious discussion of the matter. Gifts sent directly to "The United Nations" are not deductible at this time under United States income tax laws. But contributions sent to the American Association for the United Nations or to the United States Committee for UNICEF are deductible, even though the proceeds may be passed on to a United Nations agency. The same is true of gifts sent to the United States Freedom from Hunger Foundation for use by the Food and Agriculture Organization.

There has been some evidence of popular support for a move that would grant credit for income tax purposes to individuals in the United States who make contributions directly to the United Nations. A bill providing for this was first introduced into the Congress by Representative Edith Green in 1958. A similar proposal was introduced into the Eighty-seventh Congress. According to the proposed legislation, an individual would be allowed "as a credit against the tax imposed for the taxable year, an amount equal to the contributions or gifts, payment of which is made by such individual within the taxable year, to or for the use of the United Nations or its specialized agencies." The maximum credit permitted would be 5 percent of the total tax paid.

Tax experts were quick to point to several difficulties. First, they noted the already large number of exemptions granted for personal charitable gifts, including funds for the American Association for the United Nations. They also pointed out that under American tax laws deductions were not allowed for contributions to foreign charities or causes. Complications were foreseen in ascertaining tax frauds in this respect. On a broader plane, the tax experts noted that, with the exception of the United States and a few Western European countries, no nation allowed even minimum exemptions for individual charitable contributions. In view of this, it was argued that it might be advisable to press for a more general acceptance of a tax credit proposal for private contributions among member states.

In addition to the doubts that were entertained in some circles about the political or administrative wisdom of authorizing tax deduction credits, some opposition was registered to the Green bill by charitable agencies in the United States on the grounds that such credit might have a tendency to divert gifts from needy causes at home to vague and uncertain needs abroad. The opposition to tax credit is so strong that an early adoption of the Green bill or some variation of it seems unlikely.

Another proposal was made by an American scholar, Dr. Lincoln P. Bloomfield of the Massachusetts Institute of Technology, who suggested the establishment of a United Nations Endowment Fund. He visualized this as "a capital fund sufficient to provide annual income that will enable the United Nations to carry out at least a significant part of the task the nations charge it to do but without always following up with the financial wherewithal."[7] He "guessed," moreover, that a world-wide appeal for a one billion dollar capital endowment fund "would be oversubscribed by individuals, foundations, governments, and private corporations."

Few observers have been as optimistic on the amount that might be thus realized. The slowness with which subscriptions to the United Nations bond issue were bought does not suggest a vast outpouring of largesse overnight. Past gifts of individuals, groups, and foundations to the United Nations likewise do not suggest future amounts on the

[7] Letter to the Editor, *New York Times,* Feb. 25, 1962.

order of several hundred million dollars. Conceivably some sizable grants might be made to such a fund by philanthropic trusts and foundations in member countries. Perhaps a group of private philanthropies might use large initial grants as levers for matching contributions in other member countries. Many private donors might be moved to make contributions if they could be assured that others abroad would share in the burden.

Another idea is the establishment of memorial funds. The Dag Hammarskjold Foundation founded in 1962 as a "living memorial" to the late Secretary-General is of such a nature. Following initiatives taken in Sweden and in the United States, committees were set up in more than a dozen countries to appeal for funds to sustain a variety of activities that embody the late Secretary-General's deepest concerns.

The money raised for the Hammarskjold Foundation may be allocated in different ways by the various national committees. Some may contribute the portion raised in their countries directly to the United Nations or to one of the specialized agencies; others may choose to administer their funds more directly. The United States Committee of the Dag Hammarskjold Foundation is appropriately headed by Andrew W. Cordier, who, as Executive Assistant to the Secretary-General, was one of his most intimate confidants. Opportunities to achieve the goals of this memorial fund are afforded to individuals, groups, and citizens' associations in the member countries through appeals to schools, colleges, corporations, and foundations.

Conclusions

Private contributions to the United Nations, though numerous and fairly continuous in their flow, have comprised only a small fraction of the Organization's revenue. The largest single sum ever raised from these sources was $9 million given to the United Nations for World Refugee Year in 1960. The most continuous recipient of private support has been UNICEF. But the amounts donated to it added up to only $28.3 million after seventeen years of solicitation. Altogether, private contributions to the United Nations since the Organization's establishment amount to less than the equivalent of one year's regular budget. Viewed in perspective, the amounts contributed have been modest when compared to the sums given to major charitable causes in some member countries, notably the United States.

A second fact that stands out from the record of private contributions to the United Nations is that these have come almost entirely from the United States, save for specific contributions to refugee and humanitarian programs. There have been no large gifts or grants by individuals, trusts, or corporations in Europe or elsewhere comparable in any sense to those of the Rockefeller and Ford Foundations. All the initiatives on private subscription to United Nations bonds and tax deductibility credit originated in the United States. On the other hand, there is no evidence that labor unions and employer groups in the United States have made concerted efforts to obtain contributions for the United Nations as their counterparts have on occasion in the Netherlands, the United Kingdom, and other Western European countries.

It is, of course, true that no other country has a GNP per capita as high as that of the United States. But as the table below shows, in 1961 there were numerous countries with a GNP per capita in excess of $1,000 a year.[8]

The Netherlands	$1,053	Luxembourg	$1,492
Finland	1,108	Australia	1,529
Norway	1,336	New Zealand	1,557
France	1,362	Switzerland	1,726
Belgium	1,377	Sweden	1,782
Denmark	1,397	Canada	1,864
United Kingdom	1,417	United States	2,823
West Germany (including Saar)	1,436		

There are sufficient sources of wealth or income in most of these countries to warrant larger contributions to United Nations programs than have been made heretofore. In some of these, as well as in a few of the lower income states, there are large accumulated fortunes and incomes. The record indicates little or no private giving to the Organization from these sources.

It is not suggested that the principles of apportionment incorporated into the scale of member state assessments should be applied to

[8] Agency for International Development, Statistics and Reports Division, "Estimates of Gross National Product" (April 30, 1963). Switzerland and West Germany are not members of the U.N.

private support of the United Nations. But it would be desirable to have a more equitable balance among the available sources of support. Perhaps the adoption of matching formulas or the creation of an international consortium of private philanthropies might correct the present imbalance. Nongovernmental organizations the world over could play a useful role as sponsoring agencies.

Finally, in considering possible ways of increasing private support for the United Nations, one is again struck by the number and tenacity of the obstacles. While it is true that the search for additional revenue from private sources must continue, it is very likely that such income will remain a fairly modest increment to governmental support.

CHAPTER 11

New Sources of Revenue

FOR SEVERAL YEARS NOW there have been in the air a number of proposals designed to strengthen the financial structure of the United Nations by making available to the Organization new sources of funds that would make it somewhat less dependent on the contributions of member states. In view of the vagaries of state behavior, it is not surprising that many friends of the United Nations have felt that the Organization should be able to replenish its treasury from new sources of income completely independent of the control of states. So far, however, there has been no systematic exploration of these proposals nor have they been analyzed in terms of their technical and political feasibility.

Possibilities and Limits

A survey of these proposals suggests that they may be divided into three major groups. First, and least complicated, are the suggestions envisaging modest increments to United Nations income primarily through service charges. These would entail no major changes in the structure of the United Nations. Second, are more ambitious proposals advanced in 1957 by the Commission to Study the Organization of Peace—a private United States research group—which noted that there are a number of public services now provided by national governments that are international in character. The commission suggested that:

> . . . It might be feasible to allow the United Nations to share a small part of the fees or excises for international mail or passports or visas—on the rationale that the United Nations helps to maintain a world of peaceful communication, trade, and travel. A fraction of

the tolls levied upon an international waterway would be another possible source of revenue for the United Nations in this category.[1]

Most ambitious of all are a number of suggestions that envisage United Nations taxation powers or property rights over the actual and potential resources of the sea bed, Antarctica, and outer space.

Before evaluating these proposals, two important questions should be asked: First, what is the basis of the Organization's claim to such additional revenue? Second, would these new funds necessarily strengthen the Organization?

To answer the first question, tax theory must be considered briefly and related to the United Nations. The ultimate justification for any levy imposed by a particular organ of society on its members is that this organ must produce, in the language of tax theoreticians, a public good. Such a public good may be tangible, like a highway, or intangible, like public safety in the streets of a city. As noted in Chapter 1, a minimal consensus has emerged since World War II, to the effect that the United Nations should exist as a continuously operating conference machinery for most of the world's governments. What this means is that a new organ has been added to society—the United Nations. This new organ is not to be seen as being "above governments" but merely as another manifestation of our increasingly interdependent society. The consensus on the United Nations does not extend far beyond the "conference machinery" principle. But in that minimal sense international organization has definitely "arrived" as a part of human society.

In the light of this development, proponents of additional revenue for the United Nations maintain that it is reasonable to suggest that, being one of the organs of society in this sense, it should have a claim to a tiny share of public revenue. The fact that the Organization serves as a kind of global diplomatic headquarters qualifies it for the receipt of additional income.

Opponents to added United Nations income point out that member states do not receive services from the Organization free of charge. They are assessed for them. Any additional levy would in effect mean a kind of double taxation. Moreover, United Nations levies would probably be inequitable since the levies would have to be imposed on some specific type or types of international activity to the exclu-

---

[1] Commission to Study the Organization of Peace, *Strengthening the United Nations* (Harper and Bros., 1957), pp. 260-61.

sion of others. If they are imposed on travel, for example, this might harm the tourist trade. Moreover, it may be argued that the Organization helps to maintain a peaceful world just as much for those people who choose not to travel as for those who do. Hence, they too ought to be taxed. Thus, opponents state that member states pay for what they get from the United Nations and the quest for new sources of revenue would create more problems than it would solve.

The ultimate justification for additional revenue has to be based on a value judgment on the nature of the Organization itself. If the United Nations is seen primarily as "static conference machinery," then indeed there seems little justification for new sources of revenue; if, however, it is seen as a dynamic evolutionary organ of society, levies would make sense. Among those who perceived the United Nations in this evolutionary perspective was the late Secretary-General, Dag Hammarskjold. In an address at the University of Chicago Law School on May 1, 1960, he described the world as being in a state of "transition between institutional systems of international coexistence and constitutional systems of international cooperation." He suggested further that the present system clearly "carrie(d) within it the seeds for the growth of higher social organisms," and that this system "may be developed until, on single points or on a broad front, it passes over into a constitutional system of cooperation." Added revenue from new sources might be construed as one of those "single points" of breakthrough to which Dag Hammarskjold alluded.

The introduction of some levy for the United Nations would be analogous to the evolution of fiscal systems since the Middle Ages, particularly in England. At first, the king had to depend on his patrimony; when income from this source proved insufficient, he had to ask for subsidies. The funds he thus received—subsidies, grants, donations, or "benevolences"—were voluntary and could not be imposed by the king. Hence, the kings were constantly in financial straits: as late as the seventeenth century, sovereigns had to mortgage crown lands and pawn their jewels. In this way, a reliable system of public finance could not evolve, and therefore the modern state could not evolve. Much of the history of Great Britain from the Magna Carta to 1688 is the history of efforts to create, with an equitable distribution of power between king and parliament, a reliable fiscal system.

Another analogy that is sometimes made, fits less well: the transition from confederation to federation of the former colonies in

North America. This analogy exaggerates the significance of United Nations levies and hence magnifies the obstacles to be overcome, for it implies major shifts in the locus of sovereignty. The new constitution gave the federal government the authority to levy taxes without limitation or ceiling. No such shifts would be needed to obtain additional revenue for the United Nations short of direct taxation by the Organization.

For the type of revenue here contemplated, much closer analogies exist. They are numerous and, in fact, ubiquitous: the arrangements that have to be hammered out everywhere regarding the distribution and allocation of public revenue. How much of the revenue obtained in Paris is to go to the French central government? How much from the village tax to the school fund?

In the last analysis, then, the question of "Should I pay a special United Nations levy for a given international activity?" can only be answered in the affirmative if the Organization is accepted as an "organ of society" that creates a "public good" and which is conceived as evolutionary rather than static in character.

Turning to the more practical question whether such additional revenue would necessarily strengthen the United Nations, several considerations come to mind.

From one point of view, additional revenue, if sufficiently massive, would put the Organization in a much stronger position. It could afford to undertake peace-keeping operations without fear of bankruptcy, and it could advance in the areas of economic and social development. Its hand would be immensely strengthened in the peace and security as well as the economic and social fields. But from another point of view, as has been pointed out in Chapter 1, states would resent United Nations peace-keeping operations of which they disapproved and could discover other devices besides the "financial veto" to impede the work of the Organization. In other words, the issue of political control is paramount here. And in the field of development, the United Nations might, if equipped with large additional revenue, turn into a kind of international philanthropic foundation more and more removed from the center of controversy and thus less politically meaningful to the member states.

In addition to the above, two further problems must be faced: if sufficient additional income were available for the United Nations so that the bulk of its operations could be financed without assessment on the membership, would this have a tendency to promote a measure of irresponsibility among member states? For example, if countries could authorize a peace-keeping operation or a substantial program of economic aid by appropriating money from the Organization's new sources of income, they would probably do so. Is it wise to establish a system that would make it possible for programs to be voted without any real cognizance being taken of the cost?

Unless great care is taken, a system of new United Nations levies on international activities would simply alter the basis for assessing contributions from governments, substituting statistics on the volume of international mail, for example, for national income and per capita income statistics.

All this suggests that, in the quest for new sources of revenue, a careful balance must be struck. It seems indeed desirable to obtain additional funds from hitherto untapped sources in order to rescue the Organization from its present financial plight. A United Nations that is too poor cannot function effectively as an instrument of international cooperation. But care must be taken that such new funds not create a gulf between the United Nations and its membership. It is to underline the obvious to point out that the former danger is infinitely greater than the latter. With these thoughts in mind, the possibilities for new sources of revenue for the world organization will be explored.

Income From United Nations Services

The United Nations already engages in several revenue-producing activities. In 1963, the income from these sources was expected to exceed $6 million. As pointed out in Chapter 4, this money is referred to as "miscellaneous income" and is used to reduce the assessments of member states by small amounts. These activities were not primarily created in order to produce revenue. In 1955, Secretary-General Dag Hammarskjold declared:

> The extent to which the activities under consideration can be justified by the fact that they produce revenue varies, but in no case can it be said that the revenue factor is or should be the sole justification. In all cases, regard must be paid to other, and often overriding purposes of the activities which are not always consonant with a purely financial approach to management questions.

These activities include the sale of stamps by the United Nations

Postal Administration, the sale of United Nations publications and television services, the operations of a gift shop and souvenir shop, guided tours for visitors, cafeteria services, and income from investments. None of these operations is questioned by governments. Indeed, they would not exist as sources of revenue were it not for the existence of the United Nations itself. Nevertheless, these activities have established the principle that the United Nations can have independent sources of revenue. All the proposals in this chapter are based on the assumption that this principle can be expanded. Pending the adoption of any new proposals, a beginning might be made, as was suggested in Chapter 4, by changing the United Nations financial regulations and permitting the accumulation and investment of "miscellaneous income" over the years as a "nest-egg" or contingency fund.

Going beyond the presently available "miscellaneous income," are suggestions envisaging modest increments to the existing resources through United Nations service charges. For example, charges might be made for special services, such as the preparation, on request, of a paper on a given subject based on data in United Nations files, or the issuance of international health certificates through the World Health Organization (WHO), or international radio licenses through the International Telecommunication Union (ITU). At the present time, under the "funds in trust" arrangement, governments turn over funds to the Technical Assistance Board to recruit experts for purposes that cannot be encompassed in the Expanded Programme of Technical Assistance (EPTA). It has been suggested that a service charge might well be made for such activities, just as the World Bank charges interest on its loans.

On closer examination, the proposals on United Nations service charges do not stand up very well. In some instances, as in the use of United Nations files for research purposes, the amounts realized would be petty and the overhead out of proportion to the income. Second, WHO already charges a fee for the issuance of health certificates and any additional charge would have to be minimal and hence probably not worth the effort. Service charges for "funds in trust" would yield very little and would devolve largely on developing nations which are recipients of EPTA and Special Fund assistance.

The idea of ITU service charges for international radio licensing has some possibilities. Most countries have discontinued such charges because they had been resented by radio users and manufacturers.

The overhead was high and verification difficult. In the light of this experience, it would make little sense for the ITU to attempt to collect a fee from radio users; but the idea of charging a license fee for radio stations is worth considering.

One of the most important functions of the ITU is to "keep order in the air" so far as radio frequencies are concerned. The International Frequency Registration Board of the ITU handles close to 100,000 assignments a year in this area. If the ITU charged a $100 fee for each case, the additional revenue could approximate $10 million a year. It must be remembered, however, that member states are already assessed for the work of the board, which accounts for more than one-third of the annual ITU budget. Hence, any additional service charge would have to be considered a separate payment by radio stations. If the ITU would then yield this money to the United Nations, such action would set a new precedent in that it would be the first time that a specialized agency would thus raise money for the United Nations.

Considered as a whole, service charges do not promise to become a significant source of additional revenue. In most cases the yield would be small and the resistance formidable. The idea of the ITU licensing charges on radio stations seems to be the only proposal that might bring in an amount of revenue which would make the effort worthwhile.

Levies on International Activities

The possibility of United Nations levies arises in connection with three different types of international activities: mail; canal, sea, and air traffic; and travel. In all of these categories some modest precedents exist.

The Mail

By all odds the most significant backlog of experience exists in the area of stamp revenue for United Nations purposes. As noted in Chapters 8 and 9, three efforts are on record to raise funds through the simultaneous issue of special stamps in many countries: the World Refugee Year stamp scheme of 1960-61, which yielded $1.5 million; the malaria eradication stamps initiated by WHO in 1962, which yielded approximately $1 million; and the Freedom from Hunger stamp scheme launched by the Food and Agriculture Organization in 1963, which is expected to yield a similar amount. In all cases there was a coordinated effort in which most of the United Nations membership participated.

These precedents are of dubious relevance, however, since a levy on international mails would presuppose an entirely different approach. Revenue would not derive from national stamp schemes but from the postal services of governments. Only that kind of levy would bring in substantial revenue. Income from a national stamp scheme is usually a "one-shot" proposition; it is not reliable since it depends largely on the philatelic market; and it is very modest. A United Nations levy on international mails, on the other hand, would not be limited in time, would be distributed among millions of taxpayers, and might bring in considerable amounts of money.

Of the categories of international activities mentioned above, the area of mail probably would provide the best opportunity for a breakthrough in terms of a United Nations levy. The field boasts a century of extraordinary international cooperation and compliance with the regulations of the Universal Postal Union (UPU). Political matters have only rarely interfered with international postal services. Countries that do not recognize each other are members of the UPU. The world is considered by the UPU as "a single postal territory." This long tradition of cooperation has brought in its train concomitant benefits such as the UPU contributions to the unification of weights and measures, simplified techniques for settling international accounts, and greater uniformity in mail routing. This century-old consensus might provide a fertile source for a United Nations levy.

One way of imposing a United Nations levy on all international mails would be to earmark a fraction of postal revenues in all member countries for the Organization. This might be done by the equivalent of a one cent United Nations surcharge which citizens of all member nations would have to pay when using the international mails. The revenues thus collected would be turned over by governments to the Organization as supplements to their assessments. The scheme might be put into effect through a General Assembly resolution alone or through a resolution plus formal acceptance by governments, thus creating an obligation on their part vis-à-vis the United Nations. It might also be initiated through a special convention or through a resolution of the UPU.

UPU statistics indicate that such a scheme, if put into effect, might generate approximately $30 million a year. Obviously, the scheme would mean that the surcharge would not be evenly distributed among member governments.

Those which make most use of international mail would be meeting most of the costs. According to the UPU, the largest users of international mail are the United States, the United Kingdom, West Germany, France, and Canada, with roughly 12, 11, 9, 8, and 6 percent of total volume, respectively. Some countries like the Soviet Union and many of the developing nations use the international mails very little and thus would contribute only a small fraction of the costs. In small countries, international mail constitutes a higher proportion of total mail than in larger countries; moreover, some countries, like the United States, receive a great deal more mail than they send. Care would have to be taken to make the levy as equitable as possible.

Resistance to such a scheme would no doubt be considerable. In the United States—the only country where the scheme has been weighed in official circles—resistance took a number of forms. First, it was pointed out that a series of studies had shown that selling stamps was an uneconomic and inefficient method of fund raising because the costs were out of proportion to the amounts raised. For the United States, unlike most other countries where practically all international mail emanates from relatively few cities, it would mean placing stamps for sale in literally thousands of post offices with separate accounting in each one. It was also noted that postmasters' salaries were geared to the volume of stamps sold and anything that affected this relationship would cause difficulties. Moreover, there was strong congressional resistance to the idea of increasing the costs of international mail without commensurate income for the United States, especially in view of the fact that the Post Office runs an annual deficit.

A somewhat more conservative version of the above scheme would be the introduction of a voluntary feature into the picture. Citizens using the international mails would have an option on the use of the United Nations surcharge, but remittal to the Organization of the voluntary amounts thus collected would be obligatory for governments. This technique would follow the example and use the experience of several countries, notably in Western Europe, with voluntary surcharges for a variety of causes.

One of the best known precedents is the annual Swiss *Pro Juventute* ("For Youth") Drive. Since 1912, the *Pro Juventute* Foundation, in cooperation with the Swiss Postal Administration, has raised funds through surcharged postage stamps for various social service programs. The Postal Administration sells one-half of each year's issue to *Pro Juventute* at postage value, and the latter resells the stamps and retains the surcharge. The other half of the issue is sold directly by post offices to the general public. The amounts thus realized are by no means negligible.

Using some features of the Swiss plan, the United Nations Postal Administration could print stamps in different colors for different denominations, but showing neither a postal nor a surcharge value. Governments would purchase these stamps for a flat fee and then surprint them with both a postal value and a surcharge. The fee would be calculated on the assumption that governments would retain the equivalent of the postal value. This plan would give the general public the option of purchasing the stamps and paying for the surcharge. Such a scheme would probably encounter less resistance and would bring the private citizen into the picture. But the amounts realized would probably be far more modest than those derived from the obligatory plan.

Another variation would be the manufacture by the United Nations Postal Administration of stamps or other postal items that governments would purchase at a price higher than the manufacturing cost, and then resell on a voluntary basis in their national post offices. For example, governments could agree to grant the United Nations a monopoly on the printing of "air letters" and purchase them at a profit to the Organization. There would be some logic to this proposal since the UPU prescribes uniformity in "air letters" and has done a great deal to popularize them. Moreover, the UPU has long had a monopoly on the printing and furnishing of other uniform materials, such as international reply coupons, and thus could be of considerable assistance to the United Nations in setting up the necessary machinery and procedures.

Any of the above measures, if put into effect through a General Assembly resolution, would have to be coordinated with the UPU. A resolution adopted by the UPU Congress at Brussels on February 8, 1952, recommended that any:

> . . . postal activity proposed by the UN or by a specialized agency should be the subject of consultation with the UPU through its Congress or Executive and Liaison Committee, and that after such consultation any agreement should be concluded only after a favorable recommendation by the General Assembly of the UN.

A postal surcharge scheme including a voluntary feature as described above would probably require no change in UPU regulations. Up until 1957, the UPU permitted the use of surcharges only in domestic mails, but this restriction was lifted. The only requirement now is that the surcharge be clearly indicated. The 1957 UPU Convention declared in Article 186 that "Commemorative or charity stamps for which an additional charge is to be paid independently of the prepayment value, must be designed in such a way as to avoid any doubt as to that value." A completely obligatory scheme as outlined in the first proposal might give rise to some questions of interpretation. Although Article 37 of the 1957 UPU Convention declared that: "It [was] prohibited to collect charges, surcharges, and postal fees of any nature whatsoever, other than those prescribed in the Convention," a special protocol to the Convention permits surcharges up to 60 percent of postal value. Hence, a special arrangement would be necessary only if the United Nations surcharges in the obligatory scheme exceeded the postal value of the stamps by more than 60 percent.

The UPU might be of assistance in the verification process by employing its sampling technique presently used for postal accounting purposes. This procedure might be combined with yearly national reports to the UPU and occasional spot checks by UPU inspectors in member countries.

If one of the above proposals were adopted, a decision would have to be made on how the stamp revenue is to be used. Should it be placed in a special account under the authority of the General Assembly or of the Secretary-General? Should a General Assembly committee be created that would control the funds by a special voting formula based on the size of national purchases of stamps? Should the money be available for regular budget uses or should it be earmarked for special United Nations activities? These problems would have to be dealt with if a stamp scheme were to operate effectively and without legal ambiguities.

Canal, Sea, and Air Traffic

A second possibility for a United Nations levy would be a surcharge on canal, sea, and air traffic. Here an interesting precedent exists that merits careful consideration.

One of the grave results of the 1956 Israeli and Anglo-French military intervention in Egypt and the countermeasures taken by the

Egyptian government was the obstruction of the Suez Canal. On November 24, 1956, the General Assembly authorized the Secretary-General to negotiate for the speedy and effective clearance of the canal. The United Nations operation consisted in the removal of the collapsed El Ferdan Bridge and thirty-seven other obstructions and the restoration of damaged canal installations. The operation began on December 27, 1956, and was completed by April 10, 1957. An appeal was made to United Nations member states and to nonmember states as well to make advance contributions toward the expenses. In response, loans totaling $11.2 million were received from eleven governments: the United States lent $5 million; Australia, Canada, the Federal Republic of Germany, and Norway $1 million each; Sweden $750,000; Denmark and the Netherlands $500,000 each; Italy $400,000; and smaller sums were provided by Ceylon and Liberia. Actually, this was more than was needed and more than $4 million was proportionately refunded.

The total costs of the clearance operation amounted to about $7.2 million.[2] Of this, the greater part, $4.9 million, paid for the hire of thirty-two salvage vessels and other equipment from seven European countries; $970,927 was spent on restoring damaged installations. The contractual cost of technical management amounted to $682,364; and $500,00 was paid to reimburse France and the United Kingdom for salvage operations carried out at the United Nations' request. Only slightly more than 2.25 percent, $108,713 of the total expenditures, went for the salaries of United Nations personnel.

To repay the loans from the eleven governments that had financed the clearance operation, the General Assembly decided on a method new in United Nations history. It authorized the Secretary-General to negotiate an arrangement with the United Arab Republic government and the lending governments under which a surcharge of 3 percent would be levied on all shipping and trade using the canal. The arrangement was approved and went into effect on September 15, 1958. The Banque de la Société Générale de Belgique was designated by the Secretary-General as his agent for the collection and transmission to the United Nations of the surcharges. The full amount needed to repay the loans was recovered by the end of 1962.

[2] *The Worldmark Encyclopedia of the Nations* (Worldmark Press, Inc., Harper and Bros., 1960), p. 1241.

There were several special features about the Suez Canal surcharge that must be taken into account in order to complete the picture. First, the authority for the surcharge was a General Assembly resolution. Since it would be quite untenable to extend the power of the Assembly under Article 17 to private shippers in member countries, there existed, in strict law, no binding obligation on individual ship-owners or operators to pay the surcharge. Indeed, the great majority of shipping interests at first refused to pay the surcharge. Only when some governments permitted the raising of shipping rates, did the companies in these countries agree to pay the surcharge. The other governments simply "picked up the tab" for the shippers who refused to pay. In the United States, for example, only $3.9 million of the $5 million loan was recovered from United States shippers. The remaining $1.1 million was paid by the United States government. The fact that governments decided to make up the difference made the operation a success. But they did this because the economic dislocations caused by the continued closure of the Suez Canal would have cost them a great deal more. Also, the surcharge was generally considered fair and equitable: it did not alter the competitive position of the shippers; it was much too small to encourage alternative routing; had the canal not been cleared, shippers might have had to pay differential freight rates amounting to more than the surcharge.

The Suez Canal surcharge scheme was a special situation and one unlikely to be soon repeated. There existed strong inducements for governments to pay the part of the surcharge that shippers refused to pay. Such inducements would not exist in case of an obligatory United Nations canal surcharge on all international waterways. Hence, despite its success, the Suez Canal surcharge points to the tremendous obstacles which would have to be surmounted in order to impose a levy on traffic through international waterways. In the first place, international shipping interests would be almost unanimously opposed, as they were to the Suez Canal surcharge. Second, it would be very difficult to work out an equitable scale since international sea-borne traffic is unevenly divided among the members of the United Nations. Many engage in no international shipping at all. The first Inter-Governmental Maritime Consultative Organization (IMCO) Assembly in 1959 listed the United States, the United Kingdom, France, West Germany, Italy, Japan, the Netherlands, and Norway as the eight "largest ship-owning nations." A United States Department of Commerce study in 1962 added Greece, Sweden, Denmark, and the Soviet Union to the list.

Several small nations have large merchant fleets. To complicate matters further, there is the thorny issue of "flags of convenience." Panama and Liberia, for example, have invited the registration of foreign ships on easy terms and, on paper, own fleets exceeded in size only by those of the United States and the United Kingdom. Honduras and Costa Rica also have very large foreign registrations. These factors would have to be considered in the construction of a levy. A third consideration is the fact that there are only a few interoceanic canals and hence a levy imposed on shipping only through these—the Suez, Panama, Kiel, and Corinth Canals—would not yield much revenue. However, if a United Nations levy on all international shipping were contemplated, rivers and straits could be included. A levy on shipping through an interoceanic canal or through a river like the Danube or through the Dardanelles would all require the consent of the nations in whose territories the waterways are located. There is no reason to place interoceanic canals in a special category in this respect. Hence, it seems that the essential criterion of a levy on waterways ought to be the question whether the body of water is freely accessible to outside shipping. If it is, then it should become subject to the levy. The income thus derived from international shipping through canals, rivers, and straits would be more substantial. If the amount of the levy were patterned on the Suez Canal surcharge, the annual income for the United Nations might exceed $20 million.

Most of the arguments listed above also apply to a levy on international air traffic. On the one hand, it is certainly clear that such traffic depends on international peace and security and improving economic and social conditions. Thus, the existence of the United Nations certainly has relevance in this respect. Yet airlines, like shipping companies, are unanimously opposed to a levy. Moreover, problems of equity would again arise since the proportion between domestic and international air traffic is inverse to a country's size. More than 90 percent of all air services in Denmark, for example, are international, but only a very small proportion of air traffic in the Soviet Union is in that category. On the whole, the obstacles here are at least as formidable as those blocking a waterways levy. But if agreement could be reached, the revenues would be much larger. According to International Civil Aviation Organization (ICAO) statistics, international air traffic grew by 200 percent between 1954 and 1962 and continues to grow at a faster pace than domestic air traffic.

International Travel

The third international activity on which a United Nations levy might be imposed is international travel. This might be done in any one of three ways: a fee payable to the United Nations at international boundaries by travelers; a levy on passports; or a surcharge on customs duties.

The first alternative seems inadvisable. Not only would such a levy face well-nigh insurmountable opposition especially from "tourist countries," but if it were nominal, its nuisance value would be greater than its financial significance. Nevertheless, charges for tourist visas and entry permits are still made by some of these "tourist countries." Equity would again be a problem: small countries could rightly point out that their citizens cross borders more often than nationals of large countries, and some large countries whose citizens travel much, such as the United States for example, would pay a great deal more than countries like the Soviet Union, whose citizens travel little. Above all, the measure would be contrary to the salutary trend of the easing of travel across national boundaries.

There does exist a precedent on passport levies. As indicated in Chapter 2, the League of Nations charged those refugees who could afford it a modest fee for their Nansen Passports. Similarly, the International Refugee Organization received a small fee for its identity documents in lieu of passports. A United Nations levy on passports would raise fewer objections than a travel levy. In many countries, a fee is already obligatory for the issuance and renewal of passports. A United Nations surcharge could be added quite simply to the transaction. In those countries not charging a fee, a small levy might be tolerable.

The strongest negative argument is that statistics indicate the yield would be minimal. The United States, which issues the largest number of passports, issues fewer than one million every year. With a one dollar United Nations surcharge, the annual gross yield from the United States would be $1 million. Figures on international travel indicate that the total annual income from a passport levy would probably not reach the $10 million mark.

A customs surcharge has virtually no chance of success. Any device which would make the United Nations responsible for an increase in customs duties would be politically unacceptable to most of the membership. Even if a basis for agreement could be found, problems of equity would be enormous. Overhead would be costly. Perhaps the only possibility for a United Nations levy exists in the case of such traditional products for tax levies as alcohol or tobacco. Yet other countries rely heavily on the export of such goods. Hence, the distribution of the burden would be uneven.

If the possibilities for levies on international activities as a whole are considered, three basic facts emerge. First, all such levies must rest on the assumption that the United Nations has become an integral organ of society producing a "public good" and thus is deserving of additional revenue. Second, the field of international mail is probably the one in which the first attempts at a breakthrough might be made. And, third, it is clear from the above discussion that in each instance the reality must be faced that the yield would not be enormous though the resistance might be.

Long-range Possibilities

As a final step in the search for new sources of revenue, the political and technical feasibility of four ambitious proposals will be examined: first the bestowal of taxing powers on the United Nations; second, the exploration of Antarctica for United Nations revenue purposes; third, the use of ocean resources for United Nations revenue; and fourth, potentialities in outer space.

The Power to Tax

Suggestions to give the United Nations the right to establish taxes without the intervention of governments have cropped up from time to time. The best-known proposal has been advanced by Grenville Clark and Louis B. Sohn, whose scheme is predicated on successful disarmament and consequent savings in domestic budgets.[3] The authors propose a system under which the United Nations would assign annual revenue quotas, not to exceed 2 percent of estimated gross world product, to the "people of each member state." These quotas

[3] *World Peace Through World Law*, 2nd ed., rev. (Harvard University Press, 1960).

would be collected and enforced through regular governmental machinery to avoid creating an elaborate new bureaucracy, but they would be kept distinct from and would, in fact, replace some national taxes. Which specific national taxes were to be replaced would be left to the choice of governments, provided the totals involved were large enough to fill the assigned quota. The monies collected would be turned over to a United Nations fiscal office established in each member state. The authors also proposed United Nations borrowing powers up to 5 percent of gross world product.

A somewhat more modest version of the above proposal advocates that governments allocate in advance a proportion of their tax collections to the United Nations. Since this proposal would envision working through established governmental collection machinery, it claims to have the virtue of almost automatic administration.

It is readily apparent that the Clark-Sohn proposal and others hoping to invest the United Nations with taxing or borrowing powers, even indirectly, are premature. Quite apart from the fact that nations have regarded the area of taxation as exclusively within their national jurisdiction, there are other questions which must be raised. Would governments permit the United Nations to tax something that they are already taxing? Would a United Nations tax cause resentment among people and lose support for the world organization? Could agreement be found on equitable criteria of taxation for the people of countries in varying circumstances? What, if anything, can be done about states that refuse to cooperate? Is it not true that the United Nations would remain dependent on governmental cooperation in collecting and transmitting tax funds? To ponder these questions is to realize that there is little chance for adoption of any of these proposals in the foreseeable future.

Exploration of Antarctica

In 1957, the Commission to Study the Organization of Peace recommended that the United Nations be permitted to exploit the potentialities of Antarctica.[4] This might be approached through United Nations licensing rights or through direct grants of property rights to the world organization. To evaluate this proposal, the nature of the resources in Antarctica and the possibility of United Nations access to and profit from them must be considered.

[4] Commission to Study the Organization of Peace, *op. cit.*, p. 262.

Antarctica is the only polar continent, the coldest and stormiest area in the world, and technically a desert. In recent years, traces, but no sources of commercial value, of at least 176 minerals, including manganese, copper, lead, nickel, and even uranium have been found in the Antarctic.[5] There are apparently vast coal deposits, but with a few exceptions those found thus far have been of low-grade lignite which would not be commercially usable even if extraction and transportation were no problem.[6] In June 1960, a famous geologist and Antarctic expert, Laurence Gould, told the United States Senate that he "would not give a nickel for all the mineral resources" he knew of in Antarctica—but he pointed out that less than one percent of the area has been properly examined geologically.[7] Most of the continent is thus still unexplored.

The problem of exploiting these potential riches is a complex one. The costs and difficulties of exploration, the necessity of devoting so much in the way of resources merely to keeping the explorers alive, the need for geological surveys in areas covered by up to two miles of ice, all these are staggering problems which are currently being explored by governments, to the extent that such work is being done at all. The more accessible, relatively ice-free areas have thus far given no indication of mineral wealth.

All of this points to the fact that, in the near future, even if the United Nations had the right to lease out exploitation rights in the Antarctic on a royalty or other basis, it is doubtful that there would be any takers, at least not until United Nations or government-sponsored preliminary surveys and operations indicated the location and nature of mineral wealth.

Without doubt, the greatest current potential of the Antarctic lies in the field of scientific research. It provides an unexcelled natural laboratory for studies in such fields as glaciology, meteorology, geology, terrestrial magnetism and the like. While this type of basic research may eventually lead to important technological advances, it is, in its present stage, an activity requiring heavy capital expenditures rather than yielding income-producing results. This does not augur well for revenue in the foreseeable future.

---

[5] Laurence Gould, *Antarctica in World Affairs,* Foreign Policy Association Headline Series No. 128 (1958), pp. 8-9.
[6] *New York Times,* Jan. 2, 1961.
[7] *The Antarctic Treaty,* Hearings before the Senate Committee on Foreign Relations, 86 Cong. 2 sess. (1960), p. 75.

So far as access is concerned, there are now seven nations that make extensive claims to "ownership" of areas in the Antarctic. These are: Argentina, Australia, Chile, France, New Zealand, Norway, and the United Kingdom. In addition, the Union of South Africa claims certain sub-Antarctic islands near the African continent but makes no claim in Antarctica proper. Germany and Japan have in the past made claims of various types, but they are not now considered active. Both the United States and the Soviet Union have conducted extensive research in Antarctica, and both have adopted substantially similar positions with respect to claims. Neither has made a formal claim to any part of the Antarctic, but each asserts that its activities give it the right to make a claim if it should choose to do so.

The seven nations that claim ownership have shown varying degrees of interest in their Antarctic "territories." Norway asserted a claim originally to protect its whaling industry and, unlike the others, has not claimed an interest extending all the way inland to the Pole. New Zealand and Australia together claim nearly half of the continent. They remember German raiders' operations in southern waters in both World Wars and hence would not like to see an "unfriendly" government established in Antarctica. France now "administers" its relatively small Antarctic claim as an "autonomous" unit with its seat of "government" in Paris, but its claim has been substantially neglected even by its explorers.

The claims of the European nations have been mutually recognized. The prime area of political friction lies in the region called by the United States the Palmer Peninsula, the neck extending toward South America. Argentina and Chile, whose claims overlap in part, are the nations closest to Antarctica, though even they are separated from it by some 700 miles of ocean. They are seriously interested in Antarctic weather observation since their weather is influenced by Antarctic conditions. The Palmer Peninsula is also a potential source of minerals which, for Antarctica, might prove relatively accessible, though no commercial finds have thus far been made. The British claim overlaps both Latin-American claims and is also related to a British-Argentine dispute over the British-occupied Falkland Islands, which dates back to the 1830's. The British have suggested the internationalization of Antarctica and have on occasion sought to have their dispute with Argentina and Chile submitted to the International Court of Justice. Both Argentina and Chile, however, have steadfastly resisted suggestions of internationalization.

Two recent developments have advanced the cause of internationalization. First, during the International Geophysical Year, the United States, the Soviet Union, Japan, and Belgium joined with the seven claimants in the most extensive program of Antarctic research ever conducted. Despite minor political difficulties, a high level of international scientific cooperation proved possible and has been continued on a smaller scale, through a Special Committee on Antarctic Research.

Based in part on the success of the IGY in Antarctica, the United States proposed to the IGY participants that they meet together to negotiate a treaty which would create and maintain political conditions under which the scientific programs already begun could be carried forward and expanded. The resulting Antarctic Treaty, signed in 1959 and now in force for the twelve IGY participants and Poland, established an interesting political status for Antarctica. Militarization was barred; nuclear explosions were banned for the first time anywhere; all participants could freely visit and inspect each other's installations; scientists were free to move anywhere without consideration of alleged "boundaries"; and political claims were "frozen" for at least a thirty-year period. However, no procedure for international control, exploration, development, or exploitation of Antarctica was provided under the treaty.

The above discussion suggests that the prospects for early United Nations revenue from Antarctic resources are dim. First, the presence of the resources themselves is still open to question. Second, exploitation would require considerable capital investment from sources that are not made clear and on which there might be only marginal returns. The problem of access has been simplified by the Antarctic Treaty of 1959 although it must be noted that the United Nations was not brought into the settlement. At any rate, the treaty has cleared the way for continued scientific programs for at least three decades. But it is difficult to see how these programs can be converted into revenue for the United Nations even in the distant future.

Revenue from Ocean Resources

Turning to the possibilities of United Nations revenue from ocean resources, two suggestive ideas are on record. In 1957, in a bold proposal, the Commission to Study the Organization of Peace declared:

We believe that the United Nations is capable not only of administering territory, but of acquiring title under international law through cession by the state with title or through prior claim to territory or space to which no state has title. . . . With respect to the bed of the high seas beyond the continental shelf and to outer space . . . we urge the General Assembly to declare the title of the international community. . . .[8]

This idea was echoed in 1961 by Dr. Eugene Staley of the Stanford Research Institute: "The United Nations should at once be granted exclusive authority to license, regulate, and tax all exploitation of ocean resources outside presently recognized limits of national jurisdiction."[9]

To evaluate these proposals, the resources available and the problems of access and of United Nations exploitation must be examined. Ocean resources stem from two origins which must be evaluated separately: sea-life and the sea bed. The former consists of fish, whales, seals, and plankton, and the latter largely of mineral resources, including petroleum.

In the area of sea-life, while it is true that the fish of the high seas do not "belong" to any nation, special national rights in fish "farming" and conservation have already been recognized in several treaties.[10] Furthermore, a number of states are dependent on the use of their traditional fishing "rights" for food and for sale to other nations. In other words, a United Nations claim to these activities would be discriminatory, falling primarily on "fishing" nations and at least initially on one group of entrepreneurs and workers, the fishermen of all nations.

United Nations revenue from the whaling industry seems equally unlikely. The industry is subject to regulation by an International Whaling Commission established by the International Convention for the Regulation of Whaling, which entered into force in 1948. While control has been relatively ineffectual, the commission sets time and area limits to the whaling season in Antarctica and sets a maximum kill limit as well. The commission is supported by contributions from

[8] Commission to Study the Organization of Peace, *op. cit.*, pp. 6-7.

[9] Eugene Staley, "Direct Revenue for the United Nations," Stanford Research Institute, Memorandum, Nov. 13, 1961.

[10] See, for example, the Convention for the Preservation of the Halibut Fishery of the Northern Pacific Ocean and the Bering Sea (1937), U.S.T.S. No. 917; the International Convention for the High Seas Fisheries of the North Pacific Ocean (1952), T.I.A.S. No. 2786; and the International Convention for the Northwest Atlantic Fisheries (1949), T.I.A.S. No. 2089.

member states. Thus, a concept of regulation already exists, but for purposes of conservation rather than revenue. Moreover, quite apart from the fact that the yield would be nominal, it would be inequitable to call on the whaling industry to provide a basis for United Nations revenue. The same argument applies to the seal industry. Why should seal producers and consumers be major supporters of the United Nations?

Plankton, the minute life forms which sustain other sea life up to and including the largest whales, may some day become a direct source of human food. Many proposals have been made for "harvesting" and processing plankton, and it may be assumed that it is scientifically feasible to do so. At this time, however, no one exploits this resource nor is anyone likely to in the near future.

In regard to the sea beds, all nations claim sovereignty in waters adjacent to their coasts ranging in distance from 3 miles to 200 miles. The reasons range from national defense to economic requirements. The Geneva Conferences on the Law of the Sea of 1958 and 1960 demonstrated how strongly states insist on these claims. No agreement could be reached at those meetings on a uniform rule for the extent of such claims. While only a few states, mostly in Latin America, have asserted a claim to more than 12 miles, waters may be considered clearly international only if they are outside the claim of any state. This may mean that the more valuable and accessible areas must remain outside the scope of the United Nations. Furthermore, all states claim exclusive rights to the "continental shelf"—the extension of continents out under the seas—although the extent of these claims differs. The United States, for example, in 1945, defined the term "continental shelf" as the area from the shore to the 600 foot depth line. More recently, in Article 1 of the Convention on the Continental Shelf, adopted by the United Nations Conference on the Law of the Sea on April 28, 1958, it was defined as "the seabed and subsoil of the submarine areas adjacent to the coast but outside the area of the territorial sea, to a depth of 200 metres, or beyond that limit, to where the depth of the superjacent waters admits of the exploitation of the natural resources of the said areas." The "elastic clause" included in this article implies that sovereign claims to the continental shelf may extend in proportion to the advance of technology. The trend toward the extension of sovereign claims into the oceans is a continuing one. Hence, the sooner nations agree to limit their claims in favor of an international arrangement, the more likely is it that the development of a new region of power rivalry will be forestalled.

The above suggests that mineral or petroleum resources in waters within a 200 mile limit from shore would be in a legally clouded position for United Nations exploitation. Beyond this limit, a United Nations title would be possible.

So far, only two concrete possibilities have arisen in this respect, but these are very interesting. In July 1962, it was reported that twenty-one huge domes, strikingly resembling the salt domes that had made the coastal region of Texas and Louisiana one of the richest oil-producing areas in the world, were discovered in the Gulf of Mexico.[11] The domes are 400 miles away from the nearest point in the United States and 320 miles from Mexico. They are at a depth of 2,080 fathoms on the Mexican side and 1,950 fathoms on the American side, thus suggesting that they may be an extension of the American continental shelf. Hence, they are clearly within international waters unless the United States, and perhaps Mexico, decide to invoke the "elastic clause" contained in Article 1 of the 1958 Convention on the Continental Shelf. Several petroleum companies have engaged in preliminary surveys and have declared that the area is technologically accessible.

Here seems to be an opportunity for United Nations revenue that might be pursued without delay. The first step might be a General Assembly resolution declaring sea bed resources beyond a given distance as outside of national jurisdiction. Alternatively, since such a resolution technically would have the status of a recommendation only, a special convention producing a legally binding instrument might be preferable though probably more difficult to obtain. The resolution or convention might then go on to say that sea bed resources in international waters would become the property of a newly created "United Nations Resources Board." Such a step would open the way for a declaration of United Nations title to the Gulf of Mexico oil.

The derivation of revenue for the United Nations could follow a pattern well established by the United States. That country generally derives revenue from petroleum resources in two ways: first, it auctions leases to petroleum companies on a basis of competitive bidding; and second, it receives royalty payments based on production. Income from these sources ran to over $1 billion in 1962. At least one

[11] *New York Times,* July 7, 1962.

American congressman suggested that the Gulf of Mexico oil resources be made available to the United Nations by auctioning the drilling privileges.[12]

Despite the fact that the situation looks feasible it is only realistic to inject some words of caution into the discussion. First, the United States and Mexico would have to be persuaded not to invoke the "elastic clause" of Article 1 of the Convention. Second, it is important to avoid the impression that the United Nations would "enter the oil business." This would not be the case. The United Nations would merely receive title to a piece of real estate in the ocean and would benefit by sharing in its exploitation. Hence, the question of "U.N. oil" would not arise. Private companies would merely pay a "bonus" to the Organization on the granting of a concession, as well as a portion of their profits as royalties. To the extent that oil companies now make payments to national states, no extra expense would be involved for them through a United Nations title. A third consideration is the size of the royalties that the United Nations might charge. The range among oil-producing states is very wide and extends from 12 percent in the United States to 66 percent in Venezuela. The United Nations would face a delicate problem of balancing here: if it charges too much, there might be no takers; if it charged too little, it would arouse the ire of countries charging higher royalties. Fourth, serious technical and legal difficulties would have to be overcome: an artificial island group might have to be constructed to exploit the resource; and the question of what law would govern the relationships between the United Nations and the concessionaires would have to be clarified. Finally, clarity is of the essence. An early Assembly resolution or treaty would forestall much rivalry; and a clear United Nations title would be an incentive for oil companies to begin operations. So far, serious exploitation has been inhibited by the ambiguous legal status of the resource.

All things considered, the above proposal is only a long-range possibility. In view of the present oil surplus in the world, the strongest objections to it would no doubt come from oil-exporting countries. Of the 113 member states of the United Nations, only 12 fall into this category. The Soviet bloc countries would probably object for political reasons. The Arab bloc and several scattered Latin American and Asian countries would probably oppose it too. But it might be quite

[12] Letter by Congressman Ben Rosenthal (Dem., New York) to the Editor of the *New York Times*, July 15, 1962.

possible to obtain a two-thirds majority in the General Assembly and to agree on a sliding scale of royalty payments in order to accommodate those countries whose economies would suffer as a result. The first returns to the United Nations might not come in for several years. But the proposal, if adopted, would signify a momentous breakthrough in the evolution and financial independence of the United Nations.

Preliminary surveys have reached a more advanced stage in the North Sea where several oil companies are already engaged in exploratory drilling in the hope of discovering huge oil deposits. Technically, the resources would be more easily accessible than those in the Gulf of Mexico: the waters are shallower and the areas to be explored are not as far from shore. They will, however, probably be claimed by six nations under the 1958 Convention on the Continental Shelf: Britain, Norway, Denmark, West Germany, the Netherlands, and Belgium, whose continental shelves extend anywhere from twenty to one hundred miles from the coasts. These six nations would have to agree to bring the United Nations into the picture. They will certainly not yield their claims to the Organization. But in view of the fact that most of them have been staunch supporters of it, they might be persuaded to share some of the profits.

Revenue from Outer Space Activities

The "longest" of the long-range possibilities for new sources of revenue is outer space. For analytical purposes, space activities and resources that might ultimately yield revenue for the United Nations may be divided into four parts: communications satellites, meteorological systems, transportation vehicles, and resources of celestial bodies.

With regard to communications satellites, one proposal is on record. In 1961, Dr. Eugene Staley declared that:

> The use of orbiting satellites for relaying telephonic and TV signals, obviating expensive submarine cables or chains of microwave relay stations, is bound to have considerable monetary value. The UN should be given exclusive authority not only to license and regulate but also to tax this and other types of space traffic. A small percentage of the revenue from a world-wide communications network making use of space satellites might in a few years provide considerable income for the UN.[13]

[13] Staley, *op. cit.*, p. 2.

On analysis, there are several inherent difficulties with this proposal. First, it must be kept in mind that communications satellites do not create a new technological entity; rather, they offer a significant addition to an already well established and functioning world-wide communications network. Thus, while representing a new technology, the satellites will be blended into already established patterns. To tax messages using the satellites while leaving other international routings tax-free would result in an anomalous situation. It would serve only to inhibit the development of satellite systems, since existing systems of transmission by radio and cable are also being rapidly improved. On the other hand, to tax all international transmissions would probably be politically unacceptable. A light "tax" on satellite systems might perhaps be possible, but then the yield would be minimal.

If it were desired that the United Nations operate a space communications network, it would be necessary for states to donate launching vehicles, satellites, and ground reception and transmission stations, a costly procedure. Here a major problem would be the need for capital to produce the facilities which would ultimately yield revenue. And those nations now in the field that have made large research and development expenditures would be difficult to displace.

The use of satellites as parts of meteorological and navigational systems has already been accomplished. Their use will no doubt grow during the coming years. Yet, they hardly lend themselves as a source for United Nations revenue.

Governments now offer weather forecasts paid for by the general treasury as part of a necessary service to promote economic efficiency. While private weather services do exist, the public in general is not accustomed to paying for such services separately. To tax weather satellites would offer a small yield, due to the relatively small number needed. High profits would be precluded by the ability of national states to send up their own facilities. Most important, it would be undesirable to inhibit the dissemination of information in a field in which the actual gains therefrom are widespread, diffused, often not calculable and hence not suited for "fees" or "taxes." Weather forecasting is a public service industry. The problems of converting navigational satellites into revenue sources for the United Nations are similar.

The use of space-going vehicles for transportation and travel purposes between points on earth is at best a decade away. Once these become operational, however, the question will again arise whether one type of transportation facility should be taxed because it involves a new technological development while ships, trains, aircraft, and surface vehicles, which may still be operating between the same points, are not. Such a tax might inhibit technological advance into new techniques of transportation.

That man will reach the moon by 1970 seems virtually certain, but that he will also be able to exploit the resources of the celestial bodies for the benefit of planet earth within the next few decades seems far less likely. Nevertheless, the nations of the world, including the United States and the Soviet Union, voted unanimously on December 20, 1961 in favor of a General Assembly resolution which "commended" to states for their guidance in the exploration and use of outer space the following principles:

(a) International law, including the Charter of the United Nations applies to outer space and celestial bodies;
(b) Outer space and celestial bodies are free for exploration and use by all states in conformity with international law and are not subject to national appropriation.

If these principles become accepted law, a natural role for the United Nations would arise since, in the absence of national sovereignty, a control organization to make and administer rules for a population is essential. The precedents of the internationalized regimes of Leticia and the Saar under the League of Nations, the draft arrangements for Palestine and Trieste under United Nations control, and the role of the United Nations in administering West New Guinea, might serve as starting points for drafting such a regime when the time comes. But United Nations revenue from these sources is too remote even to contemplate at this time.

When long-range possibilities for United Nations revenue in Antarctica, the oceans, and outer space are surveyed, several conclusions emerge. First is the difficulty of finding resources on which states have not already taken potentially possessive positions. As a general rule, if a resource promises to yield revenue, states will tend to claim it. If they do not, it usually means that the resource is not only currently, but also potentially, useless. Second, the exploration of these areas will necessitate long-term capital expenditures. All of them would initially require great expenditures before they would yield any revenue. In this connection, the possibility of setting up a joint enterprise in which all interested nations would combine their resources for the exploration and eventual exploitation of Antarctica, outer space, or the high seas might fruitfully be pursued. Such a development company might well function under the aegis of the United Nations and could eventually contribute some of its revenues to it as an independent source of income. While prospects for the creation of such entities are now dim, further exploration of the concept of a CEMOA, an international joint stock Company for the Exploitation of the Minerals of Antarctica, or a CODEC, a Cosmic Development Corporation, might prove useful.[14]

A third conclusion which emerges is the fallacy, in most instances, of the assumption that taxes or levies may easily be imposed on new resources and the new technology. The new technology generally blends in with the old, and to tax it would be discriminatory or might even inhibit further technological developments. Fourth, there may be special cases in which a United Nations title could be obtained and a United Nations licensing arrangement consummated. The petroleum deposits in the Gulf of Mexico and in the North Sea might offer such an opportunity. They will be rare, and when they do occur, they would have to be grasped as quickly and decisively as possible. Fifth, direct United Nations exploitation seems most improbable. The vast capital necessary for such operations is not available to the Organization. Even if it were, the ethical question would have to be asked whether the development of Antarctica and of outer space ought to be given priority over the economic development of the poor and underprivileged nations of the earth.

The overall lesson that emerges from this survey of long-range possibilities for United Nations revenue is this: the resources of the frozen polar zones, of the oceans, and of outer space will not become substitutes for the failure of states to meet their financial obligations to the United Nations in the here and now. Vision demands that these possibilities be explored in order to help the United Nations to evolve toward growing strength. But realism demands with equal force that a solution to the financial crisis of the Organization be found in our own lifetime.

[14] Philip C. Jessup and Howard J. Taubenfeld, *Controls for Outer Space* (Columbia University Press, 1959), pp. 184-90 and 281-82.

CHAPTER 12

Retrospect and Prospect

THE FINANCIAL CRISIS of the United Nations has aroused acute anxiety among many observers who see it as the unmistakable symptom of an early death of the Organization. They point to the history of the League of Nations and maintain that, in its case, financial atrophy was the first harbinger of doom. They claim that the same omens, the penury of states and the mounting deficits of the Organization, are gathering now over the United Nations.

On closer scrutiny, this analogy does not hold up. Many of the symptoms are similar, to be sure, but the causes are quite different. The fiscal plight of the League was a symptom of a struggle over its very existence. Many states had questioned the *raison d'être* of the League; others had tolerated it; certainly no state had wanted it to move beyond the concept of a "static conference machinery." In that sense, the League's chronic weakness was the result of a struggle between nihilists and conservatives: those who would deny its existence altogether, and those who would relegate it to the peripheries of their national policies. The former attitude had led to active hostility, the latter to political neglect and indifference.

Summary of Major Problem Areas

The financial plight of the United Nations is not the expression of a struggle over the Organization's existence. All states have accepted its presence. The struggle is being waged between the strict constructionists of the Charter and those who wish to interpret the basic document more liberally: those who wish to maintain the United Nations as a "static conference machinery," and those who wish to give it increasing strength and executive authority. Viewed in this light, the financial crisis of the United Nations does not indicate that the Organization has fallen into political collapse, but rather that the membership has not yet been willing to ratify and sustain its rise to a higher plane of evolutionary development.

The above does not deny the existence of a major crisis. But the crisis is more constitutional and political than financial. At its heart is not so much the problem of economic incapacity to pay the rising costs, but of unwillingness to pay for politically controversial operations. The overall costs of membership have risen across the board from $50 million in 1946 to $500 million in 1963. But when considered in a broader context, these amounts are a pittance. National incomes and national budgets have also risen almost everywhere. Nations have called on the United Nations to assume increasingly greater responsibilities. In that sense, the rising costs indicate the Organization's growing vitality. Moreover, nations save money because the United Nations exists. A host country like the United States absorbs a substantial sum as feedback into its economy because it houses the United Nations. In a more fundamental sense, what would have been the costs to governments if there had been no United Nations during the Suez crisis of 1956? Or even if the crisis had been permitted to continue for several days or weeks before the Organization became involved? There are, of course, so many variables that there are no answers to these questions. But they point up the fact that any discussion of the costs of the United Nations, if divorced from the broader role that it plays in world politics, has an air of unreality.

Of all the activities of the United Nations, those subsumed under the regular budget have been the least controversial—or were until 1963, when France refused to pay for principal and interest on United Nations bonds and the Soviet bloc countries not only followed suit but also refused to pay for certain minor peace-keeping operations that heretofore had been financed through the regular budget without much difficulty.

The regular budget has risen gradually in a gentle upward curve. In 1963, it was $86 million. The most significant changes over the years have been the downward adjustment of the United States assessment percentage and the upward revision of the Soviet share. Under the present assessment pattern, a small minority of the membership still bears most of the burden: sixty countries constituting over half of the membership pay only 3 percent of the budget while twenty countries constituting less than 20 percent of the membership contribute almost 90 percent of the total. The Big Five pay almost two-thirds, the United States close to one-third.

There has been no major crisis over the regular budget. The heart of the tension lies in the area of peace-keeping. Here the United Nations has truly ventured into uncharted territory. For the first time in history, an international organization has created and financed peace forces as a collective responsibility of the world community. UNEF and ONUC have been the most controversial of these. They have raised opposition both on financial and on political grounds. The problem of relative capacity to pay has pitted the "developed" countries against the large majority of "economically less developed" members. The former group, comprising twenty-six nations in 1964, has had most of the wealth, but the latter group, comprising eighty-seven nations, has controlled most of the votes. The conflict between them has resulted in a succession of "rebate" formulas under which the richer countries have made voluntary contributions to make up the deficits created by the reductions granted the poorer ones. While each assessment since 1956 has been *ad hoc,* and no formula was ever institutionalized, these "rebate" formulas in effect have come close to establishing special assessment scales for UNEF and ONUC.

By far the most serious problem, of course, has been posed by the political attitude of the strict constructionists toward the peace-keeping functions. In oversimplified terms, they wish to deny the peace-keeping role to the United Nations while the liberals desire to extend it. The strict constructionists, however, do not always say "no" with equal sonority. The Soviet Union objected to, but until 1963 paid for, a considerable number of minor peace-keeping operations that were financed through the regular budget; it acquiesced in the establishment of the United Nations Emergency Force; and it permitted the creation of the Congo Force and only later wished to destroy it. Hence, the strict constructionist position itself ranges from reluctant acquiescence through passive resistance to active obstruction. Moreover, these categories are in constant flux. The tempering of Soviet hostility toward the Congo operation after 1962 is a case in point.

Similarly, among the liberals, "yes" is not always said with the same degree of enthusiasm. Some states support the political resolutions authorizing the establishment of the peace forces, then vote for the financing resolutions and make payment. Others have second thoughts at the second stage and abstain or even vote against payment.

And some that vote "yes" in the first two stages refuse to make payment after all. The range of liberalism, therefore, also extends along a fluid continuum of three points: enthusiastic support, moral support, and tacit consent. The more cautious form of liberalism and the permissive form of conservatism often meet in voting terms, if not in principle, on the common ground of abstention.

The financial crisis over UNEF and ONUC is first and foremost a political crisis over the proper role of these two peace forces. Only secondarily is it a crisis over money. The Soviet bloc does not oppose UNEF and ONUC and France does not oppose ONUC because they do not want to pay for them; they refuse to pay for them because they oppose them. Both liberals and strict constructionists have responded to specific cases in terms of national interest, rather than abstract principle. From the United States point of view, UNEF and ONUC sealed off a "no man's land" in the cold war from a possible East-West military confrontation and reduced the likelihood of unilateral intervention by the Soviet Union. The Soviet Union reasoned in the same manner and therefore arrived at opposite conclusions. From its point of view, UNEF and ONUC prevented Soviet bridgeheads in the Middle East and Africa. Since, in the latter case, a bridgehead had already been established and had to be liquidated under United Nations pressure, Soviet opposition to ONUC took a more active form.

The United States has never yet had to respond to the creation of a United Nations peace force that it might have regarded with ambivalence or with outright hostility. What, for example, would American policy have been toward ONUC if Kasavubu had been killed instead of Lumumba? Or what would the United States reaction have been if the General Assembly in 1961 had recommended a peace force to help forestall an American-sponsored invasion of Cuba? It would be foolhardy to suggest easy answers to questions such as these. Yet the strong pressure that the United States delegation brought to bear on the other members of the Governing Council of the United Nations Special Fund in January 1963 to cancel an agricultural assistance project in Cuba may be a straw in the wind. The point here is not to indict the policies of the two superpowers, but to suggest that it is incorrect always to associate the United States with the liberal view in the abstract and the Soviet Union with the opposite.

While it is true in principle that the United States has been fundamentally committed to the basic purposes of the United Nations Charter, and the Soviet Union, as a minority power, has been deeply suspicious of the Organization, the two superpowers have tended to react to the Suez and Congo peace-keeping challenges primarily in terms of their own national interests. The only general difference that might be postulated is the United States tendency, when there is a choice between genuine United Nations neutralization and no United Nations action, to prefer the former and for the Soviet Union to prefer the latter. But this difference too is probably the result of the specific experiences of the two superpowers.

The purely fiscal factor has assumed far greater importance in the attitudes of most of the middle and smaller powers. On the one hand, the fear that "it could happen here," has led to support for the peace forces. On the other hand, the cost of these extraordinary expenses has militated in the opposite direction. The interaction between these two conflicting pressures has led to the admixture of political support and financial delinquency that has marked the behavior of so many of these member states.

To sum up, the positions of the United States, the United Kingdom, and the Soviet Union have had relatively little to do with finances *per se.* Neither has the policy of France, which accepted and helped pay for UNEF, but not for ONUC. In the case of China and the bulk of the middle and smaller powers, money played a far larger, in some instances, even a decisive role. In terms of national income, more than one-third of the member states have borne a heavier burden than the two superpowers. Hence, while the financial crisis of UNEF and ONUC is caused primarily by the political attitudes of the few, it has deepened considerably through the financial limitations of the many.

In its two major attempts to surmount the crisis, the General Assembly has tended to embrace the liberal position. The bond issue which—at least in a single instance—endowed the Organization with major borrowing powers was an important milestone in the evolution of the United Nations. Significantly enough, the bonds were purchased not only by liberals, but also by a considerable number of middle-of-the-roaders. Similarly, the Assembly's request for an Advisory Opinion from the International Court was in essence an invitation to the Court to declare itself on the nature of the Organization. The majority opinion and its acceptance by the Assembly were clear vindications of the liberal position and acknowledged legally the Assembly's virtually unlimited fiscal authority. Yet neither the bond issue nor the Advisory Opinion provided a solution. The former was a stop-gap emergency device, and the latter did not move the majority of delinquent states to change their policies. Nor was the problem resolved by the two Working Groups or by the Special Session of the General Assembly in 1963. The mood of the Eighteenth General Assembly was definitely against any further massive appropriations for controversial peace-keeping operations. The 1964 cash appropriations for UNEF and ONUC amounted to less than one-fourth of the funds appropriated for the two forces during the previous year. ONUC was scheduled for termination in mid-1964. The total United Nations debt by the end of 1963 approached the $140 million mark. The political crisis continued unabated, with France and the Soviet bloc continuing their refusal to pay. At the heart of this crisis was the fact of international life that no power, least of all a great power, would adopt, or pay for, a policy that it considered inimical to its national interest.

In the economic and social activities of the United Nations, the dialogue between liberals and strict constructionists has taken a somewhat different form. The political division has fallen less along East-West lines than between the industrialized and the developing countries. Unlike peace and security operations, which have been unpredictable and sporadic, the economic and social activities of the United Nations have been stable and long-term commitments. The issue has not been whether they should exist but how rapidly they should grow.

Altogether, these activities, not including the International Monetary Fund and the International Bank for Reconstruction and Development, account for approximately two-thirds of the total annual expenditures of the United Nations system. The bulk of this money is raised through voluntary contributions from governments and is channeled into the special voluntary programs: United Nation Children's Fund (UNICEF), United Nations High Commissioner for Refugees (UNHCR), United Nations Relief and Works Agency for Palestine Refugees in the Near East (UNRWA), Expanded Programme of Technical Assistance (EPTA) and the Special Fund. The remainder is raised primarily by assessment for nine specialized agencies and the International Atomic Energy Agency. The IMF, the IBRD, and their affiliated bodies depend neither on annual assessments nor on voluntary contributions.

Commitments to the special voluntary programs have risen steadily, but the bases of support have been comparatively uneven. UNICEF, EPTA, and the Special Fund have won close to universal support, but the responses to UNHCR and UNRWA have been far more modest, largely because these programs had been set up for the benefit of a particular region or social group.

Comparison of the voluntary programs with the regular budget shows that most of the developing countries of Africa, Asia, the Middle East, and Latin America contribute in slightly higher proportion to the former than to the latter. The reason for this is quite obvious: most of the voluntary programs exist primarily for the benefit of the new and developing nations. The United States contribution is financially controlling in all the voluntary programs and extends from 40 percent in EPTA and the Special Fund to 70 percent in UNRWA. The United Kingdom contributes in approximately the same proportion as to the regular budget; France, China, and the Soviet Union in far smaller proportions.

The assessment pattern in the specialized agencies has followed that of the regular budget rather closely. All the budgets have risen at a moderate rate. This expansion has taken place in the face of considerable resistance from some member states. As in the voluntary programs, the position of the United States is financially controlling although its percentage contribution has been declining over the years. Some of the agencies have experimented with novel schemes for raising additional revenue and several have attempted to invoke sanctions against nations in arrears on their assessments.

On the whole, a vigorous consensus already exists on the further expansion of the economic and social operations of the United Nations. This consensus, rather than any budget consolidation or fund-raising technique, is the best guarantor of a hopeful future for these activities.

If the overall patterns of financing the peace-keeping are compared with the economic and social operations of the United Nations, it seems paradoxical that the latter, on which there exists almost universal agreement on principle, should be funded primarily by voluntary contributions, while the former, which has divided the Organization against itself, has been financed primarily through compulsory assessments. Logically, the financing principles should perhaps be reversed. In practice, however, the economic and social programs have been so diversified in their character, appeal, and membership that voluntary support probably offered the only realistic basis on which most of them could get started. By now, the pattern is firmly entrenched. Nevertheless, the question may legitimately be raised whether the expenses of bringing economic and social welfare within the reach of all mankind ought to be considered any less binding on the United Nations membership than the task of keeping the peace.

There is yet another connection between the peace-keeping operations and the economic and social programs. The implication of the World Court Advisory Opinion was clearly that the General Assembly had the power to make legally binding decisions in the financial realm. Against the background of the Development Decade and a massive majority of economically less developed nations in the United Nations, it would not be inconceivable that the eighty-seven nations in the latter group could use the precedent of the opinion to vote large funds for economic and social operations as legally binding assessments on the membership. In view of this possibility, the importance of building consensus between those who control the votes and those who control the funds will become increasingly apparent in the future. Unless this problem of political control of funds is resolved, the great power of the Assembly could be employed by impatient majorities eager to push large economic and social programs to impose heavy assessments on a reluctant minority by deciding that such expenditures were "expenses of the Organization." Justice Fitzmaurice warned against such a possibility in 1962. It is a warning not to be taken lightly by the membership. Majority rule per se does not guarantee the healthy evolution of the United Nations.

Proposals for the Future

The analysis of proposals to surmount the financial crisis proceeds on the assumption that any meaningful evaluation of fiscal policy proposals must take into account the political context of the Organization. Indeed, the political aspects of United Nations financing are so all-pervasive that there is really no such thing as an exclusively fiscal question. The truth is that virtually all questions of finance are discussed and voted on as political questions only thinly disguised as fiscal. Hence, this analysis must be concerned not only with what is fiscally desirable but also with what is politically possible.

In the regular budget, further "controlled expansion" is likely. But the positions of France and the Soviet bloc in 1963 suggest mounting resistance to this trend. The inclusion of the costs of minor peace-keeping operations and bond amortization payments in the regular budget no longer makes it possible to insulate the normal day-to-day activities of the Organization from political controversy.

The strengthening process may begin with some modest improvements. First, the various fiscal years of member states might be coordinated with the United Nations fiscal period. This would put the Organization in a better cash position. Second, while it may not be possible to increase the Working Capital Fund much above the present figure of $40 million, it may be feasible to set aside the "miscellaneous income" of roughly $6 million every year and to use it as a contingency fund under proper controls of the General Assembly. This might be easier to accomplish than an increase in the "unforeseen and extraordinary expenditures" item because the money is in existence and could accumulate every year. A sizable peace and security fund or another bond issue would meet with stiff resistance.

In the area of peace and security operations, the two toughest problems are those of cost apportionment and of unwillingness to pay. Leaving aside for the moment the problem of the politically motivated deficits, the obstacles are still formidable. The main tension is between the industrialized and the developing nations. The former feel, on the whole, that the regular scale, which makes allowances for low-income nations, is an adequate basis for cost apportionment. They are willing to give further reductions to the new nations, but hesitate to go along with a new special scale for peace-keeping purposes. The United States in particular leans toward an *ad hoc* approach, arguing that each case should be dealt with as it arises. The majority of the developing nations, on the other hand, hold that they can ill afford peace-keeping payments according to the regular scale and that the great powers, which have a primary responsibility for the maintenance of peace and security, should bear the main financial burden under a special scale.

The discussion over relative capacity to pay clearly reveals that a meeting ground between those who control the funds and those who control the votes must be found. All economic indicators suggest that the twenty-six "developed" countries were able to absorb UNEF and ONUC expenses without much difficulty. Specifically, the congressional ceiling of 33 ⅓ percent imposed on the United States does not accurately recognize American capacity to pay. While there is merit in the argument that the United Nations should not become financially dependent on any one great power, the United States was in effect paying close to 50 percent for UNEF and ONUC until 1963 and close to 40 percent thereafter. A revision of the congressional ceiling to 40 percent would not change the *de facto* picture much, but would get rid of the cumbersome device of applying for additional voluntary contributions from the United States and, most important, would place that country on record as willing to assume a leading role in further extending the peace-keeping function of the United Nations.

Most economic indicators also suggest that, while peace-keeping expenses have often imposed a hardship on the developing nations, this hardship in most instances has certainly not been extreme. Rather, most of the developing nations have tended to give the peace-keeping operations fairly low priorities in their foreign policy calculations. An upward revision of the American ceiling might well set an encouraging example and generate better payment records in the developing parts of the world.

There seem to be four possibilities of a special scale for peace-keeping operations. These try to deal with the problem of economic incapacity to pay, but do not come to grips with the politically motivated deficits. A first such type of scale might simply institutionalize the 1963 rebate formula governing UNEF and ONUC assessments, under which reductions of up to 55 percent are granted to the poorer states, and continue to rely on voluntary contributions to make up the deficit created by these reductions. This is not a dependable formula since there is no assurance that voluntary contributions will always be forthcoming. A second type of scale would use the rebate formula but apportion the deficit among the richer states not eligible for rebates. This would avoid dependence on voluntary contributions, but would in turn increase politically motivated deficits since some of the richer powers refuse to pay. A third type of scale would use the same formula and try to make up the deficit out of regular budget items such as "special missions and related activities," "unforeseen and extraordinary expenditures," and possibly "miscellaneous income." Fourth, the cumbersome rebate system might be abandoned altogether in favor of a completely new scale based primarily on GNP and GNP per capita figures.

A completely new scale would probably be the best solution since GNP figures are least permeated with political considerations and are recognized throughout the world as one index of a nation's capacity to pay. A sliding scale might be built into this or any other plan that would permit the percentages of the wealthier states to rise as the costs rise beyond certain norms, and the percentages of the poorer states to be lowered. But since agreement on such a scale would not be easy to reach, an interim solution may have to be devised. The meeting of deficits created by the rebate system through the regular budget items indicated above may provide such a transitional formula.

It may be prudent to build four safeguards into any special arrangement for the financing of peace-keeping operations. First, any special scale of contributions that might be established should have minimum and maximum percentages of contributions. Second, a sliding scale as indicated above should be a feature. Third, time limits should be fixed for review purposes by the General Assembly. And finally, it might be wise to link a future peace-keeping operation to a payment plan by including in the initial authorizing resolution a section clearly setting forth the terms under which the program would be financed.

None of the above proposals, however, comes to grips with the problem of politically motivated deficits. One way to face up to that challenge completely would be to use a system which permitted a member to refuse payment for a peace-keeping operation that it opposed. Such a solution would ignore the message of the Advisory Opinion that all member states should pay, but it would face up to the political reality that no power, certainly no great power, can be coerced into payment. In this connection, it is important to recall the distinction between passive opposition and active obstruction. If opposition remains limited to nonpayment, as was the Soviet Union's opposition to UNEF, supporters may find it prudent to override it provided they are ready to pay the share of the recalcitrant power. But if they override active opposition, they may find the operation endangered, as in the Congo, or they might even drive the obstructionist power out of the United Nations altogether. The central truth which emerges is that the launching of an operation in the face of either passive or active opposition is in fact to ask for financial crisis and any state that asks for such a crisis ought to be prepared to bail out the Organization.

The dilemma of the use of sanctions against delinquent states is a formidable one. Not to invoke Article 19 would flaunt the Charter as interpreted by the World Court in the Advisory Opinion of July 1962. On the other hand, the use of sanctions might increase the stubbornness of the politically motivated delinquents and perhaps even drive them out of the Organization.

Whether one believes that Article 19 is sufficiently clear-cut in its language to make its application unavoidable when the conditions for its application exist, it seems that the best chance of avoiding a confrontation with the issue lies in the mobilization of a broad and strong consensus that all members have an obligation to contribute to peace-keeping costs. In this respect, the United States has sacrificed a good deal of its potential for leadership toward this end because of its unwillingness to accept a commitment for the future to carry a share of peace-keeping costs greater than its contribution under the regular scale. Clearly, such a commitment could expose the United States to the risk of having to support or acquiesce in peace-keeping operations that it may find questionable in terms of its own national interest. But this is what the United States has demanded of the Soviet Union and other recalcitrant members when it has asserted the General Assembly's power to tax and the automatic application of Article 19. In the last analysis, American willingness to raise its contribution may help prevent what the majority of the membership fears most: a major constitutional and political showdown with the Soviet Union over sanctions under Article 19.

Should such a showdown be unavoidable, it should be remembered that the sanction will not be invoked *against* a given state, but *for* the law. The record of the United Nations demonstrates that the Organization has grown most as a peace-keeping mechanism when the membership has emphasized boldness rather than caution, even when such boldness temporarily strained the political consensus to the breaking point. Institutions, like people, gain in strength and depth by facing a challenge squarely.

The above discussion demonstrates that the opposition of the strict constructionists to peace and security operations to which they object has not been entirely unsuccessful. In consequence, liberals have increasingly turned to new sources for additional revenue for the United Nations.

Private support so far has been limited to the economic and social activities of the United Nations and even there the contributions, while sometimes significant, have not made possible any decisive new breakthroughs. The most generous amounts from private sources have gone to the voluntary programs for refugees and children. It is fairly safe to predict that such support will remain for a considerable time to come a modest supplement to the contributions of governments.

Some efforts have also been made in connection with the exploration of new sources of revenue. The income from these new sources would be meant to strengthen the hand of the United Nations in both the peace and security as well as the economic and social fields.

All of these proposals are based on the assumption that the United Nations has become an integral "organ of society" which is the producer of a "public good" and hence deserving of some additional revenue. Opponents maintain, on the other hand, that the Organization does not render its services free. Member states are already assessed for them. The proposals themselves fall into three major categories: income from United Nations service charges; levies on international activities; and long-range possibilities.

A systematic exploration of these potential sources of revenue leads to mixed conclusions. It becomes evident, on closer scrutiny, for example, that service charges could hardly become a significant source of additional income. In most cases, the returns would be small and the resistance great. Of the three types of levies on international activities that could be contemplated—mail, shipping, and travel—only the first shows real promise. A United Nations stamp surcharge scheme has a chance of adoption. Levies on shipping and travel would be discriminatory and might not yield enough to make the effort worthwhile. The long-range possibilities include the exploitation of the resources of Antarctica, the sea-beds, and outer space. Of these, the only one which is not hopelessly remote, economically as well as politically, is the sea-bed. Specifically, the petroleum resources discovered in the Gulf of Mexico and perhaps those in the North Sea are a possibility for potential United Nations revenue. Antarctica and outer space would necessitate huge capital investments before any returns could be realized.

The opening of these new vistas is impressive. But the fact remains that, in our lifetime at least, most of these new sources of revenue will not provide substitutes for the failure of states to pay their financial obligations. Solutions must be found now. Moreover, the liberals must ask themselves the question whether, if large new economically and politically feasible sources of revenue were found, the majority of states would be prepared to release the right to collect them to an international organization so long as there is serious controversy over its role. Once again, the problem of political consensus is central.

The vital importance of political consensus is also the lesson gleaned from a survey of the financing patterns of regional organizations. Where there is absence of consensus, there usually is penury. Where there is consensus, there usually prevails a wholesome financial climate as well. The formal structure of the organization seems to be of little relevance to the issue of financial health.

In the struggle over what the member states want the United Nations to be, it is certain that the tension between liberals and strict constructionists will continue. The progression from the League of Nations to the United Nations and the development of the United Nations itself suggest, however, that the historical trend is in the direction of the dynamic, evolutionary conception of international organization. When seen in this historical perspective, the financial crisis of the United Nations does not indicate that the Organization has fallen as low as many fear. It merely shows that it has not yet been allowed to rise as high as many had hoped.

Historical perspective also teaches that political consensus—that vital precondition for financial health—is not found. It is made. It is made primarily through a constant probing of its limits and the readiness to raise the search to a higher plane. Realism and idealism are needed in equal measure if the financial crisis is to be surmounted and if the United Nations is to move toward a better world of international order.

Appendixes

Tables

TABLE A.1. *The United Nations Emergency Force*

Member States	Vote Approving Force[a]	Vote on Financing Force[b]	Total Net Assessments for 1957–62[c]	Payments Received[c]	Balance Due June 1, 1963[c]
Afghanistan	Yes	Yes	$ 45,323	$ 6,000	$ 39,323
Albania	Abstained	No	34,108	—	34,108
Argentina	Yes	Yes	856,376	—	856,376
Australia	Yes	Yes	1,587,792	1,587,792	—
Austria	Yes	Yes	371,986	371,986	—
Belgium	Yes	Yes	1,180,820	1,022,042	158,778
Bolivia	Yes	Abstained	38,059	—	38,059
Brazil	Yes	Yes	794,195	794,195	—
Bulgaria	Abstained	No	129,306	—	129,306
Burma	Yes	Yes	68,390	68,390	—
Byelorussian Soviet Socialist Republic	Abstained	No	443,761	—	443,761
Cambodia	Yes	Abstained	30,346	30,346	—
Cameroon			8,745	8,745	—
Canada	Yes	Yes	2,897,299	2,897,299	—
Central African Republic	—	—	4,983	4,983	—
Ceylon	Yes	Yes	79,604	79,604	—
Chad	—	—	4,983	4,206	777
Chile	Yes	Yes	214,002	122,200	91,802
China	Yes	Yes	4,439,837	250,000	4,189,837
Colombia	Yes	Yes	255,425	255,425	—
Congo (Brazzaville)	—	—	8,745	8,745	—
Congo (Leopoldville)	—	—	5,568	5,568	—
Costa Rica	Yes	Yes	30,346	22,718	7,628
Cuba	Yes	Yes	218,001	27,000	191,001
Cyprus	—	—	4,983	4,983	—
Czechoslovakia	Abstained	No	822,112	—	822,112
Dahomey	—	—	4,983	3,824	1,159
Denmark	Yes	Yes	575,197	575,197	—
Dominican Republic	Yes	Yes	42,623	32,348	10,275
Ecuador	Yes	Yes	41,566	41,566	—
Egypt	Abstained	Abstained	—	—	—
El Salvador	Yes	Yes	41,688	36,311	5,377
Ethiopia	Yes	Yes	65,085	—	65,085
Federation of Malaya	—	—	121,134	121,134	—
Finland	Yes	Yes	337,485	337,485	—
France	Yes	Yes	6 238,262	6,238,262	—
Gabon	—	—	4,983	4,983	—
Ghana	—	—	46,669	46,669	—
Greece	Yes	Abstained	160,116	160,116	—
Guatemala	Yes	Yes	45,836	27,783	18,053
Guinea	—	—	19,404	11,185	8,219
Haiti	Yes	Yes	30,346	15,876	14,470
Honduras	Yes	Yes	30,346	21,938	8,408
Hungary	Abstained	—	402,928	—	402,928
Iceland	Yes	Yes	30,346	30,346	—
India	Yes	Yes	2,101,367	2,101,367	—
Indonesia	Yes	Yes	369,488	369,488	—
Iran	Yes	Yes	180,341	180,341	—
Iraq	Yes	Yes	88,598	12,000	76,598
Ireland	Yes	Yes	145,342	145,342	—
Israel	Abstained	Abstained	127,476	127,476	—
Italy	Yes	Abstained	2,013,436	2,013,436	—
Ivory Coast	—	—	7,086	7,086	—
Japan	—	Yes	1,629,897	1,629,897	—
Jordon	Yes	Yes	34,108	—	34,108

[a] General Assembly Res. 1001 (ES-I), Nov. 7, 1956.
[b] U.N. Doc. A/C.6/426.
[c] U.N. Doc. A/C.5/974 (May 14, 1963), as amended by ST/ADM/Ser. B/173 (June 5, 1963).

Member States	Vote Approving Force[a]	Vote on Financing Force[b]	Total Net Assessments for 1957–62[c]	Payments Received[c]	Balance Due June 1, 1963[c]
Laos	Yes	Yes	$ 30,346	$ 30,346	$ —
Lebanon	Yes	Yes	37,931	18,086	19,845
Liberia	Yes	Yes	30,332	30,332	—
Libya	—	Yes	34,108	—	34,108
Luxembourg	Yes	Yes	50,966	50,966	—
Madagascar	—	—	7,086	7,086	—
Mali	—	—	8,745	8,730	15
Mexico	Yes	Yes	597,028	70,000	527,028
Morocco	—	—	98,304	98,304	—
Nepal	Yes	—	30,346	29,411	935
The Netherlands	Yes	Yes	987,664	987,664	—
New Zealand	Yes	Yes	391,279	391,279	—
Nicaragua	Yes	—	30,346	27,015	3,331
Niger	—	—	4,983	—	4,983
Nigeria	—	—	26,166	26,166	—
Norway	Yes	Yes	449,648	449,648	—
Pakistan	Yes	Yes	360,620	360,620	—
Panama	Yes	Yes	34,297	6,056	28,241
Paraguay	Yes	Yes	30,346	5,876	24,470
Peru	Yes	Yes	109,408	15,000	94,408
Philippines	Yes	Yes	315,232	315,232	—
Poland	Abstained	No	1,269,004	—	1,269,004
Portugal	Yes	Yes	187,031	187,031	—
Romania	Abstained	No	375,230	—	375,230
Saudi Arabia	Yes	Yes	55,309	—	55,309
Senegal	—	—	7,281	6,310	971
Somalia	—	—	8,745	8,745	—
South Africa	Abstained	Abstained	567,589	567,589	—
Spain	Yes	Yes	867,164	—	867,164
Sudan	—	Yes	71,118	—	71,118
Sweden	Yes	Yes	1,305,078	1,305,078	—
Syria[d]	Yes	Yes	32,667	—	32,667
Thailand	Yes	Yes	121,381	118,441	2,940
Togo	—	—	4,983	—	4,983
Tunisia	—	—	37,931	37,931	—
Turkey	Yes	Abstained	454,718	454,718	—
Ukranian Soviet Socialist Republic	Abstained	No	1,700,104	—	1,700,104
Union of Soviet Socialist Republics	Abstained	No	14,218,288	—	14,218,288
United Arab Republic	—	—	284,742	—	284,742
United Kingdom	Yes	Abstained	7,954,620	7,954,620	—
United States	Yes	Yes	33,701,242	33,701,242	—
Upper Volta	—	—	8,745	—	8,745
Uruguay	Yes	Yes	106,650	81,667	24,983
Venezuela	Yes	Yes	349,550	349,550	—
Yemen	Yes	Yes	34,108	—	34,108
Yugoslavia	Yes	Yes	267,569	267,569	—
Total	Yes 63 / No 0 / Abst. 12	Yes 58 / No 8 / Abst. 9	$97,167,252	$69,831,985	$27,335,267
Mauritania			1,196	—	1,196
Mongolia			1,196	—	1,196
Sierra Leone			1,196	1,196	—
Tanganyika			1,196	1,196	—
			$97,172,036	$69,834,377	$27,337,659

[d] For the years 1960 and 1961, assessments have been shown against the United Arab Republic.

TABLE A.2. *United Nations Operations in the Congo*

Member States	Vote Approving Force[a]	Vote on Financing Force[b]	Total Net Assessments for 1960–62[c]	Payments Received[c]	Balance Due June 1, 1963[c]
Afghanistan	Yes	Abstained	$ 34,366	—	$ 34,366
Albania	Abstained	No	33,664	—	33,664
Argentina	Yes	Yes	649,372	$ 250,000	399,372
Australia	Yes	Yes	3,966,576	3,966,576	—
Austria	Yes	Yes	993,847	568,875	424,972
Belgium	Yes	Abstained	2,876,284	—	2,876,284
Bolivia	—	Yes	33,664	—	33,664
Brazil	Yes	Yes	613,023	202,080	410,943
Bulgaria	Abstained	No	141,055	—	141,055
Burma	Yes	Yes	46,355	46,355	—
Byelorussian Soviet Socialist Republic	Abstained	No	1,108,811	—	1,108,811
Cambodia	Yes	Abstained	33,664	6,366	27,298
Cameroon	—	Abstained	16,452	16,452	—
Canada	Yes	Yes	7,080,341	7,080,341	—
Central African Republic	—	—	15,387	15,387	—
Ceylon	Yes	Abstained	58,344	58,344	—
Chad	—	Abstained	15,387	2,572	12,815
Chile	Yes	Abstained	160,247	—	160,247
China	Yes	Abstained	5,751,744	—	5,751,744
Colombia	Yes	Abstained	177,826	177,826	—
Congo (Brazzaville)	—	—	16,452	16,452	—
Congo (Leopoldville)	—	Yes	20,187	20,187	—
Costa Rica	Yes	Yes	23,978	—	23,978
Cuba	Yes	Abstained	205,598	—	205,598
Cyprus	—	Abstained	15,387	15,387	—
Czechoslovakia	Abstained	Yes	2,218,437	—	2,218,437
Dahomey	—	No	15,387	9,140	6,246
Denmark	Yes	Yes	1,348,439	1,348,439	—
Dominican Republic	Yes	—	42,079	—	42,079
Ecuador	Yes	Yes	35,966	33,085	2,881
El Salvador	Yes	Yes	28,371	12,108	16,263
Ethiopia	Yes	—	34,366	—	34,366
Federation of Malaya	Yes	Yes	95,504	95,504	—
Finland	Yes	Yes	826,664	826,664	—
France	Abstained	Abstained	14,186,015	—	14,186,015
Gabon	—	—	15,387	15,387	—
Ghana	Yes	Yes	45,160	45,160	—
Greece	Yes	Yes	137,870	137,870	—
Guatemala	Yes	Abstained	29,971	—	29,971
Guinea	Yes	Abstained	33,664	33,664	—
Haiti	Yes	Yes	23,978	—	23,978
Honduras	Abstained	Yes	23,978	—	23,978
Hungary	Yes	No	734,270	—	734,270
Iceland	Yes	—	23,978	23,978	—
India	Yes	Abstained	2,624,063	2,624,063	—
Indonesia	Yes	Abstained	278,534	278,534	—
Iran	Yes	Yes	124,282	25,000	99,282
Iraq	Yes	No	75,744	—	75,744
Ireland	Yes	Yes	131,455	131,455	—
Israel	Yes	Yes	85,521	85,521	—
Italy	Yes	Yes	5,108,646	5,108,646	—
Ivory Coast	—	—	19,904	19,904	—
Japan	Yes	Yes	2,521,178	2,521,178	—
Jordan	Yes	—	33,664	—	33,664
Laos	Yes	—	23,978	23,978	—

[a] General Assembly Res. 1474 (ES-IV), Sept. 20, 1960.
[b] U.N. Doc. A/C.5/1.638 and Rev. 1, Agenda Item 49(XV) (Dec. 9 and 13, 1960).
[c] U.N. Doc. A/C.5/974 (May 14, 1963), as amended by ST/ADM/Ser. B/173 (June 5, 1963).

Member States	Vote Approving Force[a]	Vote on Financing Force[b]	Total Net Assessments for 1960–62[c]	Payments Received[c]	Balance Due June 1, 1963[c]
Lebanon	Yes	No	$ 29,971	$ 17,863	$ 12,108
Liberia	Yes	Yes	23,978	23,978	—
Libya	Yes	—	33,664	33,664	—
Luxembourg	Yes	Yes	48,895	40,946	7,949
Madagascar	—	Abstained	19,904	2,574	17,330
Mali	—	—	16,452	2,131	14,321
Mexico	Yes	Abstained	602,331	—	602,331
Morocco	Yes	Abstained	117,823	—	117,823
Nepal	Yes	—	23,978	17,474	6,503
The Netherlands	Yes	Yes	2,296,805	2,296,805	—
New Zealand	Yes	Yes	947,107	947,107	—
Nicaragua	Yes	—	23,978	—	23,978
Niger	—	Yes	15,387	—	15,387
Nigeria	—	Yes	80,828	80,828	—
Norway	Yes	Yes	1,082,292	1,082,292	—
Pakistan	Yes	Yes	242,974	242,974	—
Panama	Yes	Yes	23,978	—	23,978
Paraguay	Yes	—	23,978	9,687	14,291
Peru	Yes	Yes	64,338	—	64,338
Philippines	Yes	Abstained	252,957	252,957	—
Poland	Abstained	No	1,852,915	—	1,852,915
Portugal	Yes	No	161,919	—	161,919
Romania	Abstained	No	757,181	—	757,181
Saudi Arabia	Yes	No	52,095	—	52,095
Senegal	—	Yes	21,504	13,510	7,994
Somalia	—	Yes	16,452	8,945	7,507
South Africa	Abstained	Abstained	1,249,477	—	1,249,477
Spain	Yes	Abstained	771,483	—	771,483
Sudan	Yes	Yes	37,565	37,565	—
Sweden	Yes	Yes	3,088,949	3,088,949	—
Syria[d]	—	—	7,955	—	7,955
Thailand	Yes	Yes	95,910	70,445	25,465
Togo	—	Abstained	15,387	—	15,387
Tunisia	Yes	Yes	29,971	29,971	—
Turkey	Yes	Yes	323,266	323,266	—
Ukrainian Soviet Socialist Republic	Abstained	No	4,237,317	—	4,237,317
Union of Soviet Socialist Republics	Abstained	No	32,052,762	—	32,052,762
United Arab Republic	Yes	No	258,155	—	258,155
United Kingdom	Yes	Yes	17,532,224	17,532,224	—
United States	Yes	Yes	73,565,272	73,565,272	—
Upper Volta	—	—	16,452	—	16,452
Uruguay	Yes	Yes	70,332	—	70,332
Venezuela	Yes	Abstained	302,917	—	302,917
Yemen	Yes	No	33,664	—	33,664
Yugoslavia	Yes	Abstained	299,358	—	299,358
Total	Yes 70 / No 0 / Abst. 11	Yes 45 / No 15 / Abst. 25	$197,836,546	$125,563,896	$72,272,650
Mauritania			7,277	—	7,277
Mongolia			7,277	—	7,277
Sierra Leone			7,277	7,277	—
Tanganyika			7,277	7,277	—
			$197,865,654	$125,578,450	$72,287,204

[d] For the years 1960 and 1961, assessments have been shown against the United Arab Republic.

311

TABLE A.3. *Apportionment of the Expenses of the Operations of the United Nations Emergency Force for the Period July 1, 1963 to December 31, 1963*

Members States[a]	Scale of Assessments for 1963 (Percent)	Assessments July 1– Dec. 31, 1963
Afghanistan	0.05	$ 2,821
Albania	0.04	2,256
Argentina	1.01	56,974
Australia	1.66	157,448
Austria	0.45	42,682
Belgium	1.20	113,818
Bolivia	0.04	2,256
Brazil	1.03	58,102
Bulgaria	0.20	11,282
Burma	0.07	3,949
Byelorussian Soviet Socialist Republic	0.52	49,322
Cambodia	0.04	2,256
Cameroon	0.04	2,256
Canada	3.12	295,927
Central African Republic	0.04	2,256
Ceylon	0.09	5,077
Chad	0.04	2,256
Chile	0.26	14,667
China	4.57	257,793
Colombia	0.26	14,667
Congo (Brazzaville)	0.04	2,256
Congo (Leopoldville)	0.07	3,949
Costa Rica	0.04	2,256
Cuba	0.22	12,410
Cyprus	0.04	2,256
Czechoslovakia	1.17	110,972
Dahomey	0.04	2,256
Denmark	0.58	55,012
Dominican Republic	0.05	2,821
Ecuador	0.06	3,385
El Salvador	0.04	2,256
Ethiopia	0.05	2,821
Federation of Malaya	0.13	7,334
Finland	0.37	35,094
France	5.94	563,399
Gabon	0.04	2,256
Ghana	0.09	5,077
Greece	0.23	12,974
Guatemala	0.05	2,821
Guinea	0.04	2,256
Haiti	0.04	2,256
Honduras	0.04	2,256
Hungary	0.56	53,115
Iceland	0.04	3,794
India	2.03	114,512
Indonesia	0.45	25,384
Iran	0.20	11,282
Iraq	0.09	5,077
Ireland	0.14	13,279
Israel	0.15	8,461
Italy	2.24	212,461
Ivory Coast	0.04	2,256
Japan	2.27	215,306
Jordan	0.04	2,256
Laos	0.04	2,256

Source: U.N. Doc. ST/ADM/SER.B/183 (Jan. 10, 1964).
[a] Excluding the Member States admitted to the Organization at the seventeenth session of the General Assembly and at the fourth special session.

312

Member States[a]	Scale of Assessments for 1963 (Percent)	Assessments July 1– Dec. 31, 1963
Lebanon	0.05	$ 2,821
Liberia	0.04	2,256
Libya	0.04	2,256
Luxembourg	0.05	4,742
Madagascar	0.04	2,256
Mali	0.04	2,256
Mexico	0.74	41,744
Morocco	0.14	7,898
Nepal	0.04	2,256
The Netherlands	1.01	95,797
New Zealand	0.41	38,888
Nicaragua	0.04	2,256
Niger	0.04	2,256
Nigeria	0.21	11,846
Norway	0.45	42,682
Pakistan	0.42	23,692
Panama	0.04	2,256
Paraguay	0.04	2,256
Peru	0.10	5,641
Philippines	0.40	22,564
Poland	1.28	121,406
Portugal	0.16	9,026
Romania	0.32	30,351
Saudi Arabia	0.07	3,949
Senegal	0.05	2,821
Somalia	0.04	2,256
South Africa	0.53	50,270
Spain	0.86	48,512
Sudan	0.07	3,949
Sweden	1.30	123,303
Syria	0.05	2,821
Thailand	0.16	9,026
Togo	0.04	2,256
Tunisia	0.05	2,821
Turkey	0.40	22,564
Ukrainian Soviet Socialist Republic	1.98	187,800
Union of Soviet Socialist Republics	14.97	1,419,878
United Arab Republic	0.25	14,102
United Kingdom	7.58	718,949
United States	32.02	3,037,040
Upper Volta	0.04	2,256
Uruguay	0.11	6,205
Venezuela	0.52	29,334
Yemen	0.04	2,256
Yugoslavia	0.38	21,436
	100.00	$8,799,083
Mauritania	0.04	2,256
Mongolia	0.04	2,256
Sierra Leone	0.04	2,256
Tanganyika	0.04	2,256
Total	100.16	$8,808,107
Amount of voluntary contributions required to finance authorized expenditures in excess of the total amount assessed		691,893
Total Authorized Expenditures		$9,500,000

TABLE A.4. *Apportionment of the Expenses of the United Nations Operation in the Congo for the Period July 1, 1963 to December 31, 1963*

Member States[a]	Scale of Assessments for 1963 (Percent)	Assessments July 1– Dec. 31, 1963
Afghanistan	0.05	$ 8,238
Albania	0.04	6,589
Argentina	1.01	166,384
Australia	1.66	546,924
Austria	0.45	148,262
Belgium	1.20	395,367
Bolivia	0.04	6,589
Brazil	1.03	169,679
Bulgaria	0.20	32,947
Burma	0.07	11,532
Byelorussian Soviet Socialist Republic	0.52	171,326
Cambodia	0.04	6,589
Cameroon	0.04	6,589
Canada	3.12	1,027,955
Central African Republic	0.04	6,589
Ceylon	0.09	14,827
Chad	0.04	6,589
Chile	0.26	42,831
China	4.57	752,846
Colombia	0.26	42,831
Congo (Brazzaville)	0.04	6,589
Congo (Leopoldville)	0.07	11,532
Costa Rica	0.04	6,589
Cuba	0.22	36,242
Cyprus	0.04	6,589
Czechoslovakia	1.17	385,483
Dahomey	0.04	6,589
Denmark	0.58	191,094
Dominican Republic	0.05	8,238
Ecuador	0.06	9,884
El Salvador	0.04	6,589
Ethiopia	0.05	8,238
Federation of Malaya	0.13	21,416
Finland	0.37	121,905
France	5.94	1,957,068
Gabon	0.04	6,589
Ghana	0.09	14,827
Greece	0.23	37,889
Guatemala	0.05	8,238
Guinea	0.04	6,589
Haiti	0.04	6,589
Honduras	0.04	6,589
Hungary	0.56	184,505
Iceland	0.04	13,179
India	2.03	334,415
Indonesia	0.45	74,131
Iran	0.20	32,947
Iraq	0.09	14,827
Ireland	0.14	46,126
Israel	0.15	24,711
Italy	2.24	738,019
Ivory Coast	0.04	6,589
Japan	2.27	747,903
Jordan	0.04	6,589
Laos	0.04	6,589

Source: U.N. Doc. ST/ADM/SER.B/183 (Jan. 10, 1964).
[a] Excluding the Member States admitted to the Organization at the seventeenth session of the General Assembly and at the fourth special session.

Member States[a]	Scale of Assessments for 1963 (Percent)	Assessments July 1– Dec. 31, 1963
Lebanon	0.05	$ 8,238
Liberia	0.04	6,589
Libya	0.04	6,589
Luxembourg	0.05	16,474
Madagascar	0.04	6,589
Mali	0.04	6,589
Mexico	0.74	121,906
Morocco	0.14	23,063
Nepal	0.04	6,589
The Netherlands	1.01	332,768
New Zealand	0.41	135,084
Nicaragua	0.04	6,589
Niger	0.04	6,589
Nigeria	0.21	34,595
Norway	0.45	148,262
Pakistan	0.42	69,190
Panama	0.04	6,589
Paraguay	0.04	6,589
Peru	0.10	16,474
Philippines	0.40	65,895
Poland	1.28	421,726
Portugal	0.16	26,358
Romania	0.32	105,432
Saudi Arabia	0.07	11,532
Senegal	0.05	8,238
Somalia	0.04	6,589
South Africa	0.53	174,621
Spain	0.86	141,674
Sudan	0.07	11,532
Sweden	1.30	428,315
Syria	0.05	8,238
Thailand	0.16	26,358
Togo	0.04	6,589
Tunisia	0.05	8,238
Turkey	0.40	65,895
Ukrainian Soviet Socialist Republic	1.98	652,356
Union of Soviet Socialist Republics	14.97	4,932,209
United Arab Republic	0.25	41,184
United Kingdom	7.58	2,497,404
United States	32.02	10,549,720
Upper Volta	0.04	6,589
Uruguay	0.11	18,121
Venezuela	0.52	85,663
Yemen	0.04	6,589
Yugoslavia	0.38	62,600
	100.00	$30,008,388
Mauritania	0.04	6,589
Mongolia	0.04	6,589
Sierra Leone	0.04	6,589
Tanganyika	0.04	6,589
Total	100.16	$30,034,744
Amount of voluntary contributions required to finance authorized expenditures in excess of the total amount assessed		2,965,256
Total Authorized Expenditures		$33,000,000

315

TABLE A.5. *Special United Nations Programs Financed by Voluntary Contributions and United Nations Expenditures, Selected Years 1949–63*

(In thousands of dollars)

Agency	1949	1952	1955	1958	1961	1962[a]	1963[a]
United Nations Children's Fund	$46,665	$13,526	$14,161	$22,436	$24,449	$30,429	$30,500
United Nations Expanded Technical Assistance Program	—	22,968	25,877	33,820	38,107	51,580	53,000
United Nations High Commissioner for Refugees	—	—	1,129	5,480	3,815	3,897	4,500
United Nations Korean Reconstruction Agency	—	4,133	31,515	1,156	—	—	—
United Nations Relief and Works Agency for Palestine Refugees in the Near East	39,116	26,779	32,280	31,776	36,323	36,885	37,000
United Nations Special Fund	—	—	—	—	9,556	81,454	78,547
Total Special Programs Financed by Voluntary Contributions	$85,781	$67,406	$104,962	$94,668	$112,250	$204,245	$203,547
United Nations Regular Budget	43,204	50,548	50,228	61,122	71,096	85,818	93,911

Source: *United States Contributions to International Organizations*, H. Doc. 131, 88 Cong. 1 sess. (1963), App. Table No. 7.
[a] Estimate.

316

Voting Strength of Member States in the International Monetary Fund as of April 30, 1962

Member States	Votes		Member States	Votes	
	Number	*Percent of Total*		Number	*Percent of Total*
Afghanistan	475	0.28	Korea	437	0.26
Argentina	3,050	1.80	Laos	325	0.19
Australia	4,250	2.51	Lebanon	317	0.19
Austria	1,000	0.59	Liberia	362	0.21
Belgium	3,625	2.14	Libya	360	0.21
Bolivia	475	0.28	Luxembourg	370	0.22
Brazil	3,050	1.80	Malaya	575	0.34
Burma	550	0.32	Mexico	2,050	1.21
Canada	5,750	3.39	Morocco	775	0.46
Ceylon	700	0.41	Nepal	325	0.19
Chile	1,250	0.74	The Netherlands	4,375	2.58
China	5,750	3.39	New Zealand	1,500	0.88
Colombia	1,250	0.74	Nicaragua	362	0.21
Costa Rica	400	0.24	Nigeria	750	0.44
Cuba	750	0.44	Norway	1,250	0.74
Cyprus	362	0.21	Pakistan	1,750	1.03
Denmark	1,550	0.91	Panama	255	0.15
Dominican Republic	400	0.24	Paraguay	362	0.21
Ecuador	400	0.24	Peru	575	0.34
El Salvador	362	0.21	Philippines	1,000	0.59
Ethiopia	364	0.21	Portugal	850	0.50
Finland	820	0.48	Saudi Arabia	800	0.47
France	8,125	4.79	Spain	1,750	1.03
Germany, Federal Republic of	8,125	4.79	Sudan	400	0.24
			Sweden	1,750	1.03
Ghana	600	0.35			
			Syria	400	0.24
Greece	850	0.50	Thailand	700	0.41
Guatemala	400	0.24	Tunisia	412	0.24
Haiti	362	0.21	Turkey	1,110	0.65
Honduras	362	0.21	Union of South Africa	1,750	1.03
Iceland	362	0.21			
			United Arab Republic	1,150	0.68
India	6,250	3.69	United Kingdom	19,750	11.65
Indonesia	1,900	1.12	United States	41,500	24.47
Iran	950	0.56	Uruguay	550	0.32
Iraq	400	0.24	Venezuela	1,750	1.03
Ireland	700	0.41			
			Viet-Nam	435	0.26
Israel	500	0.29	Yugoslavia	1,450	0.86
Italy	2,950	1.74			
Japan	5,250	3.10	Total	169,564	100.00
Jordan	313	0.18			

Source: International Monetary Fund, *Annual Report 1962*, pp. 179–82.

TABLE A.7. *Voting Strength of Member States in the International Bank for Reconstruction and Development in 1962*

Member States	Votes Number	Votes Percent of Total	Member States	Votes Number	Votes Percent of Total
Afghanistan	550	0.24	Korea	500	0.22
Argentina	3,983	1.78	Laos	350	0.16
Australia	5,580	2.49	Lebanon	340	0.15
Austria	1,250	0.56	Liberia	400	0.18
Belgium	4,750	2.12	Libya	450	0.20
Bolivia	460	0.20	Luxembourg	450	0.20
Brazil	3,983	1.78	Malaya	750	0.33
Burma	650	0.29	Mexico	1,983	0.89
Canada	7,750	3.47	Morocco	950	0.42
Ceylon	850	0.38	Nepal	350	0.16
Chile	1,183	0.53	The Netherlands	5,750	2.57
China	7,750	3.47	New Zealand	1,917	0.86
Colombia	1,183	0.53	Nicaragua	310	0.14
Costa Rica	330	0.15	Nigeria	917	0.41
Cyprus	400	0.18	Norway	1,583	0.71
Denmark	1,983	0.89	Pakistan	2,250	1.01
Dominican Republic	330	0.15	Panama	254	0.11
Ecuador	378	0.17	Paraguay	310	0.14
El Salvador	310	0.14	Peru	600	0.27
Ethiopia	350	0.16	Philippines	1,250	0.56
Finland	1,010	0.45	Portugal	1,050	0.47
France	10,750	4.81	Saudi Arabia	983	0.44
Germany, Federal Republic of	10,750	4.81	South Africa	2,250	1.01
Ghana	717	0.32	Spain	2,250	1.01
Greece	750	0.33	Sudan	450	0.20
Guatemala	330	0.15	Sweden	2,250	1.01
Haiti	400	0.18	Syrian Arab Republic	450	0.20
Honduras	310	0.14	Thailand	850	0.38
Iceland	400	0.18	Tunisia	550	0.24
India	8,250	3.69	Turkey	1,400	0.63
Indonesia	2,450	1.09	United Arab Republic	1,316	0.59
Iran	1,150	0.51	United Kingdom	26,250	11.74
Iraq	400	0.18	United States	63,750	28.51
Ireland	850	0.38	Uruguay	355	0.16
Israel	583	0.26	Venezuela	1,650	0.74
Italy	3,850	1.72	Viet Nam	550	0.24
Japan	6,910	3.09	Yugoslavia	1,317	0.59
Jordan	400	0.18	Total	223,598	100.00

Source: International Bank for Reconstruction and Development, "Voting Power and Subscriptions of Member Countries April 2, 1962," *Basic Documents April 1962.*

TABLE A.8. *United Nations and Specialized Agencies, Expenditures or Authorizations, Selected Years, 1946–63*
(In thousands of dollars)

Agency	1946	1949	1952	1955	1958	1961	1962[a]	1963[a]
International Labour Organisation	$ 2,660	$ 5,034	$ 6,390	$ 7,051	$ 8,095	$ 10,205	$ 12,738	$ 14,578
Food and Agriculture Organization	377	4,655	4,830	5,974	9,147	9,490	14,368	14,595
United Nations Educational, Scientific, and Cultural Organization	1,053	7,780	8,726	9,151	12,316	16,015	16,498	19,500
International Civil Aviation Organization	980	2,681	3,266	3,223	4,001	4,720	5,336	5,827
Universal Postal Union	132	297	417	429	452	712	750	750
World Health Organization	116	4,777	7,684	9,500	13,566	19,201	24,165	30,118
International Telecommunication Union	—	2,994	1,592	1,467	2,147	3,190	3,287	3,820
World Meteorological Organization	—	—	177	383	441	643	777	990
Intergovernmental Maritime Consultative Organization	—	—	—	—	—	233	401	421
International Atomic Energy Agency	—	—	—	—	—	6,168[b]	6,161[b]	7,123[b]
Total Specialized Agencies and International Atomic Energy Agency[c]	$ 5,318	$28,218	$33,082	$37,178	$ 50,165	$ 70,577	$ 84,481	$ 97,722
United Nations Regular Budget	19,330	43,204	50,548	50,228	61,122	71,096	85,818	93,911
Grand Total	$24,648	$71,422	$83,630	$87,406	$111,287	$141,673	$170,299	$191,633

Source: *United States Contributions to International Organizations*, H. Doc. 131, 88 Cong. 1 sess. (1963), p. 87 and App. Table No. 7.
[a] Estimate.
[b] Assessment.
[c] Exclusive of the International Refugee Organization, a temporary specialized agency, for which expenditures (in thousands of dollars) were as follows: 1947—$75,676; 1948—$132,167; 1949—$119,402; 1950—$85,447.

319

TABLE A.9. *Scales of Assessments: United Nations and Specialized Agencies, 1962*

Member States[a]	United Nations (Percent)	ILO (Percent)	FAO (Percent)	UNESCO (Percent)
Afghanistan	0.05	0.12	0.07	0.06
Albania	0.04	0.12	—	0.04
Algeria	—	—	—	—
Argentina	1.01	1.42	1.35	1.07
Australia	1.66	1.86	2.22	1.73
Austria	0.45	0.35	0.60	0.42
Belgium	1.20	1.38	1.61	1.26
Bolivia	0.04	0.12	0.04	0.04
Brazil	1.03	1.38	1.38	0.99
British East African Territories, including the Seychelles	—	—	—	—
British Guiana	—	—	0.024[b]	—
Bulgaria	0.20	0.19	—	0.15
Burma	0.07	0.14	0.09	0.08
Byelorussian Soviet Socialist Republic	0.52	0.45	—	0.45
Cambodia	0.04	—	0.04	0.04
Cameroon	0.04	0.12	0.04	0.04
Canada	3.12	3.40	4.18	3.01
Central African Republic	0.04	0.12	0.04	0.04
Ceylon	0.09	0.12	0.12	0.10
Chad	0.04	0.12	0.04	0.04
Chile	0.26	0.34	0.35	0.26
China	4.57	2.04	—	2.50
Colombia	0.26	0.38	0.35	0.30
Congo (Brazzaville)	0.04	0.12	0.04	0.04
Congo (Leopoldville)	0.07	0.12	0.09	0.04
Costa Rica	0.04	0.12	0.04	0.04
Cuba	0.22	0.30	0.30	0.24
Cyprus	0.04	0.12	0.04	—
Czechoslovakia	1.17	0.92	—	0.84
Dahomey	0.04	0.12	0.04	0.04
Denmark	0.58	0.73	0.78	0.58
Dominican Republic	0.05	0.12	0.07	0.05
Ecuador	0.06	0.12	0.08	0.06
El Salvador	0.04	0.12	0.04	0.05
Ethiopia	0.05	0.12	0.07	0.06
Federation of Malaya	0.13	0.21	0.17	0.16
Federation of Rhodesia and Nyasaland	—	—	0.09[b]	—
Finland	0.37	0.30	0.50	0.35
France	5.94	6.10	7.96	6.19
France (overseas Territories)	—	—	—	—
French Polynesia	—	—	—	—
French Somaliland	—	—	—	—
Gabon	0.04	0.12	0.04	0.04
Germany (Federal Republic of)	—	4.34	7.64	5.16
Ghana	0.09	0.12	0.12	0.07

[a] A dash (—) indicates that a state is not a member of the organization in question, or that its assessment has not been determined.
[b] Associate member; contribution accruing to Miscellaneous Income.
[c] Assessment outside the 100 percent scale.
[d] Including Syria.
[e] Using Sw. fr. 4.30 = $U.S. 1.00: (No member nation currently falls into class 2)
    Class 1 = $18,587.20
    Class 3 = $11,152.32
    Class 4 = $ 7,434.88
    Class 5 = $ 3,717.44
    Class 6 = $ 2,230.46
    Class 7 = $ 743.48
[f] 1 Unit = $5,393.
[g] 1 Unit = $608.65
[h] Associate member—Territory ceased to exist on July 1, 1962—Republic of Rwanda became a full member in the ½ unit class
[i] Associate member.
[j] Percentages calculated by author on the basis of contributions to the 1962 Budget. The contributions to IMCO are apportioned, however, on the basis of a "basic assessment" (determined by the nation's contribution to the United Nations Regular Budget) plus its "gross registered tonnage."

ICAO (Percent)	WHO (Percent)	IAEA (Percent)	UPU (Class)[e]	ITU (Unit Class)[f]	WMO (Units)[g]	IMCO (Percent)[j]
0.13	0.06	0.05	6	$\frac{1}{2}$	2	—
—	0.04	0.04	6	$\frac{1}{2}$	2	—
—	—	—	3	—	—	—
1.20	1.00	1.02	1	15	19	1.09
2.50	1.62	1.65	1	20	22	0.77
0.41	0.39	0.40	5	1	7	—
1.63	1.18	1.20	3	4	16	0.83
0.13	0.04	—	6	3	4	—
1.68	0.92	0.94	1	25	19	—
—	—	—	—	$\frac{1}{2}$	5	—
—	0.14	0.15	5	1	5	0.45
0.13	0.07	0.07	6	3	4	0.45
—	0.42	0.43	5	1	7	—
0.13	0.04	0.04	7	1	2	0.45
—	0.04	—	7	1	2	0.45
4.70	2.82	2.87	1	18	28	1.80
—	0.04	—	7	$\frac{1}{2}$	1	—
0.13	0.09	0.09	5	1	4	—
—	0.04	—	7	$\frac{1}{2}$	1	—
0.39	0.24	0.25	5	3	7	—
0.67	4.54	4.62	1	15	37	1.15
0.62	0.28	0.29	5	3	—	—
—	0.04	—	7	$\frac{1}{2}$	1	—
—	—	(0.04)	6	1	7	—
0.13	0.04	—	6	3	1	—
0.41	0.23	0.23	6	1	4	—
—	0.04	—	7	$\frac{1}{2}$	—	—
0.85	0.79	0.80	3	5	10	—
—	0.04	—	7	$\frac{1}{2}$	1	—
0.93	0.54	0.55	4	5	10	1.69
0.13	0.05	0.05	6	3	2	0.45
0.13	0.06	0.05	6	1	2	0.45
0.13	0.05	0.05	6	3	2	—
0.13	0.06	0.05	6	1	3	—
0.16	0.15	—	6	3	3	—
—	0.02	—	—	1	5	—
0.42	0.32	0.33	4	3	7	0.91
7.83	5.80	5.90	1	30	47	3.65
—	—	—	3	5	—	—
—	—	—	—	—	1	—
—	—	—	—	—	1	—
—	0.04	—	7	$\frac{1}{2}$	1	—
5.17	4.83	4.91	1	20	50	3.47
0.13	0.06	0.06	6	1	3	0.45

Member States[a]	United Nations (Percent)	ILO (Percent)	FAO (Percent)	UNESCO (Percent)
Greece	0.23	0.21	0.31	0.22
Guatemala	0.05	0.12	0.07	0.05
Guinea	0.04	0.12	0.04	0.04
Haiti	0.04	0.12	0.04	0.04
Holy See	—	—	—	—
Honduras	0.04	0.12	0.04	0.04
Hong Kong	—	—	—	—
Hungary	0.56	0.42	—	0.41
Iceland	0.04	0.12	0.04	—
India	2.03	3.07	2.72	2.38
Indonesia	0.45	0.43	0.60	0.45
Iran	0.20	0.28	0.27	0.20
Iraq	0.09	0.12	0.12	0.09
Ireland	0.14	0.24	0.19	—
Israel	0.15	0.12	0.20	0.13
Italy	2.24	2.37	3.00	2.18
Ivory Coast	0.04	0.12	0.04	0.06
Jamaica	—	—	0.024[b]	—
Japan	2.27	2.00	3.04	2.12
Jordan	0.04	0.12	0.04	0.04
Korea, Republic of	—	—	0.25	0.20
Kuwait	—	0.12	0.04	0.06
Laos	0.04	—	0.04	0.04
Lebanon	0.05	0.12	0.07	0.05
Liberia	0.04	0.12	0.04	0.04
Libya	0.04	0.12	0.04	0.04
Liechtenstein	—	—	—	—
Luxembourg	0.05	0.12	0.07	0.06
Madagascar	0.04	0.12	0.04	0.06
Mali	0.04	0.12	0.04	0.04
Mauritania	—	—	0.04	—
Mauritius	—	—	0.024[b]	—
Mexico	0.74	0.76	0.99	0.69
Monaco	—	—	—	0.04
Mongolia	—	—	—	—
Morocco	0.14	0.14	0.19	0.13
Nepal	0.04	—	0.04	0.04
Netherlands	1.01	1.16	1.35	0.98
Netherlands Antilles and Surinam	—	—	—	—
Netherlands New Guinea	—	—	—	—
New Caledonia	—	—	—	—
New Zealand	0.41	0.48	0.55	0.41
Nicaragua	0.04	0.12	0.04	0.04
Niger	0.04	0.12	0.04	0.04
Nigeria	0.21	0.21	0.28	0.20

ICAO (Percent)	WHO (Percent)	IAEA (Percent)	UPU (Class)[e]	ITU (Unit Class)[f]	WMO (Units)[g]	IMCO (Percent)[j]
0.27	0.21	0.21	5	1	4	3.38
0.13	0.05	0.05	6	1	1	—
0.13	0.04	—	6	1	1	—
0.13	0.04	0.04	6	1	2	0.45
—	—	0.04	7	½	—	—
0.13	0.04	0.04	6	2	1	0.51
—	—	—	—	—	2	—
—	0.38	0.39	4	1	5	—
0.13	0.04	0.04	7	½	2	0.51
2.56	2.23	2.27	1	20	30	1.41
0.52	0.42	0.43	3	5	11	0.59
0.21	0.19	0.19	5	1	4	0.45
0.13	0.08	0.08	7	1	2	—
0.24	0.14	—	4	3	5	0.52
0.23	0.13	0.13	6	1	4	0.66
2.43	2.04	2.07	1	8	27	3.76
—	0.06	—	7	1	1	0.45
—	—	—	—	—	—	—
2.22	1.98	2.02	1	25	28	5.18
0.13	0.04	—	7	½	2	—
0.19	0.19	0.19	4	1	2	0.30
—	0.04	—	7	1	—	0.45
0.13	0.04	—	7	½	1	—
0.21	0.05	0.05	7	½	2	—
0.13	0.04	—	7	3	—	6.33
0.13	0.04	—	7	½	1	—
—	—	—	7	—	—	—
0.13	0.06	0.05	6	½	2	—
—	0.06	—	6	1	3	0.45
—	0.04	0.04	7	1	1	—
—	0.04c	—	—	½	—	0.45
—	—	—	—	—	1	—
1.34	0.64	0.65	3	8	11	0.54
—	0.04	0.04	7	½	—	—
—	—	—	—	—	—	—
0.22	0.13	0.13	4	1	4	0.18
—	0.04	—	6	½	—	—
2.51	0.91	0.93	3	10	15	3.09
—	—	—	6	—	1	—
—	—	—	—	—	1	—
—	—	—	—	—	1	—
0.51	0.38	0.39	1	5	8	0.57
0.13	0.04	0.04	6	1	1	—
—	0.04	—	7	1	1	—
—	0.19	—	5	2	3	0.39

Member States[a]	United Nations (Percent)	ILO (Percent)	FAO (Percent)	UNESCO (Percent)
Norway	0.45	0.52	0.60	0.47
Pakistan	0.42	0.62	0.56	0.39
Panama	0.04	0.12	0.04	0.04
Paraguay	0.04	0.12	0.04	0.04
Peru	0.10	0.18	0.13	0.11
Philippines	0.40	0.37	0.54	0.42
Poland	1.28	1.24	1.72	1.32
Portugal	0.16	0.28	0.21	—
Portuguese East Africa, Asia, and Oceana	—	—	—	—
Portuguese West Africa	—	—	—	—
Romania	0.32	0.45	0.43	0.33
Ruanda Urundi	—	—	—	—
San Marino	—	—	—	—
Sarawak and North Borneo[i]	—	—	—	—
Saudi Arabia	0.07	—	0.09	0.06
Senegal	0.05	0.12	0.07	0.06
Sierra Leone	—	0.12	0.04	—
Singapore, and British Territories in Borneo	—	—	—	—
Somalia	0.04	0.12	0.04	0.04
South Africa	0.53	0.80	0.71	—
Spain	0.86	1.08	1.15	0.90
Spanish Territories of Guinea	—	—	—	—
Spain (African Territories)	—	—	—	—
Sudan	0.07	0.12	0.09	0.06
Surinam	—	—	—	—
Sweden	1.30	1.63	1.74	1.34
Switzerland	—	1.30	1.27	0.94
Syria	—	—	—	—
Tanganyika	—	—	0.024[b]	—
Thailand	0.16	0.20	0.21	0.15
Togo	0.04	0.12	0.04	0.04
Tunisia	0.05	0.12	0.07	0.05
Turkey	0.40	0.72	0.54	0.57
Ukrainian Soviet Socialist Republic	1.98	1.00	—	1.74
Union of Soviet Socialist Republics	14.97	10.00	—	13.18
United Arab Republic[d]	0.30	0.51	0.40	0.31
United Kingdom	7.58	9.42	10.15	7.53
United Kingdom (Overseas Territories)	—	—	—	—
United States	32.02	25.00	32.02	31.46
United States of America (Pacific Territories)	—	—	—	—
Upper Volta	0.04	0.12	0.04	0.04
Uruguay	0.11	0.17	0.15	0.12
Venezuela	0.52	0.50	0.70	0.48
Viet-Nam (Republic of)	—	0.21	0.21	0.19
West Indies and other British Caribbean Territories	—	—	—	—
Yemen	0.04	—	0.04	—
Yugoslavia	0.38	0.40	0.51	0.34

ICAO (Percent)	WHO (Percent)	IAEA (Percent)	UPU (Class)[e]	ITU (Unit Class)[f]	WMO (Units)[g]	IMCO (Percent)[j]
0.83	0.44	0.45	4	5	8	6.92
0.48	0.36	0.37	1	15	11	0.60
—	0.04	—	6	3	—	2.63
0.13	0.04	0.04	6	1	2	—
0.14	0.10	0.10	5	2	6	—
0.44	0.39	0.40	7	1	8	—
1.22	1.24	1.26	3	3	13	0.85
0.23	0.18	0.18	4	8	8	—
—	—	—	4	8	3	—
—	—	—	4	8	2	—
—	0.31	0.31	3	1	7	—
—	0.02c	—	—	½h	1	—
—	—	—	7	—	—	—
—	0.06	—	7	1	2	0.22
—	0.06	0.05	6	1	1	0.45
—	0.02	—	7	½	—	—
—	—	—	—	½i	3	—
—	0.04	—	7	1	—	—
0.71	0.51	0.52	1	8	14	—
1.02	0.84	0.86	1	3	14	1.38
—	—	—	7	1	1	—
0.13	0.06	0.05	7	1	3	—
—	—	—	—	—	1	—
1.82	1.26	1.28	3	10	18	2.60
1.53	0.88	0.89	3	10	16	0.54
—	—	—	7	1	—	—
—	0.02c	—	—	½	—	—
0.21	0.14	0.15	6	3	5	—
—	0.04	—	7	½	1	—
0.13	0.05	0.05	5	1	2	—
0.56	0.53	0.54	3	5	11	0.81
—	1.63	1.66	3	3	17	—
—	12.34	12.54	1	30	87	4.44
0.33	0.29	0.30	3	5	12	0.56
9.88	7.05	7.17	1	30	67	12.45
—	—	—	3	1	—	—
32.95	31.71	32.27	1	30	215	15.30
—	—	—	3	25	—	—
—	0.04	—	—	1	1	—
0.13	0.11	—	6	1	6	—
0.69	0.45	0.46	6	5	7	—
0.22	0.18	0.18	6	1	3	—
—	—	—	—	½i	3	—
—	0.04	—	7	1	—	—
—	0.32	0.32	3	1	7	0.89

TABLE A.10. *United Nations Children's Fund, Private Contributions by Country, 1959–62*[a]

Contributing Country	1959	1960	1961	1962
Afghanistan	—	—	—	$ 80
Argentina	—	$ 11	$ 18	22
Australia	$ 44,809	22,958	11,424	—
Austria	100	120	—	—
Belgium	2,438	2,093	27,501	38,854
Brazil	155	—	—	2
Burma	—	63	16	—
Canada	126,497	211,116	543,594	316,057
Colombia	—	—	—	6
Costa Rica	—	—	—	37
Denmark	1,315	3,896	1,989	5,928
Ethiopia	—	—	3	—
Finland	—	—	—	37,617
France	1,368	528	618	956
Germany, Federal Republic of	4,065	6,969	23,856	150,951
Greece	—	—	—	1
Guatemala	700	—	—	1
India	2,265	369	2,564	3,720
Indonesia	—	—	33	5
Iran	118	—	13	8
Ireland	8	4,496	36	11,459
Israel	56	—	20	22
Italy	8,000	7,200	7,852	13,502
Japan	6,250	20,000	—	20,000
Lebanon	2,650	—	203	118
Luxembourg	—	299	299	492
Mexico	98	—	57	120
Netherlands	11,272	15,613	10,070	233,911
New Zealand	5,873	—	155	39,131
Nigeria	9	—	—	6
Norway	2,150	1,981	349	4,067
Pakistan	5	73	47	15
Panama	10	10	10	10
Peru	—	—	11	8
Philippines	512	66	970	774
Saudi Arabia	—	—	3,000	—
Spain	221	109	127	136
Sweden	2,243	5,858	6,936	8,619
Switzerland	35	5,983	310,170	120,389
Thailand	121	59	166	228
Uganda	—	—	10	56
Union of South Africa	21	19	25	—
United Arab Republic	—	—	9	—
United Kingdom	67,630	44,176	65,410	118,330
United States	1,225,042	1,552,344	1,647,987	2,617,744
Uruguay	—	—	—	139
Venezuela	—	—	—	24
Yugoslavia	3	121	—	25
Total	$1,516,039	$1,906,530	$2,665,548	$3,743,570
United Nations Secretariat	10,031	4,319	4,458	7,214
Grand Total	$1,526,070	$1,910,849	$2,670,006	$3,750,784

[a] Data supplied by Office of the Comptroller.

Selected References

1. League of Nations and United Nations Publications

League of Nations. *Official Journal.* Second Year (1921), "Report on the Organization of the International Force for Vilna, Approved by the Council of the League, November 25th, 1920."
——. ——. 3d Session of the Assembly (1922), Minutes of the Fourth Committee.
——. ——. Eighth Year (1927), "Legal Positions of States which do not pay their Contributions to the League," Report by the Secretary-General, Annex 943, C.36.1927, V.
——. ——. Fifteenth Year (1934), Nos. 6 and 12.
——. ——. 16th Session of the Assembly (1935), Minutes of the Fourth Committee.
——. ——. 19th Session of the Assembly (1938), Minutes of the Fourth Committee.
League of Nations Secretariat. *Financial Administration and Apportionment of Expenses.* Geneva, 1928.
United Nations. *Statistical Yearbook, 1960,* 1961.
United Nations Children's Fund. *Budget Estimates for the Financial Year 1963,* Doc. E/ICEF/AB/L.16, April 1962.
United Nations General Assembly. *Official Records.* Fifteenth Session, "First Report of the Advisory Committee on Administrative and Budgetry Questions," Supplement No. 7 (A/4408), 1960.
——. ——. Fifteenth Session, "Introduction to the Annual Report of the Secretary-General on the Work of the Organization, 16 June 1959–15 June 1960," Supplement No. 1A.
——. ——. Sixteenth Session, "Budget Estimates for the Financial Year 1962," Supplement No. 5.
——. ——. Sixteenth Session, "Introduction to the Annual Report of the Secretary-General on the Work of the Organization, 16 June 1960–15 June 1961," Supplement No. 1A.
——. ——. Sixteenth Session, "Report of the Working Group of Fifteen," Doc. A/4971, Nov. 15, 1961.
——. ——. "Supplementary Budget Estimates for the Financial Year 1962," Doc. A/5223, Sept. 24, 1962.
——. "Report of the Secretary-General on the United Nations Development Decade," Doc. E/36, May 13, 1962.
——. International Court of Justice. *Certain Expenses of the United Nations (Article 17, paragraph 2 of the Charter), Advisory Opinion of 20 July 1962: I.C.J. Reports, 1962.*

2. Publications of Other International Organizations

Council of Europe. *A Policy for Europe Today.*
———. *Ten Years of European Cooperation.*
European Coal and Steel Community. *Tenth General Report on the Activities of the Community, February 1, 1961—January 31, 1962.* Luxembourg, 1962.
Food and Agriculture Organization of the United Nations. *Forward Appraisal of FAO Programs, 1959-64.* Rome, 1959.
———. *United Nations Special Fund, Desert Locust Project, Plan of Operation.* Rome. 1960.
International Atomic Energy Agency. *Program and Budget for 1962.* Austria, 1961.
International Labour Conference. *Financial and Budgetary Questions.* 45th Session, 1961, and 46th Session, 1962.
NATO. *Facts About the North Atlantic Treaty Organization.* Paris, January 1962.
OEEC. *At Work for Europe.* Paris, 1954.
———. *The OEEC: History and Structure.* Paris, 1956.
Organization of American States. *Decisions Taken at the Meetings of the Council of the Organization of American States.*
Tenth Inter-American Conference of the Organization of American States. *Report on the Activities of the Organization of American States, 1948-1953.* Washington, D.C.: Pan American Union, 1953.
UNESCO. *Proposed Programme and Budget for 1963-64, Presented to the General Conference at its Twelfth Session.* Paris, 1962.
———. *Records of the General Conference of the United Nations Educational, Scientific and Cultural Organization,* Fifth Session, 1950; Sixth Session, 1951; Seventh Session, 1952; Eighth Session, 1954.
Universal Postal Union. "Detailed Regulations for Implementing the Universal Postal Convention," *Universal Postal Convention.* Ottawa, Oct. 3, 1957.
World Health Organization. *Official Records,* Nos. 21, 28, 33, 35, 51, 52, 106, 111, 115, 116.
———. *The First Ten Years of the World Health Organization,* 1958.

3. United States Government Publications

Commission on Organization of the Executive Branch of the Government. *Report on Overseas Economic Operations, pursuant to Public Law 180, 83d Congress,* June 1955.
U.S. Congress. *Information on the Operations and Financing of the United Nations.* Joint Committee on Printing, Committee on Foreign Relations, United States Senate, and Committee on Foreign Affairs, United States House of Representatives, 87th Congress, 2nd Session, February 6, 1962.

————. House Committee on Foreign Affairs. *Special Study Mission on International Organizations and Movements,* 1954.

————. ————. *The United Nations Specialized Agencies.* Report of the Subcommittee on International Organizations and Movements, 1957.

————. *Review of the United Nations Charter.* Compilation of Staff Studies Prepared for the Use of the Subcommittee on the United Nations Charter of the Senate Committee on Foreign Relations.

————. *The United States and the Korean Problem: Documents 1943-1953.* 83d Congress, 1st Session, Senate Document 74.

————. House of Representatives. *Purchase of United Nations Bonds.* Hearings before the Committee on Foreign Affairs, 87th Congress, 2d Session, June 27—July 26, 1962.

————. ————. *Reimbursement of Extraordinary Expenses in the City of New York.* Hearings Before the Subcommittee on International Organizations and Movements, House Committee on Foreign Affairs, 87th Congress, 1st Session, May 17, 1961.

————. Senate. *Background Documents Relating to the Organization for Economic Cooperation and Development.* Committee on Foreign Relations, 87th Congress, 1st Session, 1961.

————. ————. *Contributions to the International Labour Organisation.* Hearings Before the Committee on Foreign Relations, 85th Congress, April 16 and June 18, 1957.

————. ————. *Purchase of United Nations Bonds.* Hearings before the Committee on Foreign Relations, 87th Congress, 2d Session, 1962.

U.S. Department of State. *The International Atomic Energy Agency.* International Organization and Conference Series, Publication 6696, August 1958.

————. *United States Participation in the United Nations.* International Organization and Conference Series III, 80, Publication 4583, 1952.

4. Other Publications

Allen, Robert L. "United Nations Technical Assistance: Soviet and East European Participation," *International Organization,* Vol. XI, Autumn 1957.

Altman, Oscar L. "Quotas in the International Monetary Fund," *IMF Staff Papers,* Vol. V, No. 2, August 1956.

Ames, Herbert. *Financial Administration and Apportionment of Expenses.* League of Nations Information Section, 1928.

Béguin, Bernard. "ILO and the Tripartite System," *International Conciliation,* No. 523, May 1959.

Clark, Grenville, and Louis B. Sohn. *World Peace Through World Law.* 2d ed., rev.; Cambridge: Harvard University Press, 1960.

Commission to Study the Organization of Peace. *Strengthening the United Nations.* New York: Harper & Brothers, 1957.

Elkin, A. B. "OEEC—Its Structure and Powers," *European Yearbook,* Vol. IV, pp. 96-140.

Frye, William R. *A United Nations Peace Force.* New York: Oceana for the Carnegie Endowment for International Peace, 1957.

Goodrich, Leland M. *Korea: A Study of U.S. Policy in the United Nations.* New York: Council on Foreign Relations, 1956.

Gordon, Lincoln. "The Organization for European Economic Cooperation," *International Organization,* Vol. X, February 1956.

Gross, Leo, "The International Court of Justice and Peace-keeping Expenses of the UN." *International Organization,* Winter 1963.

Hartt, Julian, "Antarctica—Its Immediate Practicalities," *1959 Proceedings of the Institute of World Affairs,* Vol. XXXV, 1959.

Hogg, John Fergusson, "Peace-keeping Costs and Charter Obligations—Implications of the International Court of Justice Decision on Certain Expenses of the United Nations," *Columbia Law Review,* Vol. LXII, November 1962.

Howard-Ellis, C. *The Origin, Structure and Working of the League of Nations.* London: George Allen and Unwin, 1938.

Ismay, Lord. *NATO—The First Five Years.* Paris: The International Secretariat, 1958.

Jacklin, Seymour. "The Finances of the League," *International Affairs,* September, 1934.

Jackson, Elmore. "The Constitutional Development of the United Nations: The Growth of its Executive Capacity," *Proceedings of the American Society of International Law,* Vol. LV, 1961.

Jackson, John H. "The Legal Framework of United Nations Financing: Peacekeeping and Penury," *The California Law Review,* Vol. 51, No. 1, March 1963.

Jenks, C. Wilfred. "Some Legal Aspects of the Financing of International Institutions," *Transactions of the Grotius Society,* Vol. XXVIII, 1943.

Jessup, Philip C., and Howard J. Taubenfeld. *Controls for Outer Space and the Antarctic Analogy,* 1959.

Kiser, Margaret. *The Organization of American States.* Washington, D.C.: Pan American Union, 1955.

Laves, Walter, and Charles Thomson. *UNESCO.* Bloomington: Indiana University Press, 1957.

Lindsay, K. *Ten Years of European Cooperation.* Strasbourg, 1958.

Lyons, Gene M. "American Policy and the United Nations' Program for Korean Reconstruction," *International Organization,* Vol. XII, Spring 1958.

Mallett, D. "The History and Structure of OEEC," *European Yearbook,* Vol. I.

Mathijsen, Pierre. "Problems Connected with the Creation of Euratom," *Law and Contemporary Problems,* Vol. XXVI, Summer 1961.

Miller, E. M. "Legal Aspects of the United Nations Action in the Congo," *American Journal of International Law,* Vol. LV, January 1961.

Moore, Ben T. *NATO and the Future of Europe*. New York: Harper for the Council on Foreign Relations, 1958.

Nelson, G. R. "European Organization in the Field of Atomic Energy," *European Yearbook*, Vol. IV.

Nichols, Calvin J. *Financing the United Nations: Problems and Prospects*. Cambridge: M.I.T. Center for International Studies, 1961.

Padelford, Norman J. "Politics and Change in the Security Council," *International Organization*, Vol. XIV, Summer 1960.

———. "Politics and the Future of ECOSOC," *International Organization*, Vol. XV, Autumn 1961.

Ranshofen-Wertheimer, Egon. *The International Secretariat: A Great Experiment in International Administration*. Oxford: Clarendon, 1956.

Read, James M. "The United Nations and Refugees—Changing Concepts," *International Conciliation*, No. 537, March 1962.

Robertson, A. H. *European Institutions*. London: Stevens, 1959.

———. *The Council of Europe*. London: Stevens, 1961.

Rosner, Gabriella E. *The United Nations Emergency Force*. New York: Columbia University Press, 1963.

Schenkman, Jacob. *International Civil Aviation Organization*. Geneva: Librairie E. Droz, 1955.

Sertoli, Giandomenico. "The Structure and Financial Activities of the European Regional Communities," *Law and Contemporary Problems*, Vol. XXVI, Summer 1961.

Sharp, Walter R. *Field Administration in the United Nations System*. London and New York, 1961.

Singer, J. David. *Financing International Organization*. The Hague: Nijhoff, 1961.

———. "The United Nations Fiscal Process." New York University Doctoral Dissertation, 1955.

———. "The Finances of the League of Nations," *International Organization*, Vol. XIII, Spring 1959.

Staley, Eugene. *Direct Revenue for the United Nations*. Offset Memorandum, Stanford Research Institute, November 13, 1961.

Stoessinger, John G. "Financing the United Nations," *International Conciliation*, No. 535, November 1961.

———. *The Refugee and the World Community*. Minneapolis: University of Minnesota Press, 1956.

———. "Atoms for Peace: The International Atomic Energy Agency," *Organizing Peace in the Nuclear Age*. Report of the Commission to Study the Organization of Peace. New York: New York University Press, 1959.

Taubenfeld, Howard J. "A Treaty for Antarctica," *International Conciliation*, No. 531, January 1961.

Tyson, David O. "The United Nations: Big Investor in Corporates," *The Weekly Bond Buyer*, March 5, 1962.

Vogues, Daniel. *La Communauté Européenne du Charbon et de l'Acier*. Paris, 1956.

Vries, Henry P. de. *Inter-American Legal Studies*. New York: Columbia University, 1961.

Walters. Frances P. *A History of the League of Nations*. London: Oxford University Press, 1952.

Warburton, Anne M., and John B. Wood. *Paying for NATO*. London: Friends of Atlantic Union, n.d.

Whitaker, Arthur P. *The Western Hemisphere Idea*. Ithaca: Cornell University Press, 1954.

Zurcher, A. J. *The Struggle to Unite Europe—1940-1958*. New York, 1958.

Index

"Ability to pay," as assessment criterion, 19, 82, 160, 174-78

Administrative and Budgetary Questions, Advisory Committee on, 88-89, 91-93, 95, 116

Afghanistan, 125n, 132, 133, 225

African nations: Congo force, 113, 118, 122; contributions to voluntary programs, 209, 299; ILO in, 218; technical assistance in, 256, 257; UN assessment, 84

Aggressors, proposed payment by, 170-71

Agriculture. *See* Food and Agriculture Organization.

Aid: Distribution of American, 48, 49; technical (*see* Expanded Programme of Technical Assistance).

Aiken, George D., 127, 128, 130

Air: Letters, proposal re, 274; traffic, levies on, 275, 278-79

Airlifting operations, cost of, 78

Alcohol, possible tax on, 280

American Association for the United Nations, 260, 261

American States, Organization of (OAS), 43-46. 59

Ames, Herbert, 37n

Antarctica, UN interest in, 280-84, 291-92, 305

Apportionment of costs (*see also* Assessments, UN; Costs, UN; Rebate formula), 18-25, 150-52, 164-78, 301

Arab states, 108, 110, 138, 170, 288

Argentina, 103, 125n, 134, 135, 167, 234, 283

Armaments expenditures, as assessment criterion, 172-73

Arrears: Interest on, 39, 97, 235, 245; specialized agencies, 219-22, 227, 230, 231, 236, 244-45; United Nations, 76, 78, 85, 121-24

Assembly: League of Nations, 38, 39, 41; United Nations (*see* General Assembly)

Assessments: Council of Europe, 47; EEC, 54; EURATOM, 52; NATO, 57; OAS agencies, 45; OEEC and OECD, 48-49

Assessments, UN, 82-90; for peace-keeping, 19, 21, 22, 27, 29, 68, 133-38, 164-90; ONUC, 76, 114-21, 158; Peace and Security Fund, 160, 161; specialized agencies, 216, 217 (ILO), 220-21 (WHO), 227-28 (FAO), 229-30 (UNESCO), 231 (IAEA), 234 (UPU), 235 (ITU), 236 (ICAO), 239 (IMF), 244, 298, 299; UNEF, 76, 107-12, 158; World Court opinion, 145, 150-51, 300, 303, 304

Atomic Energy Agency, International (IAEA), 80, 124, 217, 219, 231-33

Atomic Energy Community, European (EURATOM), 48, 49, 52-53, 60

Australia: Antarctic claims, 283; bond issue, 125, 132; GNP per capita, 263; IRO, 200; Korea, 102, 103; ONUC, 121n, 135; specialized agencies, 200, 224n, 234, 237; Suez, 276; UNEF, 112, 135; UNICEF, 194, 195, 254-55; Worknig Group of Twenty-one, 134; World Court resolution, 123; World Refugee Year, 252

Austria: Bond issue, 125n, 132, 133; installment-payment proposal, 97; ONUC, 121, 135; regional organizations, 47, 48, 75; UNEF, 112, 135

Aviation Organization, International Civil, 234, 235-37, 244-45 278

Badawi, Judge, 141, 154

Balance of payments: As assessment criterion, 174-75; role of IMF, 238-40

Ball, M. M., 46n

Bank for Reconstruction and Development, International. *See under* International.

Basdevant, Jules, 141, 147, 150

Béguin, Bernard, 217n

Belgium: Antarctic research, 284; bond issue, 125n; Congo, 115, 116, 118, 135, 138; GNP per capita, 263; IRO, 200; Korea, 102, 103; petroleum, off-shore, 289; regional organizations, 46-48, 51, 52, 54, 55, 57, 58; specialized agencies, 223, 224n, 237; UNEF, 112, 135; UNICEF, 255

"Benefits," estimating of, 172